Re-Visioning Gower

Re-Visioning Gower

Edited by R. F. Yeager

Pegasus Press
University of North Carolina at Asheville
Asheville, NC
1998

© Copyright 1998
Pegasus Press
University of North Carolina at Asheville

Library of Congress Cataloging-in-Publication Data

Re-visioning Gower : papers presented at the meetings of the John Gower
  Society at the International Congress on Medieval Studies, Western Michi-
gan University, 1992–1997 / edited by R. F. Yeager.
      p. cm.
    Includes bibliographical references (p.).
    ISBN 1-889818-09-7 (pb : alk. paper)
    1. Gower, John, 1325?–1408—Criticism and interpretation. 2. Love
poetry, English (Middle)—History and criticism. 3. Gower, John, 1325?-
1408. Confessio Amantis. 4. Poetry, Medieval—History and criticism. 5.
Christian ethics in literature. 6. Courtly love in
literature. 7. Rhetoric, Medieval. I. Yeager, Robert F.
II. International Congress on Medieval Studies.
PR1987.R4 1998
821' .1—dc21   98–25550
                                                              CIP

This book is made to last.
It is printed on acid-free paper
to library specifications.
The typeface is Garamond Antiqua.

Printed in the United States of America

Contents

III. Texts and Manuscripts

Illustrations

"Remembering Origins: Gower's Monstrous Body Poetic"
Eve Salisbury

Figure 1: MS All Souls Col., Oxf. 98. *Vox Clamantis*, f. 126ᵛ (courtesy All Souls College).

Figure 2: MS Cotton Tiberius A.iv, British Library. *Vox Clamantis*, f. 8ᵛ (by permission of the British Library).

Figure 3: MS All Souls Col., Oxf. 98. *Vox Clamantis*, f. 116 (courtesy All Souls College).

Figure 4: MS Laud 719, Bodleian Library, Oxford (by permission of the Bodleian Library).

"Printing the *Confessio Amantis:* Caxton's Edition in Context"
Martha W. Driver

Plate 1: Drawing Added by Later Reader. John Gower, *Confessio Amantis,* f 97ᵛ. Westminster, William Caxton, 2 September 1483. PML 689 The Pierpont Morgan Library, New York (courtesy of The Pierpont Morgan Library).

Plate 2: Prologus. John Gower, *Confessio Amantis,* f 2. Westminster, William Caxton, 2 September 1483. PML 689 The Pierpont Morgan Library, New York (courtesy of The Pierpont Morgan Library).

Plate 3: Opening of Book III. Boethius, *Consolation de Philosophie,* ff 105ᵛ– 106. Bruges, Colard Mansion, 1477. Rylands 12619 The John Rylands Library, Manchester (by permission of The John Rylands Library).

Plate 4: Boccaccio Presents His Book to Mainardo Cavalcanti. Boccaccio, Giovanni, *De casibus illustrium virorum et mulierum.* Trans. Laurent de Premierfait, f 3. Bruges, Colard Mansion, 1476. Museum of Fine Arts, Boston (by permission of the Museum of Fine Arts).

Plate 5: Presentation Scene. Le Fèvre, Raoul, *Recuyell of the Histories of Troy.* Trans. William Caxton, frontispiece. Bruges, William Caxton, 1473– 1474. Henry E. Huntington Library, San Marino (courtesy of the Huntington Library and Art Gallery).

Introduction

Re-Visioning Gower continues an effort, begun with *John Gower: Recent Readings* (Kalamazoo, 1989), to widen the audience for essays first heard in sessions sponsored annually by the John Gower Society at the International Congresses on Medieval Studies held at Western Michigan University. For that earlier volume, thirteen papers read between 1983 and 1988 were selected to be recast for publication; for this present volume, fifteen studies, representing work of 1992–1997, have been chosen, each one rewritten exclusively for this collection.

The essays of *Recent Readings* and those gathered in this volume show more than a little about the shape of Gower studies today. A glance at their tables of contents reveals contributors from Germany, England, Canada, the United States—hard evidence that contemporary interest in Gower's poetry remains strong around the world. Significant, too, is the testimony both volumes offer about the changing concerns of Gower's readers. In a decade and a half, scholarly focus has shifted away from what might be called "classical" Gower studies: the identification of source texts; efforts to establish Gower as a satirist (in some part to palliate the soubriquet "moral" for modern sensibilities); the comparative evaluation of Chaucer and Gower as artists, oftenest in the past with Gower serving as a rule to measure Chaucer's greater talent.

While these topics are well represented in *Recent Readings*, here only the last appears, in one example—María Bullón-Fernández's comparison of Chaucer's Constance story with Gower's—and it is a version with a different twist. For in "Engendering Authority: Father and Daughter, State and Church in Gower's 'Tale of Constance' and Chaucer's 'Man of Law's Tale,'" Bullón-Fernández takes up, not the enhancement of Chaucer's poetic reputation at the expense of Gower's, but rather the incestuous center of the tale, in order to expose the political uses to which incest is put—by both poets, but by Gower especially. Incest, Bullón-Fernández argues, serves in the *Confessio Amantis* as an ideal metaphor for the abusive, patriarchal power of Church and monarch which are Gower's major subjects. So too Larry Scanlon, in "The Riddle of Incest: John Gower and the Problem of Medieval Sexuality," identifies incest as the master key, not only to Gower's politics in the volatile final two decades of the fourteenth century in England, but also to what Scanlon sees as the heretofore locked door of medieval psychosexuality. Scanlon situates a close reading of the "Tale of Apollonius" and its father-daughter incest in a broader context of psychoanalytic theory from Freud to Lacan, shedding light on Gower's poem and establishing "a historical and social dimension to [incest] which psychoanalysis, like the rest of modernity, has largely failed to recognize."

In their connection of incest with the wielding of power both religious and secular, Bullón-Fernández and Scanlon illustrate the importance Gower's readers currently give to his politics of institutions, of class violence and social exploitation, and of engendered demarcations of authority. Thus Gregory M. Sadlek examines how "late-medieval ideologies of labor are mediated in aristocratic love poetry employing the metaphor 'love's labor,'" and concludes that the *Confessio* presents a sharp critique of "the wastefulness of loving 'par amour'" but that Gower's "condemnation of *acedia* is rooted not only in the traditional rhetoric of 'love's labor' but also in the changing ideologies of his own culture." For David Aers, whose "Reflections on Gower as '*Sapiens* in Ethics and Politics'" seeks to revise views long held that Gower was, if not an exciting read then certainly a wise, consistently moral voice in a dark social wilderness, Gower is neither wise nor ethical, but rather almost frighteningly expressive of the conservative values of the expanding gentry class under Edward III, Richard II, and Henry IV. Like Aers, whose essay focusses on Gower's Latin as well as his English poetry, Eve Salisbury, in "Re-Membering Origins: Gower's Monstrous Body Politic," finds in the *Vox Clamantis* a strong political statement; but unlike Aers, Salisbury sees Gower's class critique as primarily self-directed, turned inward to find the social *corpus* entire at fault for its violent predicament. In her treatment (and in interesting contrast to Aers's sanguinary view) Gower steps forward as a pacifistic writer, seeking to establish universal harmony with the mirror, and the music, of his verse. Claire Fanger's study, "Magic and the Metaphysics of Gender in Gower's 'Tale of Circe and Ulysses,'" carries forward these same interests in the distribution of power and authority, while pointing out as significant contexts Gower's demonstrative erudition (both as source and as yardstick, as evaluative measure) and his complex attitudes toward women. Sexual politics are also the topic of Hugh White, whose study of "The Sympathetic Villain in *Confessio Amantis*" opens yet another corridor into Gowerian sexuality and the politics of gender relations by making the case for the seductive power of narrative to sweep even "moral Gower" along to conclusions not always morally defensible.

The political, here broadly defined and represented, is thus a strengthening focus of contemporary Gower studies. As such, it affords fresh perspective whence to view more familiar territory. For although Gower's poetic methods and effects continue to draw attention, the essays included here show plainly how thoroughly Gower's work is being reassessed in light of new discovery. Hence Patricia Batchelor, writing about "Feigned Truth and Exemplary Method in the *Confessio Amantis*" sees in Gower's handling of the *exemplum* form some measured recognition of how complex is the relationship between his didactic claims and the enterprise of making fictions. Hence too Dhira B. Mahoney, who seeks to identify in Gower's prologues the topos of "the commission … the *jussio*" or the

"Auftragstopos," cannot avoid bringing forward her persuasive argument for classification, and for the aesthetic superiority of the earlier, so-called "Ricardian" opening, in the context of politicized times. Nor do the essays of Russell A. Peck ("The Phenomenology of Make-Believe in Gower's *Confessio Amantis*") and Kurt Olsson ("Reading, Transgression, and Judgment: Gower's Case of Paris and Helen"), despite their quite different directions, present Gower's as an apolitical vision. Even Thomas Cable, whose closely argued "Metrical Similarities between Gower and Certain Sixteenth-Century Poets" is not without its own, forward-looking political bite, in that its judgments suggest possibilities for reading lines of Gowerian influence into a later time.

Finally, it should be apparent too from these contents that what we know of the dissemination and publication of Gower's work continues to grow, and to hold scholarly interest. In the third section of this volume, three essays stand as evidence of the quality, and the diversity, of current concerns. In "Glosing Gower: In Latin, in English, and *in absentia:* The Case of Bodleian Ashmole 35," Siân Echard uses the curiously glossed Ashmole manuscript, in which the "Latin programme" is diligently overridden by an Englishing scribe, to show how Gower's *Confessio* was received only a few years after his death. A.S.G. Edwards's emphasis is also on Gower's manuscripts as they were, in effect, reassembled by readers in the fifteenth century (see "Selection and Subversion in Gower's *Confessio Amantis*"); but it is Martha W. Driver who, in her essay, "Printing the *Confessio Amantis:* Caxton's Edition in Context," carries us farthest ahead in time (and farthest afield as well, for a look at Low Country patronage and techniques of book production) to establish the type of manuscript, and the compositional process, Caxton must have used for the first printed edition of Gower's English poem.

The fifteen essays here assembled, then, represent the state of contemporary Gower scholarship as practiced at its highest level. But considered another way, if its predecessor, *John Gower: Recent Readings,* is any indication, *Re-Visioning Gower* is also a sketch of where Gower studies will be headed in the years to come, as these essays are built upon and expanded by other readers, and as the store of what we know about Gower and his writing continues to grow.

PART I. POETICS AND METHOD

Feigned Truth and Exemplary Method in the *Confessio Amantis*

Patricia Batchelor

The glosses and Latin verses in Gower's *Confessio Amantis* affect the Middle English text they accompany in ways both supportive and subversive of its apparent meaning. Throughout, the Latin apparatus works to endow the fictional dialogue with the authority of truth by exploiting the forms of the scholastic commentary tradition and the prestige of the Latin language. At the same time, however, it sometimes contradicts the text or obfuscates the presumed *sentence* of the narrative or its didactic explication. Frequently the glosses or verses treat issues addressed in the narrative with a skewed emphasis, generating ambiguity rather than providing clarification. In so doing, the Latin apparatus in the *Confessio* serves a number of clearly distinct functions. As a whole, it delineates the *ordinatio* of the work; it creates a kind of dialogue with the vernacular text, contributing to the work's character as a *compilatio;* and it facilitates a *translatio auctoritatis* from the traditional, clerical, Latin culture to a modern, secular, vernacular one. Moreover, for each of these functions, although Gower's technique depends on traditional precedents for its effects, the interaction of text and apparatus ultimately constitutes a tacit challenge to the traditional forms and ideas from which each springs. Through these intermittent challenges the *Confessio* explores the relationship between truth and fiction, and, consequently, calls into question the medieval concept of *auctoritas.*

The importance of that issue to medieval literary criticism and to vernacular poetic practice has become a focus of much contemporary work in medieval studies.[1] These discussions of *auctoritas* emphasize that the term

I am indebted to Tim W. Machan who commented on a rough draft of this essay. I presented an earlier version of this paper at the Thirty-first International Congress on Medieval Studies at Kalamazoo, Michigan, in May 1996.

[1] The scope of this essay precludes a summary of this scholarship. Notable, however, for discussions of vernacular *auctoritas* as related to Gower's work are A. J. Minnis, "Authors in Love: The Exegesis of Late-Medieval Love-Poets," in *The Uses of Manuscripts in Literary Studies: Essays in Memory of Judson Boyce Allen,* ed. Charlotte Cook Morse, et al. (Kalamazoo, 1992), 161–91 and "*De vulgari auctoritate:* Chaucer, Gower and the Men of Great Authority," in *Chaucer and Gower: Difference, Mutuality, Exchange,* ed. R. F. Yeager (Victoria, B. C., 1991), 36–74; Derek Pearsall, "Gower's Latin in the *Confessio*

not only referred to the prestige of a writer or the expertise with which a given text was realized, but also imputed a certain truth value to a text. As A. J. Minnis explains, the term includes "strong connotations of veracity and sagacity."[2] It was an attribute of profound ideas articulated by the *auctores.* He notes that for Hugutio of Pisa *auctoritas* included a sense that the idea was one worthy of "imitation or implementation" and, for Giovanni de'Belli, "of belief."[3] Referring to the hostility of the medieval church toward fiction, Derek Pearsall claims that such resistance to the "unconstrained and transgressive potential of fiction" is intended "to make all writing into a demonstration of truths already known."[4] The truth-value of a text is also closely linked to the term *auctoritas* through its root word *auctor.* According to Laurent Mayali, that term originally designated, not a writer, but "the guarantor, that is, a person who attests or vouches for the truth of a statement or a situation."[5] Such a guarantee of veracity was presumed in the Latin works of the *auctores;* it is noticeably absent in vernacular works. As Tim Machan explains in a discussion of narrative techniques employed by Middle English poets, "their rhetorical strategies recognize and accept that vernacular works were precluded from authorization and vernacular writers from authorship and authoritativeness."[6] The utility of the Latin apparatus as an authorizing agent in the *Confessio* is, therefore, clear.

The effect of the apparatus on the text, its meaning within the work, is not, however, limited to this function. Like the mingled "lust" and "lore" in the work, text and apparatus are interdependent. Moreover, as text and gloss variously influence and modify each other, the work suggests instability in the relations among truth, fiction, and *auctoritas.* Genius and the Latin commentator do not always agree about the significance of the *exempla.* Often the narrative fiction describes a situation not entirely consonant with the moral truth it ostensibly demonstrates.

The resultant interpretive complications can best, perhaps only, be appreciated by attention to the way text and gloss work together in partic-

---

Amantis," in *Latin and Vernacular: Studies in Late Medieval Texts and Manuscripts,* ed. A. J. Minnis, (Cambridge, 1989), 13–25; Winthrop Wetherbee, "Latin Structure and Vernacular Space: Gower, Chaucer and the Boethian Tradition," in *Chaucer and Gower,* ed. Yeager, 7–35; and R. F. Yeager, "English, Latin, and the Text as 'Other': The Page as Sign in the Work of John Gower," *Text* 3 (1987): 251–67.

[2] Minnis, *Medieval Theory of Authorship: Scholastic Literary Attitudes in the Later Middle Ages,* 2nd ed. (Philadelphia, 1988), 10.

[3] *Medieval Theory of Authorship,* 10.

[4] Pearsall, "Gower's Latin in the *Confessio Amantis,*" 22.

[5] Laurent Mayali, "For a Political Economy of Annotation," in *Annotation and Its Texts,* ed. Stephen A. Barney (New York, 1991), 185. The etymology of this word has been the subject of much discussion. See also, Minnis, *Medieval Theory of Authorship,* n. 6, 219–20. Minnis cites the distinction made by Hugutio between *auctor,* derived from *augere,* and *autor,* derived from *autentim.* He notes further, however, that William Brito ranked the senses of the term in this order: *autentim, augeo, agere.*

[6] Machan, *Textual Criticism and Middle English Texts* (Charlottesville, 1994), 105.

ular instances. With particular force, two of Gower's *exempla*, the tale of Florent and the story of Alexander's meeting with Diogenes, illustrate how both Latin and vernacular texts contribute to the *sentence* of the work by exploiting the tension created by their juxtaposition.

The impact on the reader of Gower's "Tale of Florent," for example, is conditioned as much by discrepant details and emphases in text and gloss as by the tale's putative moral. The highly selective gloss does little more than situate the tale within a conventional literary structure and an authoritative tradition. The vernacular text is the more fully developed of the two; from it one can derive a sense of the importance of the development of Florent's character on the dramatic action.

The story of the knight who wins a young and beautiful wife when he keeps his vow to marry the old hag who saves his life is a familiar one. In Gower's version, the focus is on Florent's recourse to the virtue of obedience in his resolution of dilemmas. The actions and dialogue of all the principals in the priest's narrative *show* the rewards of such behavior. From the very beginning of the adventure, the narrative insists on the crucial role Florent's promises play in his destiny. When, for example, his efforts to resolve the riddle at his uncle's court result in discordant responses, he sets out to discover a definitive answer because he "hath levere forto dye / Than breke his trowthe and forto lye / In place ther as he was swore" (I.1511–13).[7] Later, although Florent has saved his life by using the old hag's insight, his trials are far from over. He dutifully returns to find his benefactress; when they meet again his heart breaks "For sorwe that he may noght fle, / Bot if he wolde untrewe be" (I.1701–2).

Later, the narrator also lingers over the details of Florent's reluctance to kiss the lady on their wedding night: "His body myhte wel be there, / Bot as of thoght and of memoire / His herte was in purgatoire" (I.1774–76). And, once they are in bed together, he "torneth on that other side, / For that he wolde hise yhen hyde / Fro lokynge on that foule wyht" (I.1783–85). The lady persists in her advances and "bad him thenke on that he seide, / Whan that he tok hire be the hond" (I.1796–97). For his part, Florent "herde and understod the bond" (I.1798), and responds at last, albeit "as it were a man in trance" (I.1800). His reward for honoring his promise is immediate and fabulous:

> He torneth him al sodeinly,
> And syh a lady lay him by
> Of eyhtetiene wynter age,
> Which was the faireste of visage
> That evere in al this world he syh. (I.1801–5)

At this point, Florent's young and lovely wife demands that he choose to

---

[7] All quotations from the *Confessio Amantis* are based on *The English Works of John Gower*, ed. G. C. Macaulay, 2 vols., EETS, e.s. 81–82 (Oxford, 1900–01).

"have hire such on nyht, / Or elles upon daies lyht" (I.1811–12). Again, the narrator lingers over the description of Florent's anguish over his inability to decide, and his eventual deferral to her wishes:

> 'Bot evere whil that I may live,
> I wol that ye be my maistresse,
> For I can noght miselve gesse
> Which is the beste unto my chois.
> Thus grante I yow myn hole vois,
> Ches for ous bothen, I you preie;
> And what as evere that ye seie,
> Riht as ye wole so wol I.' (I.1824–31)

His obedience, first to his own oath, and thereafter to her will, proves his worthiness. The Middle English narrative focuses on Florent, who, although sorely tried by fortune, is rewarded appropriately for his virtue and deliberate adherence to chivalrous ideals. His wife explains that she is now released from enchantment: "That nevere hierafter schal be lassed / Mi beaute, which that I now have, / Til I be take into my grave" (I.1836–38). She elaborates, then, explaining the enchantment and detailing the conditions necessary for her complete restoration:

> ' . . . til I hadde wonne
> The love and sovereinete
> Of what knyht that in his degre
> Alle othre passeth of good name:
> And, as men sein, ye ben the same,
> The dede proeveth it is so.' (I.1846–51)

She credits her recovery to the "dede," Florent's recognition of her as his "maistresse."

Thus the vernacular text illustrates, through its dramatic details, the proper exercise of the virtue of obedience. Florent emerges honest and obedient from each psychological struggle. The old hag, the vengeful queen, and finally, Fortune, in the person of his wife, reward the knight's acceptance of responsibility for his oaths. His behavior and its just recompense characterize him as a "knyht that in his degre / Alle othre passeth of good name."

Genius then extends the applicability of the story's message and asserts its *auctoritas*. He introduces his interpretation of the *moralitas* by reference to "clerkes that this chance herde" (I.1856). He claims, then, of these authorities that:

> Thei writen it in evidence,
> To teche how that obedience
> Mai wel fortune a man to love
> And sette him in his lust above,
> As it befell unto this knyht. (I.1857–61)

Florent's virtuous obedience constitutes the mechanism by which the "loathly lady" is transformed; it is his virtue that is the focal point of the tale. The subsequent written use of the *exemplum* by "clerkes" for didactic purposes defines it as credible; this authority, in turn, validates the Confessor's (and Gower's) use of it.

The dramatization of virtuous behavior does not exhaust the function of the story in the work, however effectively it satisfies the Confessor's need for an exemplary tale of obedience. Nor is Genius's invocation of written evidence the only mechanism operating here in support of Gower's establishment of *auctoritas* for his "englissh" poem. Taken as it is from the tradition of vernacular romance, the story appropriates, by functioning in this exemplary manner, the *auctoritas* of more prestigious Latin models. Gower's use of a story rooted in secular and vulgar traditions for a didactic purpose allows the whole of his vernacular work to share in the textual *auctoritas* of the ancient *exemplum* tradition. Moreover, this appropriation of the authority of tradition for the work more subtly implies a validation of the traditions of vernacular romance as well. Read as validated in this way, the romance tradition can then serve as a literary context for Gower's entire project.

The Latin prose gloss on this tale facilitates the whole sequence of transfer of power, despite its distinctly different emphasis. A shift in focus is evident from the reference to "those disobedient in love" in the commentator's first words: "Hic contra amori inobedientes" (I.1401). While Genius had proffered the *exemplum* as one demonstrating that "Obedience in love availeth, / Wher al a mannes strengthe faileth" (I.1401), the gloss introduces it as criticism of "amori inobedientes." In this way, the gloss situates the story in the context of the priest's discussion of "murmur and complaint" as aspects of Inobedience, a species of Pride, first of the seven deadly sins. The commentary stresses the story's position within the framework of the lover's confession to highlight the formal *ordinatio* of the work, thereby alluding to its character as a learned text, one participating in the scholastic tradition. Drawing attention to the *ordinatio* of the work it also highlights the Confessor's technique in accommodating his *exempla* to that structure. That beginning, however, requires an immediate transition to a positive description of the *exemplum*'s function as a story "ad commendacionem Obediencie Confessor super eodem exemplum ponit" [for the purpose of recommending obedience the confessor presents an exemplum concerning it] (I.1401).[8]

This lengthy introduction is more concerned with the situation of this *exemplum* within the framing fiction than with the tale itself. In particular, the specific identification of this portion of the vernacular narrative as an *exemplum*, sets it off from the fictional dialogue. Such attention to the

---

[8] Line numbers in the text refer to the line at which the gloss begins in Macaulay's edition. Translations are my own.

work's structure establishes a relationship between the *Confessio Amantis*
and the traditions of *exemplum* and *compilatio*.

The suggestion that it is a self-contained, discrete text is reinforced
visually in the manuscripts. Marginal identification of the speakers in the
dialogue is common even in those manuscripts in which longer commen-
tary passages appear in the text column.[9] In this instance, the Confessor is
identified in the margin (at l. 1396) when he introduces the tale. The gloss
begins at line 1408, the second line of the *exemplum* proper. In the majori-
ty of the manuscripts, it would be situated so as to separate tale from
fictional frame. Even its marginal placement in the modern edition draws
attention to the integrity of the *exemplum* as a unit within the dialogue.
When Genius next addresses Amans directly (at l. 1862), he is again
identified, signaling the end of the tale and the resumption of the fiction.
The careful distinction of each tale from the dialogue in which it is embed-
ded contributes to the work's character as a *compilatio*. Again, the allusion
is to an accepted tradition, a genre with authoritative precedents. The
implications of such an association contribute to the validation of the
vernacular text, facilitating a *translatio auctoritas* from those traditions to
this vernacular work.

The gloss on the tale of Florent proceeds, after its convoluted introduc-
tion, as a summary. It tells the story of a daughter of a king bewitched by
an evil stepmother but eventually rescued by an obedient knight.

> cum quedam Regis Cizilie filia in sue iuuentutis floribus pulcher-
> rima ex eius Nouerce incantacionibus in vetulam turpissimam
> transformata extitit, Florencius tunc Imparatoris Claudi Nepos,
> miles in armis strenuissimus amorosisque legibus intendens, ipsam
> ex sua obediencia in pulcritudinem pristinam mirabiliter reformauit.
> (I.1412)

> [Once when there was a certain most beautiful daughter of the King
> of Sicily in the flower of her youth, by the enchantment of her
> stepmother transformed into a most vile old woman, then Florent,
> nephew of the Emperor Claudius, a soldier most brave in arms and
> attending to the laws of love, by his obedience, miraculously re-
> stored this same (princess) to her original beauty.]

Introduced first, the princess appears to be the protagonist of the story.
The prominence afforded the details of her enchantment reinforces this
emphasis. Within the gloss, the original misfortune is suffered by the lady
and the final reward seems also to be hers.

---

[9] In some manuscripts the distinction between speakers is indicated only by colored
initials or paragraph symbols. In some cases the designations, "Confessor" and "Amans"
extend the line of the text; they are often abbreviated. My references here to these identi-
fying tags are to the line numbers at which they appear in Macaulay's edition. My
investigation of twenty-five manuscripts revealed a striking consistency in their treat-
ments of this feature and with that in the modern edition.

When the admirable Florent finally appears, the commentator treats the knight's genealogy with as much attention as that devoted to the description of his valor and amorous propriety. This detailing of the noble ancestry of the protagonists in the story, makes them fit subjects for classical tragedy, reflecting the learned character of the gloss and its authorizing function. However, those references to his nobility, prowess in arms, and attention to the laws of love also situate Florent within the chivalric romance tradition. This commentary passage is notable for the care with which it discloses—in the entire *exemplum*, in the individual characters, and in their personal qualities—affinities with both prestigious Latin traditions and those of more modern vernacular romance. To do so, of course, it relies on scholastic commentary conventions. Its own authoritative heritage thus enables the gloss to combine allusions to both ancient and contemporary literatures and to suggest their equivalence.

Given the dissimilarity of their emphases, the gloss closes in a manner remarkably consistent with the pagan priest's interpretation of the tale. Like the Middle English tale, it, too, credits Florent's obedience as the means by which the return of the lady to her former state is achieved: "ex sua obediencia." But there has been no mention here, as in the vernacular narrative, of Florent's trials, promise, or marriage, nor of the complexity of his decisions. Instead, although it appears only as a brief explanatory afterthought in the Middle English text, the transformations of the princess become the focus of the commentary.

One consequence of this shift is the loss of that suspense that so characterizes Genius's *exemplum*. Because Florent's adventures unfold in the Middle English tale, the narrative shows him as exemplary, obedient. In contrast, the gloss begins with the bewitched princess and so spares the reader the details of Florent's doubts, temptations, and, therefore, of his virtue. Although there are three references to obedience in this short gloss, it includes no evidence of the exercise of that virtue. This "moralized" reading of the tale, therefore, is subtly undercut by the actual emphasis in the Latin text on magic, aristocratic lineage, and the physical beauty of the princess—all characteristic of its sources and analogous to elements in vernacular romance. In the prestigious Latin context of the commentary, this emphasis cooperates with the vernacular text in endorsing a tradition which, by definition, lacks *auctoritas*.

Within the gloss, the significance of Florent's obedience is its efficacy as an antidote to the spell under which the lady lives; his virtue is fortuitous for her, an attribute no less wonderful than the miraculous transformation it effects. But the commentary, by virtue of its associations with prestigious and authoritative traditions of Latin scholasticism, appropriates for the magic of romance the validity of the *exemplum*. Its didactic interpretation of the tale is no less traditional, of course, than the form of the *exemplum* and the presumed prestige of the Latin language. All therefore, contribute to the authorizing function of the gloss and enable its validation of the Middle English narrative.

At the same time, the form of the commentary (together with its careful situation of the *exemplum* within the confessional scheme) validates the vernacular tradition on which its text depends by redefining the tale as an exemplary one possessed of *auctoritas*. While the Latin commentary ostensibly validates the text it glosses, its service to a vernacular text with vernacular romance roots also, necessarily, draws attention to potential contradictions in that validation. The reciprocal modification of text and gloss, their mutual dependence, makes as strong a statement about the instability of textual authority as either makes about obedience in love. Yet that statement, too, has traditional antecedents.

As M. B. Parkes has shown, thinking had become "a craft" in the schools by the middle of the twelfth century.[10] The focus there on meditative reading and study demanded "changes in features of layout and in the provision of apparatus for the academic reader."[11] The Latin apparatus in the *Confessio* organizes the books of the text, identifies the seven deadly sins and their multiple manifestations, and cites authoritative sources. It creates a program that mimics the revised handling of similar details in scholarly work. Stephen Nichols discusses these changes as reflective of the notion that "processes of rational thought, dialectic, and rhetoric found within the main work came to be extended to a deitic framework that became part of the textual presentation."[12] Rubrication, in particular, "offered something like a structured analysis of an ongoing 'argument.'"[13] And, indeed, in manuscripts of the *Confessio*, the Latin apparatus, which is almost always rubricated, performs just such a function.

However, in structuring the "argument" in this way, the commentary also provokes within that structure a tension between text and gloss. Glosses identify two speakers within the fictional dialogue, yet endorse neither. Moreover, the interpretation of *exempla* in the commentary sometimes contradicts or complicates the Confessor's explication. In these manuscripts, the rubrication defines the structure of the vernacular text, but also provides a conventionally didactic foil for that text.

The apparatus, colored and integrated into the text column in most witnesses, serves not only the authorizing function of the Latin texts, but also their attempt to control its meaning. That presumption is especially clear in those manuscripts in which the Latin commentary precedes the vernacular text it glosses. There, interpretation is privileged over text in a gloss that becomes visually dramatic through color and position. But the massive Middle English text, in all its particularity and narrative complex-

---

[10] Parkes, "The Influence of the Concepts of *Ordinatio* and *Compilatio* on the Development of the Book," in *Medieval Learning and Literature: Essays Presented to R. W. Hunt*, ed. J. J. G. Alexander and M. T. Gibson (Oxford, 1976), 117.

[11] Ibid., 115.

[12] Stephen Nichols, in *Annotation and Its Texts*, ed. Barney, 50.

[13] Ibid., 50.

ity, dilutes the efficacy of these "instructions for correct reading."[14] Consequently, the *mise-en-page* produces a kind of *disputatio* between the two.

The dynamic ambiguity thus generated foregrounds the issue of *auctoritas*, questioning its premises and concomitantly endowing the vernacular narrative with its own literary authority. The importance of the Latin gloss as authorizing agent diminishes as the Middle English poem is empowered. The reader must interpret gloss and text in concert to derive meaning. Here, for example, beyond its authorizing function, the gloss on the tale of Florent remains essential to the work as it makes possible a more specifically literary effect. Although it sacrifices the vernacular tale's suspense and character development, read first, the gloss makes of the entirety of the Middle English narrative a surprise for the reader.

In the vernacular account of Florent's adventures, the enchanted princess does not even appear for over four hundred lines. Consequently, although the tale and its commentary offer complementary interpretations of the *exemplum*, read together they pose for the reader an interpretive puzzle: whose story is it? The commentary tells the story of a bewitched princess, while the narrative is an account of Florent's trials. The discrepancy highlights a characteristic typical of commentary—the tendency to supplant rather than supplement the text it ostensibly exists to serve. In this instance, the gloss minimizes the knight's tribulations to which the bulk of the narrative is devoted. Pretending to discover the kernel of truth, the commentator endorses Genius's choice of the story as illustrative of the virtue of obedience. In so doing, it authorizes the pagan priest to act as interpreter. However, the terse interpretation of the tale offered by the commentary implicitly questions the focus in the Middle English narrative on Florent's psychology. Such questioning has implications for the nature and purpose of the commentary, and so constitutes a substantial contribution by the apparatus to the *sentence* of the work as a whole.

The commentary works with the text to discover traditional exercises in *disputatio* throughout the work. Here, for instance, it raises a series of questions: Does obedience in love present a challenge to one's personal integrity? Is a knight's obedience, like his other behavior, a mere convention of romance useful in the performance of miracles? Is the lady's plight an evil to be overcome by virtue, or, like the good knight's *trowthe*, a mere convention of romance? Such questions engage the reader in the discussion of the relationship between truth and fiction. By making scholarly argument out of vernacular romance, and, by doing so through an authorization of Middle English narrative by Latin commentary, Gower valorizes the popular genre's traditions and his own project. Text and gloss interact to create a complex interpretive situation; together they make of this "loathly lady" romance a matter for serious consideration with philosophical and psychological implications. Foregrounding and questioning the

---

[14] Pearsall, "Gower's Latin in the *Confessio Amantis*," 23.

concept of *auctoritas,* the reciprocal subversions and appropriations by text and gloss become as fascinating as the story each one tells.

However "plain" Gower's style, and however clear the intentions articulated by the poet of the Prologue, the exemplary method employed here confuses the truth. Fictive confessor, artificial commentary, and the texts and intertextual implications of the *exempla* themselves vie for control of each tale. The drama of that conflict becomes, itself, both topic and *sentence* in a tale told to illustrate the desirability of a preeminence of reason in human nature. The conflict between text and gloss in Gower's account of Alexander's meeting with Diogenes shows to advantage how the resultant tension figures in the *sentence* of the work.

Genius tells the story of "Diogenes and Alexander" to support his insistence that "will scholde evere be governed / Of reson more than of kinde" (III.1198–99). Again, tale and gloss agree in the substance of their expression of this philosophical ideal. Together, however, their rhetorical strategies and narrative impact foreground the instability of the concept of *auctoritas.* Gower's choice of subject matter in this tale attests to the participation of the *Confessio* in the tradition of intertextual discussion of such philosophical questions in the schools. The tale contributes to that discussion an ostensibly "correct" understanding of the issue. That understanding, however, is complicated by its context: while the *exemplum* cultivates an association with an illustrious tradition, it also modifies that tradition. The brief account of the philosopher's instruction of the emperor in the matter of reason and will typifies the poet's recurrent and artful manipulation of the relationship between text and gloss. The interdependence of narrative and commentary here creates an interpretive crux that paradoxically dramatizes its own resolution. This *exemplum* overtly addresses the traditional philosophical subject matter. More subtly, it postulates an analogous conflict between reason and the important medieval literary-critical concept of *auctoritas.* Creatively extrapolating from the accepted wisdom of the *exemplum*'s moral, Gower exploits this lesson to support his larger argument for recognition of an authoritative vernacular literature.

This tale appears in Book III of the *Confessio,* which explores aspects of the deadly sin of wrath. In the fiction's introduction to this *exemplum,* the fourth and fifth "species" of this sin are designated by Genius as "contek" and "homicide." In the ensuing discussion, which faintly mimics an academic *disputatio,* Amans admits to suffering "contek" in his heart. He explains that his wit and reason are opposed to will and hope on the subject of love, employing the image of a debate within his lover's heart. His reason urges him to desist from his fruitless efforts; yet he confesses that he is ruled by his will, which encourages him.

Amans perceives this conflict as inevitable and seemingly irreconcilable. He cites anonymous authorities—the ubiquitous "thei sein" (III.1168)—as the source of his insight into the problem. He knows that the rule of will disables understanding, and that hope places the heart in jeopardy, encouraging fantasy (III.1168–73). Yet the lover's will insists that it is cowardly to

abandon hope simply because one's suit is not encouraged. For "where an
herte sit / Al hol governed upon wit, / He hath this lyves lust forlore"
(III.1185–87). Genius immediately sympathizes with the penitent's plight.
He concedes that a lover might be excused for a weakness of will because
"love is of so gret a miht, / His lawe mai noman refuse" (III.1194–95).
Nonetheless, the priest insists that Amans be taught the proper resolution
of the dilemma.

Fiction, tale, and gloss all reiterate ideas otherwise considered elsewhere
in the work. For instance, a man's reason falls victim to vainglory personi-
fied as a hawk in Book I:

> Ther is a vice of Prides lore,
> Which lich an hauk when he wol sore,
> Fleith upon heihte in his delices
> After the likynge of his vices,
> And wol no mannes resoun knowe,
> Till he doun falle and overthrowe. (I.2671–76)

Elsewhere, Genius shows reason's vulnerability to passion. It is overruled
by beauty, mastered by love, in the "Tale of Mundus and Paulina."[15]
Wrath and melancholy conspire against reason in that of "Canace and
Machaire."[16] In those admonitory *exempla*, it is the failure of reason to
rule passion that leads to sin. The story of "Diogenes and Alexander,"
however, is a positive illustration of the power of reason to subjugate the
will.

Throughout the *Confessio*, the issue of literary authority as a measure
of truth value is both challenged and supported in a manner similar to that
by which the superiority of reason is tested in this example. Genius had
introduced this *exemplum* by attributing his information to an unnamed
authority, a written tale he found about a philosopher "of which men
tolde" (III.1201). To be sure, such attributions in medieval fictions are con-
ventional; they are, however, no less effective as a means for conferring
authority on texts because of that conventionality. Their efficacy is, in fact,
an important component of the convention. In this case, reference to un-
specified authorities conspires with the variable role of the Latin com-
mentary to convey a message mirrored in the progress of the narrative.

---

[15] Genius begins this tale with a description of Paulina's beauty, noting that "so
strong is no mannes wit, / Which thurgh beaute ne mai be drawe / To love" (I.770–72).
He later justifies the relatively mild punishment of Mundus by exile:
> For he with love was bestad,
> His dom was noght so harde lad;
> For Love put reson aweie
> And can noght se the rihte weie. (I.1049–52)

[16] In this story King Eolus becomes melancholy when he discovers the birth of his
daughter's incestuously conceived child. Succumbing to his anger, "in this wilde wode
peine, / Whanne al his resoun was untame," he resolves that she must die by her own
hand (III.244–45).

The Confessor's tale begins with the approach of Emperor Alexander and his retinue to an Axletree in which an old man is ensconced in a peculiar contraption contemplating the heavens. The knight sent by the emperor to question the man is, at first, unable to elicit from him any response. The messenger insists that the old man answer, reminding him that "It is thi king which axeth so" (III.1246). The old man, however, denies that Alexander is his king. In fact, he responds with the defiant assertion that "Mi mannes man hou that he is" (III.1251). The Middle English narrative then dramatizes Alexander's own wisdom, restraint, and courteous nature as he himself interrogates the stranger to discover the truth in this apparent riddle. The old man explains that his own will is subject to reason and therefore, "is my man and my servant" (III.1280). He then accuses Alexander, contending that "thi will is thi principal, / And hath the lordschipe of thi witt" (III.1282-83). Therefore, the emperor, ruled as he is by his will, serves the servant of the old man who is ruled by reason.

This explanation criticizes the presumptions of earthly power and questions its value. Here again, questions of truth, worth, and *auctoritas* permeate the discussion. Even more specifically, the notion of *auctoritas* dominates the conclusion of the story. After having heard the philosopher's explanation, Alexander becomes aware of the authority of its source when the old man finally identifies himself:

> 'I am,' quod he, 'that ilke same,
> The which men Diogenes calle.'
> Tho was the king riht glad withalle,
> For he hadde often herd tofore
> What man he was . . . (III.1298-1302)

The emperor responds favorably, recognizing the philosopher's reputation. However, his subsequent deference to an authority implicit in that reputation demonstrates how incompletely he has learned the lesson. Alexander's offer to Diogenes reiterates the faulty suppositions about the king's power with which the story began:

> He seide, 'O wise Diogene,
> Now schal thi grete witt be sene;
> For thou schalt of my yifte have
> What worldes thing that thou wolt crave.'
>
> (III.1303-6)

The emperor, willful as ever in his apparent magnanimity, reveals the limits of his insight.

The philosopher's reply, however, shows his independence from the influence of that power and provides an opportunity for his further mockery of such dross:

> Quod he, 'Thanne hove out of mi Sonne,
> And let it schyne into mi Tonne;

For thou benymst me thilke yifte,
Which lith noght in thi miht to schifte:
Non other good of thee me nedeth.' (III.1307–11)

The sage's curt assessment of the situation insists on the power of his reason over the Emperor's will. It effectively subverts the *auctoritas* attributed to worldly political and military power, conceding only that Alexander does have the power to move himself out of the way. Diogenes' rejection of this gesture of deference to his reputation for wisdom ironically challenges, even as it confirms, the validity of that reputation. His very disdain for Alexander's suggestion that an emperor's gift might enable his wisdom to "be sene" confirms the superiority of that wisdom to any such gift. The philosopher's lesson achieves its *auctoritas* through the consistent alliance of his speech and demeanor with reason as the sole measure of authority. Reason, not antiquity or reputation, reveals truth; only its exercise can guarantee *auctoritas*. The narration of this parable enacts the *sentence* of the *exemplum* even as the philosopher articulates it.

In his introduction to the tale, Genius had invoked the implicit *auctoritas* of a source text for his *exemplum* concerning reason and will. The superiority of reason is a principle, he claims, "Wherof a tale write I finde" (III.1200). The story opens with a characterization of its hero in terms appropriate to an *auctor:* "A Philosophre of which men tolde / Ther was whilom be daies olde, / And Diogenes thanne he hihte" (III.1202–3). The tale he tells, however, undermines the idea of any authority save reason by showing how inappropriate Alexander's deferential response to Diogenes' reputation is. The structure of the *exemplum* thereby creates an opportunity for the reader, along with Alexander, to learn the lesson of the dilemma posed by the philosopher.

As in the "Tale of Florent," the Latin gloss works in a manner unlike, yet complementary to, the narrative of the text:

> Hic ponit Confessor exemplum, quod hominis impetuosa voluntas sit discrecionis moderamine gubernanda. Et narrat qualiter Diogenes, qui motus animi sui racioni subiugarat, Regem Alexandrum super isto facto sibi opponentem plenius informauit. (III.1204)

> [Here the Confessor sets an example that the impulsive will of a man must be governed by the guidance of discretion. And he tells how Diogenes, who would subjugate the impulse of will to his reason, more fully instructed King Alexander, who opposed him concerning this idea.]

The commentator has done little more than state the *sententia*, explaining cryptically that Diogenes "more fully instructed" Alexander concerning the matter. In leaving out all details of the story, the gloss tantalizes the reader with the promise that the Middle English narrative will provide the particulars of Diogenes' pedagogical method. *How* Diogenes teaches this lesson is, in fact, evident in the very form of that narrative. The lesson

itself—embodied in the philosopher's self-possession and contentment in
solitary contemplation, in his courageous defiance of the emperor's author-
ity, in Alexander's humble attention to the lesson, and in his initial failure
to appreciate its implications—cannot be learned from the commentator's
mere summary of it. However authoritative the *sentence* reported in the
gloss, it is the way in which the narrative recounts the lesson that conveys
its truth.

Despite its brevity, the commentary performs several functions. It iden-
tifies Diogenes as a source of greater wisdom than the Emperor Alexander;
it reinforces the *ordinatio* of the work by creating a boundary for the
exemplum; and it articulates the moral of the story. By implying the truth
value in the *exemplum* toward which it merely points, the commentary
authorizes the vernacular text even as it creates mystery through its delib-
erate silence. The question at issue, a serious philosophical matter, implies
a moral authority in the Middle English narrative. The commentator's
restraint and deference to the text endows it with a rhetorical authority as
well. To understand "how" philosopher and king compare on the question
of reason and will, we must read the Middle English narrative. The profun-
dity of the *sententia* articulated in the gloss confers on the text a measure
of that *auctoritas* inherent in the philosophy of the ancients. Yet the ver-
nacular tale, thus endorsed, proceeds to undermine the validity of any such
auctoritas. It does this by detailing Diogenes' denial of Alexander's power;
it compounds the effect by relating Alexander's misinterpretation of the
philosopher's lesson, his linking of wisdom with reputation and his
mistaken perception of his own importance in the maintenance of that
reputation. Empowered by its authoritative sources in classical and scholas-
tic Latin traditions, the *exemplum* demonstrates the error of reliance on
those traditions in the determination of truth. Much as Diogenes justified
his reputation for wisdom by rejecting Alexander's proffered contribution
to that reputation, the Middle English text confirms its own *auctoritas* by
challenging the presumption of the commentary to act as an authorizing
agent.

As in these two *exempla,* throughout the work the Latin verses and
glosses overtly authorize and enable the Middle English text. At the same
time, however, the substance of the vernacular fiction—its pagan priest,
"feigned" lover, and imaginative translations of authoritative works—
continually problematizes that endorsement. The Latin commentary,
which ostensibly validates the vernacular fiction by its very presence, also
offers interpretations of themes and specific *exempla* that challenge many
of the Confessor's explications. Numerous discrepancies between text and
gloss, in particular, call into question the modification of his sources by
Genius.[17] Yet in most cases, text and commentary endorse equivalent

---

[17] The history of criticism of the *Confessio* includes numerous discussions of and
passing references to inconsistencies in interpretation of the *exempla.* Gower, Genius, and
the Latin commentator are variously held responsible for this variety. Scholarship espe-

moral lessons. Their differences, in form and content, serve most effectively to foreground the issue of literary authority.

The Middle English text depends on the prestige of its accompanying commentary for a measure of its credibility. Yet its very nature as a vernacular fiction represents a deviation from those traditions it attempts to appropriate. Because it enables the vernacular text, the commentary facilitates that appropriation, and so, paradoxically, the subversion of its own *auctoritas*. Engagement with this paradox is fundamental to the *sentence* of the *Confessio* as a whole.

Gower creates for his vernacular work an impression of philosophical import by an ostentatious exploitation of the literary and scholastic traditions most redolent of *auctoritas*. Yet the dynamic interaction of Latin and Middle English texts often problematizes the concept itself and so represents a modification of those traditions. A feigned acceptance of the stability and efficacy of authoritative truth permits Gower's successful appropriation of its power for his vernacular fiction—a fiction that persistently questions even its own hard-won *auctoritas*.

---

cially influential for my understanding of this feature in the work includes: Derek Pearsall, "Gower's Narrative Art," *PMLA* 81.7 (1966): 475–84; Winthrop Wetherbee, "Genius and Interpretation in the *Confessio Amantis*," in *Magister Regis: Studies in Honor of Robert Earl Kaske,* ed. Arthur Groos (New York, 1986), 241–60; and R. F. Yeager, *John Gower's Poetic: The Search for a New Arion* (Cambridge, 1990), esp. chap. three, "Transformations."

Gower's Two Prologues to *Confessio Amantis*

Dhira B. Mahoney

The first recension of Gower's *Confessio Amantis*, written about 1390, opens with a charming genesis narrative in which the poet describes the royal commission of his work as an actual contemporary occurrence. "He hath this charge upon me leid," writes Gower, referring to Richard II's request of Gower to write "some newe thing" for the King to read.[1] The topos of the commission, or the *jussio*, as it has been called, was a recognized conventional element of classical prologues, as Ernst Curtius has shown in his study of the inheritance of such conventions from classical rhetoric. Classical authors frequently claimed that they dared to write only because they had been urged or commanded to do so by a friend or a superior. The writer's awareness of his own inadequacy is so strong that only a commission by a friend or superior can overcome his reluctance to undertake the task.[2] This topos, which we might call a subset of the modesty topos, remained extraordinarily useful through the Middle Ages. Gertrud Simon names it the "Auftragstopos," and lists many examples of its use by monastic historians.[3] As Nancy Partner observes, "patronage and requests for literature very elegantly resolved for twelfth-century writers the tension ... between the self-effacing humility demanded by Christian propriety and the urge to excel and claim credit for one's work. By acceding to the demands of an ecclesiastical patron, [a writer could turn accomplishment into] an act of obedience. It was both proper and humble

---

[1] Quotations from *Confessio Amantis* are from *The English Works of John Gower*, ed. G. C. Macaulay, 2 vols., EETS, e.s. 81–82 (Oxford, 1900–1901; repr. London, 1979). Macaulay's edition prints the first recension text as a variant below the text, marking the line numbers with asterisks.

[2] Ernst Robert Curtius, *European Literature and the Latin Middle Ages*, trans. Willard R. Trask (Princeton, N.J., 1990), 85, and for exordial topoi in general, 83–89; for the term *jussio*, see D.W.T.C. Vessey, "William of Tyre and the Art of Historiography," *Mediaeval Studies* 35 (1973): 436.

[3] Gertrud Simon, "Untersuchungen zur Topik der Widmungsbriefe mittelalterlicher Geschichtsschreiber bis zum Ende des 12. Jahrhunderts," *Archiv für Diplomatik: Schriftgeschichte Siegel—und Wappenkunde*, Erster Teil, Vols. 3–4 (1957–58): 52–119; Zweiter Teil, Vols. 5–6 (1959–60): 73–153.

to acknowledge that subservient relationship and thus gracefully sign one's book."[4]

For later, nonmonastic, medieval writers humility was still required, though demanded by rhetorical tradition rather than by Christian propriety, and the authorizing power of the Auftragstopos was still recognized.[5] Dedicating or presenting one's work to a noble patron is one method of adducing authority, but even better is to be able to claim that a patron has requested it. Chrétien de Troyes authorizes his *Lancelot* by announcing that the subject was given him by the Countess of Champagne. She gave him both the "matiere" [subject-matter] and the "san" [meaning] but, typically, it is his "painne" [effort] that turns it into art. Later writers discovered that greater authenticity for the *jussio* could be gained by describing the circumstances in which it was delivered; thus some fourteenth- and fifteenth-century writers narrate a genesis scene, with naturalistic background and dialogue. Christine de Pizan prefaces her *Livre des fais du Charles V* with a description of Philip the Bold asking her to write a history of his brother Charles V.[6] And Osbern Bokenham describes a charming domestic scene of the Twelfth Night festivities at the house of Lady Isabel Bourchier in the "Prolocutorye" to the Life of St. Mary Magdalen in the *Legendys of Hooly Wummen*.[7] While her four sons are dancing, and others are displaying their "disguises," Lady Bourchier converses with Bokenham and delivers her request for a translation of the saint's Life. Though Bokenham remembers his "dulnesse" of wit (ll. 5079–80), he finds it impossible to deny such a "myhty comaundement" (l. 5084), asking only for a delay in order to complete his pilgrimage to Santiago. The vividness of the scene and the verisimilitude of the particulars underscore the author's familiarity with his patroness, and provide authority both for him and his commission.

More than just a charming gesture, the genesis scene has a ceremonial function. Roy Strong has described medieval royal entries into cities, noting how the ritual opens with a gesture of fealty, and includes exchanges of gifts and other gestures which emphasize the mutual obligations of ruler and city. Late medieval royal entries include pageants which emphasize the legitimate descent of the ruler and provide images of the "ideal Christian virtues" to which he should aspire.[8] Genesis scenes, though much more

---

[4] Nancy Partner, *Serious Entertainments: The Writing of History in Twelfth-Century England* (Chicago, 1977).

[5] See Curtius, *European Literature*, 407–13.

[6] Richard Firth Green, *Poets and Princepleasers: Literature and the English Court in the Late Middle Ages* (Toronto, 1980), 204; for the genesis narrative itself, see the translation of the prologue by Eric Hicks, in *The Writings of Christine de Pizan*, sel. and ed. Charity Cannon Willard (New York, 1994), 233–34.

[7] Osbern Bokenham, *Legendys of Hooly Wummen*, ed. Mary S. Serjeantson, EETS 206 (London, 1938; repr. Kraus, 1988), 136–44.

[8] Roy Strong, *Art and Power: Renaissance Festivals 1450–1650* (Woodbridge, Suffolk, 1984; repr. 1995), 7–8. See Chap. I, "The Medieval Inheritance," on the royal entry as

informal, are the literary correlative of such rituals. They dramatize the relationship of the author and patron, as well as their mutual obligations. The poet's function is to advise (as well as to entertain), and the patron's function is to reward; but even more important, the poet's function is also to instruct, to provide images of the ideal virtues to which the patron should aspire, while the patron's function in return is to benefit society by exercising those virtues. In the case of a king, he is to rule wisely and justly; in the case of a noble and devout lady, she is to further the cause of Christian society by imitating the virtuous life she reads about. Like royal entries, genesis narratives may emphasize the status or legitimacy of the patron by recounting lineage or descent (Bokenham provides an elaborate genealogy for Lady Bourchier, emphasizing her place in the line of accession to the throne); and also like royal entries, they include gestures of fealty or pledges of service.

Though Gower's genesis scene in his first recension is not as elaborate as Bokenham's, it clearly belongs to the same tradition. In his preface Gower describes how, after having decided to write a book in English, he goes rowing on the Thames, "under the toun of newe Troye" (Prol.37*).⁹ Here he meets his liege-lord Richard II, who invites him to come on to the royal barge and, after some conversation, commissions the poet to write "[s]ome newe thing" which he himself can oversee (Prol.51*–53*). Despite sickness and awareness of his inadequacy, Gower accepts the commission gladly; he could hardly refuse the task, "For that thing may nought be refused / Which that a king himselve bit" (Prol.74*–75*). The king's command will protect the poet from the envious; working in the king's service will dignify and validate the poem and offset the poet's lack of wit. These are conventional prefatory elements—the *jussio,* the fear of envious critics, the poet's inadequacy, and the impediments to his task. Yet the circumstantial details of the brief narrative are quite vivid, and the scene has a realistic feel. It has prompted John H. Fisher to write, "one would like to know more about the boating party" and to speculate who else might have been there with Richard II, perhaps his queen, his mother, even Geoffrey Chaucer.¹⁰ Richard's request to Gower in the first recension preface is balanced by the epilogue, in which Gower presents his work to the king, begging him to accept it despite its deficiencies. Thus the love allegory which frames the individual stories of the *Confessio* is itself bracketed in a larger frame, the liminal frame in which Gower addresses his audience directly in his own voice.

This liminal frame of the *Confessio* is, however, much less well known than the frame of the third recension, which has a prologue and epilogue

---

a whole, esp. 7–11.

⁹ I follow Macaulay in designating the first 92 lines of the Prologus as the "preface" and the conclusion as the "epilogue" (see xxi, n. 3).

¹⁰ John H. Fisher, *John Gower: Moral Philosopher and Friend of Chaucer* (New York, 1964), 236. Subsequent references to this work will be made parenthetically in the text.

dedicated to Henry of Lancaster, who deposed Richard and usurped the throne in 1399. As Peter Nicholson has observed, it is the Lancastrian frame which is generally privileged by Gower's editors and translators.[11] Just as the change of a picture frame affects the painting it contains, the Lancastrian liminal frame subtly reshapes the reader's approach to the poem. What follows in this essay is a reconsideration and comparison of these two liminal frames, and an analysis of the differing effect (and affect) of the frames on the text, in an attempt, if not to recuperate the Ricardian version, to at least reassess it as having equal authority to the more familiar Lancastrian one.[12]

There are fifty-one complete or nearly complete manuscripts of the *Confessio Amantis,* and the relationships between them are intricate, obscure, and disputed.[13] Macaulay classified the manuscripts according to three "recensions," corresponding to the stages of Gower's revision of his text (see xxi–xxviii, cxxvii–clxvii).[14] The first, which may be dated 1390 because of a marginal rubric (xxi–xxii), has the Ricardian preface and epilogue, containing Richard's commission of the poem and Gower's presentation of it to him. The second recension is marked by additional passages in Books V and VII, a rearranged Book VI, and a revised conclusion that cuts the presentation to and praise of Richard; some copies of this recension also include a new preface that omits the boating party episode and dedicates the work to Henry of Lancaster. As Macaulay points out, some copies of the first recension also contained a brief dedication to Henry as Earl of Derby, in the form of a short Latin envoy at the end of the text, resulting in a kind of double dedication of the work, so the effect of this second version was to make the Lancastrian dedication more prominent while suppressing the reference to Richard (xxi).[15] This second recension was begun fairly soon after the first, perhaps in the next year but

[11] Peter Nicholson, "The Dedications of Gower's *Confessio Amantis,*" *Mediaevalia* 10 (1988): 175. Subsequent references to this article will be made parenthetically in the text.

[12] Russell A. Peck provides a brief comparison of the two prefaces in his general analysis of the Prologue in *Kingship and Common Profit in Gower's "Confessio Amantis"* (Carbondale, IL, 1978), 7–9, but his focus is on the Lancastrian version.

[13] See Peter Nicholson, "Poet and Scribe in the Manuscripts of Gower's *Confessio Amantis,*" in *Manuscripts and Texts: Editorial Problems in Later Middle English Literature,* ed. Derek Pearsall (Woodbridge, 1987), 130. Subsequent references to this article will be made parenthetically in the text. The proposed *Descriptive Catalogue of the Manuscripts of the Works of John Gower,* ed. Derek Pearsall, Jeremy Griffiths, and Kate Harris, is still in preparation.

[14] See also Russell Peck's "Chronology of Gower's Life and Works" in his classroom edition of *Confessio Amantis* (Toronto, 1980), xxxii and n. 2 to the Prologue; and Fisher, *John Gower,* Appendix A.

[15] The lines begin with "Explicit iste liber" and follow with the poet's prayer that the book should find favor with readers, and remain pleasing to the Britons forever. The last two lines use the "Go litel bok" formula as they send the book to Henry, Count of Derby: "Derbeie Comiti, recolunt quem laude periti, / Vade liber purus, sub eo requiesce futurus," translated by Peck in his edition as: "Go, simple book, to the Count of Derby, whom learned men praise, and you will find refuge with him" (523, n. 9).

certainly by 1392, and long before Richard's deposition. The third recension drops the passages added to the book in the second recension, but provides the Lancastrian preface and epilogue of the second recension, finishing with the last two lines of the Latin envoy to Henry.

The first recension also contains a passage in the poem's conclusion, Book VIII, in which Venus speaks to Amans about Chaucer, who is her "disciple" and "poete" (VIII.2942*). Venus tells Amans that Chaucer wrote many songs to her in his youth, and directs Amans to tell Chaucer in his "latere age" to make his own "testament of love," just as Amans has made his confession (VIII.2941–47*). This "coterie" reference, as Anne Middleton calls it, is also excised in the later recensions.[16]

Scholars usually offer political reasons for Gower's alterations to his dedications. The common interpretation is that Gower became disillusioned with the young king during his reign and began to look to Henry for salvation for the realm. Admittedly, this view is furthered by the successive changes Gower made to the Latin colophon attached to some *Confessio Amantis* manuscripts, which, as Fisher shows, reflect a complete change in Gower's sympathy to Richard, so that by the time of his third version Richard has become "crudelissimus rex" who "in foueam quam fecit finaliter proiectus est" [the most cruel king ... who was finally thrown into the pit which he had dug].[17] Macaulay offers as one reason for Gower's disillusion the jealousy rising between Richard and his brilliant cousin and the king's displeasure when Henry left for his expedition to Prussia (xxv), and suggests that the giving of a presentation copy to Henry on his return, ca. 1393, prompted the new dedication to Henry (xxv–xxvi). The version with the new prologue and epilogue was perhaps at first intended only for private circulation, and the final conversion of the text probably took place after Richard's deposition (cxxxvii–xxxviii). Fisher cites Richard's famous quarrel with the city of London in 1392, which might have alienated Gower's sympathies from the King (118–20), and postulates Gower's "prescience" in his rededications to Henry (122–23); after Henry's accession there was "a final flurry of activity," in which a number of luxury copies of the *Confessio Amantis* were made, based on the Fairfax MS, which happened, by accident, to be the first version and which then had to be erased and corrected in the appropriate places (125–26.)[18] However, the best explanation for the changes, according to Fisher, is Gower's desire to make the *Confessio Amantis* conform in theme and vision with his other two major works, the *Vox Clamantis* and the *Mirour*

---

[16] Anne Middleton, "The Idea of Public Poetry in the Reign of Richard II," *Speculum* 53 (1978): 107.

[17] See Fisher, *John Gower*, 88–91; the Latin originals of the colophons in selected manuscripts are given in his Appendix B.

[18] Fisher suggests the choice of manuscript was made by a scribe or amanuensis in a hurry. As many scholars have pointed out, the revised passages frequently take up exactly the same amount of lines as those they replace.

de l'Omme, the latter being renamed as *Speculum Meditantis* to make the connections even clearer. "In a very real sense, Gower's three major poems are one continuous work," notes Fisher, "a systematic discourse on the nature of man and society" (135–36). The revision of the prologue and epilogue in the third recension operate "to make unmistakably clear the place of this final work in the coherent pattern evolved through the *Mirour* and the *Vox*" (121).

The concept of different recensions as representing Gower's changing attitudes to Richard's kingship and the political situation has led such scholars to see Gower as, at worst, self-serving, and at best, politically farsighted in rededicating his work long before Henry's accession. Fisher, for example, calls Gower a "sycophant" in starting out as an enthusiast for Richard and ending up as "an apologist for the Lancastrian usurpation of Henry" (133). However, the case is not as simple as it seems. The colophons which Gower apparently updated through his life were summaries of his whole work, since they mention all three major works. They could well reflect his views toward the end of his life rather than his views during Richard's reign; thus his condemnation of Richard would be written from hindsight, after Henry's accession. Furthermore, despite the marginal rubric in some copies indicating the date 1390, none of the manuscripts of the first recension are actually contemporary with Gower, but are late copies, dated by Macaulay and the catalogues to the early, middle, and even late fifteenth century.[19] "Just how or why so many of this early, politically embarrassing, version should have been produced after Richard's deposition remains a question," observes Fisher (116–17), a question which he does not attempt to answer. Nor do all the copies which Macaulay ascribes to the second recension belong to the same period. The name is used for convenience to categorize an intermediate class of texts (cxxix). And, as Nicholson has effectively demonstrated, the most important manuscripts representing the second and third recensions can themselves be shown to be composites, altered many times.[20] Thus the relationship between the manuscripts is itself obscure, and the relationship between them and the stages of Gower's text even more complex and unreliable.

Nicholson attacks the whole idea that the change of dedications was the result of Gower's political foresight, pointing out that in 1393 Henry was not yet seen as the country's savior, and arguing that Fisher exaggerated Richard's conflict with the Londoners, while Macaulay invented the idea of Richard's displeasure at Henry's chivalric exploits and departure on the crusades. Gower's "relationship with both men at the time of presentation was literary rather than political in nature" ("Dedications," 161). The revisions are due to a necessary change of patron, rather than to changes in Gower's political sympathies. Nicholson's detailed analysis of the Fairfax

---

[19] See also Fisher, *John Gower,* 116.

[20] See Nicholson, "Poet and Scribe," 130–42, also "Gower's Revisions in the *Confessio Amantis,*" *The Chaucer Review* 19 (1984): 122–43, esp. 135–39.

and Stafford manuscripts (representing Macaulay's second and third recension) refutes the idea that Gower himself prepared them for exemplars, and demonstrates that what is now called the third recension is "merely the accidental product of several different layers of textual history." It became "an identifiable 'version' of the poem not from the circumstances of its origin but from the fact that it happened to be recopied" ("Poet and Scribe," 138). Nicholson also argues that Gower's political adherence to Henry "dates only from the time of Henry's accession to the throne" ("Dedications," 174). In this period luxury copies of the poem were made, the other poems revised, and new poems written by Gower in praise of Henry and justifying the usurpation.[21] The addition of rubrics and the revision of the colophon, implying that the poem was originally written for Henry, are "disingenuous," claims Nicholson; Gower was able in this way to remind Henry of the original double dedication of the poem, suppress all references to the dedication to Richard, and "underscore his long friendship and early devotion" to Henry of Lancaster ("Dedications," 174).

Nicholson's arguments are thorough and persuasive. He challenges the whole notion of recensions, showing that they have no necessary relation to the process or stages of revision ("Poet and Scribe," 142). "In the case of the prologue and epilogue," he points out, "we do not have a simple process of revision and correction but two equally authoritative versions to choose from. The first is closer to the original moment of composition, and the second, born of particular circumstances having to do only with a new presentation, became the official version through a historical accident that placed the new dedicatee on the throne" ("Dedications," 175). It will be clear that I am following Nicholson's lead in discussing the two versions of this liminal frame separately, designating them simply as the Ricardian and Lancastrian versions, and treating them with equal respect. As scholars have come to recognize in recent years, many late medieval texts survive in differing versions from among which it is often impossible (and improper) to designate one as the authoritative text.[22] The concept that texts before the advent of printing are essentially unstable (since each new manuscript provides a new text and no text can be pronounced definitive), first articulated by Paul Zumthor as "mouvance," is now a commonplace of French medieval scholarship, and has migrated into the study of English medieval literature.[23]

---

[21] For these, see Fisher, *John Gower*, 126–27.

[22] Some random examples of such Middle English texts are *Piers Plowman* (A, B, and C texts); Chaucer's Prologue to the *Legend of Good Women* (F and G versions) and *The Canterbury Tales* (Hengwrt and Ellesmere MSS); Malory's *Morte Darthur* (the Winchester MS and Caxton's printing); the Wycliffite Bible; Julian of Norwich's *Shewings* (long and short versions); Lydgate's *Danse Macabre;* and many romances (*Ipomedon* exists in three versions, for instance, a stanzaic version, a couplet version, and a prose version). See the articles in *Crux and Controversy*, ed. A. J. Minnis and Charlotte Brewer (Woodbridge, 1992), especially those by Tim William Machan, Derek Pearsall, and Anne Hudson.

[23] See Paul Zumthor, *Essai de poétique médiévale* (Paris, 1972), 65–75, 507; also David

The Ricardian version of the liminal discourse is more personal and more charming than the Lancastrian one, and acts more effectively (and affectively) as a frame for the poem. The Prologus begins with the poet reminding us of the importance of books such as those that tell us of our predecessors, and expressing the need for "newe som matiere / Essampled of these olde wyse" (Prol.6–7); however, since wisdom alone can be too heavy for readers, he promises to go "the middel weie" and "wryte a bok betwen the tweie, / Somwhat of lust, somwhat of lore" (Prol.17–19). He will write, in English, "A bok for king Richardes sake, / To whom belongeth my ligeance" (Prol.24*–25*). This is followed by a further assertion of his loyalty, and a prayer for a long reign. Then comes the genesis narrative, which is worth quoting in full:

> As it bifel upon a tyde . . .
> Under the toun of newe Troye,
> Which tok of Brut his ferste joye,
> In Temse whan it was flowende
> As I be bote cam rowende,
> So as fortune hir tyme sette,
> My liege lord par chaunce I mette;
> And so befel, as I cam nyh,
> Out of my bot, whan he me syh,
> He bad me come in to his barge.
> And whan I was with him at large,
> Amonges othre thinges seid
> He hath this charge upon me leid,
> And bad me doo my besynesse
> That to his hihe worthinesse
> Some newe thing I scholde boke,
> That he himself it mihte loke
> After the forme of my writynge. (Prol.35*–53*)

Gower accepts the commission gladly, hoping that it will protect him from the envious, who might be ready "to feyne and blame that I write" (Prol.60*). Indeed, he prays to God "Fro suche tunges he me schilde" (Prol.67*):

> And natheles this world is wilde
> Of such jangling, and what befalle,
> My kinges heste schal nought falle,
> That I, in hope to deserve
> His thonk, ne schal his wil observe;
> And elles were I nought excused,
> For that thing may nought be refused

Hult, *Self-Fulfilling Prophecies: Readership and Authority in the First "Roman de la Rose"* (Cambridge, 1986), 66–68.

Which that a king himselve bit.
Forthi the symplesce of my wit
I thenke if that it myhte avayle
In his service to travaile;
Though I seknesse have upon honde,
And longe have had, yit wol I fonde . . .

(Prol.68*–80*)

Thus the poet resolves to write his book, so that it may be "wisdom to the wise / And pley to hem that lust to pleye" (Prol.84*–85*). This completes the ninety-two lines of the preface; the Prologus continues by examining the state of the times, which have degenerated so severely from the golden age of harmony and order. Now war and discord flourish, both in temporal affairs and in ecclesiastical ones (Gower refers bitterly to the papal Schism). Simony and greed operate: "[N]on entendeth / To that which comun profit were" (Prol.376–77). Having considered temporal rulers, the state of the church, and the commons, Gower finishes with "Nebuchadnezzar's Dream of the Ages of the World." We are now in the worst age, the age of Earth, when all is discord and instability. The cause of this evil is "divisioun," which is the "moder of confusioun" (Prol.851–52), existing in man himself, whose microcosm has affected the macrocosm (Prol.954–66). Thus the Prologus proper provides the social, political, and moral context for the love-vision, which does not begin until Book I. In the love vision, the poet as Amans, an unhappy lover, confesses himself to Genius, Venus's priest: what follows is set in the structural framework of the Seven Deadly Sins, which are explained by Genius and exemplified by individual narratives from Ovid and other sources.[24] The sins encompass not only amatory but moral and social issues as well: Book VII, for instance, is a virtual Mirror for Princes.[25]

As we have noted, the preface contains the conventional prefatory grammar; yet at the same time the conventional tropes take on a freshness and grace from the simplicity of Gower's diction and his easy versification. With his genuine devotion to Richard and its desire to trace the middle way, to produce "somwhat of lust, somwhat of lore," the preface also presents a transparent, trustworthy persona. Gower is neither asserting himself as an authority nor, despite the reference to his "symplesce,"

---

[24] The Latin sidenote emphasizes that the role of unhappy lover is assumed: "Hic quasi in persona aliorum, quos amor alligat, fingens se auctor esse Amantem ..." [From here on as if in the person of others whom Love oppresses, the author, feigning himself to be a lover] (Macaulay, ed., 30).

[25] John A. Burrow calls the scheme of the sins a "reference grid" to help the penitent recount his sins to the confessor: "So, as Genius works his way systematically across this grid, questioning Amans on the five sorts of pride, the five sorts of envy, and so on, the lover's behaviour and feelings towards his mistress ... are scanned and displayed with unusual fulness and penetration" ("The Portrayal of Amans in 'Confesssio Amantis,'" in *Gower's "Confessio Amantis": Responses and Reassessments*, ed. A. J. Minnis [Woodbridge, 1983], 8.)

presenting himself as naive and inadequate. However unsuccessful he may be as a lover (he begins Book I with his anguish during the month of May when all other creatures have their mates), he is not inadequate or insecure as a poet. The pellucid quality of the verse prevents that.

Planted in the Ricardian preface is a sense of promise and potential. It is a young king who commissions the work, and it is under the walls of "newe Troye," founded by Brutus, that the boating encounter takes place, Gower drawing on a favorite late medieval device to give authority to London and England, the *translatio imperii*.[26] Gower's "newe thing," written in the vernacular, will celebrate both England's cultural connections with antiquity and the possibilities of a new society governed according to the right principles. It will indeed be a "newe thing."

Critics have frequently complained of the poem's disunity. Gower attempts to marry three different thematic strains, the courtly love allegory, the penitential framework of the Seven Deadly Sins, and the sociopolitical commentary on the state of England, to the point that some readers focus totally on the romance plot, while others focus on the social commentary.[27] But, as Russell Peck reminds us, for Gower, man is a "double entity, both social and individual.... [T]he broad social criticism and the personal woes of the lover are part of one and the same plot." A. J. Minnis similarly observes, "For Gower, the virtues of the good lover were indistinguishable from those of the good man, and the good king was the best of men."[28] Amans's search for healing and repose is parallel to the need for peace and unity in England. For Gower, "divisioun" is the

---

[26] The myth of Trojan origin was derived ultimately from Geoffrey of Monmouth's *Historia Regum Brittaniae*, in which Brutus, the great-grandson of Aeneas, establishes the English nation and names his capital city Troynovant. The invocation of the Trojan foundation myth was very much in the air in the fourteenth century, leading even to a proposal to rename London "New Troy." See the discussion of the political implications of the issue by Lee Patterson, *Chaucer and the Subject of History* (Madison, WI, 1991), 161–62. The establishment of the new society is also linked in Gower's Ricardian prologue with his choice of the vernacular for his book: though Gower does not say explicitly that Richard ordered him to write in English, the royal commission and the choice of the vernacular are closely associated (see Prol. 22*–24*). Michael J. Bennett argues in "The Court of Richard II and the Promotion of Literature" that Richard should be given more credit for the promotion of English letters than he is usually given (*Chaucer's England: Literature in Historical Context*, ed. Barbara A. Hanawalt [Minneapolis, 1992], 10–12). Fisher has argued that Henry IV's program of encouragement of English poetry was the major influence in the development of the vernacular ("A Language Policy of Lancastrian England," *PMLA* 107 [1992]: 1168–80), but perhaps the Lancastrians were simply continuing a tradition already begun, if less aggressively, by Richard II. Robert F. Yeager suggests in "English, Latin, and the Text as 'Other': The Page as Sign in the Works of John Gower," *Text: Transactions of the Society for Textual Scholarship* 3 (1987): 251–67, that Gower may have chosen the vernacular as "an appropriately 'median' tongue," while adding the Latin hexameter verses and marginal rubrics in Latin prose to provide authority. The combination would certainly reinforce the idea of *translatio imperii*.

[27] See, e.g., Fisher criticizing C. S. Lewis in *John Gower*, 191.

[28] Peck, *Kingship*, xxi, xxiv; Minnis, *Gower's "Confessio,"* 1.

disease, whether in the microcosm of the individual man or in the body of society.

The integral connection between the healths of king and realm raised in the Ricardian prologue is revisited and intensified in the Ricardian conclusion or epilogue. It begins with a Latin prayer for the king, which alludes again to the descent of the nation from Brutus. The prayer is then expanded in English and delivered by the poet himself:

> Upon mi bare knees I preye
> That he my worthi king conveye,
> Richard by name the Secounde,
> In whom hath evere yit be founde
> Justice medled with pite,
> Largesce forth with charite. (VIII.2985*–90*)

This is followed by a long discussion of the king's good qualities, his ability to stay above dissension, like the sun above the clouds, his success in settling "many a gret debat" (VIII.3023*) among his liege men, and his desire for peace at home and abroad:

> What king that so desireth pes,
> He takth the weie which Crist ches:
> And who that Cristes weies sueth,
> It proveth wel that he eschueth
> The vices and is vertuous . . . (VIII.3029*–33*).

The emphasis is on Richard's desire for harmony and his integrity—"Thus stant he with himselve clier" (VIII.3015*). He deserves to be loved and obeyed, as indeed the poet does love and obey him. The poet is himself old and feeble—"what for seknesse and what for elde" (VIII.3042*, see also line 3070*)—but despite his unworthiness he offers his book to the king:

> But thogh me lacke to purchace
> Mi kinges thonk as by decerte,
> Yit the Simplesce of mi poverte
> Unto the love of my ligance
> Desireth forto do plesance:
> And for this cause in myn entente
> This povere bok heer I presente
> Unto his hihe worthinesse,
> Write of my simple besinesse,
> So as seknesse it suffre wolde. (VIII.3044*–53*)

The epilogue now takes up a theme from the preface, that the book should provide both mirth and wisdom, and the poet apologizes for his lack of eloquence:

> But I have do my trewe peyne
> With rude wordes and with pleyne

> To speke of thing which I have told.
>
> (VIII.3067*–69*)

The topos of inadequacy includes a reminder that he is "feble and old" (VIII.3070*), which in turn prompts Gower's farewell, not to his book but to his subject matter, love, for that topic is only suitable for a successful lover, a young man:

> But he which hath of love his make
> It sit him wel to singe and daunce,
> And do to love his entendance
> In songes bothe and in seyinges
> After the lust of his pleyinges,
> For he hath that he wolde have . . . (VIII.3078*–83*)

The renunciation of love-poetry is not a surprise; it has been prepared for, six hundred lines earlier, in Amans's expulsion from the courts of love at the ending of the allegory. It is worth reviewing this ending, in order to show how it modulates into the epilogue. Venus has appeared to Amans in response to the bill of supplication he has sent her, and as if in play, asks his name. He replies, "John Gower" (VIII.2321). She tells him he will be eased of his pain, not by being granted his wish for requited love, but by a remedy more appropriate, for he is no longer capable of the actions required of love, and it is better to "make a beau retret" (VIII.2416):

> The thing is torned into was;
> That which was whilom grene gras,
> Is welked hey at time now.
> Forthi mi conseil is that thou
> Remembre wel hou thou art old. (VIII.2435–39)

At this Amans/Gower swoons, and in a vision sees Cupid leading a procession of lovers, from the classical and romance past. They are divided into two groups, one led by Youth, the other by Elde. Youth's company includes heroes such as Tristram and Jason, unhappy women betrayed by love, and good women remembered for their fidelity. They are young and lusty:

> Al freissh I syh hem springe and dance,
> And do to love her entendance
> After the lust of youthes heste.
> Ther was ynowh of joie and feste,
> For evere among thei laghe and pleie . . .
>
> (VIII.2487–91)

Elde's company, in contrast, is wise and sober, consisting of old men besotted by their wives, like Solomon and Aristotle. It is these men who gather round Amans and pray for him, until, finally, Cupid pulls out of his body the dart with which Venus had pierced him at the beginning of the poem.

The lovers vanish, but Venus remains, to rub an ointment on Amans's heart, temples, and kidneys, and show him his reflection in a mirror:

> Wherinne anon myn hertes yhe
> I caste, and sih my colour fade,
> Myn yhen dymme and al unglade,
> Mi chiekes thinne, and al my face
> With Elde I myhte se deface,
> So riveled and so wo besein
> That ther was nothing full ne plein
> I syh also myn heres hore. (VIII.2824–31)

It is a shocking and poignant moment: the verse gives the impression that Amans sees himself being transformed into an old man as he looks. The lover can no longer put off acceptance of the knowledge that he does not belong in the court of love. He reflects that man's life is like the seasons, and gradually comfort and Reason restore his wits,

> So that of thilke fyri peine
> I was mad sobre and hol ynowh. (VIII.2868–70)

When Venus laughs and asks him what love is, he can no longer answer. As John Burrow says, "It is a wonderful moment . . . Amans cannot remember Cupid. Love itself has become like a dream from which he awakens to find it false."[29] The lover receives his absolution from Genius and kneels to Venus, who places a rosary around his neck and tells him to "make a plein reles / To love" [give up all claim on love] (VIII.2914–15), and to return home to his books and pray for peace. For a moment, Amans/Gower is dazed, but he looks on his beads, smiles a little, and returns home. The allegory then modulates into a prayer for the health of England, with which Gower winds up the themes introduced in the Prologus.

The poignancy of the ending is unmistakable. Gower's rejection by Venus is an expulsion from Paradise, and in his resignation to his new role the sadness of loss is intertwined with a Wordsworthian acquisition of wisdom. What makes it less painful is the realization that the healing provides wholeness, and brings the lover-poet to the state where he is no longer divided against himself. It is this conclusion that is recalled in the epilogue, in Gower's farewell to love-poetry quoted above, triggered by the reminder that he is old. The passage about young satisfied lovers in the epilogue (VIII.3078*–83*) echoes the description of the company led by Youth in Amans's vision (VIII.2487–91) (even to the extent of retaining the same end rhyme, "dance/entendance") thereby also recalling the inevitable progression from that joyful vision to Amans/Gower's expulsion from Venus's court. There, he was counseled by Venus to make a "beau retret" from

---

[29] Burrow, "Portrayal," 19.

love; now he recognizes that it is time to relinquish not only loving, but even writing about love:

> And thus forthi my fynal leve,
> With oute makyng eny more,
> I take now for evere more
> Of love and of his dedly hele,
> Which no phisicien can hele. (VIII.3088*-92*)

Worldly love is too "divers" (VIII.3093*) and unreliable; no man will be totally satisfied by it. But the love which is "withine a mannes herte affermed, / And stante of charite confermed" (VIII.3099*-3100*) is unchanging, will never fail us. Thus, in a modulation reminiscent of the "epilogue" of *Troilus and Criseyde,* Gower takes his readers from the realm of secular love, which he has abandoned both as fictional lover and as poet, and turns to the divine love that never fails.

Characterizing the Ricardian epilogue is the emphasis on youth and love. The poet's allegiance to Richard is not out of duty but of love: it is for the king's "worschipe" and "[i]n love above alle other thing" that he has written this book (VIII.3071*-73*; see also lines 3046*-68*). His loyalty is to a young king who seems the embodiment of justice and good government, full of potential, one who deserves that loyalty. The relationship is a personal one, expressed in verse of genuine feeling. Altogether the Ricardian liminal frame has a much stronger sense than the later version of the courtly environment, with the boating party narrative and the coterie allusion to another love-poet, Chaucer, also becoming too old for Venus's service. The poet's renunciation of (secular) love is made more touching because it so clearly evokes and associates itself with Venus's rejection of all the lovers who are too old to belong to her court.

In contrast, the Lancastrian liminal frame conveys a sense of moral strain, derived from the poet's consciousness of the world's degeneration since the Golden Age. The revised preface is only sixty-eight lines, replacing exactly the same number of lines of the Ricardian preface and starting from line twenty-four of the Prologue, but the effect is surprisingly different. Gower's relationship with his patron Henry is more distant, and therefore more conventional, because this version loses the personal references and delicately naturalistic details of the Ricardian one. The royal commission is replaced by a short dedication to Henry, which is repeated in the epilogue. The book that Gower wrote "for king Richardes sake" in the Ricardian version is now written for "Engelondes sake" (Prol.24), a substitution which happens more than once (the Latin quatrain that begins the epilogue becomes a prayer for England rather than for Richard). The genesis narrative is replaced by reflections of a more general nature, suggested by the later sections of the Prologus: the state of the world has deteriorated, for instance:

> Men se the world on every syde
> In sondry wyse so diversed,
> That it welnyh stant al reversed,
> As forto speke of tyme ago.
>
> (Prol.28–31; see also lines 56–57)

The poet has a duty to write in order to preserve the memory both of great rulers and of tyrants of the past (a conventional historical trope). There is more announcement of the poem's contents, also, than in the earlier version; the "prologe" will treat of matters that will warn the wise man of the mutability of this world:

> The fortune of this worldes chance,
> The which noman in his persone
> Mai knowe, bot the god al one [but God alone].
>
> (Prol.70–72)

After the "prologe" the book will treat of love, that has brought so many wise men low.

Most altered from the Ricardian prologue is Gower's relationship with his patron. Whereas the poet in the earlier version was on friendly terms with his king and could be called over to join him on the royal barge, here Gower is more conventionally humble and distant from his patron. He employs the appropriate modesty tropes:

> Thus I, which am a burel clerk,
> Purpose forto wryte a bok . . . (Prol.52–53)

> Bot for my wittes ben to smale
> To tellen every man his tale . . . (Prol.81–82)

and sends his book to his patron with the conventional request for correction:

> This bok, upon amendment
> To stonde at his commandement,
> With whom myn herte is of accord,
> I sende unto myn oghne lord,
> Which of Lancastre is Henri named: (Prol.83–87)

The alterations are not radical; sometimes the same phrases or the same couplets are used, in slightly different contexts (e.g., compare Prol. 89*–92* with lines 54–59, especially Prol. 90* which becomes line 54 without a change). But the effect is subtly different, since the emphases have shifted from sparkling promise to present social criticism.

Whereas the changes to the Lancastrian prologue are subtle, the changes to the Lancastrian epilogue are radical. As I have said above, the epilogue begins with a Latin quatrain praying for the health of the realm (without any reference to the founding by Brutus), and replaces the devotion to and praise of Richard with much moral and social criticism of the state of the realm. The themes of the Prologus are reprised: the clergy needs to reform itself, govern itself under the "reule of charite" (VIII.3003), the "chevalerie" should be defending the commons instead of oppressing them, the commons themselves should be obeying laws rather than pursuing "singuler profit" (VIII.3039), the population of the cities should be pursuing unity and virtue. (It is significant that whereas the Lancastrian epilogue twice extols the "comune right" as well as condemning "singuler profit" [VIII. 3013, 3023, 3039], the Ricardian epilogue never mentions these terms.) Above all, the king, who has supreme power but with it supreme responsibility, should govern himself well first before his people:

> First at hym self he mot begynne,
> To kepe and reule his owne astat,
> That in hym self be no debat
> Toward his god: for othre wise
> There may non erthly kyng suffise
> Of his kyngdom the folk to lede . . . (VIII.3082–87)

These stern moral instructions are obviously aimed at Henry but are not addressed to him directly, being couched in more general terms. The emphasis is again on wholeness, harmony, integrity: unless the king is at peace with himself, he cannot hope to keep peace in his land. Pride and greed will make his state short, but the virtuous king will govern long and be blessed by his people.

The poet now turns to his book, using much the same apology for his lack of eloquence as in the Ricardian version. The passage which expressed his unworthiness and "symplesce" in relationship to Richard is, however, now placed in relationship to a collective, unspecified noble audience:

> So preye y to my lordis alle
> Now in myn age, how so befalle,
> That y mot stonden in here grace:
> For though me lacke to purchace
> Here worthi thonk as by decerte . . . (VIII.3129–33)

As in the Ricardian epilogue, Gower conveys his renunciation of love-poetry, but where in the Ricardian version the initial announcement was followed by the charming passage of young lovers dancing and singing, here it is followed by a more general, one-note, condemnation of secular love, which is blind, opposed to reason, and causes division in the self (VIII.3144–51), reprising the application of the motif to king and society earlier in the epilogue. The passage modulates seamlessly into the final reflection on the imperfect nature of secular love and its contrast to heavenly love, which is very similar to the Ricardian version, though shorter. The text ends with a six-line Latin envoy, in which the poet hopes his book will find favor among Englishmen, and sends it to Henry, addressed as "Derbeie Comiti."[30]

Thus the Lancastrian liminal frame is more generalized, more hortatory and less commendatory than the Ricardian, and has less sense of the immediacy and presence of the court. It is less touching, particularly with the loss of the personal connection with youth and with the king. (Even the praise in the Ricardian version is poignant: the potential of youth can be sullied, the youthful promise withered.) The sterner, repetitive emphasis on the present degeneration of the world in the Lancastrian liminal frame repeats and endorses the notes struck in the Prologus and the theme of the statue in "Nebuchadnezzar's Dream." Gower becomes less an observer, less a poet, and more a prophet.[31] The authority gained by the king's personal commission in the Ricardian version has given way to a self-adduced authority gained by the poet presenting himself as a moral commentator.

I should not wish to give the impression that the Ricardian version is superior in all respects. It is the Lancastrian version that contains the longer ending to Book VIII, with Gower left "bewhapid" and "amasid" until he looks at his beads and smiles a little. In the Ricardian version the poet simply goes "[h]om fro the wode and forth" (VIII.2965*), while the Lancastrian version contains the beautiful passage of an almost Miltonic resignation and acceptance:

> And whanne y sigh non othre weie
> Bot only that y was refusid,
> Unto the life which yhadde usid
> I thoughte nevere torne ayein:
> And in this wise, soth to seyn,
> Homward a softe pas y wente,
> Wher that with al myn hol entente
> Uppon the point that y am schryve
> I thenke bidde whil y live. (VIII.2962–70)

The Lancastrian version also contains a shorter and more effective incantatory description of the love which will never fail us at the end:

> Such love is goodly forto have,
> Such love mai the bodi save,
> Such love mai the soule amende,
> The hyhe god such love ous sende . . .
>
>   (VIII.3165–68)

---

[30] Some manuscripts have only the last two lines, some four. See Macaulay, ed., notes, 549.

[31] As indeed he was in *Vox Clamantis*, where he spoke in the voices of both John the Baptist and John of the Apocalypse (see Peck, *Kingship*, xxiii). Note, though, that Robert Yeager offers a different model for Gower's final voice, that of the singer Arion, who can heal division by creating harmony, in *John Gower's Poetic: The Search for a New Arion* (Woodbridge, 1990), esp. 237–44.

Yet, as I have said above, changing a picture frame affects the painting it contains, and the substitution of the Lancastrian liminal frame subtly reshapes the reader's approach to the poem. And it is the Lancastrian text that is privileged by Gower's editors and translators as Gower's final intention. Macaulay's scholarly edition prints the Ricardian passages below as "variants"; Peck's classroom edition includes only the Chaucer passage, in his notes; and Terence Tiller's Penguin translation ignores the Ricardian version altogether. Discussions based on the Lancastrian text tend to place much greater emphasis on the sociopolitical criticism than on the theme of love.[32] It is not surprising that the official version of Gower is the "moral" Gower.

One of the questions raised by Gower's conjunction of moral and social comment with the issues of courtly love is the relationship between Gower the poet and Gower the lover. When, at the end of the narrative, Amans discovers, in a moment of pain and shock, that he is old, is he to be read by us as old from the start? Donald Schueler claims that he is, but Burrow in his perceptive essay argues that the reader is to respond to Amans as he sees himself, a young man in love's court, though unsuccessful, until the final revelations. Burrow also emphasizes the Latin sidenote which tells us the "auctor" is "feigning himself to be a lover": "The distinction between Gower as (actual) *auctor* and Gower as (feigned) *amans* is carefully preserved throughout the confession."[33] It is when his confession is over that he recommences speaking as *auctor*. "It might seem," notes Burrow, "that Gower in the closing pages of his poem, simply changes the persona of his narrator from *amans* back to *auctor*; but the beauty of his ending largely derives, in fact, from a subtle parallelism which unites the two figures in what seems almost a single act of abnegation." It is a formulation I perfectly agree with. Amans finds rest and healing (though with a sense of loss) in renouncing secular love; the *auctor* finds rest and healing for his sickness and feebleness by renouncing the writing of poetry about love. Both personae merge in the epilogue, and turn to seek unity and wholeness, which constitutes health, in the realm of England.[34] It is the Ricardian liminal frame, however, which delicately

---

[32] For example, Peck's *Kingship and Common Profit*, which assumes the Lancastrian frame; as I have noted, the term "common profit" and its variations are absent from the Ricardian epilogue.

[33] Donald G. Schueler, "The Age of the Lover in Gower's *Confessio Amantis*," *Medium Aevum* 36 (1967): 152–58; Burrow, "Portrayal," 22. For the Latin of the sidenote, see n. 24 above.

[34] Paul Strohm prefers to read three personae, Gower the poet, Amans, and the historical Gower, following Donaldson's original formulation about Chaucer. The first stage of integration between the two former personae occurs when Amans names himself "John Gower"; and when Amans looks into the mirror, he "dwindle[s] to the physical person of the aged poet" ("A Note on Gower's Persona," in *Acts of Interpretation: The Text in its Contexts, 700–1600: Essays on Medieval and Renaissance Literature in Honor of E. Talbot Donaldson*, ed. Mary J. Carruthers and Elizabeth D. Kirk [Norman, OK, 1982], 297). Yeager also recognizes "three distinct voices (Amans, the 'I' of story; Amans/John

emphasizes youth, joy, and love, making the abnegation more subtle and poignant.

Unlike Chaucer, in his liminal discourse Gower is not interested in establishing the place of his work within a literary tradition. He may speak of old books at the beginning of his poem, but only in the most general way, whereas Chaucer's relationship with the "olde bokes" of his sources is complex and intimate, whether he acknowledges his actual sources or invents fictional ones. Nor is Gower as concerned as Chaucer with defending or authorizing his position as a translator, though his choice of the vernacular for the *Confessio,* has, as we have observed, some significance in his project. I spoke above of the transparent, trustworthy persona Gower establishes in the Ricardian preface: it is related to Gower's self-portrait throughout his liminal discourse, one that is "delicately shaded and touched with naturalistic detail but not individualized."[35] Gower's persona, as Anne Middleton has brought out in her influential essay, speaks in the "common voice": "The 'I' of public poetry presents himself as, like his audience, a layman of good will, one worker among others, with a talent to be used for the common good. It is his task to find the common voice and to speak for all, but to claim no privileged position, no special revelation from God or the Muses."

Middleton asserts further that the versions of the *Confessio Amantis* are not really significantly different. "The king is not the main imagined audience, but an occasion for gathering and formulating what is on the common mind. . . . What is required is only the concrete or imagined situation of being in the royal presence or on a public platform."[36] I suggest that Middleton is unconsciously swayed by the privileging of the Lancastrian version in her view of the *Confessio Amantis* as public poetry—her last observation is more appropriate to the Lancastrian version than the Ricardian. However, her point raises a possible answer to the question that Fisher never succeeded in answering. Why were so many fine copies of the Ricardian version, a "politically embarrassing version," made after Henry's accession, two of them even owned by Henry's sons?[37]

Gower, the 'I' of the Prologue; and John Gower man and poet)" which become "conjoined" in "successive steps" to perform the modulation from fictive love-allegory to moral and political discourse (*John Gower's Poetic,* 233).

[35] Burrow, "Portrayal," 10.

[36] Middleton, "Idea of Public Poetry," 99, 107.

[37] Fisher's article on the Lancastrian encouragement of vernacular poetry as a deliberate act of language policy explains why there should be so many *Confessio Amantis* manuscripts, but not why the Ricardian version should be popular. For details of the late first recension copies, see A. I. Doyle and M. B. Parkes, "The production of copies of the *Canterbury Tales* and the *Confessio Amantis* in the early fifteenth century," in *Medieval Scribes, Manuscripts & Libraries: Essays presented to N. R. Ker,* ed. M. B. Parkes and Andrew G. Watson (London, 1978), 208-9; and Kate Harris, "Ownership and Readership: Studies in the Provenance of the Manuscripts of Gower's *Confessio Amantis,*" Ph.D. Dissertation, University of York, 1993, 129-55. Oxford, Christ Church MS 148 is associated with Thomas, Duke of Clarence, and was perhaps even commissioned

The answer I postulate is based on my consistent view of the authorizing aspect of liminal grammar and the power of convention. Perhaps it was not politically embarrassing to copy the *Confessio Amantis* with its Ricardian liminal frame after Henry's accession, because the frame was not seen, either by the writer or his audience, as a historically accurate account. In the presentation miniatures which became so popular in luxury manuscripts of the fifteenth century, the picture was not a record of an actual event, but a performance of the presentation.[38] Similarly, Gower's narrative of the boating party may be seen as symbolic and performative rather than historical. Perhaps Gower never did meet Richard in a boat on the Thames, or perhaps that was not the occasion when he suggested that Gower write his "newe thing"—it does not matter. The narrative construction of a royal commission has an authorizing value far beyond any consideration of historical actuality. Perhaps, also, the Ricardian version was not, in fact, so politically embarrassing in the mid-fifteenth century. We tend to read the *Confessio* in light of the later propaganda writing by Gower, such as the third Latin colophon and the *Cronica Tripertita*, which explicitly denigrates Richard and praises Henry at Richard's expense, and therefore to see the Ricardian version as embodying an early attitude that Gower would need to repudiate.[39] In the twentieth century the value of a political or commercial endorsement would be tainted or compromised if the endorser were a deposed or discredited leader; the fourteenth-century audience could make a clear distinction between the King's two bodies—as a sacred, anointed entity and as flawed political leader. Gower's genesis narrative draws on the authorizing power of association with the sacred entity.[40]

---

for him, after 1405 (Harris, 129); Pembroke College, Cambridge MS 307, is associated with John, Duke of Bedford (Harris, 141). These manuscripts are both first recension. A lost but recorded version of the first recension is the Portuguese translation associated with Henry IV's sister, Philippa, daughter of John of Gaunt (Harris, 153–55). Bodleian Library, MS Bodley 294 is a manuscript of the second recension (Harris, 130) associated with or actually commissioned by Humphrey, Duke of Gloucester (Doyle and Parkes, 208–9).

[38] See my essay, "Courtly Presentation and Authorial Self-Fashioning: Frontispiece Miniatures in Late Medieval French and English Manuscripts," *Mediaevalia* 21 (1996): 97–160.

[39] For the colophon, see Fisher, *John Gower*, 112; for the *Cronica Tripertita*, see Green, *Poets and Princepleasers*, 181–82. Paul Strohm points out in chap. 4 of *Hochon's Arrow: The Social Imagination of Fourteenth-Century Texts* (Princeton, 1992) that Henry's accession was "neither as inevitable nor as secure as has commonly been supposed," and that the "aura of inevitability" surrounding the accession was a result of "the Lancastrian genius for manipulating public opinion" both in the months before the accession and in retrospective writings long afterwards (75). See also the prior version of this chapter, similarly titled: "Saving the Appearances: Chaucer's *Purse* and the Fabrication of the Lancastrian Claim," in *Chaucer's England*, 21–40.

[40] Martin Gosman discusses the importance of symbolic representations of princely power in public spectacles and commissioned art of the fifteenth and sixteenth centuries. Mimesis is unnecessary, indeed avoided, since what is being evoked is the persona of the

Nicholson argues in "Gower's Revisions" that copies of the first recension must have been in the hands of booksellers even before Gower's death and that the proliferation of copies of the Ricardian version was essentially due to the commercial trade. Gower was unlikely to have "issued" a Ricardian version after 1399 himself. Kate Harris suggests that the wide dissemination of first recension copies was due simply to the greater availability of that version (the majority of the surviving manuscripts being of the first recension).[41] Nevertheless, the fact remains that the copyists and publishers of the commercial book trade clearly did not see this version as offensive to Henry. The reading public of the fifteenth century, unlike twentieth-century readers looking back on a historical situation through the distorted lenses of Lancastrian propaganda, might well have been more politically tolerant than is generally supposed. The Ricardian liminal frame accentuates Richard's personal role in the "state allegory," and evokes his persona in the act of exercising his public functions, king of England and patron of John Gower. It is more charming, more delicate, more poignant, and more appropriate to the love allegory that it frames. We should not dismiss it simply as a "variant" or a poet's discredited first draft.

---

ruler, exercising his public function, representing the *institutio:* "The king's persona was a role in a kind of state allegory" ("Some Observations Concerning the Manifestation and Exploitation of Power in the Fifteenth and Sixteenth Centuries," *Fifteenth-Century Studies* 21 [1994]: 126). Similarly, for Gower, historical reality does not have primacy over symbolic representation.

[41] Nicholson, "Gower's Revisions," 137, 139, and n. 55; Harris, "Ownership and Readership," 120–21, and n. 105.

Metrical Similarities between Gower and Certain Sixteenth-Century Poets

Thomas Cable

Comments on Gower's prosody tend more toward the level of literary effect than the level of phonological and metrical analysis. Alan T. Gaylord, for example, has a suggestive essay on Gower's "bookish prosody," which in its thirty-two pages and more than two hundred quoted lines of text indicates the metrical stressing of only nine words and the pronunciation of nine occurrences of final -e or -ed.[1] The assumption seems to be that Gower's meter is fairly clear and that the most interesting questions have to do not with its structural but with its literary and aesthetic qualities (involving matters of rhetoric, colloquial exchange, narrative summary, pacing, description, and so on). In returning the discussion downward to the level where syllables bump against other syllables and form feet (or lack of feet) and phrases (or lack of phrases), I intend to suggest that the meter is not necessarily what it may seem to a modern reader. In setting this analysis within a comparative discussion of metrical practice a century and a half later I also aim to ask higher aesthetic questions. Briefly, I shall argue that what Gower (and Chaucer) did very well can be seen in comparison with what George Gascoigne, George Turberville, and Barnabe Googe in the mid-sixteenth century did poorly, in the same meter.

The phrase "in the same meter" is important, because otherwise it would be pointless to compare Gower with these undistinguished poets. The underlying assumption that I am making is that Chaucer and Gower wrote in meters that have had a limited currency in the history of English poetry. It was not an iambic meter, either tetrameter or pentameter, as we have known iambic meters since Sidney, Spenser, and Shakespeare.[2] To say that the meter of Gower and Turberville (and the other poets named above) is an *alternating* meter may seem to advance the discussion little, because most people think of the iambic meters as more or less alternating.

---

[1] Alan T. Gaylord, "'After the forme of my writynge': Gower's Bookish Prosody," *Mediaevalia* 16 (1993): 257–88.

[2] See Thomas Cable, *The English Alliterative Tradition* (Philadelphia, 1991), 117–29. For a critique of this theory see Gilbert Youmans, "Reconsidering Chaucer's Prosody," in *English Historical Metrics*, ed. C. B. McCully and J. J. Anderson (Cambridge, 1996), 205–9.

Some people—some metrists—who have theories on the subject think of
iambic meters as *essentially* alternating.

The three-way movement, and somewhat contradictory directions, of
this essay will be first to remind readers that the meters of Chaucer and
Gower are arguably different from those of Spenser and Shakespeare (and
of Milton, Pope, Wordsworth, Keats, Tennyson, and Yeats) in ways more
than of style; further that they are arguably similar to the meters of
Gascoigne, Turberville, and Googe, also in ways more than of style; and
finally that in ways of style the meter of Gower is much more finely
modulated than the meters of these mid-sixteenth-century poets. A similar
analysis would hold for Chaucer. Whatever differences one might then
develop between Gower's meter and Chaucer's—in terms of "bookish" or
"colloquial" qualities, for example—can proceed on an understanding of
what they have in common.

Gower's eight-syllable line, often called "iambic tetrameter," is an
alternating meter, not a foot meter. Specifically this means that determina-
tions of relative stress are made between every consecutive syllable: the
second syllable is stressed more than the first, the third less than the
second, the fourth more than the third, and so on. There are a few prob-
lematic lines in Gower that do not readily fit this pattern (a pattern that
may be schematized as a/b\a/b\a/b\a/b), but the problematic lines do not
include patterns that can be interpreted as diagnostic of another meter. In
Shakespeare, by contrast, there are hundreds of lines that are clearly
diagnostic and that argue compellingly, as W. K. Wimsatt and others have
shown, for a foot meter (a meter that may be schematized as
a/b | a/b | a/b | a/b | a/b).[3] This means that in foot meter an even-
numbered syllable in a line will normally be stressed more than the odd
syllable that precedes (with several well-recognized variants) but not
necessarily more than the odd syllable that follows. Two much-discussed
examples occur in the opening lines of Shakespeare's Sonnet 30:

$$x \setminus | \quad / \quad //$$
When to the sessions of sweet silent thought

$$x \quad \setminus | \quad / \quad //$$
I summon up remembrance of things past.[4]

These rising patterns of stress through four syllables do not normally oc-
cur in alternating meter. In patterns where the odd syllable might appear
to get greater stress than the preceding even syllable, alternating meter
works to demote the odd syllable (the syllable in a position of "non-ictus")
so that it will conform to the pattern; equally the meter can work to

---

   [3] See W. K. Wimsatt, "The Rule and the Norm: Halle and Keyser on Chaucer's
Meter," *College English* 31 (1970): 774–88.

   [4] Lines from Shakespeare are cited from the edition by David Bevington, *The
Complete Works of Shakespeare,* 3rd ed. (Glenview, IL, 1980).

promote an otherwise lightly stressed even syllable (a syllable in a position of "ictus") over a following odd syllable so that the pattern is maintained. It is important to note that foot meter causes a similar kind of demotion and promotion of stress, but it does so only within feet, not between feet. This limitation of the domain of relative ictus is the main function of the foot.

Clearly the view that I am presenting is controversial, both at the level of metrical theory (Is it legitimate to assume that a meter can promote and demote the stress on syllables?) and at the level of the particular poets (Why not call the difference between Chaucer's and Shakespeare's meter a difference of style within iambic pentameter?). Because there is not space here to argue principles of metrical theory, I shall proceed directly to the comparative analysis of the particular poets and trust that it will provide evidence for returning to questions of metrical theory in a separate study.

Gower's meter, like Chaucer's, is affected by two features of late-fourteenth-century phonology: the optional sounding of final -e and the variable stress on a large part of the lexicon, especially those words of Romance origin. I shall argue that these two features reinforced each other in making an alternating meter a natural choice and that the second feature also functioned to modulate the alternating pattern, which became relentless in the poetry of George Turberville and others. To these phonological determinants one should add that Gower simply had a better ear than Turberville and was able to put together sequences of syllables that softened the pounding of an insistent meter, especially in the eight-syllable line.

Let us consider Turberville's octosyllabic lines to see what Gower does not do. The comparison has been facilitated by the computerized Chadwyck-Healey English Poetry Full-Text Database and by additional programming that allows the insertion of metrical tags showing degrees of phonological stress, the matching of phonological stress and metrical ictus, word division, word length, etc.[5] A frequent line pattern in Turberville has eight monosyllabic words in which the odd positions are occupied by function words (articles, prepositions, conjunctions, auxiliary verbs) or unstressed syllables within words, and the even positions are occupied by content words (nouns, adjectives, main verbs, adverbs); for example, from "In Prayse of the Renowmed Ladie Anne, Ladie Cowntesse Warwicke":

>   /   /   /   /
> With mowlde in hande to flee to Skies (l. 5)
>   /   /   /   /
> To see so neere the stoole of state (l. 9)

---

[5] I wish to thank Harlin Hanson for adapting the Chadwyck-Healey English Poetry Full-Text Database (Cambridge, 1992) to the needs of this particular application.

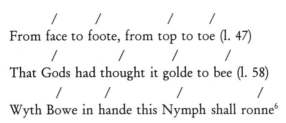

/   /   /   /
From face to foote, from top to toe (l. 47)

/   /   /   /
That Gods had thought it golde to bee (l. 58)

/   /   /   /
Wyth Bowe in hande this Nymph shall ronne[6]

In fact, this is the single most frequent pattern of stress and word division in the 642 lines of Turberville's twelve octosyllabic poems. It occurs seventy-four times.

Any count of metrical features such as this is useful only to the extent that the features constitute patterns in sound that make a difference. The history of prosodic inquiry during the past two centuries has been vexed by the fact that different systems of analysis extract different sets of features—sets that are sometimes compatible and complementary, sometimes indifferently neutral, sometimes contradictory. The goal that has determined the selection of features here is to explain why Turberville's poetry has, impressionistically, an insistent beat that goes *te tum te tum te tum te tum;* and why Gower's poetry has, impressionistically, a more varied, modulated, and subtle rhythm (despite the reading of Gower that some critics have asserted).

Among the phonological and metrical patterns that contribute to distinctly different styles in the same alternating meter of Gower and Turberville two especially are salient: the mix of monosyllabic, disyllabic, and polysyllabic words in a line; and the matching of degrees of phonological stress with metrical ictus or lack of ictus. The alternating pattern of nonictus and ictus can be thought of as a metrical template with binary values represented by whatever symbols one is accustomed to:

    x / x / x / x /
    o S o S o S o S

The most neutral stress pattern has weakly stressed syllables in odd positions and heavily stressed syllables in even positions, in these lines from Gower and Turberville respectively:

    x / x   / x / x / x
    The wyse man mai ben avised[7]

    x / x   /   x / x /
    With willing mindes they all agreede
                        (Turberville, "In Prayse," l. 41)

<hr />

[6] "In Prayse," l. 64. Quotations from Turberville are from *Epitaphes, Epigrams, Songs and Sonets (1567),* facsimile reproduction and introduction by Richard J. Panofsky (Delmore, NY, 1977).

[7] *Confessio Amantis,* Prol. 65. Lines from Gower are cited from *The English Works of John Gower,* ed. G. C. Macaulay, 2 vols., EETS, e.s. 81–82 (London, 1900–01).

To show departures from this neutral mapping, various systems could be used, some more fine-grained than others. I have marked intermediate levels of stress that might be called "tertiary" or "secondary," as opposed to "weak" and "full" stress. My own system does not pretend to more than an approximation, and even in the anchoring of metrical stress to phonological stress, which depends ultimately if indirectly on grammatical category and syntactic phrasing, the analysis is not completely determinate. Roughly, "function words" or "clitics" (modal auxiliaries, prepositions, determiners, conjunctions, etc.) are not stressed phonologically and thus are neutral in a position of non-ictus but variant in a position of ictus. The other grammatical categories (nouns, adjectives, main verbs, most adverbs) by whatever name they are called as a group (content words, major-category words, lexical category words, etc.) receive phonological stress and are thus neutral in a position of ictus but variant in a position of non-ictus. Personal pronouns are sometimes stressed and sometimes not, as are some adverbs.

The point to make is that Gower takes much fuller advantage of the variations in normal English stress than does Turberville, Googe, or Gascoigne. Gower also takes fuller advantage of different lengths of words to vary the flow of the phrasing. Whereas Turberville has seventy-four occurrences of the pattern of monosyllables noted above, "x / x / x / x /," with alternating function words and content words, Gower in a comparable selection of 642 lines, has only one.[8] Gower's verse instead is characterized by a wide variety of patterns of stress and word length that move against the binary metrical template and provide what metrists call "tension" or "counterpoint." Take for example, lines 529–43 of the Prologue to the *Confessio Amantis:*

> And natheles yet som men wryte
> And sein that fortune is to wyte,   530
> And som men holde oppinion
> That it is constellacion,
> Which causeth al that a man doth:
> God wot of bothe which is soth.
> The world as of his propre kynde   535
> Was evere untrewe, and as the blynde
> Improprelich he demeth fame,
> He blameth that is noght to blame
> And preiseth that is noght to preise:
> Thus whan he schal the thinges peise,   540
> Ther is deceipte in his balance,

---

[8] In the first 642 lines of the Prologue, line 261. Ten additional lines have this pattern plus a line-final *-e,* which of course was not possible for Turberville.

> And al is that the variance
> Of ous, that scholde ous betre avise.

With a mix of monosyllables, disyllables, and words of three, four, and five syllables, there are lines that are composed of seven words:

> And sein that fortune is to wyte (l. 530)
> God wot of bothe which is soth (l. 534)

And lines of only four words:

> That it is constellacion (l. 532)
> Improprelich he demeth fame (l. 537)

Because the form of an alternating meter does not allow the modulations that are possible in a foot meter, one expects stressed syllables to occur regularly in positions of ictus and weakly stressed syllables in positions of non-ictus. Yet Gower manages to soften the transitions between stressed and unstressed syllables with his own effective variations. Syllables that could take primary stress occur in positions of non-ictus: *men* (ll. 529, 531), *man* (l. 533), and *God* (l. 534). More frequent is a substitution that has also been noticed in Chaucer's alternating meter, the occurrence of a lightly stressed syllable in a position of ictus, as the occurrences of the preposition *of* twice in line 20 and the conjunction *as* in line 455 of the Prologue:

> That of the lasse or of the more (l. 20)
> This worldes good, so as thei telle (l. 455)

The frequent occurrence of weakly stressed syllables in positions of ictus gives a lighter feel to the line in both Chaucer and Gower. Yet there is no need to revise the traditional account of the number of ictus positions in the lines.

The couplet in lines 541–42 is interesting for questions that it raises about the changing rules of stress in Romance loanwords. Gower used the word *balance* more than any other poet in Middle English (the twenty occurrences in his poetry being more than those of all other Middle English poets combined, according to the Chadwyck-Healey database). Gower always stresses the word on the second syllable as here, presumably with pronunciation of final *-e*. Did the potential for stress on the first syllable of *balance* give a more complex feel to these two syllables than to, say, *deceipte* (stressed x /) in the same line? In any event it is a different feel from that two centuries later in Shakespeare:

> x / | x \ | ^   /
> But in the balance of great Bolingbroke
> > *(Richard II* 3.4.87)

Here not only has the stress shifted unambiguously to the first syllable but also the light stress on *-ance* is subordinated to the preposition *of* to give four rising levels of stress, as in *-brance of things past*, noted above. Similarly, *variance* in line 542 is stressed / x \ x or \ x / x to give a slower pattern than Milton's *variance* in a pattern that involves some kind of elision, or potential elision, most likely synaeresis (the change of the *i* to a *y*-glide):

<pre>
    /   /   /   \   /
Brought him so soon at variance with himself
</pre>
(Samson Agonistes, 1. 1585)

At a higher and doubtless more interesting level we should notice how Gower's syntax helps him avoid the monotony of the octosyllabic line that we find in poets like Turberville. Gaylord is especially good in describing the flow of Gower's syntax from line to line and identifying what he calls "periods" and "verse paragraphs":

> In using the term, 'period,' I am looking forward to Milton rather than back to Cicero. Gower constructs passages of clauses, dependent and independent, that are normally expansions of the common SVO syntax, not displaying short grammatical suspensions or inversions (as in Latin).[9]

Gaylord's observations can be illustrated by the passage before us: five lines begin with the coordinating conjunction *And* (529, 530, 531, 539, 542); one with the noun phrase complementizer *That* (532); one with the relative pronoun *Which* (533); and one with the conjunctive adverb *Thus* (540). This syntactic apparatus contributes to the structure of clauses that Gaylord again perceptively describes:

> They are the sort of unit-of-sense that needs to be comprehended as a whole, and might be punctuated today first with commas, then held together with semicolons or dashes. To call them 'verse paragraphs' comes close to the mark, except that Gower's manuscripts show a system of indentation that does not accord with these periods. They are related to the norms of the eight-syllable line and poetic couplets, yet by no means hemmed in by them. (262)

All this seems perfectly right until the last sentence. What does it mean to say that the periods "are related to the norms of the eight-syllable line and poetic couplets"? The patterns of syntax are not merely related to the patterns of meter but are cast strictly into them. The meter is perfectly regular. In these lines there is no "deviation" such as an "inverted first foot" or a "headless line," deviations that occur only rarely in Gower. The syntax contributes to varying the metrical style, so that the verse does not become monotonous. The reason for quibbling over this hierarchy of meter and syntax is the sense that I get from reading Gaylord of an impatience and a boredom with what metrists most often do.

---

[9] Gaylord, "Gower's Bookish Prosody," 262.

There is a way of thinking about theories of Chaucer's meter, and by implication Gower's meter, that has a certain plausibility as an intermediate course between extremes but which, I would argue, misses the music of both poets. By this view, codifications of Chaucer's meter by nineteenth-century philologists—as illustrated too fully by Bernhard ten Brink[10]—had the advantages but also the problems of nineteenth-century philology: taxonomic rigidity, mechanicalness, and an inflated estimation of rules. Mid-twentieth-century theories by James G. Southworth and Ian Robinson went too far in reaction, almost ignoring the template altogether in allowing for expressiveness.[11] The sensible compromise, then, would be to recognize an incipient meter in Chaucer and Gower but one less constrained than, say, the meter of English poets in the late-sixteenth and the seventeenth centuries (not to mention the mid-sixteenth or eighteenth centuries). This story seems compatible with Gaylord's views and with those of Susanne Woods.[12] Without naming specific errors in ten Brink's system, Gaylord mainly describes it as quaint and old-fashioned, writing wittily: "The effect is like examining some bulky engine in a museum, once designed, we are told, to perform some useful task, but whose precise function and workings are now obscure."[13] Woods sets up opposing traditions that are not quite right: "In short, Chaucer's meters are more precise than Southworth and Robinson suggest, but less prescriptive than Halle and Keyser's model would suggest" (42). Because Halle and Keyser's model is hardly prescriptive at all, one can substitute "ten Brink" or "Paull Baum," both of whom Woods sees as part of the same tradition, and have a more accurate summary of her own views and the views of others.[14]

Even with this substitution, however, I would argue that the sensible compromise has it wrong. I have reread the whole of ten Brink's treatment of Chaucer's meter and find almost nothing to contradict my own experience (a mix of impressions, tabulations, collations, grammatical parsings) in scanning thousands of lines of fourteenth-century poetry. The poetry scanned is both "syllable-stress," in Chaucer and Gower, and alliterative "strong-stress," in Langland, the *Gawain*-poet, and others. Aside from some dubious emendations and a quirky aversion to "headless" lines, ten

---

[10] Bernhard ten Brink. *The Language and Metre of Chaucer*, 2nd ed. rev. Friedrich Kluge, trans. M. Bentinck Smith (New York, 1901).

[11] See James G. Southworth, *Verses of Cadence: An Introduction to the Prosody of Chaucer and His Followers* (Oxford, 1954); see also Ian Robinson, *Chaucer's Prosody* (Cambridge, 1971).

[12] See Alan T. Gaylord, "Scanning the Prosodists: An Essay in Metacriticism," *Chaucer Review* 11 (1976): 22–82; see also Susanne Woods, *Natural Emphasis: English Versification from Chaucer to Dryden* (San Marino, CA, 1984).

[13] Gaylord, "Scanning the Prosodists," 32.

[14] See Morris Halle and Samuel Jay Keyser, "Chaucer and the Study of Prosody," *College English* 28 (1966): 187–219; see also Paull F. Baum, *Chaucer's Verse* (Durham, NC, 1961). On the Halle-Keyser theory see Derek Attridge, *The Rhythms of English Poetry* (London, 1982), 34–55, and the references there.

Brink's comments are generally accurate and adequate, if unexciting as expository prose.

Gascoigne had a notion of Chaucer's meter that is ironic to contemplate, because he thought it was so different from his own. It is hard to know if Gascoigne misread Gower in the same way, or whether the constraints of the octosyllabic line would have kept him from going astray. In any event, Gascoigne sees Chaucer as writing a line that varies in its count of syllables:

> Also our father *Chaucer* hath used the same libertie in feete and measures that the Latinists do use: and who so ever do peruse and well consider his workes, he shall finde that although his lines are not always of one selfe same number of Syllables, yet, beyng redde by one that hath understanding, the longest verse, and that which hath most Syllables in it, will fall (to the eare) correspondent unto that whiche hath fewest sillables in it: and like wise that whiche hath in it fewest syllables shalbe founde yet to consist of woordes that have such natural sounde, as may seeme equall in length to a verse which hath many moe sillables of lighter accentes.[15]

The diagram that Gower uses for the English verse of his own day is an evenly alternating one, which would not apply in Gascoigne's mind to Chaucer:

I understand your meaning by your eye.

The argument being presented here is that some such diagram captures neatly the meter used by Chaucer, Gower, Gascoigne, Turberville, and Googe. It is only in the latter part of the sixteenth century, in the works of Sidney and Spenser, that a foot-divided diagram is relevant:

$$x \; / \quad | \quad x \; / \quad | \quad x \; / \quad | \quad x \; / \quad | \quad x \; /$$

My own view is that the vertical lines representing foot boundaries provide the essential key to understanding the modulations that have been possible in iambic pentameter poetry in English for the past four centuries. In response to this view, Gilbert Youmans has argued that there is less a categorical difference between the meters of Chaucer and Shakespeare than a "strongly normative" tendency toward alternation in the foot meter of Chaucer (see n. 2). These are matters that require further empirical investigation and theoretical refinement.

Whether categorical or normative, the descriptions of Chaucer's decasyllabic line as "alternating" apply *a fortiori* to the shorter line in both

---

[15] George Gascoigne, "Certayne Notes of Instruction (1575)," in *Elizabethan Critical Essays*, ed. G. Gregory Smith, 2 vols. (Oxford, 1904), 1:50.

Chaucer and Gower. It could well be that the eight-syllable line (with an optional final unstressed syllable) does not normally allow variations, such as continually rising stress, that occur naturally in the iambic pentameter. It could be that Jonathan Swift's "iambic tetrameter" is better characterized as "octosyllabic alternating meter." These comparisons too are beyond the scope of the present essay. What can be said is that Gower worked within the constraints of a meter that allowed less flexibility than the iambic pentameter. Within those constraints he crafted happy modulations that were beyond the skill of poets a century and a half later.

The Phenomenology of Make-Believe in Gower's *Confessio Amantis*

Russell A. Peck

Oure wit may not sti3e vnto the contemplacioun of vnseye thinges
but it be ilad by consideracioun of thinges that beth iseye.
> —John Trevisa, *De proprietatibus rerum*

Often we speak of things which we do not express with precision
as they are; but by another expression we indicate what we are un-
willing or unable to express with precision, as when we speak in
riddles. And often we see a thing, not precisely as it is itself, but
through a likeness or an image, as when we look upon a face in a
mirror. And in this way, we often express and yet do not express,
see and yet do not see, one and the same object. We express and see
it through another.... An inference regarding it, which can be
reached ... as it were in a riddle, is not therefore necessarily false.
> —St. Anselm, *Monologium* LXV.

Qui habet aures audiendi audiat.
> —Jesus on John the Baptist, Matt. ll:15

Alle thing that is iwist nis nat knowen by his nature propre, but by
the nature of hem that comprehenden it.
> —Boethius, *Consolation of Philosophy* Bk. V, prosa 6[1]

An early version of this essay was presented at the 1991 International Congress at Kal-
amazoo. A revised version was presented at Pennsylvania State University in the fall of
1992. The essay was published in *Studies in Philology* 91.3 (summer 1994): 250–69. I have
made some revisions of the text and have added a couple of notes, though for the most
part the argument is as it was in its first published form. I am grateful to Eve Salisbury
for discussion of "the new medievalism" and to Gerald Bond for comments on the
general goals of the essay.
   [1] Sources for the epigrams are as follows: *On the Properties of Things: John Trevisa's
translation of Bartholomaeus Anglicus De Proprietatibus Rerum*, ed. M. C. Seymour
(Oxford, 1975), I, 41. *St. Anselm: Basic Writings*, trans. S. N. Deane (La Salle, IL, 1962),
129–31. The citation of Matt. ll:15 occurs at the end of Trevisa's initial epigram to his
translation of Bartholomaeus Anglicus' *De proprietatibus rerum* and functions as the
rhetorician's admonition to read well; the sense of the Latin is: "He who has ears to
hear, let him hear"—Douai translation. The passage from Boethius is from Chaucer's
translation, *The Riverside Chaucer*, ed. Larry Benson (Boston, 1987), 466; the *Boece* in this

In an attempt to define a "new medievalism," Stephen Nichols comments on the need "to interrogate the nature of medieval representation in its differences and continuities with classical and Renaissance mimesis."[2] What strikes him as a characteristic feature of medieval discourse is not simply its strongly traditionalist orientation, but rather its remarkably flexible sense of boundaries within the dynamics of cultural expression. "In the Middle Ages, one senses a fascination with the potential for representation, even more than with theories or modes of representation" (Nichols, 2). Nichols acknowledges the powerful shadow of tradition in the Middle Ages, but, following Brian Stock,[3] suggests that for medieval writers tradition "is far from static." Rather, it is "very much a phenomenon of the present ... and, as such, is also an agent of cultural change" (Nichols, 10). To illustrate this vital reciprocity between tradition and the potentialities of representation that lead to cultural change, Nichols points to medieval attempts to extend the range of what was known of the material world through their challenges to ontological boundaries, social boundaries, boundaries of religious orthodoxy and also of gender, even to boundaries between humans and animals.[4] Human irrationality seems a greater preoccupation than proofs of rationality.

The most fascinating area of liminal exploration in fourteenth-century England is, to my way of thinking, the recurrent challenging by various writers not only of humankind's rational-animal nature, but of the very workings of the human mind itself. They explore ways in which the mind appropriates languages to represent itself. Characteristically, human thoughts are shown to contain not substantialities, but only linguistic representations of things; the logic of the potentialities of representation is, moreover, fundamentally suppositional, rather than reific. And, almost in the manner of *ordo repraesentationis* found in church drama of the previous century, fourteenth-century fiction writers represent the potentialities of

---

edition is edited by Ralph Hanna III and Traugott Lawler.

[2] Nichols, "The New Medievalism: Tradition and Discontinuity in Medieval Culture," in *The New Medievalism*, ed. Marina S. Brownlee, Kevin Brownlee, and Stephen G. Nichols (Baltimore, 1991), 1–26. The lines quoted are found on 1–2.

[3] Nichols draws particularly on the opening chapter of Brian Stock, *Listening for the Text: On the Uses of the Past* (Baltimore, 1990). "One of the features of traditionalistic action is that norms are consciously selected from the fund of traditional knowledge in order to serve present needs.... Viewed in the light of their [the traditional models'] common features, they constitute one of the period's strongest endogenous forces for change" (38–39).

[4] This medieval representation of animality's challenge to social ratiocination is a topic that bears on fourteenth-century English intellectual topology, not just in such discourse as John Gower's "Tale of Adrian and Bardus" or his story of Nebuchadnezzars's instruction as an ox, but in English "Breton Lays" like *Sir Orfeo*, where the king leaves his throne to dwell with beasts until he learns to see in a new way, or *Sir Gowther*, where the monster becomes the saint of civility through discourse with animals as he's fed by dogs, or in the Middle English adaptation of Chrétien's Ywain and his lion. That is, in the latter fourteenth-century English writers challenge human rationality from all sides.

mental behavior theatrically through figura and the histrionics of opposi-
tional dialogue.

In this essay I examine innovative uses of tradition that reflect an in-
tense preoccupation with questions of ontology and epistemology among
late-fourteenth-century English writers, especially the ways in which they
represent their powers of representation. The material world of immediate
experience, even as much as the past with its cultural ideologies, lies apart
from individual human perception. Although in some ways the mind's per-
ception may be said to unite what is outside the mind with what is inside,
the converse is likewise true in very basic ways. That is, from the instant
of induction, the mind definitively isolates itself from what it beholds by
substituting self-generated abstractions for the thing experienced, abstrac-
tions that only seem to represent what the mind thought it perceived. One
looks to the words even as much as the deed.

This sort of epistemological proposition has been much commented up-
on in Chaucer.[5] In this essay I wish to demonstrate a comparable fascina-
tion with the mind's capacity to abstract signs from things in the fiction
making (representation) of Chaucer's contemporary, John Gower, a writer
who perpetually boasts about his backward glance toward books, the past,
and what they have to tell him. I hope to demonstrate that Gower, even
as much as Chaucer, exemplifies a medieval fascination with the potentiali-
ties of representation in conjunction with the liminality of human percep-
tion. Gower's approach to the processing of ideas is more "conventional"
than Chaucer's, but that conventionality illustrates all the more surely
Nichols's and Stock's insights into the vitality of tradition as perpetrator
of cultural change.

In his recent analysis of Gower's *Confessio Amantis,* Kurt Olsson ex-
plores admirably Gower's skill in creating moral uncertainty through com-
plex voicing.[6] Olsson approaches the nexus of uncertainty in the poem
through practices of medieval rhetoric, a rhetoric often founded in the con-
ventions of the *Roman de la Rose.* My point shifts the issues of uncertainty
more from rhetoric toward concerns of philosophy. In his bookish tradi-
tionalism, Gower aligns himself with the complexities of late medieval re-
ception theory. He acknowledges repeatedly that tradition (history, tales
of the past, ideologies of the past) resides in books, books that he re-

---

[5] See, for example, my "Chaucer and the Nominalist Questions," *Speculum* 53
(1978): 745–60; Judith Ferster, *Chaucer on Interpretation* (Cambridge, 1985), and *Fictions
of Advice: The Literature of Politics of Counsel in Late Medieval England* (Philadelphia,
1996); J. Stephen Russell, *The English Dream Vision: Anatomy of a Form* (Columbus,
1988); and Robert R. Edwards, *The Dream of Chaucer: Representation and Reflection in
the Early Narratives* (Durham, 1989). See also Peggy Knapp, *Chaucer and the Social
Contest* (London, 1990), on Chaucer's exploration of boundaries between traditions and
insight. And see Robert Myles, *Chaucerian Realism* (Woodbridge, Suffolk; Rochester,
NY, 1994), on Chaucer's insights into the relationships of intentionality and language.

[6] Kurt Olsson, *John Gower and the Structures of Conversion: A Reading of the
"Confessio Amantis"* (Cambridge, 1992).

presents through his poetry. But in the *Confessio Amantis* he dramatizes radically fresh insights into fourteenth-century empirical semantics, as the recipient of knowledge reencounters in his head whatever the mind intuit-ed, converting that experience into a fiction of his own making, a fiction through which he then interrogates his desires, predilections, and blind spots. Such a relativistic epistemology was not unknown among the ancients (certainly Boethius had given the matter careful thought), but that sort of relativistic sign theory assumes fresh and distinctively new potenti-alities for English writers in the latter fourteenth century, particularly the mystics, Trevisa, Langland, Chaucer, and Gower. Empirical sign theory becomes central both to the way they think and, of equal importance, to the ways in which they represent what they think. If there is such a thing as a medieval poetic, it is intrinsically bound up in their theories of percep-tion and the relative interiority of representation, a representation that they explore through dramatic, dialogic exchange.

Part One: How We Know What We Know

Trevisa's proposition, cited in the headnote to this essay, that we know what is hidden in terms of what is seen is the basic proposition underlying all medieval epistemology. At the risk of "doing the magpie" (the phrase is David Aers's),[7] I use the term "phenomenology" to represent this pro-cess. My choice is deliberately anachronistic. The Greek word *phaeno-menon*, meaning to show or make apparent, is, according to the OED, first derived into French as *phénomène* (1570), and then into English in Bacon (1625) as a term for external data which the mind attempts to accommo-date. *Phenomenology*, the science of observing the mind's processes of intu-iting and generalizing, is a late-eighteenth-century designation that is juxta-posed to *ontology*. That distinction is not unlike the juxtaposition of words and things in medieval debates on nominalism and realism, insofar as it is restricted to a mental science. As a term, phenomenology is particularly useful to the medievalist because of its distinction between phenomena inside and outside the brain, and its focus on intuition, intention, appear-ance, and perception, these being precisely the considerations of epistemol-ogy commonly explored in the fourteenth century.[8] As Trevisa explains, we see one thing and think another, but *what* we think, we think in images derived from the seen. Corollary to this proposition is its linguistic mirror, namely, that we say things not as they are, but in terms of signs and imagined likenesses that we know. That is, to talk about what *is*, one

---

[7] See Aers, "Medievalists and Deconstruction: *An Exemplum*," in *From Medieval to Medievalism*, ed. John Simons (New York, 1992).

[8] On relativity of linguistic perceptual processes as they are reflected in the history of realist and nominalist thought, see Robert Myles, "The Thesis of Intentionality: Medieval and Modern," *Chaucerian Realism*, 33–54.

addresses what *is* is *not*—a verbal corollary, a likeness, or even an anti-thesis. Thought requires a representation, a dramatic action between what is intuited and what is perceived, the plotting of which is bound to inten-tionality.

The thinking and saying of one thing in terms of another and of re-lying upon phenomena of the senses to imply ideas in the mind are fundamental principals of this process of understanding. In *Piers Plowman,* Will sets out to learn how he might save his soul. Even before he perceives that that is his quest, he discovers himself immersed in the flux of phenom-ena, in an in–between place, "a faire felde ful of folke ... / Of alle maner of men, the mene and the riche, / Worchyng and wandryng as the worlde asketh" (B.Prol.17–19), all engaged in the busyness of phenomena, in look-ing and lurking. When Holicherche appears and identifies herself, Will asks, "kenne me kyndeli ... How I may saue my soule?" (B.I.81–84). Holi-cherche replies by telling him that "whan alle tresores aren tried ... trewthe is the best" (B.I.85). But Will doubts whether he has any "kynde knowing"; he knows not "by what craft in my corps it comseth and where" (B.I.135–36). Through metaphor Holicherche tries to explain to him that "triacle of heuene" (B.I.146) called love, then, as last resort, teaches him "somme crafte to knowe the Fals" (B.II.4). The Fals is not the Trewe, but it helps, at least, in the unknowing of what is not. And, even so, the knowing of false still requires "somme craft," some representation.

Let me shift momentarily to another window, from the twelfth century this time, that sheds a traditional light on Langland's fourteenth-century problem. In his treatise *De Arca Noe Morali,* Hugh of St. Victor explains that this weird circumstance, where we know *this* through the *other* pro-viding we have some skill, is a consequence of the fall.[9] Hugh's idea is essentially realist in its assumptions about external reality, but it drama-tizes the relativity of perception and knowledge represented through lan-guage. Knowledge is in itself a *kind* of sin, a perversion of what *is* that causes instability and anxiety in the human heart. Yet knowledge can also provide a way back toward home. Knowledge creates a world apart from what is, a world in the brain—a world of its own.[10] Knowledge is thus

---

[9] *De Arca Noe Morali,* I.2, *Hugh of St. Victor: Selected Spiritual Writings,* trans. by a religious of C.S.M.V. with intro. by Aelred Squire, O.P. (London, 1962), 46. As quests in understanding *De Arca Noe Morali* and *Piers Plowman* share many common concerns. I recognize that the juxtaposition of Hugh and Langland might be construed as more "doing of the magpie," but such elision works well, it seems to me, not as an attempt to universalize ideas but rather to juxtapose phenomena in a manner whereby tradition butts in to open up and clarify the potentialities of representation.

[10] A good fourteenth-century literary example of the relativity of brain-knowledge may be found in Chaucer's *Hous of Fame,* where Geoffrey, caught up in the images in his head cries out for divine help to save him from "fantome and illusion" (492–94), and, subsequently, in a take-off on Dante's celebration of his powers of thought, ridicules through hyperbole the great capacity of his brain (523–28). For discussion of Chaucer's play with mental relativities, see Peck, "Chaucer and the Nominalist Questions," 745–60.

paradoxical. In our anxiety, since we know, even in sin, only through metaphor (through mental signs rather than through the things themselves—does anyone know "love in dede"?[11]), stability, or at least the illusion of it, may be restored, Hugh suggests, through a kind of word game:

> Now, therefore, enter your own inmost heart, and make a dwelling-place for God. Make Him a temple, make Him a house, make Him a pavilion. Make Him an ark of the covenant, make Him an ark of the flood; *no matter what you call it*, it is all one house of God. In the temple let the creature adore the Creator, in the house let the son revere the Father, in the pavilion let the knight adore the King. Under the covenant, let the disciple listen to the Teacher. In the flood, let him that is shipwrecked beseech Him who guides the helm.[12]

Hugh's way of counteracting the instability of the heart layers one analogy upon another upon another, then expands each—"no matter what you call it"—requiring the mind to make linguistic leaps between the structures being formulated, between familiar things (temples, houses, pavilions, arks), to perceive in the strange area of the unsaid what can not be said, only implied. The familiar things are not simply things of nature or of the material world, however, but things given a local color, in this instance a biblical color, a color contextualized through the Christian culture of its conception—not just an ark, but Noah's ark, the ark of salvation, etc. The phenomena are not simply things seen, but things read.

The fourteenth-century English mystics offer a variation on this same epistemological idea. Since knowledge is a kind of sin and therefore a condition of non-being, that is, a substitution of *what is not* for *what is*, to know is to miss, to miss the highest good. The happiest human exercise thus becomes a procedure not of knowing but of unknowing:

> Of alle other creatures and their werkes—ye, and of the werkes of God self—may a man thorou grace haue fulheed of knowing, and wel to kon thinke on hem; bot of God him-self can no man thinke. And therfore I wole leue al that thing that I can think, and chese to my loue that thing that I cannot think. For whi he may wel be loued, bot not thought. By loue may he be getyn and holden; bot bi thought neither. And therfore, thof al it be good sumtyme to think of the kyndness and the worthines of God *in special,* and thof al it be a light and a party of contemplacion: nevertheles in this werk it schal be casten down and keuerid with a cloude of forgetyng. And thou schalt step abouen it stalworthly, bot listely, with a

---

[11] My allusion in this aside is to Chaucer's *Parliament of Fowls,* line 8, where the implication seems to be that humankind knows love only in fantasy, rather than in deed, despite the sore strokes Cupid so insistently inflicts upon us as individuals.

[12] *Noah's Ark* I.5 (Squire, 51); emphasis my own.

deuoute and a plesing stering of loue, and fonde for to peerse that
derknes abouen thee. And smyte apon that thicke cloude of vn-
knowyng with a scharp darte of longing loue, and go not thens *for
thing that befalleth.*[13]

As with Hugh of St. Victor and Langland, love becomes the only means of
possession, or, rather, of approaching or participating, an attempt through
locatable feeling to move beyond phenomena toward the source, knowing
that experience is simultaneously a kind of having and losing.

In the *Confessio Amantis* Gower's epistemology shares little with the
mystic way. Gower locates knowledge firmly in activities of the pheno-
menal world, the dark wood in which Amans dotes on his feelings. He
concentrates on the "thing that befalleth," that which exists for the *Cloud
of Unknowing* author "in special." Gower's epistemology is akin to the
mystic's, however, and to Hugh's, and Chaucer's, and Langland's as well,
in voicing a cumulative what-is-not fiction to approach what is. Like the
lot of them, Gower addresses Truth by exploring false, all the while
privileging love as the motivating and guiding intention, the only certain
hope. As with the others, Gower's concern is with what goes on inside
Amans's head amidst the flux of phenomena. What is in the lover's head
is fiction. That is, one does not have rocks in one's head, unless one is
Dorigen, and even there the rocks are ideas of rocks, which may be a
greater problem than real rocks.[14] Gower's attitude toward the flux of
phenomena affecting Amans is fundamentally akin to Langland's, Chau-
cer's, and the mystic's. Although Gower is, without a doubt, a conceptual
realist, he is keenly aware of distinctions between phenomena inside and
outside the mind. His Genius will create fictions as phenomenal as
Amans's mental extractions from the world around him, fictions to address
fictions within the precincts of Amans's and the reader's brain.

Part Two: Gower's "middel weie": Fiction as Mediator

Like the *Cloud of Unknowing* author, Gower, in the *Confessio Amantis,*
approaches knowing through love, but as he sets out his fiction he is
careful, in his Latin voice, to differentiate kinds of love:

Postquam in Prologo tractatum hactenus existit, qualiter hodierne
condicionis diuisio caritatis dileccionem superauit, intendit auctor
ad presens suum libellum, cuius nomen Confessio Amantis nuncu-
patur, componere de illo amore, a quo non solum humanum genus,

---

[13] *The Cloud of Unknowing*, chap. vi, ed. Phyllis Hodgson, EETS o.s. 218 (London,
1958), 25–26. Emphasis my own.
[14] The allusion is to Chaucer's "Franklin's Tale," where Dorigen sees the crux of her
problems as lying in nature rather than her comprehension, and scolds God for making
"this werk unresonable" (V[F]872).

sed eciam cuncta animancia naturaliter subiciuntur. Et quia nonnulli amantes ultra quam expedit desiderii passionibus crebro stimulantur, materia libri per totum super hiis specialius diffunditur.[15]

[Now that the treatise has shown thus far in the Prologue how the present division of the conditional situation has overcome love of charity, the author intends at present to write his book, the name of which is called *Confessio Amantis,* on that love by which not only humankind, but also all animals are naturally subjected. And because all lovers are repeatedly aroused by the passion of desire more than is good for them, the matter of the book as a whole will be laid out according to these particular passions.]

Gower says he will speak *quasi in persona aliorum, quos amor alligat,*[16] "as if in the dramatic role of others whom love binds." The love he addresses is passionate love, *naturatus amor,* a love that "is blind and may noght se" (I.47). The fiction dramatized will be exemplary "of my woful care, / Mi wofull day, my wofull chance, / That men mowe take remembrance" of what they read and "ensample take / Of wisdom" (I.74–80). That is, his poem will become phenomena for the reader's eye and ear, brain food which may nourish the alert reader's intelligence.

Gower stresses emphatically that the epistemology of *naturatus amor* works through the senses, particularly the eyes and ears.[17] Venus sends Amans to Genius, who begins by instructing him "touchende of my wittes fyve ... the gates / Thurgh whiche as to the herte algates / Comth alle thing unto the feire / Which may the mannes Soule empeire" (I.296–302). Genius begins with sight, since it is "moste principal of alle" (I.307). Genius's admonitory advice is largely against "misloke"—"Betre is to winke than to loke" (I.384)—warning Amans "That thou thi sihte noght misuse" (I.436–7). That is, Genius is mindful that one sees what one intends; indeed, most of the wit of the dialogue will hinge upon Amans's comically biased intention. The ear too is a powerful source of error; Amans must guard ears as well as eyes, if the approximations he conceives are to accord with what *is;* otherwise he will be deceived by both ears and eyes and, in his confused intention be subject to fear.

Genius's admonitions acknowledge a vast discrepancy between what lies inside and outside the orifices of the body. Amans needs some kind of interior defense for dealing with the prejudicial interpretations his desires

---

[15] *Confessio Amantis,* adjacent to lines I.9–26. All references to *Confessio Amantis* are taken from *The English Works of John Gower,* in 2 volumes, ed. G. C. Macaulay (Oxford, 1900; repr. 1957), and are cited hereafter by book and line number within the context of my argument. Volume I includes Prologue to V.1970; volume II, V.1971 to the end. Macaulay's edition appears in the Early English Text Society, extra series nos. 81–82.

[16] Adjacent to *CA* I.59–60.

[17] See Olsson, *John Gower and the Structures of Conversion,* 63–72, for an excellent discussion of Amans's vulnerability through his eyes and ears.

impose upon what the senses convey. Since reason, or charity, or higher love has been somewhat arbitrarily excluded from the fiction of *naturatus amor,* that is, none is the starting point or the impetus, what we are perpetually entertained with in Gower's dialogue is lies. Genius will address Amans's lies with fictions adapted from past time. In effect the poem's rhetoric will consist of fictions measuring fictions in search of a moderating accord. It is not a lofty way, but in its mediocrity it sustains a pleasing balancing act. Amans will respond to Genius's stories with glimpses into the ways he views himself, glimpses which are quite wonderful fantasies in themselves that are answered with Genius's equally fantastic stories, brought with a fresh warp from the past, as the two weave together a politics of make-believe.

Part Three: Gower's Epistemology of Make-Believe

To demonstrate more precisely Gower's uses of false as a means toward discovering the true, I would like to examine two sections of the *Confessio,* the latter part of Book II (those sections dealing with Falssemblant, Fa Crere, and Supplantation—all sub-species of Envy) and the latter part of Book VI (the discussion of sorcery as a delicate kind of Gluttony). In both sections the agencies of "sin" use the same rhetoric as Gower the poet in constructing make-believe as a means of instructing and thus controlling their victims (read: audience, those who give ear); or, to put it another way, as a means of fulfilling their pleasure (their love)—of making the outside seem to accord with will on the inside. These internal, imagined structures may not be exactly the temples, pavilions, or arks of the covenant that Hugh of St. Victor spoke of, but the processes of mental architecture are the same. Genius imagines Envy as a barge on a stormy sea, "Wher Falssemblant with Ore on honde / It roweth" (II.1902–5), making the wind seem soft to man's ear and the weather fair through "faire wordes"; "Bot thogh it *seme,* it is noght so" (II.1889, emphasis mine).

The literary source of Genius's Falssemblant (in part the source for Genius himself) is the *Roman de la Rose.* Kevin Brownlee has recently explored Faux Semblant's narrative functions in the *Roman* in terms of his diegetic status, his historical subtext, and his linguistic-poetic significance, placing that discourse in the historical context of debate between the secular masters and the mendicant orders for control of the University of Paris in the mid-1250s.[18] Gower's adaptation of Jean de Meun's monster has nothing to do with the University of Paris, but it does serve his purposes in ways akin to Jean's uses of his creation. Gower's Falssemblant is recontextualized in terms of an incipient capitalist economy that he, and

---

[18] Kevin Brownlee, "The Problem of Faux Semblant: Language, History, and Truth in the *Roman de la Rose,*" in *The New Medievalism,* ed. Brownlee, Brownlee, and Nichols (Baltimore, 1991), 253–71.

Chaucer too, for that matter, sees as a threat to traditional morality. Genius would have Amans "Let thi Semblant be trewe and plein" (II.1911) and use "thi conscience" (II.1926) as helpmate, "If thou were evere Custummer / To Falssemblant in eny wise" (II. 1928–29). Semblant, as Genius uses the term, equates perhaps with good intention. That is, Genius is suggesting that Amans attempt to see without prejudice what is being intuited, knowing, of course, that that is impossible. Conscience *might* govern Amans's intentions, thereby helping the percepter to be objectively self-critical, but the process will go awry, revealing rather that Amans's eager emotional investment is rather in false-seeming, through which he gets his kicks.

In presenting Falssemblant, Gower takes a character from his books and conflates him with a local situation (the Lombard bankers, to whom the English throne is much indebted) as part of his analysis of the moral welfare of his distraught lover, that fiction called Amans. The mercantile metaphor ("if thou were evere Custummer to Faussemblant") is important to Gower's purpose, since the lover's fantasy is inevitably what he buys into. That capitalist metaphor in turn establishes a political context for ethical behavior. Falssemblant flourishes most, Genius says, among Lombards and merchants, who make profit from other people's land (II.2093 ff.). They are especially versed in Fa crere "To voide with a soubtil hond / The beste goodes of the lond / And bringe chaf and take corn" (II.2125–27). They are like the master rhetorician who "makth believe ... Er that he mai ben aperceived" (II.2136–37).

In Book II, especially, Gower presents the phenomonology of desire as a commerce in make-believe and political aggression. Envy, the topic of Book II, is the most politic of sins, always preoccupied with others' domains. As such, it exemplifies precisely the phenomenology of fantasy's juxtapositioning of inside-outside that is my essay's concern.[19] Amans responds to Genius's discussion of Falssemblant with an enthusiastic celebration of his guilt, explaining how he feigns friendship in order to get information about his lady and to keep others from having access to her. Amans is deeply committed to a politics of power. He would find out what he can about those with whom she converses so that he can slander them "in forthringe of myn oghne astat" (II.204-8). From a moral point of view his confession illustrates admirably the subtle workings of Envy and its crafty displacements. But his confession also demonstrates the political complexity of Gower's epistemology of make-believe, as the lover intuits evidences and attempts to negotiate what he conceives the intuited images of others might be in order to affect the imaginations of his Lady and his rivals, those complex phenomena outside himself that so infect (or

---

[19] In working through this idea I have come to a renewed admiration for R. A. Shoaf's study of the language of commerce in Chaucer's poetic, *Dante, Chaucer, and the Currency of the Word: Money, Images, and Reference in Late Medieval Poetry* (Norman, OK, 1983).

seem to) his own imagined structures. This lover is indeed a shaper of politic fictions. Amans acknowledges his preference for his own make-believe, but in doing so he must recognize that others likewise dwell within their own interiority which he, with his antics, hopes to infiltrate, perhaps even own. Genius attempts to modify Amans's aggression by introducing to his ken the ancient story of Deianira and Nessus, a tale that juxtaposes a host of agents vying for control and dominion within the imaginations of others.[20]

The "Tale of Deianira and Nessus" is a study in the political aggression of mind games: The giant Nessus meets Hercules and Deianira as they come to a river, but do not know how to cross. As he reads their dilemma he feigns good cheer, thereby hoping, for the moment at least, to gain Hercules' confidence. But in his heart he "thoughte al an other wise" (II.2198). He shows Hercules the wrong way to cross while volunteering to carry Deianira himself, hoping to enjoy her on the far bank while Hercules founders in deep water. But Nessus's interior scenario misfires as Hercules' bow does not, and he is slain by Hercules' long shot. At his death, however, Nessus invades Deianira's mind with another feigned "chiere," promising her a guarantee of love (his blood-soaked shirt), which he claims will make whoever wears it return the love of the giver. What he has done, of course, is to read Deianira's anxiety and to play upon it. His words prove potent because of the anxieties of her desire: "Who was tho glad bot Deianira. / Hire thoughte hire herte was afyre / Til it was in hire cofre loke, / So that no word therof was spoke" (II.2255–58). Gower's point is nicely articulated here, what with the exchange and storage of goods in coffers and hot ideas in brains. But Deianira's eager heart is none so hot as Hercules' soon will be, once he puts on the shirt. He will be so hot as to be consumed by fire. The prefigurative irony through the juxtapositioning of interior and exterior phenomena sets nicely the incongruities of the several individuals' interior readings as they cheer themselves with their private thoughts, heedless of what is going on before their very eyes. Hercules is shortly self-beguiled as he puts Deianira aside to take a new love, Eolen:

> sche made Hercules so nyce
> Upon hir Love and so assote,
> That he him clotheth in hire cote
> And sche in his was clothed ofte. (II.2268–71)

As with the fire allusion, so too here the clothing imagery is cozy in its figuration of private enraptures and anticipates the conclusion where Deianira presents to Hercules the charmed shirt, confident in her fantasy that it will restore his love to her. Both Hercules and Deianira are caught up in

---

[20] I have discussed this story in some detail in *Kingship and Common Profit* (Carbondale, IL, 1978), 60–62. But my emphasis here is somewhat different.

false-seeming and are self-destroyed through false dress. In balance they are as much victims of their own staged fantasies as they are of Nessus's agenda.[21]

Genius calls his story of Deianira a "grete conceite" (II.2311); with it he imagines that he will change Amans's behavior. But Genius is less "successful" in his mental invasion of Amans, than were Nessus, Hercules, or Deianira of each other; his fiction produces no result at all in Amans, except for a momentary feeling. Amans's self-determined infatuation is sufficiently powerful to insulate him from all remedies.

Genius thought to introduce his conceit so that Amans might "be more war / Of alle tho that feigne chiere" (II.2142–43). Genius is himself feigning "chiere," of course, but his conceit can guarantee no success, for the listener hears only what he is predisposed to hear. "He that mysconceyveth, he mysdemeth," May warns Januarie, as she leaps down from the tree ("Merchant's Tale" IV [E] 2410). Amans claims to be so moved by Deianira's pitiful sorrow that he will make no more feigned cheer. But he has learned nothing. He supplants his anxiety by simply asking to be filled in on what comes next. Ironically, the next topic is Supplantation, the fifth form of Envy.

Supplantation is a political consequence of Falssemblant. Like Falssemblant, Supplantation uses the rhetoric of make-believe for territorial aggrandizement—"chalk for chese / He changeth with ful litel cost / Wherof an other hath the lost / And he the profit schal receive" (II.2346–49). The Supplantor is a manipulator of forms. Through deceit he hopes to appropriate dominion in the mind of his consort, as the "Tale of the False Bachelor" exemplifies. But Genius's grand example of all forms of Envy, but especially of Falssemblant and Supplantation, is Cardinal Boniface's displacement of Pope Celestin by placing a "Trompe into his Ere, / Fro hevene as thogh a vois it were" (II.2873–74) to infect his conscience "thurgh fals ymaginacioun" (II.2845).[22]

---

[21] This proposition is in keeping with Gower's notion that people shape their own fates: "Each man shapes for himself his own destiny, incurs his own lot according to his desire, and creates his own fate (*fata*). In fact, a free mind voluntarily claims what it does for its various deserts in the name of fate (*sortis*). In truth, fate (*sors*) ought always to be handmaiden to the mind, from which the name itself which will be its own is chosen" *Vox Clamantis*, II.iv.203–8, in *The Major Latin Works of John Gower*, trans. Stockton (Seattle, 1962), 102. The idea lies at the heart of Gower's treatment of sorcery at the end of *CA* VI and reflects his notion of the ethical implications of the individual's isolation within his own interiority.

[22] It is perhaps noteworthy that several of Genius's key exemplifications in Book II are taken from chronicles—the tales of Constance, Celestine, Constantine, and Sylvester. That is, they are "histories." Gower ends Book II, as he had done Book I, with a summary tale that ties felicitously together all aspects of Envy: As an antidote to the dispossessions effected by Envy, Genius tells the "Tale of Constantine and Silvester," where conscience, guided by charity and pity, heals the Emperor's leprous deformity to establish a healthy community where all parts pray for rather than prey upon each other. But unlike the "Tale of Three Questions" at the end of Book I, in this wrap up the voice of history intrudes like an arctic chill, as Genius recalls the evil effects upon

As Genius explains these matters with his well-formed stories, he would place in Amans's head fictional forms that address the fantasies of "mislok" and miss-hearing that have usurped the lover's sanity. The effect of Genius's strategy is to create a comic warfare by means of complication. If the fiend would in his duplicity use knowledge to divide and conquer (I am thinking of those passages in the Prologue to Confessio Amantis where sin is "modor of division"), then so too would Genius immobilize sin's conquest of Amans's fractious mind with further, less harmful, multiplication. Gower's "middel weie" is a most gentle mode of psychopolitical infiltration by exemplification, a rhetorical reorchestration that may not prove what is, or even show what should be, apart from traditional stories. But his bookish fictions revitalize potentialities in precisely the way Nichols says medieval tradition might do, thus making more possible the reordering of Amans's inward territories through a kind of protocolonialist policy.

At the end of Book VI Gower focuses such pleasant conjurings of his Genius by introducing another form of make-believe—sorcery. In Gower's scheme the discussion of sorcery offers Amans a means of deconstructing potentially harmful mental conjurations in preparation for Genius's sermon on the instruction of the King (i.e., the wise architect of mental phenomena) in Book VII. Here, as prelude to embarking upon his most ingenious device of resurrecting Aristotle to address the hopeless lover, Gower assails the very proposition of the Confessio, namely the conjuring of images for purposes of mind control. As in Book II, Gower focuses on processes of inception and manipulation of what one hears, sees, and, thus, thinks. At first it may seem odd to the reader that Gower would introduce his discussion of sorcery in a book disposed to Gluttony, at least until we recognize in this anatomy of naturatus amor that the mind is a creature of appetite whose food is images and whose happiest digestion is the processing of images into food for the mind.[23] "Thoght" is a "lusti coke" (VI.913–14), Genius says, who ever keeps "hise pottes hote / Of love buillende on the fyr / With fantasie and with desir" (VI.913–15), a cook who works with ingredients supplied by eye and ear. Amans's lady's voice "is to min Ere a lusti foode," a "deynte feste" (VI.846–48), a food delicate enough to make Amans think he is in Paradise before the Fall (VI.867–72). Certainly, in the delicate habitation of Amans's fantasy, it seems a food sufficient to sustain life.

---

the Christian Church of the donation of Constantine. Tradition, which had enabled Gower to achieve his rosy fiction of Constantine's cure, simultaneously introduces the voice of complaint for which Gower had become famous in his Vox Clamantis, which pipes up now even through his more courtly Genius as a chilly warning to the reader of how tricky the commerce of the world and language can be amongst greedy people.

[23] See R. F. Yeager on a tradition linking necromancy, sorcery, and witchcraft as sins of the mouth, and, thus, as subdivisions of gluttony in John Gower's Poetic: The Search for a New Arion (Cambridge, 1990), 187–95. Gower's phenomenological approach shifts the focus from mouth to brain, but still in terms of lusty ingestion.

Genius tells two stories to exemplify the dangers of such mental conjuring and beguilement, the "Tale of Ulysses and Telegonus" and the "Tale of Nectanabus." Both tales demonstrate how "he that wol beguile / Is guiled with the same guile, / And thus the guilour is beguiled" (VI.1379–81). Both narratives focus on the interiority of reading signs. Both Ulysses and Nectanabus have dreams, but neither sees well how their dreams apply to themselves, largely because of the cluttered foreground and their engrossed desire. Ultimately, both conjurers are destroyed by their children, children who were products of their fantasies.

Nectanabus foresees an attack upon Egypt by an enemy against whom he thinks he has no defense. So, assuming a disguise, he flees to Macedoine. It thus seems he has looked after himself well. But it is not so simple. His politically aggressive sorcery becomes a matter of self possession as well as appetite (see n. 30). Like the fiend in Chaucer's "Friar's Tale," who, having lost his own form must go in someone else's, the dispossessed Nectanabus, to make up for his own lack, now fiendishly seeks to possess others. He invades Olympias, Queen of Macedoine, first through her eyes, then her ears, stepping toward the utter invasion of her body in his would-be rape:

> The queene on him hire yhe caste,
> And knew that he was strange anon:
> Bot he behield hire evere in on
> Withoute blenchinge of his chere. (VI.1864–66)

In this instance Olympias would perhaps have been better off had she remembered that "betre is to winke than to loke" (I.384). With Nectanabus's strange image in her mind she summons him to her. He comes equipped with images of power—his astrolabe and instruments for reading the heavens—which assist him through her eyes in establishing his authority. She listens "with gret affeccion" (VI.1898) as he plants in her mind the idea she desires, an idea she will subsequently translate into dream. As she sleeps, Nectanabus makes subtle images to appear before her that seem to confirm the prophesy.

Gower's narrative sequence is particularly interesting here as he takes the reader through the event twice, first outside Olympias's head, and then a second time inside her dream. So it is that guile works, as the beguiled relives the scenario of the beguiler. The Queen worries what King Philippe will think, but Nectanabus takes care of that by beguiling him through a "See foul" (a gull, I presume), who addresses the king through images in a dream, then, upon his return, through "facts" (Olympias's pregnancy), and, finally, through a miraculous display of further images at court and in the field. Like Olympias, the king too is taken in by his eyes and ears ("al this [he] sih and herde" [VI.2247])—impregnated, so to speak, as he too comes to believe. These are miraculous conceptions, indeed.

Nectanabus has, of course, no real power over his victims. His success is utterly dependent upon their willingness to believe, or, rather, to make-believe. He, like the poet Gower, is only a manipulator of illusions. In fact, he is twice removed as an agency of power. He is dependent upon the will of his victim, but also, as Gower presents it, upon the license of God. Genius acknowledges that:

> The hihe creatour of thinges,
> Which is the king of alle kinges,
> Ful many a wonder worldes chance
> Let slyden under his suffrance;
> Ther wot noman the cause why,
> Bot he the which is almyhty. (VI.1789–94)

The issue is not simply that God permits weird things to happen that people cannot explain. God has foresight, and thus is able to know and, presumably, to judge accurately. The sorcerer also has a kind of foresight. But he lacks discretion to read well what stands before him. He, despite his preview, is not able to "tak hiede how that it is" (VI.1779) for himself. His conjurings blind him to his own inner welfare in the same way that they affect the perceptions of his victims. That is, he follows his desire and, like those he manipulates, imagines it for the best.

This latter point is rather subtle. Nectanabus makes much of his being the agent of Anubus. What he does not perceive is that God permits these things to happen for reasons of His own, a point Gower is insistent upon. That is, Nectanabus's lie—that he is God's agent—is not a lie, though he does not know it. He just imagines it through make-believe. In his presentation of the tale Genius is careful to keep the reader aware that although it seems that Nectanabus is the instigator of most of the action, he is not, in fact, the power that enables it to happen. When Nectanabus does his will with Olympias and Olympias conceives, she, we are told, is only "in part deceived" (VI.2085). The point seems to be that God permits this to happen, and Alexander will become a world conqueror. But also, she is perhaps more savvy of Nectanabus's craftiness than she lets on, even though Genius does conclude that she has been beguiled. She admits the entrance. Subsequently, the people of the court, including Nectanabus, are treated to a strange sight as a flying pheasant drops an egg from which a small serpent emerges only to be shriveled by the burning sun. The event is interpreted as one further prediction of the miraculous birth of Alexander and his death in an alien land. But this latter demonstration, which Nectanabus does not invent, could stand as well for the fate of Nectanabus himself, who likewise dies, ignorant of his fate, in an alien land.

Genius concludes his narrative with an explicit moral: "Lo, what profit him is belaft" (VI.2346). Rather than being a maker of fictions harmful to others, Nectanabus is self-destructive: he becomes an exile from his own land, a thrall rather than a king, a deceiver on behalf of his foolish lust, an invader of others' domains, and he dies an inglorious death. The make-believe that seemed to help him escape proved ultimately, in Gower's view, to be only a kind of escapism. In the words of Chaucer's Miller,

"Men may dyen of ymaginacioun, / So depe may impressioun be take" (CT I [A] 3612–13). In Gower, everyone creates his own fate, even in ignorance, as false is mistaken for true.

A fitting contrast to Nectanabus is the figure of Apollonius in Book VIII, a man who is likewise in possession of a great talent, who is forced into exile and who, through his wisdom, obtains new possessions. But Apollonius's politics of possession are quite different from those of Nectanabus. Though he plays upon the ears and eyes of others he meets in an effort to secure himself, he is not a manipulator with the same intent as the sorcerer. Rather than being an invader of others' territory to supplant them, he is more concerned with maintaining his own inner kingdom, which he takes with him. In his ship he brings grain, not chaff. He intends well, has discretion, and learns to understand the relativity of his perceptions as Nectanabus does not do. Thus, rather than being destroyed by his own generation, he is mysteriously saved by it. He is restored to his throne and full family, rather than dying from an ignominious fall.

The crucial difference between the two protagonists lies in their attitudes, their "semblant," toward the people around them as the phenomena is projected within their own heads. In his conclusion Gower seems to be working with the proposition of Boethius cited in the headnote "that alle thing that is iwist nis nat knowen by his nature propre, but by the nature of hem that comprehenden it" (*Boece* V.pr.6.2–3). Although Genius tells hundreds of exemplary stories to Amans (and thus hundreds for us as readers), the stories make little impression upon Amans until he wills that they do. That is, Amans cannot be said to be victim of Falssemblant or Supplantation or Sorcery except by his own choices. The phenomena (i.e., that which comes from the outside), for all its pluralism, simply passes by, unknown in its "nature propre." Amans himself is aware of the problem. At the end of Book VII, even after all Genius's good instruction on kingship and just governance, he responds: "The tales sounen in myn Ere, / Bot yit myn herte is elleswhere, I mai miselve noght restreigne" (VII. 5411–13). What matters is what Amans (seer/reader, hearer/audience) chooses to "comprehend."

This distinction between inside and outside explains why it is that Gower as poet/sorcerer, manipulating so craftily all these fictions with which he hopes to enter the minds of his readers, finally puts his magic aside at the end, when Genius, Venus, Amans, and the stories disappear, and he becomes once again "John Gower" (VIII.2908). All the poet can, in fact, do is to present himself humbly as a man of loving conscience, of "Semblant trew and plein" (II.1911), a supplicant rather than a supplanter, praying charitably for the welfare of the domain he loves—England. Knowing that he cannot effect change in his audience (only they can do that), he dramatizes instead a change from *naturatus amor* to *caritas* within himself, and takes another name—John Gower. This new fictive voice, who seems to be none other than the historical man himself, would be a grain supplier whose desire for the good, like that of Apollonius, is made plainly evident. How that desire of this new voice might be accomplished is left hidden, however, not only to the audience of Gower's poem but to Gower himself. We, as readers, are simply left with his riddles which, though lies, are not necessarily false. Their truth lies solely in the audience's capacity to understand them.

This relativistic conclusion of the *Confessio Amantis* shares much in common with the conclusion of Chaucer's *Canterbury Tales*, or *Troilus and Criseyde*, or *The Book of the Duchess* and *The Hous of Fame*. In fact, it seems likely to me that Gower may have gotten many of his ideas of phenomenology and the relativity of knowing and comprehending from Chaucer. Certainly there was not much of this sort of preoccupation in the *Vox Clamantis*. The shift away from the fictive voices of Amans and Genius to a fiction in his own "John Gower" voice, after the elaborate instruction on kingship in Book VII, is comparable in its function to the "Parson's Tale" and Retraction as conclusion to the *Canterbury Tales*. Although Gower lacks the brilliance of Chaucer in incorporating philosophical matter into fictive comedies (I am thinking of the ludicrous perspective of Geoffrey dangling from the claw of the eagle, or May pronouncing Scripture from the pear tree), his understanding of the relativity of perception to inception and intention is subtle indeed and lies at the heart of the poetic against which the *Confessio Amantis* is framed. Like Chaucer, Gower's sense of incongruity and irony is highly refined, and his awareness of the politics of fiction making, albeit quite different from Chaucer's practice, is, nonetheless, richly sophisticated.[24] Both poets delight in the phenomena of comprehension and celebrate through wit the relativity of what is known. Both recognize how much of what we call judgment hinges upon just such matters. And both, sometimes with a wry wit, turn to faith as the only source of true knowledge: "O Crist," thoughte I, "that art in blysse, / Fro fantome and illusion / Me save" (*HF*.492–4).

The philosophical context of Gower's phenomenology of make-believe was commonplace, especially after the epochal success of Jean de Meun's *Roman de la Rose*. In his revision of the opening section of the *Confessio*, written after he had completed the poem, he added a passage about the "wyse" man's understanding of the particularities of the world:

> yit woll I fonde
> To wryte and do my bisinesse,
> That in som part, so as I gesse,
> The wyse man mai ben avised.
> For this prologe is so assised
> That it to wisdom al belongeth:
> What wysman that it underfongeth,

---

[24] I have recently attempted to demonstrate the rich sophistication of Gower's subtle use of irony in "The Problematics of Irony in Gower's *Confessio Amantis*," *Mediaevalia* 15 (1993): 207–29.

He schal drawe into remembrance
The fortune of this worldes chance,
The which noman *in his persone*
Mai knowe, bot the god al one. (Prol.62–72)

The "wysman" intuits wisdom, may draw it into his remembrance, but he does not understand it "in his persone." The point is like Geoffrey's not knowing "Love in dede" in *Parliament of Fowls* (1.8). Man "mai ben avised," but that avisement is relative, a configuration of potentialities. Troilus sees "with ful avysement" only after death, when he has moved beyond the "erratik sterres" (*TC* V.1811–12). On earth, in Fortune's domain, only God may *know* the "worldes chance." In mutability's domain people are left with only likenesses stored in their brain. But Gower goes on to assert that "this bok schal afterward ben ended / Of love, which doth many a wonder / And many a wys man hath put under" (Prol.74–76). The "wys man ... put under" reminds one of the *Lay of Aristotle*, with the philosopher on his hands and knees playing horse to the mistress of his fantasy, which is simply a variation of Amans lying in the bush lamenting to Venus—a matter of love *in special*. But the line also anticipates the conclusion to the *Confessio Amantis*, where the wise man (once Venus has fled) moves beyond *naturatus amor* and, in his prayer of submission to God for England's sake, is put under love in another way. There the implication is that although he may not know "this worldes chance ... in his persone," through make-belief (i.e., love of God, who alone knows all), he has the potentiality to participate in full knowledge, even without knowing. In the meantime, we, like Gower, have other potentialities, stories of the past—all lies—with which to fill our brains and amuse our own fantasies. Good commerce indeed! Such pastime engages phenomena of the present through traditions of the past in a manner of representation akin to that which permitted Gower to represent old men as new and thereby reopen his culture to the vital changes Stephen Nichols, with his new medievalism, sees as characteristic of that tradition-rich society.

Reading, Transgression, and Judgment: Gower's Case of Paris and Helen

Kurt Olsson

At the outset of the tale that concludes Book I of the *Confessio Amantis*, Genius describes a young king who delights in posing riddles:

> Of depe ymaginaciouns
> And strange interpretaciouns,
> Problemes and demandes eke
> His wisdom was to find and seke;
> Wherof he wolde in sondri wise
> Opposen hem that weren wise. (I.3069–74)[1]

The delight in such a "game," created to fill leisure, mirrors a larger delight that Gower fashions in this poem, in setting "problemes and demandes" and advancing interpretations that will serve his purpose of confronting the wise—his readers—not merely to his delight and benefit, but to theirs.

Among the meanings that Gower assigns to wisdom in the *Confessio* is the capacity to make good ethical decisions, without the prospect of ever achieving certainty, or locating and then merely applying to such cases a certain, incontrovertible knowledge. The task for those who are wise in this sense is to interpret "problemes and demandes" in human experience and discover a "rihte weie" or "beste weie" through them, recognizing all the while that "what schal fallen ate laste, / The sothe can no wisdom caste" (I.39–40). Such practical wisdom is not merely a body of precepts, "lore," or knowledge to be gleaned from a text: it is a capacity to judge soundly; ultimately, it is a capacity, based on sound judgment, to rule oneself and, in political settings, govern others well.[2] Gower challenges

---

[1] Quotations from the *Confessio Amantis* are from *The English Works of John Gower*, ed. G. C. Macaulay, 2 vols., EETS, e.s. 81–82 (Oxford, 1900–01).

[2] "Vero finis & perfectio, sapientiae est facere hominem habilem ad seipsum & ad alios gubernandum virtuose." Robert Holkot, *In librum Sapientiae regis Salomonis praelectiones CCXIII*, lect. 74 (Basle, 1586), 261; cf. lect. 75, 264. See also *The Pseudo-Ovidian De vetula* 10, ed. Dorothy M. Robathan (Amsterdam, 1968), 48; Pierre Bersuire, *Dictionarium, seu Repertorium morale*, 3 vols. (Lyons, 1516–17), s.v. *regere*, 3: fol. 142ᵛ; John Bromyard, *Summa praedicantium*, 2 vols. (Antwerp, 1614), s.v. *sapientia*, 2:345–46.

readers not only to reflect upon practical wisdom as a major subject of his poem, but also to exercise it, to sharpen their judgment through the very process of reading.

If, as we read the *Confessio,* we follow the popular advice of the *Disticha Catonis* and "draw close" to "learn from reading what wisdom is,"[3] we shall have to do so in reference to Gower's other subject, love. That subject is itself a vexing one, and not merely because, as the poet claims, love "many a wys man hath put under" (Prol.76), or because the changing, variable nature of the passions, which he explores in the various "distinctions" of this book, adds another uncertainty to knowing and judging. As Genius applies the vices to love in order to discover what they mean, he bases judgment on rules he has taken from different, often conflicting, "codes." The precepts for gentle manners and conduct associated with the court of Venus, who is the goddess of "gentilesse" as well as love, do not always accord with ethical precepts derived from a learned and largely ecclesiastical tradition. Genius is himself a judge who, in repeatedly crossing judicial boundaries such as these, breaks rules. For the reading of this poem, the poet confronts the wise by forcing them to do likewise: reading, interpretation, and judgment become transgressive activities.

Gower thus discourages us from limiting our "reading to learn what wisdom is" to a single regimen. Learning will require a multifaceted exercise of interpretation, involving the building of a memory-store and a sustained exercise of both ingenuity (or *ingenium* more broadly) and judgment. Over the course of the work, these powers will be ordered and re-ordered to effect a greater delight and benefit. The challenge for readers is to sort through and "put things in order."[4] The challenge for Gower is to create for his poem an order that is not only noetic, ethical, and poetic, but rhetorical; he must make each of his competing claims on his readers' attention compelling, and thereby make their task of judging difficult, but also meaningful and productive.

For his manner of presenting this material, we might include Gower among a group of late medieval writers who make medieval reading, in Lee Patterson's words, "a dangerous enterprise."[5] There is some impishness in

---

[3] "Ades, et quae sit sapientia disce legendo," *Disticha Catonis* 2, praefatio, ed. Marcus Boas (Amsterdam, 1952), 90; trans. Ian Thomson and Louis Perraud, *Ten Latin Schooltexts of the Later Middle Ages: Translated Selections* (Lewiston, NY, 1990), 67.

[4] "Sicut dicit philosophus in principio Metaphysicae, 'sapientis est ordinare.'" Thomas Aquinas, *In decem libris Ethicorum Aristotelis ad Nicomachum expositio,* lect. 1, ed. Raymund M. Spiazzi, 3rd ed. (Turin, 1964), 3; trans. Armand Maurer, *St. Thomas Aquinas: The Division and Methods of the Sciences,* 4th rev. ed. (Toronto, 1986), 94. A. J. Minnis, drawing upon the same quotation ("sapientis est ordinare") from the *Summa contra Gentiles,* applies it to the linked prologues not only of that work but of the *Confessio.* "'Moral Gower' and Medieval Literary Theory, in Gower's *"Confessio Amantis": Responses and Reassessments,* ed. A. J. Minnis (Cambridge, 1983), 68.

[5] Lee Patterson, *Negotiating the Past: The Historical Understanding of Medieval Literature* (Madison, WI, 1987), 141. From the class of writers who make reading dangerous, Patterson excludes John Gower. "Given this (Ovidian) complexity of form, we should

the poet's opposing "hem that weren wise," for he provides clues to reading that may, unless we are wary, mislead. The *Confessio* is not a poem through which readers can easily find the "rihte weie." The danger lies not only in the clash of values reflected in the content, but in the multiple aids to reading that the poet builds into the English text and also around it, in its Latin apparatus. Gower probably wrote the latter at least in part "to commit himself to posterity as a poet worthy to stand beside his classical forbears."[6] The Latin prose summaries and glosses and verse section-headings seem designed to imitate commentaries on the *auctores* and thereby to situate the *Confessio* among those books. But things said in that apparatus, as well as in commentaries within the text, also destabilize the work by providing competing frameworks for interpretation.

In recent decades, we have learned much from looking closely at the work's interpreters—Genius as a "reader," the Latin prose glosses, the author of the Prologue—either in isolation, or in juxtaposition with one or two other "voices" in the work. An examination of the fuller array of voices and their interpretive "codes," as interrelated and applied to the multifaceted content of a single narrative or section of the work, might shed new light on this wise poet's unusual method of putting things in order. In this essay I propose to focus on a single narrative, that of Paris and Helen, and the "readings" and judgments it contains and elicits. This case richly illustrates how the poet sets "problemes" to confront the wise.

The tale of Paris and Helen is the last story told in Book V, and we would expect it to have a special importance for the work as a whole. In its own right, the story carried great weight throughout the period, and Gower has awarded his own version of it the ultimate position in a very important part of his work. Book V, more than twice the length of any other book in the *Confessio*, treats avarice in ten species, "Mor than of eny other vice" (V.7612); the subject has a special relevance, Genius maintains, because throughout the world, companies of avarice "Ben nou the leders overal" (V.7616). The book is certainly important, but it is also troublesome. Contributing to its length, for example, is what Macaulay found to be a "very ill-advised digression ... about the various forms of Religion,"[7] a digression in which Genius denounces the goddess he serves. The argu-

---

not be surprised to find an alternative tradition of consistent anti-Ovidianism in a group of texts that offer an unmistakable condemnation of *fole amor* in favor of marital *amicitia*. . . . The best known of these poems is the *Traitié selonc les auctours pour essampler les amantz mariez* that Gower appends to the *Confessio amantis,* a praise of married love set against the *Confessio*'s exposure of 'la sotie de cellui qui par amours aime par especial.' The straightforward moralism of these texts makes explicit the anti-Ovidianism that remains only an implication in more subtly wrought (and interesting) poems, but the differences in method cannot disguise the basic similarity of attitude" (137–38).

   [6] Derek Pearsall, "The Gower Tradition," in *Gower's "Confessio Amantis": Responses and Reassessments,* ed. A. J. Minnis (Cambridge, 1983), 182.

   [7] Macaulay, *English Works,* 1:515.

ments of this book, variously reflecting such uncertainty about his status as Venus's "oghne Prest," further threaten his already fragile relationship with Amans. The tale of Paris and Helen does not restore confidence in that relationship; indeed, for all its potential, it has not competed well against other excellent stories in the book for the attention of critics. To some readers, the tale ultimately seems mismatched with its topic, anti-climactic, and flat.

It is not that the telling lacks virtues. The story is relatively long, though a good deal shorter than the version presented in Gower's primary source, Benoît de Sainte-Maure's *Roman de Troie*. Macaulay praised Gow-er's selective use of his source and the power of his revisions, and Derek Pearsall has seen in Gower's telling "a most consummate demonstration of his power of economical narrative."[8] Russell Peck has also noted that Gower's tale of Paris and Helen not only "ties together a nexus of Trojan materials, bad marriages, and stories of crumbling societies prominent in Book V," but seems to illustrate most of the divisions of Avarice treated in the book's preceding narratives: Coveitise, Fals Brocage, Stelthe, Ravine, Skarsnesse, Unkindschipe, Robberie.[9] One may ask, nevertheless, what purpose the narrative is really supposed to serve, especially because there is some doubt that Gower's revision of his source adequately focuses read-ers' attention on the topic he has announced as his subject.

That subject is sacrilege and the "wreche" it "hath aboght" (V.7190–91). Because Paris abducted Helen from Venus's temple, the priest con-cludes in the tale, the Greeks besiege Troy "And wolden nevere parte aweie" until they have won it "And brent and slayn that was withinne" (V.7582, 7584). And, as if this message were not strong enough, the confes-sor then draws on other cases to reinforce it: Achilles died "And al his lust was leyd asyde" (V.7596) because he chose Polixena in Apollo's temple; Troilus was forsaken by Criseide because he "his ferste love leide / In holi place" (V.7598–99).

As a reader of the stories he tells, Genius often misses much, and this case is no exception. As a teller, he seems for almost three-fourths of the narrative to be less interested in sacrilege than in other major events in the history of the Trojan-Greek conflict: the affront by King Lamedon, Pri-am's father, that led to the Greeks' first destruction of Troy; the rebuilding of the city; Priam's failed attempt to reclaim Esiona, his dishonored sister; the debate in parliament over pursuing "werre" or "reste"; and the deci-sion to support Paris in taking from the Greeks the woman "Of al this Erthe the faireste" (V.7427). This narrative prepares readers for an abduc-tion. When at last Paris "into Grece goth," it merely "fell upon his chance" (V.7468) that he landed on an island where Helen had recently

---

[8] Macaulay, *English Works*, 2:509; Derek Pearsall, "Gower's Narrative Art," *PMLA* 81 (1966): 481.

[9] Russell A. Peck, *Kingship and Common Profit in Gower's "Confessio Amantis"* (Carbondale, IL, 1978), 120, 122.

arrived to worship Venus. Although Paris abducts her from a temple, the materials provided in the early stages of the narrative make the fact of an abduction seem more important than the place where the abduction occurs. At the same time, Genius, in framing the tale, is so emphatic about suitable behavior in a "holi stede" that he has left at least one critic with the impression that "the rape would have been just fine had it taken place elsewhere."[10] The pieces of this narrative do not seem to fit together.

I

We obviously must look at the narrative more closely, but before we do so, it will be useful to reflect on the Latin prose glosses which frame the section and the tale within it. For this section of the *Confessio*, the prose comments are brief. The first one, at V.6962, introduces the vice:

> Hic tractat super vltima Cupiditatis specie, que Sacrilegium dicta est, cuius furtum ea que altissimo sanctificantur bona depredans ecclesie tantum spoliis insidiatur.

> [Here (the confessor) treats the last species of Avarice, which is called Sacrilege, whose theft, pillaging those goods of the church which are consecrated to the most high, lies in wait only for spoils.]

This is a counterpart to Genius's statement in the text; God's law that man "noght be thefte stele" (V.6969) is broken

> With hem that so untrewely
> The goodes robbe of holi cherche.
> The thefte which thei thanne werche
> By name is cleped Sacrilegge. (V.6976–79)

The second gloss, at V.7197, describes the tale and its message:

> Hic in amoris causa super istius vicii articulo ponit exemplum. Et narrat, pro eo quod Paris Priami Regis filius Helenam Menelai vxorem in quadam Grecie insula a templo Veneris Sacrilegus abduxit, illa Troie famosissima obsidio per vniuersi orbis climata divulgata precipue causabatur. Ita quod huiusmodi Sacrilegium non solum ad ipsius regis Priami omniumque suorum interitum, set eciam ad perpetuam vrbis desolacionem vindicte fomitem ministrabat.

> [Here in love's cause he poses an example on the point of that vice. And he recounts that especially because the sacrilegious Paris, the son of King Priam, abducted Helen, the wife of Menelaus, from the temple of Venus on a certain Greek island, that most famous siege

---

[10] David W. Hiscoe, "The Ovidian Comic Strategy of Gower's *Confessio Amantis*," *PQ* 64 (1985): 368.

of Troy, proclaimed throughout the world, occurred. Sacrilege of this kind thus contributed tinder of retribution not only to the violent death of King Priam and all his people, but also to the permanent destruction of the city.]

This "summary," like Genius's reading of the narrative, tells us little about the story's content. Indeed, it appears to follow the priest's own emphases in focusing chiefly on the consequences of Paris's sacrilege. Those consequences are not directly represented in the narrative, however, but are described in a prophecy uttered by Cassandra and her brother, the priest Helenus, after Paris returns to Troy with the abducted queen. For his action, they warn, Paris

> schal lese his lif
> And many a worthi man therto,
> And al the Cite be fordo,
> Which nevere schal be mad ayein. (V.7574–77)

In ending the story, Genius simply confirms that this is what happened: "And so it fell, riht as thei sein" (V.7578).

It may be the case that Latin glosses like these complement statements in the English text, but, as Pearsall has aptly cautioned us, the Latin apparatus is not "the means to the understanding of the poem, but another view of what the poem means."[11] The Latin prose glosses, prominently featured on the manuscript pages, together articulate such a view. That warrants further consideration, for the meaning emerging from the glosses may color our reading of the other interpretations Gower has supplied for his work.

The prose glosses represent an instance of Gower's use of the ancient and medieval rhetorical device of *ethopoeia*, a feigning of the speech of another person.[12] This rhetorical figure comes into play repeatedly in the fashioning of characters for the tales, of course, but Gower also uses it in another important way in the glosses, as when he applies it to himself as author, in the famous comment at I.59: "Here as it were in the person of other people, who are held fast by love, the author, feigning himself to be

---

[11] Derek Pearsall, "Gower's Latin in the *Confessio Amantis*," in *Latin and Vernacular: Studies in Late-Medieval Texts and Manuscripts*, ed. A. J. Minnis (Cambridge, 1989), 16.

[12] "Ethopoeia est, cum sermonem ex aliena persona inducimus"; and again, "ethopoeiam vero illam vocamus, in qua hominis personam fingimus pro exprimendis affectibus aetatis, studii, fortunae, laetitiae, sexus, maeroris, audaciae. . . . iam vero adolescentis et senis, et militis et imperatoris, et parasiti et rustici et philosophi diversa oratio dicenda est. . . . In quo genere dictionis illa sunt maxime cogitanda, quis loquatur et apud quem, de quo et ubi et quo tempore: quid egeri, quid acturus sit, aut quid pati possit, si haec consulta neclexerit." Isidore of Seville, *Etymologiae* 2.21.32, 2.14.1, ed. W. M. Lindsay, 2 vols. (Oxford, 1911). Priscian calls this same figure *adlocutio*, "imitatio sermonis ad mores et suppositas personas accommodata." *Praeexercitamina ex Hermogene versa* 9.27, ed. Carolus Halm, *Rhetores latini minores* (Leipzig, 1863), 557.

a lover, proposes to write of their various passions one by one in the various distinctions of this book."[13] As many critics have observed, through this note and others like it, Gower strives to keep the poem directed to its serious moral purpose. He does so in two senses. In this example, he focuses on the role of another person that he assumes in the text, thereby upholding his own separate status as a serious author. While calling attention to the use of such a device in the English text, however, the note itself represents an instance of *ethopoeia* as well. The gloss is a "speech," consistent with the "speech" of the other glosses, uttered by the persona of an interpreter (even a professional interpreter) of the text. In a restricted sense, this *aliena persona* is cast in the likeness of a grammarian, a teacher of literature who, through paraphrase and commentary, confers authority on the text, making it worthy to stand beside other texts that have been similarly expounded by grammar masters in the schools.[14]

In this framework, the persona and his glosses become a fiction, consistent with and limited to tasks performed according to a regimen established by a specific group of learned men. The persona on the margins is not a "character" in the usual sense. He does not expressly fashion or talk about himself, and neither does Gower comment on him: the poet cannot do so, of course, because these glosses, as a fiction, postdate the composition of the *Confessio*. The marginal commentator's tasks are limited, moreover, to one of the grammarian's two major offices, and the restriction is an important one: his field is *enarratio poetarum* or the interpretation of the poets, not *scientia recte loquendi* or the science of speaking correctly; to borrow Quintilian's alternative terms, his field is *historike*, not *methodike*.[15] Grammarians are expected to possess extensive knowledge—didascalic, cultural, historical, linguistic—for their tasks of interpreting the poets (or, more broadly, the authors) and thereby sustaining the cultural tradition.[16] In the ancient world, the *enarratio poetarum* was largely a descrip-

---

[13] "Hic quasi in persona aliorum, quos amor alligat, fingens se auctor esse Amantem, varias eorum passiones variis huius libri distinccionibus per singula scribere proponit." Trans. A. J. Minnis, *Medieval Theory of Authorship: Scholastic Literary Attitudes in the Later Middle Ages*, 2nd ed. (Philadelphia, 1988), 189.

[14] Alastair Minnis thus observes that "the commentator on the *Confessio amantis* was determined to prove that Gower ... was a good *auctor*. A clear distinction is therefore made between what Gower says in his own person (the *sapiens* of the *Prologus*) and what he says in the persons of those that are subject to love (including Amans and the Confessor) in the course of the treatise." *Medieval Theory of Authorship*, 189. The persona Gower devises to present his glosses represents a teacher who effectively authorizes the text by initiating a tradition of expounding it.

[15] Quintilian, *Institutio oratoria* 1.4.2, 1.9.1, ed. and trans. H. E. Butler, 4 vols., Loeb Classical Library (Cambridge, MA, 1963), 1:62–63, 156–57.

[16] In Thierry of Chartres, a supposition of such learning underlies the claim of the allegorical figure Grammatica that her prerogative is "the exposition of all authors." Trans. from the *Heptateuchon* by Jan Ziolkowski, *Alan of Lille's Grammar of Sex: The Meaning of Grammar to a Twelfth-Century Intellectual* (Cambridge, MA, 1985), 92. A like premise leads John of Salisbury to assert that the grammarian's task is to "shake out" the authors, identifying what they "have borrowed from the several branches of

tive activity, providing information necessary to a basic understanding of
the text: in addition to speaking about matters of style, the grammarian
expounds disputed passages, explains stories, paraphrases poems.[17] The
practice changes in late antiquity, Rita Copeland notes, with "the need to
reconstruct the meanings and contexts of a historically distant classical
literature." Indeed, "by the time of Isidore of Seville, such *enarratio* is no
longer a simple propaedeutic," but grounds "the most advanced textual
study and becomes, in turn, a model for literary historians and scriptural
exegetes."[18]

The prose commentaries of the *Confessio* initially appear to serve the
humbler and more ancient purpose, as a propaedeutic to reading and not
as a prescriptive or authoritative interpretation. The glosses do not present
or explore possible allegorical meanings, as medieval exegetical practice
would have allowed, but simply explain literally the elements of the
narrative or argument. Clearly, the English text they introduce does not
represent an "historically distant ... literature." The glosses function not
so much to draw a cultural past into the present, as to connect Gower's
present work with its cultural past, "to stabilise [the] poem within the
Latin learned tradition."[19] In the margins, the persona of grammarian-
glossator does this by performing many different tasks.[20]

By far the largest number of his entries introduce the topics and pro-
vide summaries of the tales. One might suppose that the summaries are
bound, for the most part, to being condensed, matter-of-fact statements of
what the confessor presents in the English text ("Hic tractat," "Hic ...
ponit," "Et narrat"). That, however, is not the case, as the present instance
reveals. The commentator, as he connects the poem with its cultural past,
sometimes introduces details in the summaries that are absent from the
tales; throughout he makes a special point of naming people and places and
situating cases historically, sometimes at the expense of accounting for
what actually occurs in the tale; he shifts emphases, focusing on "what is
morally excellent"[21] as another means to stabilize the narrative in a cul-
tural tradition, and thereby reminds readers to keep their judgment, or the

---

learning." *Metalogicon* 1.24, trans. Daniel D. McGarry (Berkeley, 1962), 66; ed. Clemens
C. I. Webb (Oxford, 1929), 54. A *grammaticus,* using that store of knowledge, helps
ensure that "all elements of the cultural tradition continue as living presences." Robert
A. Kaster, "The Grammarian's Authority," *Classical Philology* 75 (1980): 219.

[17] Quintilian, *Institutio oratoria* 1.2.14, ed. and trans. Butler, 1:46–47. For the empha-
sis on interpreting the poets, see Stanley F. Bonner, *Education in Ancient Rome: From the
Elder Cato to the Younger Pliny* (Berkeley, 1977), 58.

[18] Rita Copeland, *Rhetoric, Hermeneutics and Translation in the Middle Ages: Academic
Traditions and Vernacular Texts* (Cambridge, 1991), 21, 56, 57.

[19] Pearsall, "Gower Tradition," 182.

[20] He identifies *auctores,* names speakers, supplies the original Latin version or a para-
phrase of "sentences" here rendered in English, explains references, divides arguments
into their component parts, highlights items catalogued and more fully expounded in the
text, elucidates difficult passages, and sometimes simply enters a "Nota."

[21] Quintilian, *Institutio oratoria* 1.8.4, ed. and trans. Butler, 1:148–49.

interpretations they construct from reading, in order. As Robert Yeager has remarked, the glosses "represent Gower's solution to the problem of didactic precision which confronts all moralists who trust important lessons to unavoidably misreadable fictions."[22] Copeland has argued similarly that Gower's "Latin apparatus can be seen as a mechanism for controlling the potential subversiveness of the poetic fiction."[23] Pearsall sees the glosses in a somewhat different light, arguing that "the proses formalise the exemplary *function* of the stories in a manner that could be said deliberately to miss their *point*" and suggests, as a cause of this, that "the Latin acts as the agent of that general hostility toward narrative fiction which is characteristic of medieval ecclesiastical orthodoxy," an orthodoxy whose "object is to make all writing into a demonstration of truths already known."[24] The commentator in the *Confessio*, consistent with the role of *grammaticus*, thinks in terms of rules and categories, and it should not surprise us that he locks into what Genius purportedly offers, "truths already known." Sometimes, to make such truths even more apparent, he overrules Genius's judgment and introduces a stark moral thinking of his own, one that connects the particular moral act to a motive or a result by a simple, inexorable cause-and-effect logic. The product can be a rewritten narrative that ignores significant ambiguities and complexities in Genius's telling.[25]

It is unlikely, however, that Gower wrote the Latin glosses merely to warn us against reading his text as the glossator does. In a manuscript culture, such glosses are commonly employed to help readers find, gather, and learn things the author presents. The combined prose glosses on Sacrilege, exemplifying a pattern of commentary that is recurrent though not unvarying in the *Confessio*, introduce the topic (e.g., "Sacrilegium");

---

[22] Robert F. Yeager, "English, Latin, and the Text as 'Other': The Page as Sign in the Work of John Gower," *Text* 3 (1987): 262.

[23] Copeland, *Rhetoric, Hermeneutics and Translation*, 217.

[24] Pearsall, "Gower's Latin," 22.

[25] For example, on Genius's tale of Albinus and Rosemund, an exemplum about boasting, the commentator records that Albinus, having killed his enemy Gurmond, carries off Gurmond's daughter, Rosemund, by force, perfunctorily marries and beds her ("insuper et ipsius Gurmundi filiam Rosemundam rapiens, maritali thoro in coniugem sibi copulauit"), and then, at a public banquet, boasts of his victory over Gurmond by having Rosemund drink from a cup made from the skull of her father. The sequence of events is compressed, and the tale rewritten in the summary to make the crime explicable: simply, Albinus is a man obsessed with trophies. For Genius the matter is more complex. The love between Albinus and Rosemund matures over time:

His herte fell to hire anon,
And such a love on hire he caste,
That hire he weddeth ate laste;
And after that long time in reste
With hire he duelte, and to the beste
Thei love ech other wonder wel. (I.2484–89)

In the context of this love, the boast is inexplicable: the sudden change in the relationship can be attributed only to Venus's turning her "blinde whel" (I.2490).

identify its place in a frame of such topics (e.g., "super vltima Cupiditatis specie"); summarize the story briefly; and point the moral ("Sacrilegium ... vindicte fomitem ministrabat"). Such entries mark divisions of the text that become key both to reading—"Modus legendi in dividendo constat"[26]—and to the exercise of a trained memory. The divisions, fit in a whole, constitute the places where one discovers what is to be remembered, and the glosses provide "finding devices" that allow readers to get to those places and discover what they seek quickly.[27] Together these Latin comments represent a "gathering" or, in Hugh of St. Victor's terms, a "brief and compendious outline [of] things which have been written or discussed at some length." It is from such "brief and dependable abstracts," stored in memory, that we can "later on, when need arises,... derive everything else."[28]

While one may seriously doubt that Gower's prose glosses are uniformly "dependable" in providing the gist of a given section, they remain useful in providing memory places and helping readers find items in the whole work. In the simplest terms, these glosses form aids to the "trained and well-provided memory," which in the culture was thought to be "the essential foundation of prudence, *sapientia*, ethical judgment."[29]

If we think we should limit what we glean from a section to what the Latin prose glosses state, we miss the point of the gathering. The "abstracts" become points of origin for finding other things, for getting to and remembering "truths" that perhaps have never been presented elsewhere in quite the way that Genius presents them here. The glosses are not *the* means to the understanding of the poem, but they are *a* means.

The marginal grammarian follows Genius as "reader," but he also fulfills his role as a keeper of memory: dividing, indexing, categorizing to make things fit in a memory-store that represents the cultural tradition. The story of Paris and Helen has a special importance in that store, the glossator reminds us: the tale identifies what caused the world-famous siege of Troy. Certainly, the persona represented through the Latin glosses and summaries in one sense exemplifies readers, condemned by Seneca, who merely "have exercised their memories on other men's material,"[30] who remember but do not know. In another sense, however, the marginal grammarian "speaks" only by virtue of an office; his service is to open the

---

[26] "The method of reading consists in dividing." Hugh of St. Victor, *Didascalicon: De studio legendi* 3.9, ed. Charles Henry Buttimer (Washington, DC, 1939), 58; trans. Mary J. Carruthers, *The Book of Memory: A Study of Medieval Culture* (Cambridge, 1990), 174.

[27] Richard H. Rouse and Mary A. Rouse, "*Statim invenire:* Schools, Preachers, and New Attitudes to the Page," in *Renaissance and Renewal in the Twelfth Century,* ed. Robert L. Benson and Giles Constable (Cambridge, MA, 1982), 201–25.

[28] Hugh of St. Victor, *Didascalicon* 3.11, trans. Jerome Taylor (New York, 1961), 93–94; ed. Buttimer, 60–61.

[29] Carruthers, *Book of Memory*, 176.

[30] Seneca, *Ad Lucilium epistulae morales* 33.8, ed. and trans. Richard Gummere, 3 vols., Loeb Classical Library (Cambridge, MA, 1962–67), 1:238–39.

text, to initiate the reading. We might therefore begin a reading of the
Confessio with the glosses, but we would be well-advised not to end with
them.

II

Gower's rewriting of the tale to fit this section of his English poem may
have been inspired by a passage in the *Roman de Troie*, where Benoît de-
scribes the immediate Greek reaction to Paris's sacrilege:

> Par tote Grece a reconté
> Coment le temple orent robé,
> Com Paris e sa compaignie
> Ont Heleine prise e ravie;
> Tot a conté, tot a retrait,
> Ensi come il l'aveient fait.
> Mout en furent Grezeis irié. (4755–61)[31]

[Throughout Greece everyone recounted how Paris and his com-
pany, as they seized and carried Helen away by force, had robbed
the temple; just as they had done it, everyone recalled, everyone
reported it. About it the Greeks were much enraged.]

Gower does not adapt this passage to his English narrative, however;
indeed, it is the Latin commentator who captures the spirit of the French
text when he remarks that Paris's sacrilege contributed the "tinder of
vengeance" to Troy's fall. The gloss, in reflecting the *Roman*, calls atten-
tion to "difference," to the independence of the English tale from its
source, as well as to its constructedness.[32]

Gower's challenge as a storyteller is to respond to his delimiting topic
of sacrilege while also developing a full narrative, with elements that may
not expressly serve his exemplary purpose. As he realizes what Pearsall has
termed the "unconstrained and transgressive potential of fiction" in devel-
oping that narrative, however, Gower simultaneously broadens the para-
meters within which sacrilege is traditionally understood. In the episodes
preceding the abduction and sacrilege, he raises questions about political
advantage, will, and posturing—all related to uses and abuses of power—
that will recast our perception of the announced topic and eventually force
us to refine our interpretation and judgment of Paris's crime.

The case of King Lamedon sets the course for that broader reading.
When Jason and Hercules, on their voyage to Colchos, "reste preide" in

---

[31] Benoît de Sainte-Maure, *Le Roman de Troie*, ed. Léopold Constans, 6 vols. (Paris,
1904), 1:246.

[32] On the glosses as calling attention to the "craftedness" of Gower's English narra-
tives, see Yeager, "English, Latin, and the Text," 259.

Troy, Lamedon "wrathfulli" dismissed them, and for his obvious violation of basic rules of hospitality in failing to show "courtesy and reasonable generosity" to his foreign guests[33] the Greeks later take their vengeance. They raze Troy, destroy "king and al," and take Lamedon's daughter, Esiona, captive, granting her to the Greek king, Thelamon, to serve "at his wille." Lamedon, earlier described as "noght curteis" (V.3312) and here as "so vilein" (V.7203), exhibits a mean-spiritedness from which "fell the dissencion" that "after was destruccion / Of that Cite" (V.3307–9).

The razing of Troy for Lamedon's crime obviously relates to two important later events in this history: the rebuilding of the city and its prophesied final destruction. We know from the Latin gloss that because of Paris's action, Troy will be destroyed, never to be rebuilt. The image of a city in total ruin (reported in the prose summary and later predicted in the English text) carries a special poignancy for those who have read Genius's description of Priam's re-creation of Troy after its first destruction. It is made into "a cite newe" (V.7231), attracting to itself a "Gret presse" of people and a wealth of goods. It is so well fortified that "A fewe men it mihte kepe / From al the world, as semeth tho, / Bot if the goddes weren fo" (V.7250–52). Not only is Troy protected and safe, but Priam is "of children riche" (V.7317): a prosperous future seems assured. Forewarned by the Latin summary, however, we look ahead to an event that this magnificent rebuilding makes all the more tragic, and we look back to Lamedon, who also felt secure enough when he denied "reste" to his more powerful Greek visitors.

Lamedon's dismissal of Jason and Hercules, in addition to breaching the rules of "courtesie," is a bluff, an exercise of power that he does not truly possess: indeed, the Greek reprisal against him demonstrates that his wrathful "vileinie" is no match for their ire. This episode further reveals, on the Trojan side, a tendency to a "streit holdinge" (V.7655) manifested not merely in avarice, but in an insularity of attitude and an ostentatious display of self-sufficiency; it also manifests the Trojans' tendency to act rashly to keep or gain an advantage over a greater opponent. On the Greek side, it reveals a tendency to retaliate ruthlessly and absolutely for an affront, regardless of its degree of seriousness.

Lacking on both sides is a reflection of *curialitas*, a courtliness that might help ease the tension. To be sure, once Troy has been rebuilt and Priam calls a parliament to determine how to reclaim his sister, his people advise a strategy of "Acord and pes" (V.7270). When Priam sends Antenor to Greece to discuss Esiona's return, however, Thelamon and his people

---

[33] "Est itaque in hospitem peregrinum omnis humanitas et sobria liberalitas exercenda." John of Salisbury, *Policratici siue De nugis curialium et vestigiis philosophorum* 8.13, ed. Clemens C. I. Webb, 2 vols. (Oxford, 1909), 2:325; trans. Joseph B. Pike, *Frivolities of Courtiers and Footprints of Philosophers: A Translation of Books I, II, and III, and selections from Books VII and VIII of the Policraticus of John of Salisbury* (Minneapolis, 1938), 381.

curtly dismiss him with "wordes stoute" (V.7282). The Greeks are no less arrogant and "vilein" in their behavior than were the Trojans under Lamedon. The major difference between these powers lies in their relative strength, and that is the focal issue of a second parliament convened by Priam to address the Greek affront.

Gower's treatment of the latter event, much shortened from the version in the *Roman de Troie,* alludes to the turmoil of those gathered, as they voice "many a doute" and "many a proud word" (V.7326–27), but it presents only two major speeches. In these, Hector and Paris represent the opposed sides on the question, "what was the beste, / Or forto werre or forto reste" (V.7329–30). Their speeches thus form a *disputatio in utremque partem.* Simultaneously they do more, for the personae projected by the speakers, partly through the contrast, provide "readings" of what will become Paris's crime.

Hector's speech, only about half the length of its counterpart in Benoît, focuses immediately on the great "manhode," "worthinesse," and "knihthode" of the Greeks (V.7337–38). Basing his claim upon facts that Paris will not dispute, he argues that the Greeks are extremely powerful relative to the Trojans ("To hem belongeth al Europe" [V.7340]) and "we be bot of folk a fewe" (V.7343). Hector underscores this point because "were it reson forto schewe / The peril, er we falle thrinne" (V.7344–45). Indeed, with Greek power as his given, Hector issues a series of similarly directed, commonsensical reminders: it is foolish for an aggrieved person to act "so that his grief be more" (V.7349), for example, and again, a person who "loketh al tofore / And wol noght se what is behinde, / He mai fulofte hise harmes finde" (V.7350–52). This string of maxims has a particular power for the context. The Trojans would be well-advised, for example, to remember that the Greeks have hurt the Trojans before (the "cite newe" is a present reminder), and they are the world's greatest power now. Each maxim becomes a glass providing a different perspective on that power and the need to exercise great caution before provoking it.

Hector shows a keen awareness not only of his basic argument and the evidence he must present to support it, but also of his auditors and the self he must project to win them to his side. He is no less outraged by the Greeks' insults than they are, and indeed, should the Trojans decide to "taken werre on honde" (V.7362), he will be the first to "grieven" their enemies. At the same time, however, he encourages each of them to reflect carefully on the likely consequences of aggression against "hem that ben of such a myht" (V.7357). He will not oppose their counsel and urges them to shape "the beste weie" (V.7372). Given his goal in this speech, it may seem curious that Hector should call attention to his own readiness, even eagerness, to fight. Nevertheless, this statement effectively "authorizes" his argument. Because he is, as Genius has testified and the statement now intimates, a man "withoute fere" (V.7331), his warnings about the might of the Greeks should be taken very seriously.

In the last analysis, Hector's interest throughout this speech is not personal; his concern is the common weal. Keeping his will in check, he exemplifies a responsible courage, a mean between vices at opposite extremes; timidity on the one side, rashness on the other. This is part of the fuller presentation of his character: as presented through the speech, he almost becomes a textbook exemplar of prudence. He anticipates the future, clearly recollects the past, and uses both to determine a "rihte weie" through a great difficulty. He has no inflated opinion of himself. He advises his fellow Trojans, but does not claim he has the only solution to this question; nor does he wander from the point of what might best serve Troy, manipulating the case to serve his own advantage. He states his argument and then is prepared to accede to what the parliament's "counseil demeth" (V.7367).[34] While Genius represents these various qualities, however, he does not use the speech to preach the virtue of prudence. We witness virtue enacted, but the virtue remains unnamed. Most importantly, as we are drawn into the narrative to interpret this speech, argument, and character, we also frame a "reading" of the next speaker.

Paris recognizes the might of the Greeks, but in his speech he enlarges the issue to include the "truth" of the Trojans' quarrel. Whereas Hector calmly urges his auditors to be prudent, Paris immediately projects a deep sense of outrage over the wrongs the Trojans have suffered, and he inflames a like passion in his auditors. He stresses the "strength" of their endurance, a suffering that has implicitly reached its breaking point:

> Strong thing it is to soffre wrong,
> And suffre schame is more strong,
> Bot we have suffred bothe tuo. (V.7377–79)

Although the Trojans have sought peace by sending Antenor to the Greeks, the Greeks "grete wordes blowe / Upon her wrongful dedes eke" (V.7384–85). The Trojans have acted reasonably, while the Greeks have not: "who that wole himself noght meke / To pes, and list no reson take, / Men sein reson him wol forsake" (V.7386–88). The Trojans have pursued peace; the Greeks have rejected it.

In these statements, no less emotionally charged for their advocacy of reason, Paris prepares his auditors to support the action he will now propose. The Greeks are powerful, but the Trojans are right. Ten men engaged in a true "querele" against one hundred who are false may indeed have "the betre of goddes grace" (V.7393), and on that supposition, Paris volunteers to defend the truth of the Trojans' "querele." His claim that "I wole assaie, hou so it falle, / Oure enemis if I mai grieve" (V.7396–97) bespeaks his courage, of course. It also does more. By a backward proof, he now shows that the Trojans have effectively won "goddes grace," that their truth has been proven, and that they will get the "betre" of their

---

[34] These aspects of Prudence are presented, for example, in *Moralium dogma philosophorum,* ed. John Holmberg (Uppsala, 1929), 8–12.

enemies in this conflict.

This proof—"I have cawht a gret believe / Upon a point" (V.7398–99)—rests on his famous Judgment. In his capsule account of that event, he reports that he gave the golden apple to Venus, "So that me thoughte it for the beste" (V.7428). Venus "wolde it neveremor foryete" (V.7424) that he has declared her the most beautiful of the three goddesses, and Paris turns into the principal warrant for his argument Venus's promise that in Greece she will "bringe unto my hond / Of al this Erthe the faireste" (V.7426–27). In this pledge lies a response to the Trojans' quandary over what to do about the abducted Esiona: as the Greeks have stolen one of our noblewomen, so we shall steal one of theirs. By such an action, vengeance will be achieved, justice served, and a people with the true "querele" vindicated, all with the sanction of divine authority. Thus, when Paris, less deferential than Hector, demands of his fellow Trojans, "Sey ye what stant in youre avis" (V.7435), their response appears to be a forgone conclusion. Hector has seemed concerned less about the good or the "true querele" than about the *utile*, about survival. Paris seems more concerned about the right, the *honestum*. Unlike Hector, who urges caution and yet declares his readiness to fight, Paris does not vacillate: he seems in the force of his rhetoric the stronger character.

At a deeper level, of course, Hector, in his practical focus on the realities of Greek power, serves the good of his people; Paris, despite his apparent investment in the right, is an opportunist who serves only his own advantage. In contrast to Hector, Paris is short-sighted, presumptuous, and rash. Nevertheless, Genius, just as he does not directly judge Paris's speech, does not, at this point, judge his character. The task of judging is assigned only to Cassandra, who apparently is alone in seeing the outcome of pursuing this course of impetuous self-interest: "if Paris his weie take, / As it is seide that he schal do, / We ben for evere thanne undo" (V.7448–50). When her brother steps forward to support her prophecy, "al was holde bot a jape" (V.7463). The surest judgment against Paris in the narrative is "pointed" at the moment of sacrilege, but the rest of the action significantly informs that judgment. To discover how these elements are drawn together, we might now be guided by another of Gower's internal "readers."

III

The Latin verses that head this section of the *Confessio* provide some hints about the connection between Paris's speech and his later action.

> Sacrilegus tantum furto loca sacra prophanat;
>   Vt sibi sunt agri, sic domus alma dei.
> Nec locus est, in quo non temptat amans quod amatur,
>   Et que posse nequit carpere, velle capit.

[Sacrilege profanes the shrine by theft,
God's sacred house is as his fields to him.
No place where Love won't grope for what is loved,
And wanting seize what power cannot pluck.][35]

Verses like these throughout the poem explore the mystery of why people behave the way they do, and they often do so through enigmas of their own, alluding "to ideas or situations that they do not explain" (Echard and Fanger, xxviii). The Latin versifier is, as a persona, a *vir* or *poeta fecetus*, a literate, urbane, and often witty commentator and question-poser. He does not advance a rhetoric of deterrence such as Genius the reader, the Latin grammarian, and, to some degree, the seers in the narrative employ in this section of the work. Rather than dissuade readers from sacrilege by arousing a fear of punishment, he simply explores the attitude or *intentio* that is realized in the vice.

Here, as elsewhere, the couplets implicitly raise questions that will be answered tentatively, if they are answered at all, in the section of the English text they introduce. As throughout the work, the verses are, to borrow Siân Echard and Claire Fanger's terms, proverbial, drawing on the root term as meaning not only an "adage or maxim," but "a parabolic statement in which a profound truth is cloaked" (ibid., xxxii–xxxiii). For the verses on Sacrilege, we might usefully consider the latter element, the parabolic, following the root sense of *parabola* as "a comparison." As is the case for works like Alan of Lille's *Parabola*, readers are expected to find and reflect upon a "likeness" in the conjoined couplets. In this instance, the couplets are separated by their respective subjects, *Sacrilegus* and *amans;* "church-robber" (or, as a personification, "Sacrilege") and "lover" are coequivalent terms, and in the juxtaposition the poet encourages a comparison. His style is paratactic, and the meaning of the conjunction between the two halves of the statement must be supplied by the interpreter.

In these lines, the couplets are linked by the term *locus,* the *loca sacra* or sacred places of line 1, and the *locus* or place of line 3. The sacrilegious person desecrates holy places by theft and, as the second line shows, collapses a hierarchical order and perceives obviously different places similarly. As are his own fields to the sacrileger, so is God's house: each is a source of plunder. *Nec* "And not," the coordinating conjunction joining the couplets, effectively reinforces "place" as the connecting theme. "And there is not a place where" of the second couplet now requires a subject for the clause that follows; we expect *sacrilegus,* but are given another, *amans.* On the strength of this statement, every lover, if the opportunity arises, is a *sacrilegus,* a desecrator of sacred places, in those, indeed in all places "groping," "handling," "testing by touch," "examining to discover

---

[35] Trans. Siân Echard and Claire Fanger, *The Latin Verses in the "Confessio Amantis": An Annotated Translation* (East Lansing, MI, 1991), 67.

the feelings of," "making a bid for," "attempting to influence," "making an attempt on," "attacking," even "making a sexual assault on"[36] what is loved. Whereas the word "temptat" in the third line opens up this range of meanings, a first reading is most likely to yield the broadest, perhaps gentlest meaning of "temptat" as referring to the lover merely "testing" what is loved. The fourth line then startles with its double paradox of a rapacious, potentially destructive love, applied with force even when power is lacking: in effect, the lover seizes what he cannot seize.

The meaning of this "sentence" is not apparent, but the case of Paris provides an interpretation. Against the might of the Greeks, Paris is powerless. The "hihe feste" in Venus's temple provides an opportunity for him to do what he cannot otherwise do, "safely" abduct Helen from Menelaus and the Greeks. It is not merely that he seizes her in a place sacred to Venus, paradoxically through an act of sacrilege that the goddess has seemingly authorized against herself. Nor is it merely that in this place, Helen, through her expressed devotion to Venus, is presumably more susceptible to Paris's advances. It is also, very simply, that the act occurs in a temple, a place of "reste" that also happens to be situated in a "lond of pes" (V.7492): those who enter this sacred place are, as expected, unarmed, so that "of defense was no bote, / So soffren thei that soffre mote" (V.7549–50). Helen here lacks the protection of the Greek powers that usually surround her. "To want" thus displaces "to be able": the lover's will, appetite, or desire (velle) takes what his power (posse) cannot.

Paris's act requires a denial that greater powers exist outside himself. Such denial has surfaced in the parliament, not merely in his rejecting the might of the Greeks, but in his co-opting the gods to establish that he and the Trojans have won "goddes grace." What Venus has promised to deliver "unto my hond" is his, and he calls the gods, as well as the Trojans, into the service of his will in taking it. His implied boast in the parliament—that his judgment in the dispute of the three goddesses has provided the solution to the Trojans' "querele"—is masked by another display, a claim that from his vision of this judgment, he has caught a "gret believe." Later, when he discovers who the people are who have gathered at Venus's temple, he plans also to "don his obeissance" (V.7486) to the goddess. Putting on "his beste aray" and adorning himself "With great richesse ...,/ As it to such a lord belongeth" (V.7488–90), he enters the temple "with his felaschipe" (V.7494). His devotion, whether initially real or only apparent, becomes a stratagem, a display of lordship and "gret richesse" that he carries over into his first meeting with Helen. We shall return to that encounter presently.

The critical turn in Paris's thinking occurs just after that event, when he leaves the temple: "So goth he forth and tok his leve, / And thoghte ...

---

[36] For this range of possibilities, see the *Oxford Latin Dictionary*, ed. P. G. W. Glare (Oxford, 1982), s.v. *tempto*.

/ He wolde don his Sacrilegge" (V.7519-21). Even the two coordinating conjunctions, the "and ... And" connecting two commonplace acts, prosaically described, with the sudden, impulsive planning of a sacrilege (a notion unexpectedly introduced, seemingly as an afterthought) reveal in Paris a flattening of perception that is also betrayed in the speech before the parliament and in the enactment of this vice. With his thought of sacrilege, Paris resets his course and later returns to the temple, breaking into the world "of devocion / Heleine in contemplacion" has created around herself (V.7537-38). The place, the goddess it honors, and her authority are now matters of indifference to him. As in his speech before the parliament, so in Venus's temple, he desecrates the source of his "gret believe."

The Latin verses, in evoking this possible reading of the narrative, go beyond the prose glosses, though they are not inconsistent with them, by hinting at the attitude, inclination of will, or intention that leads people to act sacrilegiously. The Latin poetry, in "revising" or shifting the jurisdiction of the prose summaries, probes, questions, raises doubts that one can begin to settle tentatively through a closer reading of the English narrative. While the Latin verses do not tell us what the text means, they provide topics that may help us discover meaning.

IV

The Latin verses also shed light on the confessional dialogue preceding the narrative. By parataxis, the two Latin couplets separate elements that will be similarly introduced in the organization of Genius's speech. In this confessional argument, Genius separately treats sacrilege in general and sacrilege in love's cause, and he focuses respectively on *sacrilegus* and *amans*, but does not fully explore the nature of the relationship. He defines the vice in the very broad context of the eighth commandment—"Thou shalt not steal"—and the practice of those who "nou adaies" refuse to work: "what thei mai be Stelthe take / Thei holde it sikerliche wonne" (V.6972-73). The *sacrilegus*, or the thief who steals goods from "holi cherche," will not be deterred by a greater power, by a commandment, or by any "cursednesse." Without conscience, he "brekth the holinesse / And doth to god no reverence" (V.6990-91); he takes the "Pourpartie" of goods from God "Which unto Crist himself is due" (V.7001); he defies the priest's curse, saying "he fareth noght the wurse" for his theft (V.6994). This introduction repeats, for the *sacrilegus* of the English text, the contrast between *posse* and *velle;* the church-robber is driven, and he apparently succeeds, exclusively by his will and a succession of denials. For such defiance, Genius puzzles, "I not what bedes he schal preie" (V.6998). Again, the priest focuses on consequences. Warning of the "peine comende afterward" and the "heritage in helle," and citing three instances of princes "Coupable sore in this degre" (V.7010), Genius minces no words in showing the heinousness of this sin and the severity of its punishment: this is clearly not a subject one should take lightly.

That, however, is what he appears to do when he shifts the subject to "loves cause," *amans*, and the pursuit of love in church. Genius's tone is now lighter, and aspects of his subject also seem so. One might suppose a lesser degree of guilt, a lesser sacrilege, in the lover whose "pilage" from the beloved in church amounts to nothing more than her freely given "goodli word," "beheste," or "tokne" (V.7045, 7050).[37] This section is "ernest," but it also includes "game," and where the one ends and the other begins is not easily determined.

Genius distinguishes between two kinds of men who commit sacrilege in love: those who find in church a means to advance an existing love, and those who enter a church seeking a woman to seduce. The former find there the leisure to test the beloved, perhaps even "to influence" her, but they are implicitly "true" lovers who observe rules of "courtesie" and genteel behavior, who do not overreach in their courtship. Their sacrilege, such as it is, is perhaps identified in the priest's final statement about them: "Thus halwe thei the highe feste" (V.7051); more particularly, their fault lies in using rites of the church to gain "som avantage" (V.7043) over the lady. In contrast to these, the "lovers" in the latter group do not love at all; they act, in the priest's terms, "Riht as an hauk" looking "Upon the foul, ther he schal lihte" (V.7071–72); in their actions, *temptare* means "to make a sexual assault."

Amans claims that he belongs to the former group: he loves one woman alone, and he can prove it. In church, he sets all his devotion only on her image (V.7128), and as he describes that worship, he confesses not to idolatry (though Genius's recent teaching on false religion might have evoked such a response) but to "covoitise" and sacrilege, which he commits as the lady inspires him. The thefts he contemplates are modest: he would even be content with "a goodly syhte" (V.7138). More serious, though he does not acknowledge it, is his praying "unto mi god" as well as reciting the Paternoster and the Creed, "Al ... for that I wolde spede" in love (V.7120). This, again, is sacrilege, an appropriation of rites of the church to advance his suit. Throughout, however, the lover comically

---

[37] In the second recension of the work, Gower has the priest make a three-part distinction regarding sacrilege: it may be regarded as the theft of a sacred object from a sacred place, a nonsacred object from such a place, or a sacred object from a nonsacred place. The "sacred," in Genius's terms, is whatever "halwed is to the servise / Of god" (*V.7028–29). The distinction and definition are traditional. See, for example, Peter Lombard: "Sacrilegium tribus modis committitur: quando scilicet vel sacrum de sacro, vel non sacrum de sacro, vel sacrum de non sacro aufertur. Sacrum vero dicitur quidquid mancipatum est cultui divino, ut ecclesia vel res ecclesiae." *Sententiae in IV libris distinctae* 3.37.5.2, ed. Ignatius Brady, 3rd ed., Spicilegium Bonaventurianum 4 (Grottaferrata, 1971–1981), 2:210–11. In the *Confessio,* this three-part distinction might have helped clarify the nature and degree of the sacrilege of lovers, but Gower dropped it in the third recension. Later in this essay, I shall suggest why a distinction implying degrees of guilt may have run counter to the confessor's argument.

exudes a confidence that his churchly behavior is entirely appropriate, especially because it affords new evidence of his truth, "gentilesse," and worthiness in love.

Genius's implied contrast between supposedly "true" lovers and false ones develops into a contrast between Amans and the Paris of the tale that follows this confession. Both of these lovers are powerless: Amans against the strength of his lady's heart, which, he admits, will take a miracle "forto chaunge" (V.7123), and Paris against the Greeks. Amans and Paris also begin their testing similarly. Amans, with his "contienance" on the book, shifts his gaze ("al [his] lok") to his lady (V.7116). Paris, arriving at the temple to "do sacrifise to Venus," prays, "And thanne aside he gan be-holde, / And sih wher that this ladi stod" (V.7509–10). In each case, the look slides laterally, disrupting the hierarchies of prayer and meditation, and attitudinally betraying what could readily become sacrilege, an appro-priation of the sacred for personal gain. The subsequent behavior of these two lovers, however, is clearly very different. Amans seeks no more "avantage" in church than does Genius's better suitor; though he seizes what he wants in a sacred place, his desire and action are inhibited, and to some may seem innocuous. His "test" occurs at the offering, certainly when the lady is least able to resist, but there, as he would perceive it, he steals no more than a "lusti touch" when he puts his arm around her waist, and also a good word, the gentle rebuke of her "grant mercy" (V.7145).

By contrast, Paris takes what he wants by assault. With his men "redy armed" he enters the temple "al sodeinly" (V.7545), seizes Helen, and "with his felaschipe" bears her to the ship (V.7552–54). His earlier action in the temple, when he first meets Helen, provides a hint of this later action. There is something sinister about Paris as, "In his freisshe mod," he approaches Helen

> and made hir chiere,
> As he wel couthe in his manere,
> That of his wordes such plesance
> Sche tok, that al hire aqueintance,
> As ferforth as the herte lay,
> He stal er that he wente away. (V.7513–18)

On leaving her, he thinks only of doing "his Sacrilegge" that evening, "That many a man it scholde abegge" (V.7522). Even in this thought, Helen herself has diminished in importance.

In similar fashion, the suitor from Genius's class of "lusti folk" parades before the "faireste of the route" in church, "Wher as thei sitten alle arewe" (V.7062–63):

> Ther wol he most his bodi schewe,
> His croket kembd and theron set
> A Nouche with a chapelet,

Or elles on of grene leves,
Which late com out of the greves. (V.7064–68)

He does all of this because he, like Paris, would "seme freissh" (V.7069). His goal, before he leaves the church, is "forto stele an herte or tuo" (V.7087), though "he loveth non of alle" (V.7083). His chaplet of flowers or "grene leves" suggests an indifference about the choice, about serving either the "Flour" or the "Lef" in that game of love which had become popular in the courts of late medieval Europe, including the court of Richard II.[38] This lover's implied service to either is mere display, and for him, ostentation is power. Once again, we are led back to the paradox of *posse-velle*, but now it is presented in the context of courtly behavior. The lover with the chaplet steals a magnificence to impress, indeed enchant the fairest of the company, "as he were of faierie" (V.7073), and thereby to cloak another theft, that of "an herte or tuo."

The distinction between the lovers in Genius's introduction to sacrilege *in amoris causa*, subsequently revealed in the behavior of Amans and Paris, presumably holds much potential for refining our sense of what sacrilege means, and also for ferreting out, in these cases, where the truly ethical issues lie. At least initially, however, Genius disappoints us. He does not elaborate further on his distinction, and he appears to pick up on the lover's confession in only one particular. His approach to the lady, and presumably his worship of her, occurs in church, the wrong place to advance one's love: "The cherche serveth for the bede, / The chambre is of an other speche" (V.7188–89). If the prose commentator seems stilted in his interpretation of the English text, Genius here seems just as wooden in judging the lover and framing the narrative. Whatever power his narrative contains, he seems incapable of seeing it as emerging from and, in turn, redefining a moral context. In this instance, his imagination appears to be place-bound. Idolatry is not the issue. Nor is rape. Nor are courtly "styles." Nor, in looking ahead to the tale, is Paris's particular action in seeking Helen, or the fact that Venus has authorized rape, or the fact that the temple where the rape occurs is *her* temple. In the *moralitas*, these are complexities that seem beyond the comprehension of Amans's priest. His energies now seem to be focused merely on a distinction of place.

There is another apparent confusion in Genius's teaching. Although he chastises Amans for pursuing his love in church, he considers Amans's thefts of look, word, or touch as mere "game." The sin, for the priest, lies in Amans's will. But Amans has said that he is content with what he has taken: "al the remenant to seke / Is fro mi pourpos wonder ferr" (V.7148–49).

Where, then, is the poet headed with this argument? A closer look at

---

[38] See D. A. Pearsall, ed. *"The Floure and the Leafe"* and *"The Assembly of Ladies"* (London and Edinburgh, 1962), 23. Gower refers again to the garlands of "lef" and "flour" at VIII.2467–69.

the confession reveals that there are moments in Amans's statements when he does indeed talk about his will. If the lady pays him attention, he is so smitten "that me were lief / To ben in holy cherche a thief" (V.7133–34); his conscience will allow him to woo the lady "In holy cherche,"

> Be so that up amendement
> I mihte gete assignement
> Wher forto spede in other place. (V.7153–55)

He possesses "no holinesse" when he sees the lady "in eny sted" (V.7163). He takes only small things (look, touch, word) in church, but he wants more: "thogh I wolde oght elles have" (V.7171), he admits, he does not attempt more, simply because the rest is "kept with such a privilege" that he can do no sacrilege.

What Genius has "discovered" for this case is what the Latin poet of the apparatus has remarked, that underlying the theft of sacrilege, "to want" may be more critical than "to be able." The priest is not always inclined to make or uphold distinctions, for reasons we shall note later. What he often does best is find a likeness in differences, and that is what he does here. Thus, however great the difference between Paris's and Amans's acts of sacrilege (reflecting extremes in the range of meanings for the Latin word *temptat*), they share a deeper likeness. Beneath their acts, they are alike in their *intentiones,* or inclinations of will. Given the penchant of Genius to find such likeness, it should not surprise us that in his introduction to the two types of sacrilegious "lover," he launches into his treatment of the second and ostensibly more wicked exemplar with the observation, "And ek riht in the selve kinde" (V.7055).

V

The implications of Genius's collapsing distinctions he himself has proposed extend far beyond the treatment of sacrilege. Gower's fictive priest is a figure more enigmatic in his consistent "plain-speaking" than is his counterpart in the Latin apparatus, the parabolist of the verse section-headings. To be sure, some parts of his "expertise" are less controversial than others. From what appears to be a capacious memory, for example, he calls up whatever "lore" the occasion seems to demand. He is presented as a thesaurus of information, a font of literary learning, and in his acts of drawing upon the *auctores* and a store of encyclopedic knowledge to explain a "text," even he resembles a *grammaticus*. In exposition and definition, he organizes and classifies. It is he who divides the confession and finds stories in the "public memory" to fill the divisions. Sometimes his answers to the queries of his inquisitive "pupil" seem better suited to a grammar-school collation than to a confession. Amans's question about how the golden fleece appeared in Colchos, a question based on Jason's quest in the tale he has just heard, leads to the story of Helle and Phrixus.

The latter story provides information, exposition; the moralization of the tale of Jason and Medea is effectively deferred until Amans's curiosity about the history of the fleece is satisfied. Amans's question about the gods, after he has heard the tale of Vulcan and Venus, leads to the digression on religions. And in explaining that digression, the grammarian on the margins effectively describes Genius as a grammarian: through this catalogue of the gods, the priest supplies readers with a vocabulary that will help them understand what occurs elsewhere in the work.[39]

Nevertheless, the priest does not always connect the new matter and the old in ways we expect. His mode of connecting is a function of *ingenium*, of a "natural ability," "poetic talent," "ingenuity," and, of course, "genius" that lift explanation, or a provision of information, into a field of imagination and poetry. For a traditional grammarian engaged in retrieving and preserving a cultural past, "any exercise of *ingenium* is bound to be viewed as less successful and rewarding than an application of *diligentia* which finds a way of translating the past, in the form of *auctoritas*, into the present."[40] Gower effectively advances a like distinction in his work, namely between his Latin prose grammarian-commentator, who, through a diligence in connecting the poem with its cultural heritage, confers authority on the English text, and Genius, who, because of the idiosyncracies of his *ingenium*, sometimes reinforces and sometimes undermines that authoritative status.

To pursue this analogy, Genius advances from a field of grammar to that of poetry and is there given the license that *grammatici* accorded to the poets.[41] His faults—his repeated solecisms on questions of manners and conduct—may be given other names because of his unique function. Because of his ambiguous prerogative as a Christian confessor and as Venus's "oghne Prest," he can do what those locked into a single jurisdiction cannot always do: invent. For Gower, it is not enough to have the provision of a text "divided" into places and "gathered" by memory, and then to have "hem that weren wise" stop with the memorizing, with an accretion of what Seneca condemns as mere "note-book knowledge," as something not digested, but only tasted from a commentary.[42] What

---

[39] "Quia secundum Poetarum fabulas in huius libelli locis quampluribus nomina et gestus deorum falsorum intitulantur, quorum infidelitas vt Cristianis clarius innotescat, intendit de ipsorum origine secundum varias Paganorum Sectas scribere consequenter" (at V.749).

[40] Robert Kaster, "Macrobius and Servius: Verecundia and the Grammarian's Function," *Harvard Studies in Classical Philology* 84 (1980): 236.

[41] Quintilian thus writes that the teacher of grammar "will point out what words are barbarous, what improperly used, and what are contrary to the laws of language. He will not do this by way of censuring the poets for such peculiarities, for poets are usually the servants of their metres and are allowed such license that faults are given other names when they occur in poetry." *Institutio oratoria* 1.8.13–14, ed. and trans. Butler, 1:152–53. John of Salisbury refines the statement by Quintilian in *Metalogicon* 1.24, ed. Webb, 54; trans. McGarry, 66.

[42] Seneca, *Ep.* 33.7, ed. and trans. Gummere, 1:236–39.

Seneca describes as missing from that process is relevant to Gower's figure of Genius: "we should see to it that whatever we have absorbed should not be allowed to remain unchanged, or it will be no part of us. We must digest it; otherwise it will merely pass into memory [*memoria*] and not into our very being [*ingenium*]."[43] In that sense, reading is an act of making the common "propre": it is an act of appropriation.

In another sense, however, reading is also an act of making what is one's own (what is "propre") common, in the sense of opening up places for new invention. Reflection on a text, as it advances from reading and interpretation to meditation, is a transgressive act, as Hugh of St. Victor remarks in writing on this last step:

> Meditation takes its start from reading but is bound by none of reading's rules or precepts. For it delights to range along open ground, where it fixes its free gaze upon the contemplation of truth, drawing together now these, now those causes of things, or now penetrating into profundities, leaving nothing doubtful, nothing obscure.[44]

It is doubtful that such activity, as inspired by the *Confessio,* can ever achieve such finality: Gower never encourages his wise readers to presume that they have left "nothing doubtful, nothing obscure" in the field of meditation that most concerns him, the "consideration of morals." Genius helps keep us from such a presumption.

Whatever jurisdiction readers select for their interpretation of this poem, if they select only one, they will discover that within that jurisdiction Genius is not always wrong, but neither is he always right. On some matters, he shows acute insight; on others, he is extraordinarily obtuse. And that, in one sense, is because from place to place in his argument he changes codes, co-opting material either from the Christian religion or from his goddess of love and "gentilesse," as suits a given purpose. We may well ask which value system he most strives to inculcate, even as he appears to commit sacrilege in relation to each. The answer is probably neither, or both. Genius is certainly drawn to both, and he judges each of them to be good. To be sure, he tries, "for schame," to evade speaking about Venus and Cupid in his treatise on the gods, but soon after that he quickly restores these deities to their former status as grounding certain of his arguments. What Gower keeps open, through these mixtures of fictions and codes, is the exercise of an imagination that crosses memory-places, and a capacity for reflection, for "ranging along open ground." Genius's power resides more in conjoining things than in separating them, more in coordinating than in discriminating or subordinating: he is a persona who, in his own domain, reflects the stylistic feature of parataxis in the Latin verses. As he brings unlike things together, he fosters discovery. But he is

---

[43] Ibid., 84.6–7, ed. and trans. Gummere, 2:280–81.
[44] *Didascalicon* 3.10, trans. Taylor, 92–93; ed. Buttimer, 59–60.

limited in his power to differentiate, to perceive or identify unlikeness, to weigh degrees of importance and value. This limitation sometimes leads to major lapses of consistency, of course. For the poem, however, it also introduces larger complexities, more reflective of experience, that require from "hem that weren wise" a stronger capacity to judge.

Regarding Genius's role in this section of the work, Larry Scanlon has observed that "in his explicit exposure of Paris's sacrilege, he implicitly exposes the sacrilegious status of his own authority, and in so doing indicates his capacity to see beyond it."[45] It is in that seeing beyond—that double transgression of breaking rules set either by the false goddess or by the "true" religion he serves—that we shall find the connections that will make sense of this tale as the culminating narrative in this critical book.

In refusing to credit Amans's claim of worthiness in love, here manifested in his "gentil" behavior toward the beloved in church, and in collapsing the distinction between Amans and the preening, self-indulgent, womanizing suitor from among the "lusti folk," the priest goes beyond what the Court of Love authorizes. Lovers admitted to Venus's court suffer passions, but they also observe rules that make them "gentil" in conduct and manners; that observance, together with their capacity to produce sexually, form the test of worthiness. Genius has here dropped from consideration Amans's enactment of the accepted manners of *curialitas* and finds against the sacrilege in the lover's will. It is unlikely that a "pure" venerean would reach a similar verdict. Amans is a lover after all: what is most critical is that he orders his passion in deed, observing a standard of "gentilesse" and respecting the "privilege" of the beloved.

In judging Amans's will to commit sacrilege, Genius also counts the "remenant," his petty larcenies, "bot a game" (V.7184). A churchman would not. In those acts, though they may be wonderful amusements in the "game" of love, a cleric would be much more likely to see the inappropriateness: a misuse of rites, false worship, and idolatry, perhaps, but at the very least a violation of the rule that forms only one part of Genius's judgment: "The cherche serveth for the bede, / The chambre is of an other speche."

Genius's separation of sacrilege in general and sacrilege "in loves cause" appears to carry with it a tonal as well as subject distinction, between *gravitas*, "ernest," and "lore" on the one hand, and *levitas*, "game," and "lust" on the other. What is ultimately more important than the division, however, is the reconnection. To forgive Amans's behavior in church as "game," while also attacking the tendency of his will, Genius must honor conflicting premises in two discrete jurisdictions. In the process, however, he adds weight to the code of amorous etiquette while he also lightens the code of moral prescriptions drawn from "ecclesiastical orthodoxy." He

---

[45] Larry Scanlon, *Narrative, Authority, and Power: The Medieval Exemplum and the Chaucerian Tradition* (Cambridge, 1994), 276–77.

does the latter by enlarging the field of sacrilege to include a whole range of misappropriations of power, each involving a manipulation of codes. It is perhaps no accident that the Latin couplets foreshadow this in a particular way. Whereas the first couplet focuses directly on the *Sacrilegus* who has a very particular place-bound intent of robbing a church or temple, the second couplet, which like the first could stand on its own, offers no such restriction: a lover will test the beloved in any place. As the subject opens up to the question of *posse-velle*, explored in so many different ways by Genius, beginning with the seemingly unrelated case of Lamedon, we begin to see that simple prescriptions cannot adequately address the complex, changing particularities of experience. A lightening—a game about the "ernest"—can improve our capacity for sound judgment. In joining teachings from competing jurisdictions, Genius can show why sacrilege is "vltima Cupiditatis specie" and represents the worst kind of theft, an application of that "low cunning supported by talent"[46] that ultimately denies the existence of every distinction, privilege, and "cursedness."

The debate Gower encourages through the multiple interpreters he represents in his work is consistent with the end he envisions as the poem concludes, when the persona of Amans/"John Gower" becomes a "reader" of his own confession. This work fosters an exercise of reading and, even more importantly, re-reading, inspiring the use of a variety of "medieval reading strategies"[47] to sharpen our capacity for ethical judgment. In focusing on the crossing of boundaries, an action that is always transgressive, Gower creates for his many examples "in amoris causa," indeed for all the cases he presents, changes of jurisdiction or venue that encourage us to reperceive issues. Yeager, citing Derrida's notion of a "jurisdiction of frames," has suggested that the *Confessio*, as presented on the manuscript page, involves a "dissolution of jurisdictions."[48] Those jurisdictions never dissolve totally, but form the basis for the re-creation of new ones. That re-creation is the task Gower assigns his readers. Relevant to that task is a recent comment by John Dagenais about reading in a manuscript culture: "the nature of Glosynge and some specific instances of glossing in medieval manuscripts reveal a textual world that is not self-sufficient, not completed, not even intended to be complete, until an individual reader intervenes 'ethically' in the text."[49] Perhaps no medieval poet contributes more than Gower to creating a "complete" work that is so incomplete, a text enlarged and "finished" through an apparatus probably of his own devising that forces readers not only to learn from reading what wisdom is, but to intervene, judge wisely, and thereby become wise.

---

[46] Cicero, *De inventione* 1.2.3, ed. and trans. H. M. Hubbell, Loeb Classical Library (Cambridge, MA, 1961), 8–9.

[47] John Dagenais, *The Ethics of Reading in Manuscript Culture: Glossing the Libro de buen amor* (Princeton, 1994), 88.

[48] Yeager, "English, Latin, and the Text," 263.

[49] Dagenais, *Ethics of Reading*, 61.

PART II. POLITICS

The Riddle of Incest: John Gower and the Problem of Medieval Sexuality

Larry Scanlon

Freud and Gower: The Return of the Repressed

Nietzsche once claimed, "you can explain the past only by what is most powerful in the present."[1] If that is true, then any study of incest in the Middle Ages must contend with the prominence of the topic in recent public debate. Incest is a central category in modern thought, but for most of this century its centrality has been defined as fantasmatic and mythological. As recently as the early sixties most social scientists and psychologists considered it "a rare sexual perversion, a one-in-a-million occurrence."[2] That view has now been almost entirely superseded, largely as the result of the women's movement which began later in the same decade. By the middle of the 1980s, an "explosion" of clinical and epidemiological research had established that "sexual assaults against women and children were ... pervasive and endemic to our culture."[3] Feminist psychotherapists developed treatment strategies that challenged some of the central philosophical tenets of classical psychoanalysis, even as they affirmed its most basic technique, "the talking cure."[4] Seeking recovery in speech, they urge their clients to "break the silence," to recall memories of abuse often long repressed. They treat repression more as a social force: in the case of incest, the pressure to forget often literally begins with the threats of the abuser, and a large part of the trauma of incest lies in the refusal of

---

[1] Friedrich Nietzsche, *The Use and Abuse of History*, trans. Adrian Collins, with an introduction by Julian Kraft (Indianapolis, 1957), 40.

[2] Linda Gordon, *Heroes of Their Own Lives: The Politics and History of Family Violence, Boston 1880–1960* (New York, 1988), 207–9. Cf. Rosaria Champagne, *The Politics of Survivorship: Incest, Women's Literature, and Feminist Theory* (New York, 1996), 15–17.

[3] Judith Lewis Herman, *Trauma and Recovery: The Aftermath of Violence from Domestic Abuse to Political Terror* (New York, 1992), 30; D. E. H. Russell, *The Secret Trauma: Incest in the Lives of Girls and Women* (New York, 1986).

[4] This term was coined by "Anna O." (Bertha Pappenheim), a patient of Freud's early collaborator Joseph Breuer. Joseph Breuer and Sigmund Freud, *Studies on Hysteria* in *The Standard Edition of the Complete Psychological Works of Sigmund Freud*, trans. James Strachey (London, 1962), v. 2, 30. Cf. Herman, *Secret Trauma*, 12–13, and Champagne, *Politics of Survivorship*, 20–29.

others to recognize its actuality. These therapists sometimes include psycho-analysis itself in this widespread cultural repression, "confronting" it in a manner analogous to the strategies of confrontation they recommend incest survivors pursue in relation to their families and abuser.[5] At bottom this confrontation pits one narrative type against another. In place of the largely fantasmatic Oedipal model of mother-son incest, this new school offers actual case histories, whose most typical form is father-daughter, the possibility that Freud initially acknowledged in his earlier "seduction theory," but later largely abandoned.[6]

Nevertheless, these two narratives are not mutually exclusive, nor are these therapists universally hostile to Freud. Indeed, their confrontation with his incest story might itself be explained in psychoanalytic terms. We could call it a return of the repressed. Father-daughter incest has haunted psychoanalysis from its inception. Jacqueline Rose has suggested that Freud abandoned the "seduction theory" only to the extent necessary to concentrate his attention on the Unconscious. That would mean that psycho-analysis remained energized in implicit ways from the theory's repressed contents.[7] And the recent feminist recovery of the incest issue draws strength not only from its own clinical and sociological testimony, but also from the issue's unacknowledged potential within psychoanalytical thought itself. Here we can find a corollary to Nietzsche's dictum: what is most powerful in the present often becomes so because its power in the past has been forgotten.

This corollary sheds surprising new light on Chaucer's half-forgotten contemporary, John Gower. The Middle Ages had its own incest stories—many of them. The most dominant was a father-daughter incest narrative,

---

[5] One can find the notions of "confrontation" and "breaking silence" throughout the considerable literature of self-help for incest survivors. The most famous of these works is Ellen Bass and Laura Davis, *The Courage to Heal: A Guide for Women Survivors of Child Sexual Abuse* (New York, 1988).

[6] The fate of the "seduction theory" has been the focus of intense controversy. For a fairly neutral account see Peter Gay, *Freud: A Life for Our Time* (New York and London, 1988), 90–96. For the fullest and most notorious condemnation of Freud, see Jeffrey Moussaiff Masson, *Freud: The Assault on Truth; Freud's Suppression of the Seduction Theory* (Boston and London: Farrar, Straus and Giroux, 1984). For Alice Miller (*For Your Own Good: Hidden Cruelty in Child Rearing and the Roots of Violence*, trans. Hildegarde and Hunter Hannum (New York, 1983); and *Thou Shalt Not Be Aware: Society's Betrayal of the Child*, trans. Hildegarde and Hunter Hannum (New York, 1984) the Oedipal theory is merely symptomatic of a comprehensive cultural denial of the violence inherent in modern child-rearing practices. For more measured assessments of Freud's abandonment of the seduction theory, see Champagne, *Politics of Survivorship*, 21–51; Herman, *Trauma and Recovery*, 18–20, and Peter L. Rudnytsky, *Freud and Oedipus* (New York, 1989), 23–39. For an incisive feminist response to Masson, see Jacqueline Rose, *Sexuality in the Field of Vision* (New York and London, 1986), 1–23.

[7] Rose, *Sexuality* (New York and London, 1986), 12–15. I should add, as Rose and many others have pointed out, it was never the case that Freud flatly denied the actual occurrence of incest. See Linda Ruth Williams, *Critical Desire: Psychoanalysis and the Literary Subject* (London, New York, Sydney and Auckland, 1995), 10–17.

the story of Apollonius, centering precisely on the blind violence of paternal power. And John Gower was the author of the most widely disseminated vernacular version of this story.[8] It occurs in the last book of his *Confessio Amantis,* the encyclopedic poem he wrote in English for "Englonde's sake" at the request of Richard II. As I have argued elsewhere, this poem, which was almost exactly contemporary with the *Canterbury Tales,* played an equal role in the founding of the vernacular tradition which subsequent history was to assign to Chaucer alone.[9] Gower's interest in incest is obviously not the only issue at stake in his long eclipse. However, it is just as obviously the most prominent one, especially given Chaucer's own systematic avoidance of "swiche unkynde abhomynacions," as he himself expressed it, speaking through his Man of Law.[10] By contrast, Gower speaks of them throughout the *Confessio,* and they dominate Book VIII. The "Tale of Apollonius" is by a wide margin the longest narrative in the entire poem, and it is preceded by an overview of the history of marital regulation, interpreted through the categories of Christian salvation, where Gower engages briefly but significantly with the extensive tradition of patristic commentary on incest.

The notion of John Gower as an object of repression will no doubt strike some readers as a bit grandiose. Yet we might usefully cite Jane Smiley's celebrated novel, *Thousand Acres,* for its treatment of incest implicates Gower but does not acknowledge him. Smiley draws heavily on both clinical and self-help literature in constructing her story of an Iowa farmer's long-hidden sexual abuse of his two teenage daughters and the subsequent role it plays in the catastrophic destruction of his extended family. But she reshapes the confrontation with Freud into a confrontation with an even more monumental cultural patriarch: Shakespeare. She structures the novel as a retelling of *King Lear,* with the farmer, Larry Cook, as the Lear figure, who on a whim transfers his property to his married daughters. Told from the point of view of Ginny, the Goneril character, the novel offers the earlier abuse as the source of the tensions which make this transfer's results catastrophic. As Diane Purkiss notes in her review of the book in *The Times Literary Supplement,* "Smiley makes the silences of *King Lear* a metaphor for the unspeakableness of incest and rape.... In giving Goneril a voice, Smiley joins the distinguished line of women writers who have written new parts for Shakespeare's women."[11] Purkiss aptly characterizes Smiley's "confrontation" with "the silences" of Shakespeare. Yet

---

[8] The Apollonius story has its own long history prior to Gower's version, a history ably chronicled in Elizabeth Archibald, *Apollonius of Tyre: Medieval and Renaissance Themes and Variations; Including the text of "Historia Apolloni Regis Tyri" with an English Translation* (Cambridge, 1990).

[9] Larry Scanlon, *Narrative, Authority, and Power: The Medieval Exemplum and the Chaucerian Tradition* (Cambridge, 1994), 245–350.

[10] Geoffrey Chaucer, *Introduction to the Man of Law's Tale,* in *The Riverside Chaucer,* ed. Larry Benson, et al. (Boston, 1987), 88, l. 88.

[11] Purkiss, Review, *The Times Literary Supplement,* 4674: 20 (30 October 1992).

this confrontation is not without its own overtones of repressive mastery.

The Shakespeare who represses the possibility of father-daughter incest is largely a fiction, an artifact of his reception by modernity. To this extent, Smiley's stance is a feminist version of a twentieth-century cliché: the past is essentially repressed and repressive, and the role of the modernist— and now postmodernist—is to speak the unspoken, to make the repressed return. A more properly historical understanding, however, must recognize that the Shakespeare of *Lear* is also the Shakespeare of *Pericles of Tyre,* and this recognition must bring us right back to Gower. The play was Shakespeare's version of the Apollonius story. He explicitly offers it as an homage to Gower, who speaks both the play's prologue and its epilogue. While this play is now largely forgotten, in the first half of the seventeenth century it was one of Shakespeare's most frequently performed. I want to insist on this lost history not to make a pedantic point at Smiley's expense, but to make the more obvious one that without the modernist repression of the Shakespeare of *Pericles,* her novel would lack some of its considerable power. Remarkable as it may seem, it appears that on the specific question of father-daughter incest medieval culture was in some ways less repressed than late modernity.

This fact certainly tells us something very important about the Middle Ages. But it also tells us something important about repression: the "degree" of repression cannot be used in any simple way as the basis for differentiating historical periods. Foucault's famous deconstruction of the "repressive hypothesis" vis-à-vis the Victorians applies across the board.[12] To argue that some moment in the past was more repressed than the present is to risk misrecognizing the repressiveness structuring one's own present. It is also to misconstrue the normative nature of repression itself. For Freud, the purpose of repression was the avoidance of psychic pain, and he defines it as "the function of rejecting and keeping something out of consciousness."[13] The "something" is an idea invested with libidinal energy, which conscious thought would find dangerous or threatening, and which is therefore banished to the Unconscious. The repressed can return because it never really goes anywhere. Instead, it "exercises a continuous striving in the direction of consciousness, so that the balance has to be kept by means of a steady counterpressure." When, because of other stresses, or the intervention of an analyst, the counterpressure weakens, the repressed material returns, though characteristically as "substitute-formations" or symptoms.[14] For Lacan, "repression and the return of the re-

---

[12] Michel Foucault, *The History of Sexuality; Volume I: An Introduction,* trans. Robert Hurley (New York, 1980), 1–49.

[13] Sigmund Freud, "Repression," in *General Psychological Theory,* ed. Philip Rieff [trans. James Strachey] (New York, 1963), 104–5.

[14] Freud, "Repression," 111–12. See also *Moses and Monotheism,* trans. Katherine Jones (New York, 1939), 160–176, where Freud argues the development of monotheism can be viewed as a "slow 'return of the repressed.'" He concedes "it is not easy to

pressed are the same thing."[15] He can make this equivalence because he defines repression in terms even more rigorously linguistic: what gets repressed is not an "idea" but a signifier. One can repress a signifier only by eliding it, that is, by putting another signifier in its place—which makes repression essentially metaphoric. The signifier which repression banishes to the Unconscious returns as a symptom, that is, as another signifier— "the symptom *is* a metaphor" (emphasis original).[16] Repression's essentially linguistic character links it to the entry into the symbolic order, which for Lacan constitutes the origin of human selfhood. Repression ceases to be purely a defense mechanism devoted to the avoidance of psychic pain. Instead, it becomes a form of mastery, devoted to achieving and maintaining a coherent identity.

The Lacanian version of repression makes it easier to see how the process could be social as well as psychic, how it could lend itself to the consolidation of power over others—although this was not a possibility in which Lacan himself was very interested. If we momentarily turn this possibility back to Freud's own repression of the "seduction theory" (if "repression" is the right term for it), we find an open question: what was psychoanalysis's investment in the reigning domestic ideologies of nineteenth-century Europe, and in the longer history of Western culture which had produced them? From this perspective, a consideration of John Gower's relation to psychoanalysis may seem a bit less far-fetched. This essay reconsiders Gower's view of incest, concentrating on Book VIII of the *Confessio*, both the "Tale of Apollonius," and the brief history of incest regulation which precedes it. I have framed my argument with psychoanalytic categories, especially that of repression. But my goal is to demonstrate what a historically informed reading of Gower can tell us about those categories no less than it is to demonstrate what these categories can tell us about Gower.[17]

---

translate the concepts of individual psychology into mass psychology," but nevertheless insists that "the processes we study here in the life of a people are very similar to those we know from psychopathology" (170). As he points out somewhat earlier, the "limits between" the "normal" and the "pathological ... are not strictly defined, and the mechanisms are to a certain extent the same" (160). This similarity, which is one of psychoanalysis's founding insights, forms the basis of the analogies Freud draws between individual psychology and the mass psychology of tradition. I offer my appeal to psychoanalytic concepts in the same suggestive spirit. I would, however, add another justification. In this essay I am using psychoanalysis to interrogate John Gower and the Middle Ages, but the reverse is also true. I am also using John Gower to interrogate psychoanalysis.

[15] Jacques Lacan, *The Seminar of Jacques Lacan; Book I: Freud's Papers on Technique 1953–54,* ed. Jacques-Alain Miller, and trans. John Forrester (New York, 1991), 191.

[16] Jacques Lacan, *Écrits: A Selection,* trans. Alan Sheridan (New York and London, 1977), 175.

[17] Psychoanalysis is an ostentatiously modernist discourse, and any medievalist who has recourse to it immediately risks the charge of anachronism—Medieval Studies' most powerful (and therefore most seductive) taboo. There is a standard objection: as a modernist discourse, psychoanalysis simply does not "apply" to the Middle Ages. Yet this

I. Nature's Lore: Confessio Amantis, *Book VIII*

During the same years that Freud was founding psychoanalysis, G. C. Macaulay completed the considerable scholarly task of editing what is still the standard edition of Gower's poetry. For some of Macaulay's immediate predecessors, Gower's interest in incest had proved so difficult to deal with that they responded to it with editorial repression of the most radical sort: excision. Macaulay's approach was more modulated. He begins the notes to the eighth book of the *Confessio Amantis* in this way:

> We may suppose that our author had some embarrassment as re-
> gards the subject of his eighth book. It should properly have dealt
> with the Seventh Deadly Sin [i.e., lechery] and its various branches.
> Nearly all of these subjects, however, have already been treated of
> more or less fully, either in the fifth book ... or in the seventh....
> There remained only Incest and of this unpromising subject he has
> made the best he could, first tracing out the gradual development of
> the moral (or rather the ecclesiastical) law with regard to it, and
> then making it an excuse for the Tale of Apollonius ... of Tyre,
> which extends over the larger half of the book.[18]

One might well ask where the "embarrassment" actually lay, with Gower, or with Macaulay himself. For Macaulay the topic is so obviously unprom-ising that the possibility Gower might have actually been interested in in-cest is one he never considers. Instead he floats the half-hearted hypothesis that Gower, a poet intensely interested in the intricacies of penitential taxonomy, somehow forgot in the course of treating the first six of the Deadly Sins that there was a seventh, and thus arrived at the final book bereft of a suitable topic. Then he compounded this negligence by making the already inappropriate focus on incest "an excuse" for the apparently inexcusable "Tale of Apollonius."

This sort of easy presumption of authorial incompetence has long gone out of critical fashion, and by calling attention to Macaulay's recourse to it, I may seem to be picking an easy target. I do so because in my view Macaulay's "embarrassment" continues to inform Gower's critical recep-tion. Although many of the best recent studies of the *Confessio Amantis* stress the integral connections between Book VIII and the rest of the

---

objection is less a sensible precaution than a simple refusal to engage with psychoanalytic claims. Psychoanalysis aspires to provide a comprehensive account of human subjectivity. If it applies anywhere, it applies everywhere. I am in no way suggesting psychoanalysis is infallible, nor that its claims shouldn't be subject to historical analysis. On the con-trary—what I have tried to demonstrate throughout this introduction is that historical analysis is precisely what the lacunae in the psychoanalytic tradition invite. Moreover, as the reading to follow should demonstrate, the problem is ultimately not that psycho-analysis doesn't apply to medieval texts, but that it applies all too well.

[18] G. C. Macaulay, *The Complete Works of John Gower*, 4 vols. (Oxford, 1899–1902), III, 536.

poem, they nevertheless do so on the basis of a variety of philosophical rationales that generally elude the question of Gower's interest in incest *qua* incest. Thus, Georgiana Donavin, Kurt Olsson, Russell Peck, Elizabeth Porter, and R. F. Yeager, in the course of quite distinct readings treat incest primarily as a typification or epitome of something else, such as "lack of critical governance" or "the selfishness of all sins," and even then they are interested in it mainly as a foil to the "exemplary *summa*" offered by the "Tale of Apollonius" and the "model of ethical self-governance" offered by its title character.[19] In the reading to follow I take Gower's interest in incest at face value, and I argue that it is less philosophical than political in the broadest sense. Incest for Gower is both a penitential category and a complex social reality. Yet even as a penitential category it is a historically variable discursive reflex rather than a stable conceptual unity, and what interests Gower is precisely the relation between the category's variability and its social efficacy. Thus, I find H. A. Kelly's conclusion that Gower's attitude toward incest was "the received theological one" accurate but misleading.[20] The claim is misleading because it imputes a stable coherence both to Church doctrine and Gower's poem, when it was precisely the variabilities and contradictions of Church doctrine that motivated his poetic redeployment of it. These contradictions were political in origin; the Church's extraordinary interest in incest proceeding from its institutional role as late medieval society's chief regulator of marriage. In the opening of Book VIII, Gower briefly charts the development of this clerical regulation. He then uses the Apollonius story to redefine the boundaries of marriage regulation in less clerical terms.

The shift begins with the displacement of lechery by incest as the seventh Deadly Sin. This displacement radically reduces the general focus on spiritual behavior to the law of exogamy specifically, the fundamental institutional principle of marriage. While this change does not ultimately undermine the authority of penitential discourse, it does focus attention exclusively on the social and political effects of that discourse. That is, Gower is less interested in sexual desire as a general disposition than in the more specific question of how it is disciplined through the institution of marriage. Accordingly, this Book represents Gower's engagement with the Church at its most complicated. In contrast to the fairly fierce anti-clericalism that dominates the prologue and reappears at key moments such as the end of Book II, here Gower finds himself not only largely dependent on

---

[19] Elizabeth Porter, "Gower's Ethical Microcosm and Political Macrocosm," in *Gower's "Confessio Amantis": Responses and Reassessments*, ed. Alistair Minnis (Cambridge, 1983), 160; Russell Peck, *Kingship and Common Profit in Gower's "Confessio Amantis"* (Carbondale, IL, 1978), 165; R. F. Yeager, *John Gower's Poetic: The Search for a New Arion* (Cambridge, 1990), 217–18. See also Georgiana Donavin, *Incest Narratives and the Structure of Gower's "Confessio Amantis"* (Victoria, BC, 1993); and Kurt Olsson, *John Gower and Structures of Conversion: A Reading of the "Confessio Amantis"* (Cambridge, 1992), 215.

[20] Henry Ansgar Kelly, *Love and Marriage in the Age of Chaucer* (Ithaca, 1975), 33.

clerical tradition, but also broadly sympathetic to its policies.[21] In some respects this sympathy reflects the accommodation that the laity as a whole was beginning to reach with the Church regarding the regulation of marriage. It will be helpful to review that history briefly before proceeding with Book VIII itself.

Although marriage was an important conceptual and ideological focus of the Christian tradition from its inception, engagement with marriage as a social structure was sporadic until the period of the Gregorian reforms, when the systematic regulation of marriage became one of the Church's central institutional goals. Through the implementation of canon law by the ecclesiastical courts the Church became for the next three centuries society's primary regulator of marriage. Making marriage a sacrament, the Church succeeded in investing with its own particular forms of spirituality an institution devoted primarily to the transmission of property. When after 1350 lay authorities began to reclaim some of this regulatory power, they nevertheless retained the Church's redefinitions. As James Brundage observes at the beginning of his magisterial study, *Law, Sex, and Christian Society in Medieval Europe,* "In the process of secularizing marriage law and sex law, modern states appropriated much medieval canonistic doctrine. A substantial part of legal doctrine about sexual activity and about matrimony in the Western world remains bound by its medieval Christian origins to this day."[22]

This fact is thoroughly remarkable—especially since it is almost universally ignored. Its neglect by scholars working in post-medieval fields is regrettable but perhaps not surprising. What is quite surprising is how few medievalists themselves have shown interest in this continuity. Those who have are mainly intellectual historians like Brundage, and even they are less interested in exploring its implications than in simply asserting it. The continuity has particular significance for Gower, for it places him in the first few decades of the long "secularizing process" Brundage invokes. It suggests, among other things, that Gower's relative obscurity may be related to a much broader desire to repress the continuities between modern sexuality and the medieval Church. For Book VIII of the *Confessio Amantis* engages one of the Church's most distinctive and puzzling features, its extreme commitment to exogamy. Until the Fourth Lateran Council in 1215, the Church prohibited intermarriage among those related up to the seventh degree of consanguinity. Thereafter, it reduced the prohibition to the fourth degree, which, roughly speaking, would include all relatives up to third cousins. The Church also forbade intermarriage on the basis of affinity, or relation by marriage, and compaternity, or sponsorship at baptism or confirmation. (Thus, a man was prohibited from marrying not only his cousins, but also in-laws like his brother's widow, or "spiritual"

---

[21] Scanlon, *Narrative, Authority and Power,* 257–67.

[22] James A. Brundage, *Law, Sex, and Christian Society in Medieval Europe* (Chicago and London, 1987), 4.

relatives like a goddaughter.)

The sheer range of these prohibitions was extraordinary. Yet they have received little direct study, and there has been almost no attempt to link their doctrinal rationales to their social effects. Nevertheless, even the most cursory examination confirms that the two were linked. The authorities who offer doctrinal rationales also make their policy concerns explicit. Thus in the *Ecclesiastical History* Bede presents the *Responsa Gregorii,* an early redefinition of consanguinity and affinity requirements, as Gregory's ecclesiological instructions to St. Augustine for dealing with endogamous unions which predated the English conversion.[23] Some centuries later, Peter Damian, in the last major apologia for the prohibition to the seventh degree, makes clear from the beginning of his argument that for all their complexities, the Church's prohibitions have the simple goal of preventing marriage within the same kinship group:

> ... what could be more clear than the statement made by Pope Calixtus: "We consider those related by blood whom the laws of God and of the state call blood relations, and accept them as heirs, who cannot be rejected." Let us now inquire of judges who sit in court, who adjust affairs at law, and who devote themselves to scrutinizing legal decrees, whether failing closer relations, relatives in the seventh degree are admitted as heirs, or whether they are granted a guardian? How do you allow the marriage with this presumed non-blood relative whose inheritance, however, you will admit by right of blood relationship?[24]

Among those to whom an inheritance can pass there can be no inter-marriage: it is as simple as that, and the seven prohibited degrees are largely a precaution against the tenacity of inheritance rights. A bit later Damian justifies the number of degrees by appeal to the human body, which he claims has "six members below, and the same number above,"

---

[23] *Bede's Ecclesiastical History of the English People,* ed. Bertram Colgrave and R. A. B. Mynors (Oxford, 1969), i. 27, 82–87. On the *Responsa,* see Brundage, *Law,* 140–44; and David Herhily, "Making Sense of Incest: Women and the Marriage Rules of the Early Middle Ages," in *Law, Custom, and the Social Fabric in Medieval Europe: Essays in Honor of Bryce Lyon,* ed. Bernard S. Bachrach and David Nicholas (Kalamazoo, Michigan: Medieval Institute Publications, 1990), 5–7.

[24] Peter Damian, "Letter 19" in *The Letters of Peter Damian,* trans. Owen J. Blum (Washington, DC, 1988), I, 173.

Quid enim apertius eo, quod papa Calixtus asserit dicens: *Eos autem consanguineos dicimus, quos divinae et saeculi leges consanguineos appellant et in haereditatem susci-piunt nec repelli possunt.* Interrogentur igitur, qui in tribunalibus iudicant, qui cau-sarum negotia dirimunt, qui scrutandis legum decretis insistunt, numquid si pro-pinquiores desint usque ad septimum gradum agnati, sive in hereditatem sive in tute-lam non admittuntur. In cuius autem haereditatem ex iure consanguinitatis admit-teris, quo pacto velut extraneus eius coniugium sortiaris?

(*Die Briefe des Petrus Damani,* ed. Kurt Reindel; *1: nos. 1–40* [Munich: Monumenta Germaniae Historica, 1983], 19, 181.)

adding that "for the sake of greater precaution a seventh generation is added to them."[25] Aquinas, writing a half-century after the Fourth Lateran Council, frankly acknowledges the variability of the Church's teachings. He observes that the Old Law required that "each man should take a woman from his kindred," while at first under the New Law, "marriage was forbidden even to the more remote degrees of consanguinity" in order to promote "natural friendship" among a greater number. Then "towards these latter times ... it became useless and dangerous to extend the prohibition to further degrees of consanguinity."[26] When he explains exogamy's rationale, he almost sounds like a modern anthropologist:

> ... the accidental end of marriage is the alliance of men and the extension of friendship: for a husband regards his wife's kindred as his own. Hence it would be prejudicial to this extension of friendship if someone were to marry a wife connected by blood, because no new friendship would accrue to anyone from such a marriage.[27]

As it happens, it is to a modern anthropologist that we owe the only extended treatment of this issue within recent memory. In *The Development of the Family and Marriage in Europe* Jack Goody argues that the Church devised its exogamous policies in order to break up concentrations of aristocratic property and divert them into its own hands.[28] This thesis has been widely criticized as reductive—with some justice. Despite the extended justifications clerical tradition offers for its radical expansion of incest taboos, Goody can find no articulation whatever of the strategy he proposes. Nor, given their intricacy, can these rationales be dismissed as mere alibis for that strategy. Goody's argument is a fairly straightforward application of the base/superstructure model of classical Marxism. While

---

[25] Peter Damian, "Letter 19," 174–75.
Unde mos inolevit, ut sub figura humani corporis illa consanguinitatis descriptio pingeretur. Sicut enim corpus hominis sex infra totidemque supra, qui et ipsi ex latere dicuntur, articulis constat, unde et sexus dicitur, qui in medio est quasi sextus. Quod nimirum a secundis manuum sive pedum digitis facile est inveniri, ita nimirum et illa successionis humanae figure senis utique superius et inferius atque in his, qui ex latere veniunt, gradibus terminatur; quamquam ad propensioris cautelae gratiam et septima his sit generatio consequenter adnumerata (*Die Briefe*, 19, 183).
[26] Saint Thomas Aquinas, *Summa Theologica*, (Turin, 1933), Suppl. Q. 54 Art. 4, 497:
Sed alios consanguinitatis gradus lex vetus permisit, imo quodammodo praecepit, ut scilicet de cognatione sua unusquisque uxorem acciperet.... Sed postmodum lege nova ... Et ideo antiquitus usque ad remotiores gradus consanguinitatis matrimonium impedietabur, ut ad plures per consanguinitatem et affinitatem naturalis amicitia promaneret....
[27] Aquinas, *Summa Theol.*, Suppl. Q. 54 Art. 3, 495:
Sed per accidens finis matrimonii est confoederatio hominum, et amicitiae multiplicatio; dum homo ad consanguineos uxoris, sicut ad suos, se habet. Et ideo huic multiplicationi amicitiae praejudicium fieret, si aliquis sanguine conjunctam uxorem duceret, quia ex hoc nova amicitia per matrimonium nulli accresceret.
[28] Jack Goody, *The Development of the Family and Marriage in Europe* (Cambridge, 1983).

I would certainly concede that the distortions such a model produces are lamentable, I find it equally lametable that it took a scholar outside the field of Medieval Studies to raise the issue of power in relation to Church's incest prohibitions. For too many medievalists, the Middle Ages continues to function as a lost ideal, the nostalgia for which is so strong it often approaches the status of a methodological principle. According to this ideal, medieval society and especially the medieval Church were transcendent entities interested in neither sexuality nor power. But an adequate explanation of the Church's extreme investment in incest prohibitions obviously requires one to view it as intensely interested in both.

In the best recent treatment of the problem, the late David Herlihy recasts Goody's thesis in more gendered terms, then incorporates it into the larger argument of his magisterial study *Medieval Households*. Noting that the prohibitions of early Church councils concentrated particularly on sisters-in-law, daughters-in-law, stepsisters, stepmothers, and stepdaughters, Herlihy suggests they were intended to increase the circulation of women across kindreds. They were thus designed particularly to combat the "resource polygyny" of early Germanic, Celtic, and Gallo-Roman society, the tendency to accumulate women in the most powerful households.[29] By thwarting this tendency the Church's prohibitions helped it enforce the movement toward commensurability which Herlihy detects among European households from the eighth century onward. At this point medieval society began definitively to move away from the asymmetric "household system of antiquity," in which "different sectors of society possessed fundamentally different domestic units," toward a domestic system "commensurable and comparable" across "all levels of the social heirarchy."[30] Although this change was driven by a number of factors, chief among them was the Church, which "sought to impose a common rule of marriage upon all the faithful in all social classes. Two of its commands had a powerful impact upon marriages and the formation of households: exogamy and monogamy."[31]

Yet even Herlihy hesitates to explore the connections between this slow shift in social structure and the theological justifications by which clerical commentators explained and facilitated it. Thus, on the specific question of affinity relations he comments,

> Marriage made husband and wife two in one flesh, and thus the husband became a brother to his wife's sisters. Hence, if his wife should die, he had to look beyond the circle of her sisters if he wished to remarry. But was this metaphor cogent enough to determine policy?[32]

---

[29] Herlihy, "Making Sense," 1–16, esp. 8–11.
[30] David Herlihy, *Medieval Households* (Cambridge, MA, and London, 1985), v.
[31] Herlihy, *Households*, 61.
[32] Herlihy, "Making Sense," 6.

Herlihy's question is worth pausing over. Metaphors of the flesh are among the most "cogent" Christianity has to offer. The assumption that even these metaphors are nevertheless not cogent enough to motivate social policy betrays a peculiarly modernist anxiety—one which postmodern theory has thrown into high relief. In seeking to break away from a past it views as irrational, mystified, and theocentric, modernity seeks forms of social organization based on more rational grounds, grounds that are "realer" than language, that stand beyond what Nietzsche called its seduction.[33] Thus Herlihy, in an odd, deferential moment, refuses to believe that even the Middle Ages, for all of its irrational devotion to spiritual metaphors, could actually have based social policy on them. Instead, he simply accepts Christianity's transcendent aspirations as a given, leaving as an unanswered question the relation between those aspirations and the Church's incest prohibitions.

If we are to have any hope of understanding this relation we must begin by defining Christianity's transcendent ideals in exactly the same terms in which Christianity itself defined them: as a form of desire. We need to take the notion of spiritual desire literally, that is, as not only as a form of spirituality but also as a form of desire. Then we will be much better placed to understand how Christian ideals could draw so often on sexual metaphors. The metaphor of husband and wife as one flesh rises out of and reinforces Christianity's incarnational theology.

> Being subject one to another, in the fear of Christ.
> Let women be subject to their husbands, as to the Lord:
> Because the husband is the head of the wife, as Christ is the head of the church. He *is* the savior of his body.
> Therefore as the church is subject to Christ: so also let the wives be to their husbands in all things.
> Husbands, love your wives, as Christ also loved the church and delivered himself up for it:
> That he might sanctify it, cleansing it by the laver of water in the word of life:
> That he might present it to himself, a glorious church, not having spot or wrinkle or any such thing; but that it should be holy and without blemish.
> So also ought men to love their wives as their own bodies. He that loveth his wife loveth himself.
> For no man ever hated his own flesh, but nourisheth and cherisheth it, as also Christ doth the church:
> Because we are members of his body, of his flesh and of his bones.
> *For this cause shall a man leave his father and mother: and shall*

[33] Nietzsche, *On the Genealogy of Morals*, I, 13.

cleave to his wife. And they shall be two in one flesh (Eph., 5:21–31).[34]

These metaphors of one flesh have traditionally been read as sublimely asexual, indeed, antisexual. This reading is not so much wrong as incomplete. It is certainly true that to construe these metaphors as a desire to transcend the body is to read past the letter, in accordance with the basic principle of Christian exegesis. But paradoxically, this reading is also a reading to the letter, for in it, *flesh* signifies twice. It designates both the state of transcendence (where Christ and the Church become one flesh), and the carnal state which is to be transcended. Thus the metaphor of the flesh is at once an escape from the letter and a return to it.

Modern scholars who ignore this paradox actually oversimplify medieval Christian spirituality. For they fail to acknowledge that its desire to transcend social reality is also a desire to reshape that reality. In this passage from Ephesians, Paul begins by affirming marriage's internal hierarchy, its subjection of women to men, and by buttressing that hierarchy with the vastly incommensurable superiority of Christ to the Church. Yet Paul's rhetorical goal is not hierarchy and division but unity and the collapse of distinction. Leaving mother and father, the moment of full individuation, becomes simultaneously its collapse—a collapse which promises an ever greater one in the transcendent merging of Christ and his Church. As the rhetorical agent of these collapses, marriage transforms husband into wife. The husband who becomes one flesh with his wife from a position of masculine privilege is simultaneously feminized as part of the Church which becomes one body with Christ. The metaphor of the flesh treats marriage as transformative and transformable. It is true this rhetorical logic does not by itself explain the myriad of specific decisions that came to constitute Church policy on incest, much less the complex circumstances of its adoption and enforcement, and major shifts in direction. But if we view the metaphor as expressing a desire that defines itself through relations of gender and aspires both to police and, at least in part, to transform them, we can begin to understand how it and others like it

---

[34] Subiecti invicem in timore Christi.
     Mulieres viris suis subditae sint, sicut Domino: quoniam vir caput est mulieris: sicut Christus caput est Ecclesiae: ipse, salvator corporis eius. Sed sicut Ecclesia subiecta est Christo, ita et mulieres viris suis in omnibus
     Viri diligite uxores vestras, sicut et Christus dilexit Ecclesiam, et seipsum tradidit pro ea, ut illam sanctificaret, mundans lavacro aquae in verbo vitae, ut exhiberet ipse sibi gloriosam Ecclesiam, non habentem maculam, aut rugam, aut aliquid huiusmodi, sed ut sit sancta et immaculata. Ita et viri debent diligere uxores suas ut corpora sua. Qui suam uxorem diligit, seipsum diligit. Nemo enim unquam carnem suam odio habuit: sed nutrit et fovet eam, sicut et Christus Ecclesiam: quia membra sumus corporis eius, de carne eius et de ossibus eius. Propter hoc relinquet homo patrem et matrem suam, et adhaerebit uxori suae, et erunt duo in carne una.
Biblia Sacra iuxta vulgatam clementinam, ed. Alberto Colunga and Laurentio Turrado (Madrid, 1965). The translation is Douai\Rheims.

provided the force driving Church policy. Moreover, in providing that driving force, these metaphors also reveal that far from accepting gender relations as given, Christianity recognized their contingency and actively involved itself in reshaping them. In his treatment of incest, Gower draws heavily on this recognition.

Gower makes the complexities of clerical regulation one of the poem's central issues from the beginning. The figure Genius, its main voice of didactic authority, is the Priest of Venus "touchende of love" (I.236). This allegorical conflation of the clerical and the erotic is the primary structural device whereby Gower accomplishes his "middel weie" between "lust and lore." But he makes it clear throughout that this middle way is a disrupted and disruptive one. No sooner has Genius introduced himself to Amans than he declares he "mot algate and nedes wile" not only make his "spekinges / Of love, bot of othre thinges / That toucheth to the cause of vice," as properly belongs to the office of Priest (I.237–43). Gower thus founds Genius's allegorical identity around the split between the erotic and the clerical, anticipating the many tensions that will subsequently arise between Genius's exempla and the *sententiae* he assigns them, and between his penitential discourse and the specific biographical circumstances of Amans. Indeed, we can find an even earlier anticipation of these fissures in the description of love which opens Book I. Speaking in his own voice Gower declares "love's lawe is out of reule" (I.18). Love is at once lawful and out of rule, that is, its law is defined precisely by its resistance to regulation. Since by "love" Gower clearly intends the earthly and erotic, it is certainly possible to argue, as many scholars have, that this initial tension is transcended by some turn toward *caritas* later in the poem—for example the moment at the very end where Venus dismisses Gower from further service at her court. However, such readings do not so much resolve the tension between the clerical and the erotic as simply repress the latter. They also ignore the very specific problem of the eighth book. As the final book of the poem, it moves closer to the social actualities structuring erotic experience rather than further away.

For this very reason, Book VIII also comes closest to Genius's split significance and the instability of the middle way Gower follows throughout the poem. As the fundamental social constraint on erotic experience, the law of exogamy indeed constitutes the contested middle ground between lust and lore, desire and the law. Unlike the other six deadly sins, incest is not only a sin but also a crime. It is the site where the Church's penitential authority merges with its juridical power. Thus it signifies the concrete contribution the Church's spiritual teachings make to the production of social order. In this way Book VIII's disruption of the penitential schema balances, albeit precariously, the earlier disruption of Book VII, which departed from the schema altogether to deliver a brief *Fürstenspiegel*. Book VII marks the furthest reaches of Gower's anticlericalism, locating the source of social order in the figure of the King rather than the Church. But it is haunted throughout by the problem of sexual regulation. The

dramatic occasion for the book is the "Tale of Nectanabus," which ends
Book VI, and details both the secret of Alexander's illegitimate birth and
his eventual unsuspecting murder of his real father, the Egyptian sorcerer-
king, Nectanabus. Since Alexander knew Nectanabus only as his tutor and
advisor, the tale leads naturally to Alexander's later advisor, Aristotle, and
to the work he was reputed to have written for Alexander, the *Secretum
secretorum,* one of the most widely disseminated and celebrated of *Fürsten-
spiegel* in the later Middle Ages. This occasion obviously throws a shadow
over the entire book since it presents one of the genre's model monarchs
as illegitimate, and so contemptuous of moral authority that he throws an
advisor over a balcony to test the accuracy of his advice. In turn, Book VII
ends with the stories of Lucretia and Virginia, two exempla from Livy of
tyranny overthrown by its own lechery. The two tales present the inconti-
nence they illustrate as a violation not only of their female protagonists,
but as an attack on the patriarchs who head their households, Lucretia's
husband, and Virginia's father. The book thus ends with an implicit
acknowledgement that lay authority in its highest form depends on the
institutional integrity of the patriarchal family and the law of exogamy
which founds it. This necessity brings Gower back to the central role the
Church plays in the maintenance of social order. Book VIII will constitute
his most modulated engagement with clerical tradition.

Gower opens the book with a brief history of marital regulation from
Creation to his own present. He draws it from three sources, the *Historia
Scholastica* of Peter Comestor, the *De Sacramentiis* of Hugh of St. Victor,
and the figure of *Natura* as *doctor,* a commonplace of the canonistic and
scholastic tradition that begins with the late Roman jurist Ulpian.

> Natural law is what nature has taught all animals. For this law is
> not peculiar to the human race but common to all animals that are
> born on land or sea and to birds. From this comes the union of
> man and woman that we call matrimony, from this the procreation
> and the upbringing of children.[35]

While Gratian, the first systematic compiler of canon law, does not himself
use this definition, subsequent commentators return to it in order to clar-
ify the definitions he does offer. As Brian Tierney has made clear, what
they get from Ulpian is precisely his pedagogical metaphor, nature's
agency as a form of indoctrination, "the *regimen* established in all creatures
according to which birds fly, fish swim and so on."[36] Its most famous

---

[35] *Corpus Juris Civilis* (Leipzig, 1887), *Digest* 1.1.1.3. Trans. Brian Tierney in "*Natura
id est Deus:* A Case of Juristic Pantheism?" in *Church Law and Constitutional Thought in
the Middle Ages* (repr. London, 1979), 309.
  Ius naturale est, quod natura omnia animalia docuit; nam ius istud non humani
generis proprium, sed omnium animalium, quae in terra, quae in mari nascuntur,
avium quoque commune est. Hinc descendit maris atque feminae coniunctio, quam
nos matrimonium appelamus, hinc liberorum procreatio, hinc educatio.
[36] Tierney, "*Natura id est Deus,*" 316. Gratian offers two definitions, identifying

instance is Alain de Lille's *De planctu Naturae*, where the figure of Genius's priesthood originates.[37] Yet without in any way deviating from "received theological doctrine," Gower exploits the ambiguities in these three sources to produce a decidedly laicist version of incest prohibitions and the Church's role in maintaining them. The most important juxtaposition is the prominent insertion of doctrinal assertions about natural law into the chronological frameworks of biblical commentary. As Brundage observes, the appeal to Nature is necessarily contradictory: "in point of fact ... every 'unnatural' deviation that can be imagined occurs somewhere in 'nature.'"[38] Canonistic tradition managed this contradiction by dividing natural law into a hierarchy of categories from the "law of animal nature" to "natural reason ... or the power to choose good over evil."[39] Gower's chronological treatment breaks down the hierarchy. It not only focuses attention on the variability of incest prohibitions, which scholastic writers like Aquinas readily conceded, but it also fashions that variability into a coherent narrative, which they did not.

The narrative begins by defining God in Aristotelian terms, as the unmoved mover, a definition which Gower may well have drawn from Peter Comestor:

> The myhti god, which unbegunne
> Stant of himself and hath begunne
> Alle othre thinges at his wille ... (VIII.1–3)

It then moves immediately to the fall of Satan and the Creation of Adam and Eve. God

> ... bad hem cresce and multiplie.
> For of the mannes Progenie,
> Which of the womman schal be bore,
> The nombre of Angles which was lore... (VIII.29–32)

The command to increase and multiply is the motivating principle of the narrative which follows. It explains the variability of incest prohibitions until the Third Age, when "The nede thos was overrunne, / For ther was

---

natural law first with the Law and the Gospel and then, somewhat confusingly, created reason. (Gratian, *Concordia discordantium canonum*, v. 1 of *Corpus iuris canonici*, ed. Emil Friedberg, [Leipzig, 1879, Rpt. Graz, 1959], *Dist.* 1 *dictum ante* c. 1, *Dist.* 1 c. 1, *Dist.* 5 *dictum ante* c. 1. Cf. Tierney, "*Natura id est Deus*," 309–10.) Nevertheless, I would argue Ulpian's metaphor hovers behind Gratian's text as well, precisely in the ambiguity of this double formulation. If natural law originates both in the command of the Divine Word, and in the internal workings of created reason, that can only be because reason has been instructed by this command, and has internalized it. There is still an intermediary stage more amenable to human control than God.

[37] Larry Scanlon, "Unspeakable Pleasures: Alain de Lille, Sexual Regulation, and the Priesthood of Genius," *Romanic Review* 86 (1995): 230–33.

[38] Brundage, *Law, Sex, and Society*, 7.

[39] Kurt O. Olsson, "Natural Law and John Gower's *Confessio Amantis*," *Medievalia et Humanistica*, n.s. 11 (1982), 230–43.

poeple ynouh in londe" (VIII.100–101). Gower draws his emphasis on the command from the *Historia Scholastica,* where it plays a prominent role. However, the *Historia* makes no mention of the idea of humanity as the replacement for the fallen angels. Gower's conflation of these two ideas connects the natural process of procreation directly to God's redemptive designs in creating Adam and Eve. Gower makes this connection even tighter in his most direct borrowing from Comestor, the citation of the *Revelations* of the pseudo-Methodius. The citation occurs immediately after the expulsion from Paradise.

> Metodre seith to this matiere,
> As he be revelacion
> It hadde upon avision,
> Hou that Adam and Eve also
> Virgines comen bothe tuo
> Into the world and were aschamed,
> Til that nature hem hath reclamed
> To love, and tauht hem thilke lore,
> That ferst thei keste, and overmore
> Thei don that is to kinde due,
> Wherof thei hadden fair issue. (VIII.48–58)

The Historia credits Methodius only with discovering that Adam and Eve were still virgins at the moment of their expulsion; it does not mention nature. Gower's addition, seamlessly incorporated into a subordinate clause, makes nature at once a sign of the first couple's fallenness and the agent of their redemption. Moreover, the same thing is true of the sexual act, upon whose biological actuality these lines insist, albeit somewhat euphemistically. The introduction of *Natura doctor* enables Gower to establish a continuous narrative chain between God's replacement of Lucifer and the act of procreation, and if this claim makes procreation redemptive, it makes redemption implicitly dependent on the chaotic processes "to kinde due." For all of its implication in the taint of the Fall, sexuality becomes an autonomous source of order operating from within history. As the "lore" of nature, it is less an irresistible urge than a discipline in the Foucaultian sense: a set of discursive practices mobilized by some powerful authority.

Throughout the period of the Old Testament, the incest prohibition was secondary to the imperative to increase and multiply. Gower divides the period into three ages: the First, which lasts until the Flood; the Second, which lasts until the time of Abraham; and the Third, which lasts until the coming of Christ. He derives this schema from Hugh of St. Victor, but revises it substantially. For Hugh, the First Age was the time of natural law and extended from Adam to Moses. The Second Age was the age of written law extending from Moses to Christ. The Third was the

age of grace and extends from Christ to the end of the World.[40] By giving
the period from Noah to Abraham its own age, Gower has effectively
added a fourth age to this schema. More importantly, he has completely
elided the doctrinal significance Hugh assigned to it. During the first age,
"Nature so the cause ladde / .... that time it was no Sinne / The soster for
to take her brother" (VIII.63, 68–69). In the second, because of the need to
repopulate after the Flood, the same thing was true:

> Thei token thanne litel hiede,
> The brother of the Sosterhiede
> To wedde wyves ... (VIII.95–97)

By the third, as I have already noted, the need was "overrunne," and
intermarriage was forbidden in the first degree, but not the second: "Sos-
terhode of mariage / Was torned into cousinage" (VIII.103–4). Gower
presents the Christian portion of this history almost as if it were an
afterthought. "The tribes tuelve of Irahel," he concludes,

> For evere kepten thilke usance
> Most comunly, til Crist was bore.
> But afterward it was forbore
> Amonges ous that ben baptized;
> For of the lawe canonized
> The Pope hath bede to the men
> That non schal wedden of his ken
> Ne the seconde ne the thridde. (VIII.142–47)

Moreover, this moment is also superogatory, insofar as the narrative logic
of this brief history is concerned. It is unclear what relation if any the
additional degrees of prohibition bear to the imperative to increase and
multiply, whose ends had already been fulfilled in the Third Age. No
doubt Gower, following Aquinas, viewed these extra degrees as emblematic
of the grace of the New Law. In contrast with the Old, where "divine
worship was handed down as the inheritance of the race," under the New
Law, it is maintained by "spiritual grace," rather than "carnal birth."
While the Old Law required endogamy "to avoid the confusion of inheri-
tances," the New requires exogamy "that love should have a yet wider
play."[41] Nevertheless, Gower is concerned less with salvific transcendence

---

[40] Hugh of St. Victor, *De sacramentis, PL* 176, 312:
Tria enim sunt tempora per quae praesentis saeculi spatium decurrit. Primum est
tempus naturalis legis; secundum tempus scriptae legis; tertium tempus gratiae.
Primum ab Adam usque ad Moysen. Secundum a Moyse usque ad Christum. Ter-
tium a Christo usque ad finem saeculi.
This parallel was discovered by Olsson ("Natural Law," 237).
[41] Aquinas, *Summa Theol.*, Suppl. Q. 54, 4:
Sed alios consanguinitatis gradus lex vetus permisit, imo quodammodo praecepit, ut
scilicet de cognatione sua unusquisque uxorem acciperet, ne succesionum confusio
esset; tunc temporis cultus divinus per succesionem generis propagabatur. Sed post-

codified in canon law, and more concerned with the durability of erotic resistance. He concludes by observing that despite the restraint of "holy cherche," many continue to take "wher thei take may" (VIII.148–52). Love, "unbesein / Of alle reson," spares no condition

> Of ken ne yit religion,
> Bot as a Cock among the Hennes,
> Or as a Stalon in the Fennes
> Which goth amonges al the Stod,
> Riht so can he nomore good,
> Both takth what thing comth next to honde.
>
> (VIII.153–63)

These two concluding similes, the cock among the hens, and the stallion among the stud obviously connect human erotic resistance to irrational nature, but they do so in a way that also affirms human regulatory control. Both of these similes involve domestic animals, that is, nature not in an autonomous state, but already under human regulation. Moreover, in the movement from the first simile to the second, there is an increase in resistance which matches an intensification of regulation. The random sexual activity of the cock among hens is a constant within the domestic space which contains him. The activity of the stallion, by contrast, represents a slippage. He goes among the stud in the fens, at the boundary of the domestic, beyond the human control that would ordinarily be exercised in the breeding of horses.

In this final simile, then, the resistance of the natural is imagined as a response to human regulation. The implicit association of this resistance with human love returns us to the opening definition of love as a law out of rule. Sexuality remains an autonomous force that must be governed from within history, even if the restraint comes from the "lawe canonized." Restraint must occur by refraining from "what thing comth next to honde," by carnal exertions defined by the social boundaries within which they occur. It is less about transcendence than about distance and duration. The repeated operation of Nature's lore, in response to the injunction to increase and multiply, of itself produces the historical transformation necessary to make exogamy feasible. Without this transformation the moral authority which exogamy acquires would be impossible. It is true Gower never makes these points entirely explicit. They are conveyed largely, though by no means exclusively, through the narrative logic which holds this overview together, and which elides key elements of patristic tradition even as it derives its authority from others. Although the narrative focuses our attention on the importance of the secular effects of

---

modum lege nova, quae est lex spiritus et amoris, plures gradus consanguinitatis sunt prohibiti, quia jam per spiritualem gratiam, non per carnis originem, cultus Dei derivatur et multiplicatur: unde oportet ut homines etiam magis a carnalibus retrahantur, spiritualibus vacantes, et ut amor amplius diffundatur.

marital regulation, it really does not go much further in specifying the structural support for those effects. Paradoxically, that specificity will come in even more implicit form, through the long narrative to follow, the "Tale of Apollonius."

II. The Durable Riddles of Incest: The "Tale of Apollonius"

Evaluating the narrative specificity of the exempla in the *Confessio Amantis* has long been the central formal problem in Gower scholarship. The field has been reluctant to grant these narratives any independent weight and has largely restricted its interrogations to readings that could be explicitly sustained by the poem's *sententiae*. I would be the last to argue Gower's didactic ambitions should be slighted. Nevertheless, I am convinced that the reluctance to confront his narratives on their own is an instance of a more general problem modern scholars have had in dealing with medieval narrative. This problem results from a misapplication of the otherwise salubrious principle of medieval alterity. In contrast to the anti-didacticism that is supposed to define modern narratives, medievalists have routinely interpreted medieval didacticism as an interest solely in a narrative's moral, to the exclusion of the rest of its formal features. As is the case with any polar opposition, the problem with this one is that it oversimplifies the phenomena on either side of the divide. Medieval culture was intensely interested in stories as stories, and modern culture has been just as interested in morals, despite its protestations to the contrary. This point is crucial to my concern in this essay, because few stories anywhere have been more moralized than the Oedipus story within the traditions of psychoanalysis. Moreover, the story has operated within those traditions in much the same way dominant stories operated in medieval traditions: not as a locus of unchanging meaning, but precisely as the common ground over which doctrinal battles were fought. I have already suggested the Apollonius story is part of psychoanalysis's repressed past. In the argument to follow I will juxtapose the two stories in order to make two further, complementary suggestions: first, that the psychoanalytic Oedipus provides a conceptual framework with which to understand the vectors of power and desire driving Gower's narrative; but second, that the Apollonius story foregrounds the issues of female subjectivity and paternal power which the Oedipus story has had notorious difficulty addressing.

In *The Incest Theme in Literature and Legend*, Otto Rank notes with some distaste the prevalence of medieval incest stories.

> Like antiquity, the Christian Middle Ages are rich in popular stories, legends and literary works dealing with the incest theme in its many guises.... Although the development of these legends was partially influenced by the traditions of antiquity, the continual assimilation of these themes and their special treatment under the influence of the Christian world view demonstrate the active uncon-

scious role of narrator and listener in these stories, which differ
displeasingly from the naive antique traditions in their voluptuous
and torrid fantasies. If we were dealing simply with the assimilation
of existing traditions and their extension to the passive Christian
heroes—the saints—there would be no explanation for the burning
sensuality with which incestuous crimes were aligned one upon the
other, approaching the limits of the humanly conceivable. Based on
this excess, we must assume that the great repression of drives ex-
pressed in Christianity could be maintained only at the cost of a
fantasy life pouring forth to the most voluptuous degree; here the
repressed drives found a place where they could be played out.[42]

In this passage we can find a concrete illustration of the contradictions in
which a repressive hypothesis soon finds itself embroiled. Rank character-
izes the Middle Ages as a time of "great repression"; he thus appropriates
to himself the standpoint of liberality and freedom. Yet what he objects to
in medieval stories of incest is not their repressiveness, but precisely their
license. They are "voluptuous and torrid fantasies"; they exhibit a "burn-
ing sensuality ... approaching the limits of the humanly conceivable."
Thus, the opposition which structures this passage is not freedom vs. re-
pression, but one norm of repression vs. another. Moreover, it is not
simply the residual moralist in Rank which the medieval stories threaten.
Because these stories "differ displeasingly from the naive antique tradi-
tions" they also threaten his desire for a simple origin.

For Rank the "naive mode of thinking" of ancient Greek legend makes
the Oedipus story a reliable reflection of the Unconscious.[43] But this as-
sumption of naiveté obscures the sophisticated use to which psychoanaly-
sis actually puts the Oedipus story. Taking only the story's premise and
the name of its hero, psychoanalysis gives Oedipus a new adventure and a
happier fate. What was tragedy becomes romance: the psychoanalytic
Oedipus succeeds where the classical Oedipus failed. He manages to avoid
both marrying his mother and killing his father. He renounces his desire
for his mother by realizing he can become his father. Lacan takes the story
even further from the Greek version. Adding the categories of Saussurean
linguistics, he makes the father entirely symbolic. It is not the father
himself, but the Name of the Father which the Oedipal subject seeks. And
because like any signifier, the Name of the Father assumes the absence of
its signified, the Name of the Father is in fact the Name of the Dead
Father. For Lacan, Oedipus can renounce his mother and avoid killing his
father because the father is already dead: death is paternity's symbolic
precondition.[44]

---

[42] Otto Rank, *The Incest Theme in Literature and Legend: Fundamentals of a Psychology of Literary Creation,* trans. Gregory C. Richter (Baltimore and London, 1992), 271.

[43] Rank, *Incest Theme,* 33.

[44] Lacan, "The subversion of the subject and the dialectic of desire in the Freudian

In her justly celebrated essay "Desire in Narrative," Teresa de Lauretis offers a feminist critique of these moralizations. She suggests Freud was driven to the Oedipus story by a desire to solve "the riddle of the nature of femininity," a desire which Oedipus's own drive for knowledge re-enacts.

> The Oedipus of psychoanalysis is the *Oedipus Rex* [which is] sharply focused on the hero as mover of the narrative, the center and term of reference of consciousness and desire. And indeed in the drama it is Oedipus who asks the question and presses for an answer that will come back to him with a vengeance....
>
> But whose desire is it that speaks, and whom does that desire address? The received interpretations of the Oedipus story, Freud's among others, leave no doubt. The desire is Oedipus's, and though its object may be woman (or Truth or knowledge or power), its term of reference and address is man: man as social being and mythical subject, founder of the social order, and source of mimetic violence; hence the institution of the incest prohibition, its maintenance in Sophocles' Oedipus as in Hamlet's revenge of his father, its costs and benefits, again for man.[45]

For de Lauretis, the male desire she identifies is less a reason to reject the Oedipus story than a means of deconstructing it. She finds in the Sphinx and her riddle an echo of the riddle of femininity and suggests the Sphinx expresses the story's internal acknowledgment that female subjectivity eludes it. I want to suggest the Apollonius story has a similar value. De Lauretis draws historical support for her suggestion from Vladimir Propp. In an essay written nearly two decades after *The Morphology of the Folk-Tale*, Propp argues the Sphinx is a residue from an earlier folktale. The tale concerned the courtship of a princess and the obstacles she and her father placed before her suitor, Oedipus's forerunner.[46] While this earlier tale does not specifically concern incest it plainly resembles the Apollonius story in its portrayal of father and daughter resistance to the prospect of exogamy. It has been suggested that the Apollonius story evolved out of Oedipus. If that is true, then what we have is not the fixed teleology

---

unconscious," in *Ecrits*, 310. See also in the same collection, "On a question preliminary to any possible treatment of psychosis," 199.

[45] Teresa de Lauretis, *Alice Doesn't: Feminism, Semiotics, Cinema* (Bloomington, 1984), 111, 112.

[46] de Lauretis, "Desire," 113–16; Vladimir Propp, "Oedipus in the Light of Folklore," in *Oedipus: A Folklore Casebook*, ed. Lowell Edmunds and Alan Dundes (Madison, WI, 1983), 108–10. Propp's conclusion has been called into question (see, in the same volume, Edmunds and Dundes, headnote to this essay, and Edmunds, "The Sphinx in the Oedipus Legend," 147–73). The objections, however, concern the "core" of the legend and do not necessarily bear directly on de Lauretis's argument or mine. Whether the Sphinx was in Sophocles's sources, or was something he added, is less crucial than the obvious fact that the figure has remained intertwined with the tradition ever since.

Propp assumes but a more complex alternation. The Apollonius story exfoliates the knot of concerns the Oedipus story has condensed in the single figure of the Sphinx. That exfoliation quite clearly corresponds to the heightened medieval concern with the incest taboo, and its constitution of marriage and paternity. But even if the similarities between the Apollonius tale and the classical Oepidus are purely coincidental, those between the medieval tale and the psychoanalytic Oedipus are not. The Apollonius story is part of what psychoanalysis's embrace of Oedipus represses, both as narrative possibility and historical fact.

Gower's overriding interest in moralization makes his version of the Apollonius story apposite to juxtapose to the psychoanalytic Oedipus. Gower's version differs from most of its predecessors in two main respects. First, his Latin gloss actually entitles the story the "mirabile exemplum de magno Rege Antiocho," identifying the incest episode as its subject. Second, as this title also indicates he treats the story as an exemplum rather than a romance.[47] He is thus most concerned with this story as a story of incest, and most concerned with incest in its relation to moral order. This insistence on the moral value of the story's most scandalous event exacerbates another of its extraordinary features: its extreme compression. As Archibald notes, the story "reads like an epitome."[48] While relatively short in absolute terms, it nevertheless gives the impression of an epic scope. The compression is disorienting. It makes the story as difficult to remember in all its details as it is to forget in its entirety. But as we shall see, this effect itself has ideological value. It foregrounds the narrative's tendency toward repetition, as we can confirm by examining the plot in detail.

The plot transverses at least three decades and the enormous distances of numerous sea voyages back and forth across the eastern Mediterranean from Tyre, Antioch, and Tarsus to Pentapolis, in North Africa and Mytilene in the eastern Adriatic. Yet each of these many journeys is repeated at least once, and these repetitions enable others, which make the narrative, for all of its expansiveness, almost claustrophobic. The story begins with the violent disintegration of the family of King Antiochus. After the death of his wife, a "worthy quene" (VIII.282), he forces himself repeatedly on their "piereles" daughter (VIII.288), who "couthe noght hir Maidenhede / Defende" (VIII.302–3). Because of the daughter's great beauty, the king is soon forced to deal with the problem of suitors. To prevent any possibility of marriage, he devises a deadly test: a riddle no one can answer. The many who try and fail are executed, their heads left "stondende on the gate" (VIII.364). Finally, no one else will try until Apollonius, a "lusti knyht" of "hihe mod" and "hote blood," hears "tidinges" of the test, and decides to attempt it, as much for the adventure as for love of the princess.

---

[47] Cf. Archibald, *Apollonius*, 90–98.
[48] Archibald, *Apollonius*, 12.

Eloquent and accomplished in "every natureel" science, as soon as he hears the riddle he recognizes it as a veiled confession. He warns Antiochus: "It toucheth al the privete / Betwen thin oghne childe and thee" (425–26). Antiochus will not concede defeat, but neither will he execute Apollonius for fear of exposure. Instead, feigning magnanimity, he gives Apollonius a thirty-day grace period.

Apollonius sneaks back to Tyre immediately, then flees to Tarsus with ships laden with wheat. As it happens, Tarsus is in the grips of a famine, and hails Apollonius as its savior, erecting a brass statue of him in a public square. However, he soon receives word that one of Antiochus's henchmen had been looking for him in Tyre and he flees again. This time he is shipwrecked, loses all his goods, and ends up naked on the coast of Pentapolis, where he will find the royal wife he failed to find at Antioch. Rescued by a fisherman, he proceeds to the court and surpasses all the competitors at the athletic contests sponsored by the king. At the banquet which follows, he displays his virtuosity on the harp and his "vois celestial" (VIII.780). The princess asks that he become her tutor, and after some time in his tutelage she is smitten: "Thenkende upon this man of Tyr, / Hire herte is hot as eny fyr" (VIII.845–46). What attracts her is precisely what enabled him to solve Antiochus's riddle: "the wisdom of his lore," which testifies to his "gret gentillesse" (VIII.789, 791). The circumstances of their betrothal also mirror the unhappy confrontation at Antioch. Apollonius emerges as the Princess's choice only after three other suitors have failed; and once again he gains access to a "privete" between father and daughter (VIII.918), this time the secret letter the princess sends to the king to announce

> Bot if I have Appolinus
> Of al this world, what so betyde,
> I wol non other man abide. (VIII.898–900)

At Antioch the desires of the daughter were obliterated; at Pentapolis they are determinative. After the marriage the court receives word from Tyre that Antiochus and his daughter have been struck by lightning. Apollonius decides to return home with his now-pregnant bride.

At this point, the story is considerably less than half over, if we measure its length by its sheer number of lines. Yet what happens from this point onward bears almost no causal connection with what has gone before. With the death of Antiochus, the narrative element motivating Apollonius's wanderings disappear. Yet his wanderings continue and come to include his wife and daughter as well. What motivates these wanderings are random catastrophes which bear little relation either to the first part of the story or to each other. On the voyage to Tyre a storm causes Apollonius's wife to fall ill and apparently die. Her body is thrown overboard in a well-appointed casket, and it washes ashore at Ephesus where she is revived by a clerk who is a "gret Phisicien" (VIII.1164). Believing herself the sole survivor of the shipwreck, she enters the local Temple of Diana.

Meanwhile, Apollonius diverts to Tarsus where he asks Strangulio, his closest friend from his earlier visit, to raise his daughter, Thais.

When Thais reaches the age of fourteen, Strangulio's wife, Dionise, jealous that Thais's beauty and accomplishments overshadow those of her own daughter, conspires to have her murdered. A bondman leads Thais to the shore, but when he unsheathes "his rusti swerd," her screams attract some passing pirates, who rescue her only to sell her to the master of a brothel in Mytilene. He expects great profits from both her virginity and her beauty, but her weeping so overpowers the desire of all prospective customers that she remains inviolate. She then offers him a deal: if he will set her up as a tutor of young gentleman, she will give him the proceeds. Believing Thais dead, Strangulio and Dionise stage a mock-burial to hide their guilt, a rich tomb of brass adorned with her image.

Apollonius returns to Tarsus shortly thereafter. He is heartbroken, but believes their deception. A storm on the return voyage drives his ship to Mytilene, but he will not leave his cabin "for pure sorwe" (VIII.1599), and lies alone weeping. Athenagoras, the city's lord, suggests Thais be sent to cheer him up. After initially being unable to move him, she reveals her circumstances and he realizes who she is. In the joy accompanying their reunion Athenagoras proposes to her, and both father and daughter accept. As Apollonius is about to return to Tarsus for revenge, a vision directs him to Ephesus, where he is reunited with his wife, now "Abesse" at the Temple (VIII.1849). They return to Tyre, and after Thais and Athenagoras are married, Apollonius revenges himself upon Strangulio and Dionise. The story ends with his ascension to the throne of Pentapolis after the old king dies.

This second part of the narrative is even more a story of wandering than the first. It is only the depth and frequency of its thematic repetitions which make the second half of the story seem at all connected to the first.[49] This part of the story also begins with the death of a wife and mother, although a putative death rather than an actual one. This death also gives way to the betrayal of a daughter. It is true that in this case the narrative distances the father from the betrayal. Nevertheless, the betrayal still takes the form of a sexual degradation, albeit one slightly more putative than actual. These repetitions of plot motifs are supplemented by a set of characterological repetitions. The characterological repetitions are striking precisely because they straddle the divide between father and daughter, the tale's central gender boundary. Like her father, Thais is memorialized in brass at Tarsus. Like her father, she is thrust from Tarsus into a state of near total abjection. Like her father, she escapes this state by virtue of her courtly accomplishments, especially her proficiency with the harp, which leads us to the most striking repetition of all. At Mytilene, Thais is Apollonius's way out of abjection. That is, she assumes the role once played by

---

[49] Cf. Rank, *Incest Theme,* 308.

her mother. Sent by Athenagoras to comfort Apollonius, as her mother had been sent by her grandfather at the court of Pentapolis, she secures for him the full coherence of paternity which the tale promises from the beginning but repeatedly fails to deliver. Yet even this deliverance is haunted by an incestuous echo. Not only must Apollonius endure the suffering that comes from confronting Antiochus's incest, but he must pass through a residue of it with his own daughter before he can finally put it behind him.

It has sometimes been suggested that Apollonius's sufferings have for their purpose educating him about the proper attitude to take toward the random reversals of Fortune. I see two problems with this reading. First, medieval exempla of Fortuna tended to be tragic, and this tale, like most of the medieval tales of incest, is comic.[50] Second, while this reading accounts for the causal randomness of the second half of the narrative, it doesn't account either for its duration or its repetitiveness. Let me offer a stark alternative: what the tale enacts is the return of the repressed. It structures its narrative around paternal desire for the daughter—the desire which the law of exogamy both defines and forbids. This desire is sexual, certainly. It is a desire to have the daughter, in the sense of sexually possessing her. But it also has a more transcendent aspect, one which nevertheless may be equally aggressive. It is a desire not only to *have* the daughter, but to *be* the daughter as well, a protective desire to see things from her point of view, or a more domineering desire to occupy her subject position. The law of exogamy requires the father to assume power over the daughter for her protection. The question which the Apollonius story raises is whether this protective desire doesn't give way to a desire for dominance ultimately indistinguishable from the illicit sexual desires the father's protection is meant to prevent. As a possibility which the law of exogamy can never coherently acknowledge, this question must continually return.

Almost all of the tale's protagonists, Antiochus, Apollonius, the king of Pentapolis, and Athenagoras are all male, and mostly paternal. Yet their actions are repeatedly "focalized" through the tale's daughters.[51] Thus, the narrative leading up to the rape analyzes Antiochus's motives in detail, but what we get afterward are not his reactions but his daughter's, while he becomes a cipher, an agent of mere blind violence. The shift occurs at the exact moment of the rape, which Genius explains as an affect of power:

---

[50] The paradigmatic collection relating Fortuna to tragedy is Boccaccio's *De casibus virorum illustrium*. See Renate Haas, "Chaucer's *Monk's Tale*: An Ingenious Criticism of Early Humanist Conceptions of Tragedy," *Humanistica Lovaniensia* 36 (1987): 44–70. On the comic character of medieval incest tales see Elizabeth Archibald, "Incest in Medieval Literature and Society," *Forum for Modern Language Studies* 25 (1989): 2.

[51] I take this term from Gerard Genette's *Narrative Discourse: An Essay in Method*, trans. Jane E. Lewin (Ithaca, 1980).

Bot whanne a man hath welthe at wille,
The fleissh is frele and falleth ofte....
This king hath leisir at his wille
With strengthe, and whanne he time sih,
This yonge maiden he forlih:
And sche was tendre and full of drede,
Sche couthe noght hir Maidenhede
Defende, and thus sche hat forlore
The flour which sche hath longe bore.
It helpeth noght althogh sche wepe,
For thei that scholde hir bodi kepe
Of wommen were absent as thanne;
And thus this maiden goth to manne ...
                              (VIII.288–89, 298–308)

Strength, wealth and leisure at will on one side; dread, weeping and utter defenselessness on the other. The stark contrast—made all the starker by the shift in narrative focus—defines incest not as a form of pleasure, but as a pure expression of power. Yet what makes this power so horrifying is that it proceeds not from strength but from weakness. Antiochus "falleth ofte" because he is frail, and it is the frailness which motivates the rape, while his wealth and strength are only enabling conditions. What the narrator presents is effectively a regression, where the father, deprived of his wife by her death, becomes even more childlike than the daughter, and all of his patriarchal power is driven by an infantile desire to swallow up his whole family. "The wylde fader thus devoureth / His oghne flesh ..." (VIII.309–10).

For what it's worth, this psychological profile of Antiochus anticipates the views both of classical psychoanalysis, and of current feminist clinicians. Rank observes "the act of incest itself ... is the direct realization of an incestuous wish that has remained alive since childhood."[52] More recent clinical evidence suggests the moment of this regression is often triggered by some episode of extreme stress such as the death of a spouse.[53] The stress produces an infantile rage which the adult manages precisely by making the child its target. No less than these modern accounts, Gower's narrative reveals the tenuousness of the restraint the law of exogamy actually exerts over paternal power. It depends on the inhibiting presence of women, whom it nevertheless subordinates to the paternal will. Gower's shift in narrative focus enables him to foreground this peculiar dependence. The treatment of Antiochus's abuse ends with the entrance of his daughter's old nurse and her entirely futile efforts at consolation:

---

[52] Rank, *Incest Theme*, 30.

[53] For an overview and further bibliography, see Sandra L. Ingersoll and Susan O. Patton, *Treating Perpetrators of Sexual Abuse* (Lexington, MA, and Toronto, 1990), 15.

That other, which hire wordes herde,
In confortinge of hire ansuerde,
To lette hire fadres fol desir
Sche wiste no recoverir:
Whan thing is done ther is no bote,
So suffren thei that suffre mote... (VIII.339–40).

There is no "bote": Gower's extended depiction of this daughter's abjection makes vivid and indisputable the thorough destruction her father has caused. Worse: in its shift to her point of view, the narrative exposes its own entanglement in the very form of desire it documents and would escape. Like Antiochus the narrative seeks solace in the daughter. As the originary source of order in a fallen world, the law of exogamy is nature's guilty lore—only slightly less guilty in its observance than in its breach. Rank observes, "The difference between normal love for relatives and incestuous love for them lies only in the original intensity of the sexual drive and in how far the individual is able to sublimate it and give it a culturally acceptable form."[54] Adherence to the law of exogamy is precisely not a matter of absolute right, but instead a matter of degree. That is why the only solution to the ideological abyss which Antiochus's crime opens up is distance and duration. This partial and necessarily contingent solution recapitulates, in the history of one family, the progressive distancing chronicled by the brief history of marital regulation which opened this final book.

The daughter is the paradoxical guarantor of this therapeutic distance. For it is in her that the law of exogamy must find its ultimate confirmation. If its designation of the daughter as the forbidden object of desire is to have a meaning beyond its own privilege, it must find that meaning in its protection of daughters, that is, of those it makes the object of its policing. Yet in seeking that meaning it always risks exposing the originating violence that makes the second necessary. This is the paradox around which the "Tale of Apollonius" is built and which it at once expresses and exploits. Apollonius the good father must atone for the sins of Antiochus. Yet Apollonius's status as father depends on the possibility of violent superiority which Antiochus enacts. As Apollonius completes his atonement, the narrative repeatedly makes him dependent on daughters, ironically exposing his dependence on Antiochus as well.

As I have already observed, Apollonius arrives at Pentapolis in a state of almost pure abjection. The agent of his reintegration in human community is the king's daughter, albeit at the king's bidding. Like the image in a mirror, the situation at Pentapolis both replicates and reverses the one at Antioch. Where Antiochus represented the law of exogamy at its most violent and incoherent, the king of Pentapolis represents it at its most orderly and generous. He provides social contact with his daughter as the

---

[54] Rank, *Incest Theme*, 30.

most prominent feature of the hospitality offered to a guest who has suffered misfortune. When her suitors come to call, he not only welcomes them, but he also leaves the final choice entirely up to her. Antiochus's riddle revealed the "privete" he intended to hide. The king of Pentapolis, by contrast, wholeheartedly offers to Apollonius, "The lettre and al the privete, / The which his dowhter to him sent" (VIII.918–19). What is striking about this gesture is its radically antithetical double meaning. On the one hand, it is an assertion of patriarchal privilege of the most burtal and naked sort. He displays his daughter's "privete" as if she were live-stock at auction. On the other hand, this gesture also constitutes a radical abdication. The king reduces his role to that of obedient go-between. He becomes the transparent signifier of his daughter's desire. Neither of these meanings can be subsumed by the other; they are irreducible components of the same act. If the three-way exchange among Apollonius, the king, and the princess shows the patriarchal law of exogamy at its most benefi-cent, the exchange also reveals its violent underside. Even the best of the good fathers bears this violent stain.

Thus the narrative cannot end when Antiochus dies. The violent excess he embodied outlives him, and Apollonius and his family must continue to atone for it. By an insidious patriarchal logic, the burden of atonement falls heaviest on the daughter. Although Apollonius is nominally the pro-tagonist, this second part of the narrative is the story of Thais. Her abjec-tion sets in motion the chain of events that will eventually enable Apollo-nius to constitute himself as a successful patriarch. He experiences that abjection as her death. The reader, however, experiences it as her confine-ment to a bordello, that is, as a literalization of the traffic in women which the law of exogamy underwrites. This split recombines once again the desire to be the daughter with the desire to have her. For the selling of Thais into sexual slavery is, like so much else in this tale, excessive and arbitrary. How else to explain it except as the guilty pleasure this narrative takes in imagining the possible violation of even this most virtuous of daughters. Her improbable means of protection, her weeping and her "wofull pleintes" (VIII.1442), certainly attest to the nearly miraculous power of her chaste virtue; but they attest just as certainly to the narra-tive's need to police its guilty desires, to see things from her point of view. Her tears recall those of Antiochus's daughter, but these have an efficacy the earlier ones completely lacked. This efficacy expresses more positively the desire to be the daughter which lies behind the simulation of loss to Apollonius. It is because in some way he shares Antiochus's guilt that he must also share his punishment. Because Antiochus intended "His oghne doghter forto spille" (VIII.297), Apollonius must believe his own daughter spilt. His own desire to become the father necessarily means a murderous obliteration of the desires of the daughter. His only hope then is that she withstand that obliteration, which is precisely what the narrative achieves.

He arrives at Mytilene in the same abject state in which he arrived at Pentapolis. Once again it is a daughter who brings him back to human

community, again at the behest of a monarchical figure, this time Athen-
agoras. But here it is his own daughter, and her recapitulation of her
mother's role lends an incestuous horizon to the very act of reintegration
that ostensibly will finally put the vicarious guilt of Antiochus behind
him. Once again the medium of reintegration is the harp, but this time it
is the daughter who is the master. In fact, Thais has taken over entirely the
gentle lore that had defined Apollonius even in abjection. She sings like an
angel and is the master of riddles ("sondri bordes"), "demandes strange,"
and many "soubtil question" (VIII.1675–83). Their recovery of each other
occurs as a fusion of identity, whereby she takes on his mastery and ini-
tiates his recognition precisely by invoking her lineage, that is, her embodi-
ment of his patriarchal accomplishment:

> Avoi, mi lord, I am a Maide;
> And if ye wiste what I am,
> And out of what lignage I cam,
> Ye wolde noght be so salvage. (VIII.1696–99)

These lines express literally the figural argument the narrative has been
making throughout. Apollonius remains "salvage" until he recognizes
Thais as his daughter. Yet this recognition occurs only after she prolep-
tically claims his lineage:

> With that he sobreth his corage
> And put awey his hevy chiere....
> Non wiste of other hou it stod,
> And yit the fader ate laste
> His herte upon this maide caste,
> That he hire loveth kindely,
> And yit he wiste nevere why. (VIII.1700–1, 1704–9)

Apollonius begins to love Thais "kindely," but only after she has focused
his attention with the language of lineage. Even so, once his attention his
focused, there is still no spontaneous recognition: he loves her "kindely,"
but has no idea why. Moreover, while "kindely" here obviously means
"like a father," we cannot completely dismiss the incestuous possibility of
"kindely" as "carnally," which is exactly the sense Gower employs at the
opening of Book VIII, when Nature "hath reclamed" Adam and Eve and
"Thei don that is to kinde due" (54–57). Gower's point in his historical
survey was that the distinction between incest and marriage is historically
variable. This ambiguity heightens the suggestion here that incestuous
desire cannot ultimately be separated from familial devotion. It is only
through the discourse of lineage that the ambiguity gets resolved, as Thais
recounts her biography in response to Apollonius's questions:

> This king unto this maide opposeth,
> And axeth ferst what was hire name,
> And wher sche lerned al this game,
> And of what ken that sche was come. (VIII.1712–15)

The effect on Apollonius of learning Thais's name and "ken" is nothing less than a rebirth:

> This king hath founde newe grace,
> So that out of his derke place
> He goth him up into the liht,
> And with him cam that swete wiht,
> His doghter Thaise, and forth anon
> Thei bothe into the Caban gon
> Which was ordeigned for the king,
> And ther he dede of al his thing,
> And was arraied realy. (VIII.1739–47)

As the very hyperbole of the term makes clear, there is more to this "newe grace" than the simple recovery of a daughter. Thais brings Apollonius out of "his derke place" into the cabin "ordeigned for the king" where he reassumes all the trappings of power. She literally returns him to himself. In naming herself she enables him to recognize his own name and subject position once again. It is as if, as the agent of this rebirth, Thais has become parent to Apollonius—bespeaking a narrative desire as extravagant and guilty as the earlier one that put her in the brothel.

Moreover, this extravagant desire also drives the narrative's most astonishing recognition, its insistence on the precarious, contingent nature of the identity Apollonius recovers. His paternity is by no means some ineradicable essence. On the contrary, it is an entirely discursive structure which he inhabits only with difficulty, and what finally secures him to it are not his own efforts but those of his daughter. If the narrative seeks a good father in Apollonius to expiate the sins of the bad father Antiochus, then what it offers as the ultimate proof of the good father is his redemption by the good daughter. This point cannot be overemphasized. In achieving its resolution the narrative does not demonstrate the essential justice of the patriarchal law of exogamy. On the contrary, the narrative comes to resolution by demonstrating the law's essential injustice, then counterpoising it with the figure of the good daughter, who absorbs that injustice and transcends it. I draw this conclusion on the basis of the long close reading I have almost finished—that is, on internal evidence interpreted largely in psychoanalytic categories. Nevertheless, I intend it as a historical claim as well, one for which external confirmation is not far to seek. Thais resembles Constance, another good daughter, whose sufferings also restore and secure the transmission of dynastic rights. Both figures are related somewhat more distantly to Griselda, the archetypal domestic heroine, whose dominance of western European literary culture was already well underway. All three represent lay appropriations of the hagiographical, and because they focus that appropriation on the domestic and the familial, they correspond neatly to the contemporaneous laicization of marriage regulation we have already noted. It is true that the Apollonius story is much older than either that of Constance or Griselda. Nevertheless, Gower's version differs from most of its predecessors in that it is cast as an exemplum rather than a romance. In this way he gives its desire for the good daughter a moral force. The good daughter becomes a substitute for the regulatory power of the Church, a source of moral order operating with secular history and within the lay structure of the family. She enables Gower to offer the "Tale of Apollonius" as a specifically narrative confirmation of the doctrinal revisions which open the Book.

Some may object that even in this more explicitly historical form, my reading presumes a distinctly modern interest in linguistic and semantic instability. But that is precisely my point. There is little distinctly modern about such an interest, and it is only by repressing considerable evidence to the contrary that modernity has been able to appropriate this interest to itself. While I might appeal for support for this point to much of the best medieval literary scholarship of the past two decades, the most cogent evidence for my purposes can be found in the Apollonius tale itself. For like the Oedipus story, the tale links incest to the riddle, a genre founded on the possibility of linguistic instability. The riddle enacts in its own semiotic structure the very breakdown in gender and familial boundaries that drives the entire narrative. And as Georgiana Donavin has astutely noted, it does so in Oedipal terms.[55]

Riddles typically operate like algebra problems or brainteasers. Their pleasure lies in drawing a single, unambiguous solution out of what initially appears to be an irresolvable confusion. Thus, though they are founded on the possibility of instability, they depend just as much on the capacity of language to stabilize meaning as they do on the capacity to destabilize it. In this riddle, by contrast, instability is all.

> With felonie I am upbore
> I ete and have it noght forbore
> Mi modres fleissh, whos housebonde
> Mi fader forto seche I fonde,
> Which is the Sone ek of my wif.... (VIII.405-10)

It is clear, as Apollonius puts it, that the riddle "toucheth al the privete" between Antiochus and his daughter, but we cannot say exactly how. Does the "I" refer to Antiochus himself, or to a possible son of this incestuous union? If we take it to refer to Antiochus, the more likely of the two possibilities, we will nevertheless still find it impossible to follow a single line of reference through the whole riddle. There is simply no "I" that can fill all the slots the riddle requires. "Eating my mother's flesh" is a circumlocution for "sleeping with my daughter": it repeats the metaphor used earlier in the lines "The wylde fader thus devoureth / His oghne fleissh ..." (VIII.305-6). Then there are two possibilities for the rest of the riddle, both of which produce a contradiction in terms. If the phrase "whos

[55] Donavin, *Incest Narratives*, 71.

housebonde / Mi fader" refers to the daughter, then the contradiction lies in this phrase itself. If, on the other hand, the phrase refers to the mother, then the contradiction shifts to "Sone ek of my wif."

The most plausible explanation of these contradictions is that the point of the riddle is precisely that it is irresolvable. Father-daughter incest radically collapses the distinctions on which familial categories depend. Because paternal authority logically depends on the law of exogamy, the father who assaults his daughter not only destroys his own nuclear family, but also the dynastic relations that holds the nuclear unit in place. Once he ruptures the exogamous boundary which separates him from his children, all generational distinctions collapse. By effectively becoming his daughter's husband, he also becomes his own father, because the law which separated him from his father has lost its force. Likewise, his father might as well become the son of his own daughter, since she has now become his wife. The distinctions among all these categories depend in the first instance upon the father acting like a father, upon his restraint of his own power, his categorical refusal to take advantage of the violent possibilities which paternal authority must necessarily open up to him. Father-daughter incest throws familial categories into complete disarray because they depend on its refusal.

The paternal "I" of this riddle seeks the "housebonde / Mi fader." Why should a father's incestuous desire for his daughter also be a quest for his own father? And why should the object of this quest be imagined not only as the father but the husband of the mother? It is impossible to answer these questions without assigning to this riddle an understanding of incestuous desire that is essentially the same as that of psychoanalysis. Regressively fulfilling his desire for his mother with his daughter, the incestuous father is also still seeking to displace his own father. Moreover, given the riddle's insistence on the purely discursive status of a familial categories, we might make the anticipation of psychoanalysis even more precise. What the incestuous father of this riddle seeks is the Name of the Father. If the historicity of this claim seems dubious, I would suggest once again that that has less to do with its ostensible anachronism, than with the pressure this tale places on the received notion of the distinction between medieval and modern. The parallel between this riddle and Lacan's revision of the Oedipal story is literally uncanny, in the psychoanalytic sense of that term. The uncanny is a feeling produced by the return of repressed material.[56] To find such heightened awareness of the essentially discursive status of familial categories in a medieval text is to confront an aspect of medieval culture modernity has failed to recognize.

Accordingly, we should not be surprised to find this riddle foregrounds an aspect of incestuous desire which the psychoanalytic account assumes

---

[56] Sigmund Freud, "The Uncanny," trans. Alix Strachey, in *Psychological Writings and Letters*, ed. Sander L. Gilman (New York, 1995), 142–46.

but never makes explicit. The riddle equates the quest for the father with the cannibalization of the mother. It thereby tells us something which the psychoanalytic Oedipus wants to tell us but cannot quite articulate. Behind the son's desire to marry his mother lies an even more archaic, pregenital desire to devour her. Psychoanalysis, especially in its Lacanian version, recognizes the implacability of this aggression in many other ways (it is the dynamic driving the Mirror Stage, for example). But the Oedipus story nevertheless takes the son's desire for his mother as an end in itself, and to that extent idealizes it. By refusing that idealization the Apollonius story concentrates our attention on the son's desire to replace the father. It links the impotent rage of the entirely dependent nurseling to the unrestrained power of the mature patriarch. Indeed, it explains the latter as a residual expression of the former. In this way the Apollonius story offers a much more direct explanation of the social effectivity of the incest taboo than the Oedipus story has been able to. For it makes both the enforcement and the violation of the incest taboo expressions of the same regressive desire. It unites the Law of the Father with the unruly desires of the son in a way which the Oedipus story, with its exclusive focalization through the son, cannot.

It is perhaps not so surprising after all that medieval culture should have more easily sustained a narrative recognition of this unity than modernity. Its feudal structure demanded the conflation of familial and social authority: it located the source of public order in the figure of the father. By contrast, there is a strong tendency in modern culture to idealize the private as a transcendent space beyond the power relations of the public sphere. Modernity may experience father-daughter incest as such a scandal because it violently ruptures this idealization. Medieval power relations overtly depended on familial structures. That may well have meant that medieval culture could not afford similar illusions. While the "Tale of Apollonius" certainly treats Antiochus's actions as scandalous, its riddle nevertheless presents the scandal as a largely necessary cost of the only imaginable form of social order.

Rank observes perceptively that "solving [the riddle] proves just as fatal as not solving it."[57] This paradox points to a more profound one, which may provide the ultimate explanation for Apollonius's long atonement. His very attempt to solve the riddle implicates him in Antiochus's guilt. As Antiochus's barrier to his daughter, the riddle expresses his paternal power no less than the incest it at once discloses and reveals. In pitting his lore against that of Antiochus, Apollonius literally expresses a desire to displace him, a desire necessarily tainted by the guilty power which is its object. Apollonius seeks to acquire the patriarchal authority over the daughter which Antiochus holds; that authority assumes the possibility of abuse which Antiochus has made actual. Apollonius must atone for so long

---

[57] Rank, *Incest Theme*, 313.

because Antiochus's guilt is ultimately also his own. Antiochus's secret can never be truly hidden, because it implicates in its guilt all of patriarchal authority.

What is the function of this guilty knowledge? The eventual affirmative conclusion of the story suggests that for Gower, as for the tradition he inherited, it was ultimately expiable. But the long effort which that resolution requires suggests that whatever expiation is achievable comes at a tremendous cost. Either way, this was a poet for whom incest was a nearly intractable problem implicating the mechanisms of social order in their most basic operations. Moreover, his profound attention to the problem drew upon a cultural repository of equal depth. Obviously, there is no point in arguing that Gower's view of incest, or that of the traditions he recapitulates, was somehow fuller than that afforded by modern traditions like psychoanalysis. At the same time, it is equally important to acknowledge that he reveals a historical and social dimension to the problem, which psychoanalysis, like the rest of modernity, has largely failed to recognize. If the more recent revelations about repressed memories of incest are any indication, the guilt of Antiochus is a specter from which modernity is still in flight.

Engendering Authority: Father and Daughter, State and Church in Gower's "Tale of Constance" and Chaucer's "Man of Law's Tale"

María Bullón-Fernández

In an essay entitled "The Question of Authority and 'The Man of Law's Tale,'" Patricia Eberle has argued that the three different versions of the story of Constance that we find in Nicholas Trivet's Anglo-Norman *Chronique,* Gower's "Tale of Constance," and Chaucer's "Man of Law's Tale" are all stories of "origins."[1] Following Brian Tierney's definition of a story of origins, Eberle explains that, "[this] is a story told in order to lend legitimacy to a particular view on the question of authority" (Eberle, 124). This type of narrative is "related to a tendency in medieval political thought to found a theory of political authority on a hypothesis about its beginnings in a primitive state" (ibid., 125). Using Walter Ullmann's definition of authority, Eberle distinguishes between two views of authority: "ascending" and "descending." According to the "ascending" view, power ascends from the subjects to the king. Hence, the subjects have the power to depose a king who does not comply with the law. According to the "descending" view, the king has absolute power over his subjects; power descends from the monarch (ibid., 116–17). While Trivet's and Gower's versions support slightly different versions of the "descending view," Eberle argues, Chaucer's version questions this view. Chaucer's "Man of Law's Tale," she points out, "rewrites the view of the heroine found in his sources in order to offer a reexamination of the descending view of the question of authority that she represents" (ibid., 125).

Although Eberle's essay represents an important new approach to the

This essay draws in part from two different papers I have presented: "Telling Silences: Gower's Constance vs. Chaucer's Custance," read at the 29th International Congress on Medieval Studies, Kalamazoo, May 1994, and "Gower's 'Tale of Constance': Father and Daughter, State and Church," read at the 111th MLA convention, Chicago, December 1995. I would like to express my sincere gratitude to Winthrop Wetherbee. We have had numerous conversations about the story of Constance and he has patiently and enthusiastically read and commented on several drafts of this essay.

[1] Patricia J. Eberle, "The Question of Authority and 'The Man of Law's Tale,'" in *The Centre and Its Compass: Studies in Medieval Literature in Honor of Professor John Leyerle,* ed. Robert A. Taylor, et al., *Studies in Medieval Culture* 33 (Kalamazoo, 1993).

Constance narrative, its exclusive focus on state politics understates the crucial role of the Church in the tale. Indeed, Eberle's study points to a fundamental aspect of the story to which critics have paid little attention: its political dimension. In doing so, she departs from traditional criticism of both tales, which has often centered on the religious aspect of the story.[2] Eberle rightly demonstrates that an exclusive focus on the role of the Church in the tale leaves out a fundamental dimension of the story. Nevertheless, her focus on the examination of authority in a strictly lay context in turn suggests that the Church only serves as a backdrop to this examination, that Church politics itself is not part of the subject of the story. The Church, however, does play a fundamental role in the legend of Constance, whichever version we examine. It is, indeed, significant that the two major authority figures in the tale are the respective representatives of the State and the Church, an emperor and the pope. Thus while the analysis of the religious dimension needs to take state politics into account, the analysis of state politics also needs to take Church politics into account. More specifically, an analysis of any version of the story needs to situate it within the context of the power struggle towards the end of the Middle Ages between the emperor and kings, on the one hand, and the pope, on the other.[3] We need to recognize and examine this context in order to understand the significance of Gower's tale.

Before continuing, I should mention that in this essay I will be primarily concerned with Gower's and Chaucer's versions, both of which were written within a few years, in the last quarter of the fourteenth century.[4] Trivet's *Chronique* was written earlier in the same century, probably around 1334, and it is addressed to a specific audience; it was written for

---

[2] As V. A. Kolve puts it, some critics "examine [the tale] through the lenses of religious skepticism." See V. A. Kolve, *Chaucer and the Imagery of Narrative: The First Five "Canterbury Tales"* (Stanford, 1984), 297–98. However, many critics, like Kolve himself, or, for instance, Morton W. Bloomfield, have analyzed the tale from a more orthodox Christian viewpoint. See Morton W. Bloomfield, "The Man of Law's Tale: A Tragedy of Victimization and a Christian Comedy," *PMLA* 87 (1972): 384–90.

[3] As R. N. Swanson has noted, "[t]he debates between 'papalists' and 'royalists' in the thirteenth to fifteenth centuries were essentially about the structure of Christendom and the relations between the various fragments (the kingdoms) and its religious head (the pope)." See R. N. Swanson, *Church and Society in Late Medieval England* (Oxford, 1989), 91. Some of the most influential studies of Church-State relationships in the Middle Ages are: Walter Ullmann, *Principles of Government and Politics in the Middle Ages* (London, 1961); Brian Tierney, *The Crisis of Church and State, 1050–1300* (Toronto, 1988); Michael Wilks, *The Problem of Sovereignty in the Later Middle Ages* (Cambridge, 1963).

[4] We do not know the exact dates of composition of these two versions. However, we know that Gower must have written the first recension of the *Confessio Amantis* in the 1380s and must have finished it by 1390. Critics generally agree that Chaucer wrote his "Man of Law's Tale" around 1390 and thus that Chaucer knew Gower's "Tale of Constance" when he wrote his version of it. For a discussion of the dates of composition of the two tales, see Patricia J. Eberle's introduction to her explanatory notes on "The Man of Law's Tale" in *The Riverside Chaucer*, ed. L. D. Benson (Boston, 1987), 856–57.

princess Marie, the daughter of Edward I.[5] Although in light of my analysis of the Constance story in the following pages, it is significant that Trivet's story is part of a work that is dedicated to the daughter of a king, an interpretation of this Anglo-Norman version would demand a careful and lengthy consideration of the circumstances in which it was written, something that is beyond the scope of this essay. My aim here is to offer new interpretations of Gower's and Chaucer's versions.

The tensions and struggle for power between State and Church are more evident in Gower's "Tale of Constance," which fully examines these issues, than in Chaucer's "Man of Law's Tale," which only hints at them. That the Man of Law's version only hints at the conflict, or, to put it more accurately, as I will argue, that his version suppresses it, is probably one of the reasons why critics have neglected to study the State-Church relationship in the story. Since critical studies have usually focused on Chaucer's version, while discussing Gower's only as it mirrors, or fails to mirror, Chaucer's, these studies have themselves failed to notice the relevance of the conflict in the story. However, if we start from Gower's tale, as I intend to do here, we will not only illuminate his version in new and insightful ways but we will also open up new possibilities in Chaucer's version. This essay will show that the depiction of Christian religion and its representative institution, the Church, in Gower's "Tale of Constance" carries significant political implications. Gower's version offers a complex comment on State-Church relationships.[6] It uses the story as a "story of origins" in Tierney's sense, and it does so not in order to support the "descending" view of authority, as Eberle has argued, but to describe and examine the myth of another origin: that of the political subordination of the Church to the State. Gower, I will argue, does so neither to justify this subordination nor to defend the opposite form of subordination, that of the State to the Church, but to question the royal absolutist implications of this particular story of origins.

The following analysis, moreover, will show how lay power uses gender to articulate its vision of State-Church relationships.[7] Gower's

---

[5] For an analysis of the date and circumstances in which Trivet's *Chronique* was produced, see Ruth Dean, "Nicholas Trevet, Historian," in *Medieval Learning and Literature: Essays Presented to Richard William Hunt*, eds. J. J. G. Alexander and M. T. Gibson (Oxford, 1976), 339–49.

[6] Larry Scanlon, *Narrative, Authority, and Power: The Medieval Exemplum and the Chaucerian Tradition* (Cambridge, 1994), has analyzed the conflict between lay and clerical power in the Middle Ages, paying special attention to Chaucer and Gower. Scanlon's analysis, though, does not deal with either version of the story of Constance. This essay will show the relevance of this conflict for the story of Constance.

[7] While several recent studies of the Man of Law's version have focused on issues of gender from various viewpoints, none of them has analyzed their intersection with State politics. See, for instance, the chapter entitled "The Law of Man and Its 'Abhomynacions' " in Carolyn Dinshaw, *Chaucer's Sexual Poetics* (Madison, 1989), 88–112; the chapter entitled "Womanliness in the Man of Law's Tale" in Sheila Delany, *Writing Woman: Women Writers and Women in Literature, Medieval to Modern* (New York, 1983), 36–46;

"Tale of Constance" examines the uses of gender in the institutional con-
flict between State and Church at the end of the Middle Ages. The political
implications of the tale, I will show, are imbricated in the tale's father-
daughter theme that Margaret Schlauch brought to our attention many
years ago.[8] Indeed, Gower's version of the Constance story uses the
father-daughter relationship as a metaphor for the relationship between
State and Church, the Church representing the feminine in its relationship
with State masculine power.

It is no coincidence that Gower uses a woman to represent the Church.
In "Custance and History: Woman as Outsider in Chaucer's 'Man of
Law's Tale,'" David Raybin has argued that Chaucer's tale treats Con-
stance as an outsider, as someone ahistorical.[9] During her voyages "[s]he
is exiled from the temporal world and thus unconstrained by time, bound
to her faith and thus spiritually free, existing in an emblematic position
largely outside human contact, outside history" (Raybin, 69). And, when
she is ashore, "it is to live in the margins, both spatially and, in spite of
her royal birth, socially" (ibid., 69). Raybin sees Constance's ahistoricity
as a positive feature: "The tale ... demonstrates the insufficiency of patriar-
chal history, the limitations of institutionalized religion, the more positive
values in femaleness and sexuality, and ultimately the necessity for a wom-
an's spiritual power in the context of such a world" (ibid., 65). I have no
contention with Raybin's argument that Chaucer's tale emphasizes Cus-
tance's timelessness, her ahistoricity. In fact, an emphasis on Constance's
timelessness is also evident in Gower's version. I disagree with him,
though, in another respect. Raybin's suggestion that Chaucer's version ulti-
mately demonstrates the value and necessity of women's spiritual power
does not recognize the subordinate status of such power. In both Chaucer's
and Gower's versions, Constance is divested of power, of self-willed
influence on historical and political events. I should qualify this assertion
by noting that I am not denying that Constance influences history, that
she does take an active part at times. Her influence, however, is always an
act of obedience to male authority, whether to the authority of her biolog-
ical father or of her Divine Father. Carolyn Dinshaw has argued, referring
to the Man of Law's version, that "Constance's limited self-consciousness

---

and, more recently, Susan Schibanoff, "Worlds Apart: Orientalism, Antifeminism, and
Heresy in Chaucer's Man of Law's Tale," *Exemplaria* 8.1 (1996): 59–96.

   [8] See Margaret Schlauch, *Chaucer's Constance and Accused Queens* (New York, 1927),
133. More recently, Elizabeth Archibald, "The Flight from Incest: Two Late Classical
Precursors of the Constance Theme," *Chaucer Review* 20 (1986), 259–72, has expanded
on Schlauch's suggestions. The function of the incest motif has been more frequently
analyzed in the past years by critics of Chaucer's tale than by Gower scholars. See, for
example, R. A. Shoaf, "'Unwemmed Custance': Circulation, Property, and Incest in the
Man of Law's Tale," *Exemplaria* 2.1 (1990): 287–302; and, especially, Dinshaw, *Chaucer's
Sexual Poetics*.

   [9] David Raybin, "Custance and History: Woman as Outsider in Chaucer's Man
of Law's Tale," *Studies in the Age of Chaucer* 12 (1990): 65–84.

in fact serves patriarchy well."[10] Gower's Constance has a similarly limit-ed self-consciousness. In her case, though, her limitations also have further implications. In Gower's tale, it is not just women who are divested of power; the Church itself is made subordinate to the State, to royal power.

The question of the distribution of power between State and Church was a major source of political debate and tension throughout the Middle Ages. Where does the power of the pope end and where does that of the king begin? In his influential study, *The Problem of Sovereignty in the Later Middle Ages,* Michael Wilks has analyzed the debates that arose around the struggle for power and sovereignty between State and Church toward the end of the Middle Ages. Significantly, in order to define the distribution of power, theorists, and those in political positions of authority, frequently resorted to familial metaphors. The pope was the great father, the patriarch who, as representative of God, ruled over his children, the whole of Christian society, including kings and emperors.[11]

Of course, kings and emperors did not like such a role and tried to minimize the extent of the pope's power. One of the ways in which they did this was by redefining the traditional distinction between temporal and spiritual power to their own advantage. Traditionally, in drawing the distinction between temporal and spiritual power, popes did not renounce legislative and political authority. As Wilks has put it, "[t]he famous 'Render unto Caesar' text, the allegories of the two swords, or the sun and the moon, are for the papalists simply means of expressing this distinction of functions, but they do not deny the overriding papal right to exercise both himself" (Wilks, 267). Lay rulers, though, tried to counter this conception of papal rights by redefining the limits of the spiritual realm. They sought to limit the pope's authority, Wilks observes, "by making a rigid separation between the provinces of pope and lay ruler, to create in effect autonomous spheres of temporal and spiritual in which emperor and pope could reign supreme" (ibid., 70–71). Thus, lay rulers tried to relegate the pope to a confined and strictly spiritual role. The pope was the father for spiritual matters, he was the one to consult on spiritual concerns, but he would have no power in terms of practical and immediate political decision-making (ibid., 285 ff.).

The "Tale of Constance" relegates the pope to a strictly spiritual role, but this is not the only tale in Gower's *Confessio Amantis* which does so. Larry Scanlon has argued that two crucial tales in Book II of the *Confessio Amantis,* the "Donation of Constantine" and "Pope Boniface" also

---

[10] Dinshaw, *Chaucer's Sexual Poetics,* 112

[11] Wilks, *The Problem of Sovereignty,* 159. See also Alexander de S. Elpidio's remarks in *De ecclesiastica potestate:* "Et secundum hanc acceptionem ecclesia Romana est ... universalis ecclesia prima ... Et sicut eius episcopus pater est et pastor omnium pasto-rum, ita Romana ecclesia mater et caput est omnium ecclesiarum" (quoted in Wilks, 397). [And in this sense, the Roman church is ... the first universal church ... And as its bishop is the father and the shepherd of all shepherds, so the Roman church is the mother and the head of all churches (translation mine)].

examine this theme.[12] These two tales, according to Scanlon, show Gower
delimiting and reducing the power of the Church over temporal matters to
the benefit of kings. The story of Pope Boniface, especially, manifests "a
particularly extreme version of the royalist position" (ibid., 258). In this
story, Scanlon observes, "Gower disenfranchises clerical power by making
it entirely spiritual" (ibid., 262). It is this disenfranchisement, this confine-
ment of the pope and the Church to a purely spiritual role, that is also
working in the "Tale of Constance," a tale included in Book II of the
Confessio, as well. But there is also something quite distinctive about the
"Tale of Constance," something that one does not find in the stories of
Pope Boniface or of Constantine and Sylvester. This tale illustrates the
proper relation of lay and spiritual power through the use of a father-
daughter relationship, and in significantly gendered terms.

In a fundamental though not exclusive way, the "Tale of Constance"
is about a daughter's perfect compliance with her father's exacting de-
mands. When the sultan of Persia wants to marry her, the father only
shows concern about the sultan's conversion, never about the advantages
or disadvantages of this marriage for his daughter. When Constantine hears
about the sultan's interest in his daughter, Genius notes:

> ... the fader in himselve
> Was glad, and with the Pope avised
> Tuo Cardinals he hath assissed
> With othre lordes many mo,
> That with his doghter scholden go,
> To se the Souldan be converted. (ll. 634–39)[13]

His main worry is "To se the Souldan be converted." Since the sultan
promises he will, Constantine gives his daughter in marriage and sends her
to "Barbarie." We never know what Constance thinks about this marriage
arrangement. She just obeys.

The father's seemingly ruthless separation from his daughter at the
beginning of Gower's tale, though, should not be taken as a sign that for
him their bond has no significance. Quite to the contrary, at the end of the
tale we learn that Constantine had been extremely sad since the day his
daughter left: "This Emperour fro thilke day / That ferst his dowhter
wente away / He was thanne after nevere glad" (ll. 1465–67). This remark
contrasts with the one found at the same point in Gower's source, Trivet's
Chronique. Trivet notes that Constantine was sad, not because his daughter
had left, but because he thought she had been killed: "[F]or the grief which
he had taken for his daughter whom he thought dead, he would never after
eat at a joyful feast nor hear minstrelsy" (48) ["pur ceo que pur le doel qe
il auoit pris pur sa fille, quil quida morte, vnqes apres ne voleit a feste de

---

[12] Scanlon, *Narrative, Authority, and Power,* 256–67.

[13] Quotations from the *Confessio Amantis* are taken from *The English Works of John
Gower,* ed. G. C. Macaulay, 2 vols., EETS, e.s. 81–82 (Oxford, 1900–01).

ioie manger ne Mynistraucie oyer," 49].[14] At the end of Gower's tale, moreover, when father and daughter reunite, the father's reaction suggests again the importance of their bond: "Was nevere father half so blithe / Wepende he keste hire ofte sithe, / So was his herte al overcome" (ll. 1521–23).

For Constance, too, her relationship with her father carries a special weight. This becomes more evident when we compare it to her relationship with her own son. Let us examine the monologue she delivers when she is put on a ship and set adrift with her son Moris. This constitutes one of the rare moments in which Genius permits his heroine to speak at any length. And yet the monologue, as her words show, does not reveal much about herself as an independent individual with her own desires. The entire passage is worth quoting:

> 'Of me no maner charge it is
> What sorwe I soffre, bot of thee
> Me thenkth it is a gret pite,
> For if I sterve thou schalt deie:
> So mot I nedes be that weie
> For Moderhed and for tendresse
> With al myn hole besinesse
> Ordeigne me for thilke office,
> As sche which schal be thi Norrice.' (ll. 1068–77)

Constance is reacting here as a perfect nurturing mother; her worries are for her son, not for herself. However, the words she uses to describe her situation reveal an impersonal sense of duty. Words like "mot I nedes be," "besinesse," or "office" suggest that her mothering role is an injunction by society, a duty she has to perform, rather than her own individual choice.[15] The line "sche which schal be thi Norrice" also reveals this impersonal sense. She refers to herself and her duty in the detached third person, "sche," as if the person performing the nourishing function were not herself but someone else. Constance's impersonal sense of duty overrides her own thoughts and feelings in this dramatic moment.

It is only when she speaks about her attachment to her father, Constan-

---

[14] Both the translated and the original quotations from Trivet's "Life of Constance" are taken from the facing-page translation in "Trivet's Life of Constance," Edmund Brock, ed. and trans., in *Originals and Analogues of Some of Chaucer's "Canterbury Tales,"* ed. F. J. Furnivall, Edmund Brock, and W. A. Clouston (London, 1872–87). All further quotations from Trivet's work are taken from the same edition.

[15] Commenting on Genius's depiction of the moment when the sultan decides to marry Constance, Arno Esch has noticed that "Gower's narrative manner resembles an impersonal report" (100). The same sense of impersonality tinges Constance's own words in this passage. Esch also notes that, unlike Chaucer's depiction of this scene, which "borders on sentimentality ... Gower aims at a typical and conventional picture" (104). See Esch, "John Gower's Narrative Art," trans. Linda Barney Burke, in *Gower's "Confessio Amantis": A Critical Anthology,* ed. Peter Nicholson (Suffolk, 1991).

tine, that we hear what could arguably be called Constance's personal voice. When father and daughter reunite, Constance uses a significant word, "querele," to describe what she feels about her father:

> Mi lord, mi fader, wel you be!
> And of this time that I se
> Youre honoure and your goode hele
> Which is the helpe of my querele,
> I thonke unto the goddes myht. (ll. 1513–17)

The noun "querele" is sometimes associated with love and with the inner, personal struggles of the lover in the *Confessio*. In Book I, for instance, Amans, complaining about his love-sickness, asks Venus: "Behold my cause and my querele" (I.134).[16] In the "Tale of Rosiphelee" when the heroine begins to feel love, Genius says: "And so began ther a querele / Betwen love and hir oghne herte" (IV.1302–3). Notice also Constance's conspicuous use of "I" and "my" in this short speech by contrast with the "sche" in the monologue just quoted. Constance's reaction upon seeing her father, moreover, also contrasts with the detachment she had shown earlier when she was reunited with her husband. Genius notes that when they met again, Allee "joie made" (l. 1443) and everybody was happy, but he does not specify how Constance reacted. He only remarks that she "hadde a gret part of his wille" (l. 1447). In this sense, as Peter Goodall has observed, "the reunion of husband and wife is overshadowed by the reunion of father and daughter."[17]

We see an even more individual Constance when she decides to return home after the death of her husband Allee, following their return to England. Allee's death signifies that Constance, having converted England and having given an heir not just to her husband but to her father as well, has fulfilled her duties and that thus she can finally make her own decisions about her life and return once and for all to her father. Genius describes her decision to go back to Rome as a personal one. Here we should note significant differences among Trivet's, the Man of Law's, and Gower's versions. Trivet provides a "good," dutiful reason for her to go back: "[she] returned to Rome by reason of the news which she heard of her father's sickness" (52) ["pur la nouele qe ele oy de la maladie son piere," 53]. The Man of Law remarks that when Alla died, Custance had "greet hevynesse" (l. 1145), and then simply notes that, "dame Custance, finally to seye, / Toward the toun of Rome goth hir weye" (ll. 1146–47).[18] No

---

[16] Other examples of Amans's use of "querele" in the same sense can be found in VIII.2173, where he asks Genius to intercede with Cupid and Venus for him and "Be frendlich toward mi querele," and in Amans's "Supplication" to Venus when he complains that Cupid "somdiel is cause of mi querele" (VIII.2272).

[17] Peter Goodall, " 'Unkynde Abhomynaciouns' in Chaucer and Gower," *Parergon*, n.s. 5 (1985): 97.

[18] All quotations from the "Man of Law's Tale" are taken from *The Riverside*

specific reasons are given. In Genius's version, however, her reasons for returning to Rome and to her father carry a significant weight. Genius notes that after Allee died Constance "made sorrwe ynogh" (l. 1579); then he remarks that "therupon *hire herte drowh* / To leven Engelond for ever / And go *wher that sche hadde levere*" (ll. 1580–82, emphasis mine). She decides to return to Rome. This time, we should note, her reason to act is not a response to someone else's demands; no duty determines her decision. It is a personal decision: "hire herte" decides. Constance, the woman who had been moved back and forth by others and who had taken few initiatives of her own, finally decides all by herself to follow her own desire, to go where "sche hadde levere."

The bond between father and daughter is underscored once again by the final image that describes Constantine dying in Constance's arms, an image also found in Trivet, but not in the "Man of Law's Tale." Shortly after Constance returns, Genius tells us, "deth of kinde hath overthrowe / Hir worthi fader, which men seide / That he betwen hire armes deide" (ll. 1588–90). The reunion of Constance and Constantine hints at a kind of incestuous love. This hint is reinforced by the fact that Moris inherits directly from Constantine, as if he were the offspring of the father and the daughter. By giving him an heir, Constance performs the role of wife for her father. In this sense, Constance's obedience to her father at the beginning of the tale could be seen as a Griselda-like proof of her love for him.

In addition to being the daughter and, figuratively, the wife of the emperor, Constance also appears as Constantine's mother at one point. Genius's use of this other familial role to refer to the relationship between Constantine and Constance is the more remarkable because it is completely original with him. Neither Trivet nor Chaucer's Man of Law uses it. When Constantine recognizes his daughter at the end of the tale, Genius remarks:

> For thogh his Moder were come
> Fro deth to lyve out of the grave,
> He mihte nomor wonder have
> Than he hath whan that he hire sih. (ll. 1524–27)

Russell Peck has noted that in this passage it seems that "[t]o the emperor, reclaiming his daughter is like a resurrection," a resurrection of Constance, her husband and child, and of himself.[19] I would argue, though, that what is remarkable about this unparalleled passage is that it points to Constance's third familial role in her relationship with her father: as the one who gives him life again, Constance becomes now her father's mother.

Throughout Gower's tale, then, Constance performs the roles of daughter, wife, and mother of the emperor in a mysterious riddle that reminds

---

Chaucer, ed. L. D. Benson.

[19] Russell Peck, *Kingship and Common Profit in Gower's "Confessio Amantis"* (Carbondale, IL, 1978), 69.

us of the different roles assigned to the Virgin Mary and the Church. The roles of mother, wife, and daughter were invoked to define the Virgin Mary's relationship with Christ; the Church, also identified with Mary, was similarly seen as bride, mother, and daughter of God, and of the Christian community.[20] In this respect, Julia Kristeva has argued in her essay "Stabat Mater" that, "[t]he highly complex relationship between Christ and his Mother served as a matrix within which various other relations—God to mankind, man to woman, son to mother, etc.—took shape."[21] I would suggest that the relationship between Christ and His Mother is also the matrix that in the "Tale of Constance" defines the relationship between Constantine and Constance and, figuratively, State and Church. Of course, throughout the Middle Ages, the Church was also conceived in other terms, as, for instance, *corpus Christi mysticum*.[22] But I would like to stress here that, of all the different metaphorical interpretations of the function of the Church that Gower could have drawn from, in the "Tale of Constance" he represents the Church as the feminine mother-wife-daughter.

Significantly, as Gower stresses the importance of Constance/the Church as feminine spiritual leader rather than as a patriarchal and political institution, he reduces the pope's role in the tale. This telling characteristic also greatly distinguishes Gower's from Trivet's rendering of the story of Constance, and, to a lesser extent, from Chaucer's. In Nicholas Trivet's version, before the marriage of Constance to the sultan is decided upon, the pope is consulted along with "the other great ones of Holy Church" (6) ["les autres grantz de seint esglise," 7]. Moreover, the sultan sends letters indicating his desire to marry Constance to the emperor, to Constance herself, and, we should note, also to the pope. Thus, the pope and other officials of the Church are present and play a role almost as important as that of the emperor. In the "Man of Law's Tale" the role of the pope is also prominent; he is the mediator: "... by tretys and embassadrie,

---

[20] On the identification of the Church and Mary, and their characterization as mother-wife-daughter, see Marina Warner, *Alone of All Her Sex: The Myth and the Cult of the Virgin Mary* (New York, 1983), esp. 17–18, 105–11. Warner notes that,

> [i]n iconography of medieval Christendom and later, she often holds the centre stage, both at the Ascension and at the gift of tongues; a towering figure, she becomes the very embodiment of *Mater Ecclesia*, brimming over with the grace and power of the Spirit, and before whom the apostles sometimes kneel in awe (18).

This identification of *Ecclesia* and Mary is also particularly evident in commentaries on the Song of Songs in the Middle Ages, like those of Bruno of Segni in the late eleventh century. See Ann W. Astell, *The Song of Songs in the Middle Ages* (Ithaca, 1990). See also, Michael Wilks, "Chaucer and the Mystical Marriage in Medieval Political Thought," *Bulletin of the John Rylands Library* 44 (1962): 489–530.

[21] Julia Kristeva, "Stabat Mater," in *The Female Body in Western Culture*, ed. Susan Rubin Suleiman (Cambridge, 1985).

[22] On the Church as *corpus Christi mysticum* and other similar metaphors, see, for instance, Francis Oakley, *The Western Church in the Later Middle Ages* (Ithaca, 1979), esp. 159–63.

/ And by the popes mediacioun, / And al the chirche, and al the chivalrie
... They been acorded" (ll. 233–35, 237).

In Gower's version, by contrast, the pope is pushed to the margins of
the events, playing a strictly spiritual and symbolic role. In response to the
sultan's letter, it is the emperor, the father, who takes the initiative and
makes decisions. As quoted above, when Constantine learns about the sul-
tan's intentions, Genius notes,

> ...the fader in himselve
> Was glad, and with the Pope avised
> Tuo Cardinals he hath assissed
> With othre lordes many mo. (ll. 634–37)

Notice that the "he" in line 636, the one who sends the cardinals, as well
as the lords, is the emperor rather than the pope, while the pope is only
consulted once. He does not mediate; he is only consulted and he gives his
advice. Thus, rather than exerting actual power, he is scarcely more than
a point of reference, a symbolic representation of power.

In Trivet's version, moreover, the institutional presence of the Church
is also more salient during Constance's stay in England. When Constance
converts Hermingheld and Elda, after the miracle of the blind man, the
bishop of Bangor is immediately called upon to sanction their conversion
by baptizing them. In Gower's version, however, both Hermingheld and
Elda are considered to be fully converted without the intervention of the
bishop (ll. 751–78). The bishop only appears later when he is to marry
Constance and the king, and it is during that trip that he baptizes the king
and many others (ll. 903 ff.). The "Man of Law's Tale," interestingly
enough, differs from both Trivet's and Gower's versions; the work of
conversion is ultimately ascribed to Jesus' intervention rather than to
Custance's: "Custance hath so longe sojourned there, / In orisons, with
many a bitter teere, / Til Jhesu hath converted thrugh his grace / Dame
Hermengyld" (ll. 536–38). In this case, both the Church and Custance
herself are divested of power. It is Jesus who converts Hermingheld.

Another significant example of the limited role of the institutional
authorities of the Church in Gower's version occurs toward the end of the
tale. In Trivet's *Chronique*, when the Emperor Tiberius decides to appoint
Maurice as his heir, he does so "by the consent of Pope Pelagius and all
the senate of Rome" (50) ["par assent le pape pelagie e de tout le senat de
Rome," 51]. In Gower's tale the Pope has nothing to do with this decision.
Only the parliament is consulted:

> A parlement er that thei wente,
> Thei setten unto this entent,
> To puten Rome in full espeir
> That Moris was apparant heir. (ll. 1549–52)

Chaucer's version, we should note, departs here from Gower's in a signifi-
cant way. His Man of Law does not mention the emperor's and the parlia-
ment's deliberations, but mentions and foregrounds the pope's role by
remarking, "This child Maurice was sithen Emperour / Maad by the
Pope" (ll. 1121–22). Gower's version does not even mention the pope at
this point.

The marginal function of the pope is even represented textually in
Gower's tale. I mentioned before that in his version the emperor is the one
who actually makes the decision to marry his daughter off to the sultan.
Significantly, the first Latin gloss to the tale disagrees on this point; after
noting that the sultan had promised to convert to Christianity, the gloss
remarks: "cuius accepta caucione consilio Pelagii tunc pape dicta filia vna
cum duobus Cardinalibus aliisque Rome proceribus in Persiam maritagii
causa nauigio honorifice destinata fuit" [the pledge being accepted by the
counsel of Pelagius, who was Pope then, the said daughter with two cardi-
nals and other Roman officials was sent to Persia with honor in a ship for
marriage (translation mine)]. Notice that the gloss, unlike the tale itself,
does not even mention the father and that it gives more relevance to the
pope by specifying his name. The discrepancy between the Latin gloss and
the vernacular tale thus reproduces textually the tension between clerical
and lay power. It enacts the struggle for sovereignty between pope and
emperor, or between Church and State, showing the "royalist" displace-
ment of "papalist" power. The pope is literally marginalized.

In addition to marginalizing the pope, Gower's tale suggests the subor-
dination and dependence of the Church on paternal, royal power, not only
through the father-daughter relationship central to the tale, but also by
ascribing the roles of mother and wife to Constance in her relation with
Constantine. Commenting on Dante's line "Vergine Madre, figlia del tuo
Figlio" as a line that "perhaps best captures the combination of the three
feminine roles—daughter-wife-mother—within a whole," Kristeva argues
that "[t]he nexus of these three functions is the basis of immutable and
atemporal spirituality: 'the fixed term of an eternal design,' as *The Divine
Comedy* magisterially puts it."[23] The combination of the three roles in the
case of Constance, similarly, puts her in an atemporal, ahistorical plane
that divests her of immediate, independent power and confines her mainly
to a spiritual role.[24] I do not mean to suggest, though, that her actions do
not affect history. Her work of conversion has definite political effects.

[23] Kristeva, "Stabat Mater," 105.
[24] This effect is similar to the effect that, as Howard Bloch has pointed out, the com-
peting discourses of misogyny and courtly love have on women: "essentialist definitions
of gender [whether positive or negative] are dangerous not only because they are wrong
or undifferentiated but ... because historically they have worked to eliminate the subject
from history" (6). And Bloch continues, "the denial of history to women entails an ab-
straction that also denies the being of any individual woman, and is therefore the stuff
of a disenfranchising objectification" (11). See R. Howard Bloch, *Medieval Misogyny and
the Invention of Western Romantic Love* (Chicago, 1991).

Indeed, Constance's marriage with Allee not only brings about the conversion of England, but also unites eventually, through the inheritance of her son Moris, two political powers: England and Rome. But the political effects of Constance's actions respond to the interests of the Church—she realizes the command to spread the faith. The tale also responds to the interests of lay political power. Constance obeys the authority of her father, the political authority in Rome, and her obedience provides Constantine and Rome with an heir who guarantees the stability and the political advancement of the Roman empire.

Constance's roles as daughter and figurative mother, furthermore, provide a comment on the authority of English royal power. As mentioned at the beginning of this analysis, the story of Constance is a "story of origins," that is, a story that attempts to legitimize a certain form of authority. Constance, according to the tale, brought Christianity to England. She is in this sense the origin, the spiritual mother who gave birth to the authority of the Christian monarchs of medieval England, and the one who thus validates royal authority. It is significant, of course, that a woman sent by an emperor, a lay political authority, should function as the symbolic origin of the Christian English state, rather than a man sent by the pope (as was historically the case with Saint Augustine's conversion of the English). No imposition from the pope turned England to Christianity but the faith of an obedient daughter who had less to do with the institutional and political power of the Church and its patriarchal authority than with lay authority. Moreover, as a woman, Constance not only validates royal authority, but also affirms the subordination of the Church to the male king.

Gower's tale thus offers a complex comment on the relationship between State and Church. His version deemphasizes the role of the patriarchal figure of authority within the Church, the pope, and, through Constance, foregrounds the Church's feminine (meaning here subordinate) role in its relationship with lay masculine power. However, that Gower's tale does this does not mean that he enacts lay power's form of appropriation in an uncritical way, as I will show.

So far, this essay has only alluded to the incestuous connotations in the tale. I want to return now to the incest theme and analyze those allusions to articulate my final argument about the tale and its ultimate implications. R. N. Swanson has observed that,

> The slow development towards a lay—but not secular—view of the state, with the emphasis on royal power proceeding directly from God rather than being mediated through the church, challenged, and then shattered, the church's hold on the succession, and on the legitimization of regimes.[25]

---

[25] Swanson, *Church and Society,* 121.

The emphasis on royal power proceeding directly from God and circumventing the pope's power, as I have shown, is clear in Gower's version. The one who institutes the beginning of Christian monarchy in England is Constance, a woman sent by the emperor, not by the pope himself. The pope's authority is thus circumvented. Swanson has also pointed out that in emphasizing, "the prince's duty as *rex Christianissimus* ... [Christian monarchs had] purely practical aims[;] the most important political theorizing was propounded for a very specific end: effective royal control over Parliament" (Swanson, 93). The tensions between the two powers as articulated in different treatises tended to justify lay power on the basis of its Christian origins and this justification was used to control parliament. If, as Swanson argues, at least one of the purposes of political theorizing in late medieval England was the establishment and justification of effective royal control over parliament, then a fundamental question inevitably arises: Is Gower's purpose in the tale to give English monarchs the necessary justification, based on a myth of origins, for ruling over parliament?

An analysis of the incest theme in the tale and in the *Confessio Amantis* as a whole suggests that we should not hasten to answer this question in the affirmative; in fact, when one examines the suppressed incest theme in the tale and compares it to the explicit condemnation of father-daughter incest in another tale in the *Confessio,* the answer turns out to be negative. In the story of Apollonius (VIII.271–2008), Genius depicts father-daughter incest as a most horrible and unnatural act: "The wylde fader thus devoureth / His oghne fleissh" (ll. 309–10). He also describes it as an "unkinde fare" (l. 312), a "horrible vice" (l. 317). I have argued elsewhere that, in addition to explicitly condemning father-daughter incest in this tale, Genius also uses incest in other tales as a metaphor to condemn other fathers' oppressive and, in a sense absolutist, relationships with their daughters, most notably in the "Tale of Canace and Machaire" (III.143–336).[26] These fathers tend to be rulers with significant political power. In these cases, as in the case of the actual incestuous relationship between Antiochus and his daughter in the story of "Apollonius," Genius condemns the father as well as the ruler. The metaphor of incest thus serves to denounce absolutist political power.

Incest does not occur in the "Tale of Constance" as it does in earlier versions of this narrative studied by Schlauch. However, as Peter Goodall has noted, while "[t]he Man of Law explicitly differentiates the Constance story from a story like Apollonius of Tyre ... Gower, far from differentiating them, links them closely."[27] The incestuous connotations in Gower's version of the story have not been completely suppressed. In fact, the

---

[26] María Bullón-Fernández, "Confining the Daughter: Gower's 'Tale of Canace and Machaire' and the Politics of the Body," *Essays in Medieval Studies* 11, 1994 Proceedings of the Illinois Medieval Association, eds. Allen J. Frantzen and David A. Robertson (Chicago, 1995), 75–85.

[27] Goodall, "Unkynde Abhomynaciouns," 96.

links between the narratives of Constance and Apollonius as well as Genius's condemnation of father-daughter incest elsewhere in the *Confessio* cast a very dubious light over the "Tale of Constance" and its fantasy of self-reproducing, in other words, incestuous, royal power. Scanlon has shown that in its reappropriation of clerical power one of lay power's most important strategies was to sacralize itself.[28] He notes that, initially, in the Carolingian period, as it became part of the ruling class, clerical power produced conceptions of power for lay rulers. It did not do so without reaping its own benefits: "There is no doubt this process involved an ecclesiastical appropriation of major proportions, as clerics invested pre-existent lay political forms with sacral and ecclesiological significance" (Scanlon, 86). In the fourteenth century, lay power tried to reappropriate clerical power by taking control of sacred symbols:

> The laicization of the later period should ... be seen, at least in part, as a reappropriation rather than a simple act of resistance, as the growing power of royal courts enabled them to take fuller control of the legitimating functions that had earlier been provided by the Church (ibid., 86).

In the "Tale of Constance," lay power, or more appropriately, royalist ideology, as defined by Swanson, that is, the ideology that tries to establish effective royal control over parliament, appropriates the God-Mary relationship as a matrix to explain the relationship between Constantine and Constance, thus reappropriating sacral images and stories for lay purposes.

But the question still remains: does the tale show this reappropriation uncritically? Because of its use of familial metaphors, the God-Mary-Christ riddle could be interpreted as a symbolic and religious story of incest—God the Father conceived a son through his own daughter. However, this relationship is rarely understood to be incestuous, because, among other reasons, the relationship situates itself in a different, suprahuman plane. The father-daughter relationship between God and Mary is not a father-daughter relationship in a literal, biological sense. This does not mean that one could not deconstruct the metaphoric-literal opposition that seems to be at work here. However, my point is different. Whether we do not consider the God-Mary relationship as a case of incest because it situates itself in a suprahuman plane, or for other reasons, what interests me here is that in the case of Constance and Constantine it is impossible to ignore the human dimension of their relationship. Their father-daughter relationship in their case is literal, rather than metaphorical, and human, rather than suprahuman. Some might argue that the point of the Constance-Constantine story is precisely to create that opposition and to make us see the Constance and Constantine relationship as having a different, suprahuman quality. After all, Constance seems like a suprahuman heroine and

---

[28] Scanlon, *Narrative, Authority, and Power,* 86.

the tale encourages us to compare her to the Virgin Mary. However, that Gower's story tries to make, or is even interested in making, Constance exclusively saintly or suprahuman is certainly not evident. Throughout Gower's tale, Constance is driven not just by a sense of religious duty but also by a sense of social obligation. She is not just a saint. As Winthrop Wetherbee has argued, Gower's version "emphasi[zes] ... Constance's active, public role," by contrast with Chaucer's version in which the Man of Law has "a tendency to fetishize her helplessness and underplay her normal social relations."[29] Her role goes beyond the religious function of converting others. It is also social and political as she becomes a mother and provides an heir for her father.

Furthermore, Constantine himself is far from being a figure for God, someone with suprahuman or divine qualities. Constantine is very "human" and political when he arranges a convenient match for his daughter by marrying her to the sultan. The marriage ensures the advancement of his religion, but this advancement also has obvious political and economic advantages for Rome. Constantine's humanity is further emphasized at the end. When he dies in his daughter's arms, we are reminded of a Pietá scene: Mary/Constance has the dead Christ/Constantine in her arms. However, the parallel between the Jesus-Mary and the Constance-Constantine Pietás is not perfect. The son/father in the Constance-Constantine Pietá scene is all too human. Notice how, by using the noun "kinde," Genius emphasizes the natural character of Constantine's death: "deth of kinde hath overthrowe / Hir worthi fader, which men seide / That he between hire armes deide" (ll. 1588–90). Thus Gower's depiction of their appropriation of the God-Mary relationship as a matrix to explain their relationship cannot be considered purely and uncritically allegorical. The human dimension is always there and reminds us that Constance and Constantine have a literally familial relationship, thus foregrounding the incestuous connotations of their relationship.

If one examines the incest theme, then, the ultimate political implications of Gower's tale do not necessarily entail the uncritical support of royalist aspirations. As I have argued, Gower uses the father-daughter relationship in the "Tale of Constance" as a matrix not just for the examination but also for the definition and delimitation of power relationships between State and Church. But he does so not in order to justify royalist absolute power. Quite to the contrary, it becomes evident that Gower's version questions the model of self-reproducing, incestuous, royal power that the Constance story presents. This further suggests that, *contra* Eberle, he is not supporting the "descending" view of authority, according to which the king has absolute power over his subjects. Rather, in questioning the self-sufficiency and incestuous character of a power concentrat-

[29] Winthrop Wetherbee, "Constance and the World in Chaucer and Gower," in *John Gower: Recent Readings,* ed. R. F. Yeager (Kalamazoo, 1989), 69.

ed in royal families, Gower questions the ideology behind the mode of the royalist appropriation of papal power. The incestuous character of their relationship suggests an absolutist model that Gower did not support.

It needs to be emphasized here that Gower's questioning of this appropriation does not imply that he supports clerical power over *temporalia*. Gower makes explicit his disapproval of clerical appropriation of lay power through the prophecy mentioned at the end of the story of another Constantine, the one who, supposedly, had donated his power to the Church. Genius says that he read in a chronicle that as soon as Constantine made his donation of *temporalia* to the Church,

> A vois was herd on hih the lifte,
> Of which al Rome was adrad,
> And seith: 'To day is venym schad
> In holi cherche of temporal,
> Which medleth with the spiral' (ll. 3488–92)

According to Genius, the Donation had been a well-meaning mistake—"[Constantine's] will was good" (l. 3482), he remarks. But this mistake became the source of a host of problems, which Genius hopes "God mai amende it, whan he wile, / I can ther to non other skile" (ll. 3495–96).

There are significant links between the story of the "Donation of Constantine" and the "Tale of Constance" that further illuminate Gower's complex analysis. As noted, the Constantine of the Donation is not the same as Constance's father. He is the one who converted to Christianity. Nevertheless, the coincidence in the names as well as the proximity of the tales within the *Confessio* encourage us to see links between them. Both tales are in Book II, the book about the sin of Envy; one illustrates an example of a branch of Envy, backbiting, the other an example of the opposite of Envy in a general sense, Charity. Furthermore, the "Donation of Constantine" is one of the most important narratives representing clerical appropriation of lay power. As noted, the story was used by the Church to justify its supremacy over lay rulers. It is thus significant that the "Tale of Constance" presents the opposite move, that is, the reappropriation of clerical power by lay rulers. This parallel, nevertheless, is not meant to delegitimize this reappropriation of power.

There is, of course, no condemnation of the reappropriation of clerical power by lay rulers in the "Tale of Constance." As the prophecy in the "Tale of Constantine and Sylvester" suggests, and as Scanlon has amply illustrated, Gower definitely condemned the Church's use of temporal power. But Gower's criticism of the Church's use of temporal power does not lead him to a blind support of any form of royal power. What the "Tale of Constance" does, I suggest, is question the model used to justify the appropriation. It hints at the dangers of using a model that in suggesting the incestuous, self-reproducing character of a power concentrated in royal families carries absolutist political implications. Gower's condemnation of father-daughter incest and his use of it as a metaphor to condemn absolutist use of royal power in other tales suggests that his support of royalist reappropriation of *temporalia* in the "Tale of Constance" is not an uncritical acceptance of lay pretensions to power. At the same time that the tale supports those pretensions, it also points to the need to delimit them.

Questions about the relationship between State and Church inevitably emerge in all three versions of the Constance story as the emperor and the pope, as well as the work of conversion of the English monarchy, play important and explicit roles in all of them. I have shown that these questions are most clearly raised and dealt with in Gower's version. But what about Chaucer's "Man of Law's Tale"? In light of my reading of Gower's tale, one might expect a similar reflection on State-Church power conflicts at the end of the fourteenth century in Chaucer's version. And yet there is no such reflection in it. Quite the opposite: again and again the Man of Law avoids alluding to the conflict. While his tale, like Gower's, finds a new origin in the conversion of England, an origin that itself originates in lay power, that is, in Constantine rather than in the pope himself, it does also allow the pope an important role in the Constance story, as I have shown. By doing so, the Man of Law tries to avoid suggesting any tensions between lay and clerical power.

Avoiding conflict seems a typical strategy of the Man of Law. Susan Schibanoff has recently offered a new reading of the "Man of Law's Tale" according to which "the Man of Law uses a discourse of orientalism to issue a clarion call for unity—not among the general *communitas* of the faithful but specifically among the Christian men of his audience."[30] The lawyer aims at making peace, at remedying "the overt divisiveness that has broken out among [the] narrators [of the previous tales]" (Schibanoff, 60). Schibanoff convincingly sees the potential divisiveness in terms of class rivalry among the Knight, the Miller, the Reeve, the Cook, and the Host. In light of Gower's "Tale of Constance," I suggest that there is another potential type of rivalry among Christian men that the tale tries to suppress, and that is the rivalry between the representative authorities of the Church and the State. Gower's complex tackling of the conflict makes the Man of Law's avoidance of it all the more significant.

---

[30] Schibanoff, "Worlds Apart," 60.

John Gower's *Confessio Amantis*, Ideology, and the "Labor" of "Love's Labor"

Gregory M. Sadlek

> Nowher so bisy a man as he ther nas,
> And yet he semed bisier than he was.
> —Geoffrey Chaucer

One of the clearest trends in recent critical practice has been, in the words of Anne Middleton, to see works of literature not as tranquil artifacts but as "sites of action, a locus of complex agencies" in which social and literary forces "act and modify each other through sustained literary engagement."[1] For some works this approach is more self-evident than for others. For example, it is easy to perceive that *Piers Plowman,* a poem that self-consciously agonizes over the problems of labor and social unrest, is a site of mediation between various English literary traditions, William Langland's personal and class interests, and late-medieval ideologies of labor. It is less easy—but, I would argue, just as profitable—to see that late-medieval ideologies of labor are mediated in aristocratic love poetry employing the metaphor of "love's labor."

In Book IV of John Gower's *Confessio Amantis,* for example, the confessor Genius focuses his treatment of the Seven Deadly Sins *in amoris causa* on the sin of *acedia,* a vice roughly equivalent to our modern "sloth."[2] Within

---

[1] Ann Middleton, "Medieval Studies," in *Redrawing the Boundaries: The Transformation of English and American Literary Studies,* ed. Stephen Greenblatt and Giles Gunn (New York, 1992), 26.

[2] The best and most comprehensive treatment of this vice is still found in Siegfried Wenzel, *The Sin of Sloth: Acedia in Medieval Thought and Literature* (Chapel Hill, 1967).

Several notable treatments of Book IV of the *Confessio* serve as the background to this study. Rozalyn Levin ("The Passive Poet: Amans as Narrator in Book 4 of the *Confessio Amantis*" in *Proceedings of the Illinois Medieval Association* [DeKalb, IL, 1986], III.114–29) argues that Book IV reveals Gower's understanding of the courtly concept of "gentilesse." Linda Marie Zaerr's dissertation "The Dynamics of Sloth: *Fin amour* and Divine Mercy in John Gower's *Confessio Amantis*" (Diss. Univ. of Washington, 1987) analyzes Gower's adaptation in Book IV of Christian teachings regarding *acedia,* particularly the relationship of the *exempla* and the frame narrative and finds that the book reveals fatal inconsistencies and flaws in the concept of *fin amour.* Robert Yeager (*John Gower's Poetic: The Search for a New Arion* [Cambridge, 1990]) points out Gower's debt in Book IV to Dame Nature's discussion of "labor" in the *Roman de la Rose* and sees

this framework he is eventually forced to analyze the concept of "love's labor" in some detail. In Book VIII, the penitant Amans, who becomes identified with the poet himself, is forced not only to confront his age, the major reason for his lack of productivity in love, but also to accept a forced retirement from love's labor altogether. One aspect of the paradoxical nature of these books, and to some extent of the whole *Confessio,* is rooted in Gower's attempt, whether in jest or in earnest, to analyze and illustrate the virtues and vices of a romantic lover in terms of a Christian moral paradigm. As many critics have noted, however, the mix can appear at times both clever and downright wrongheaded. Why Gower took this approach and what was its artistic effect have been of continual interest to Gower critics at least since the publication of Macaulay's standard edition.[3] To discuss sloth as a vice in the religion of love is paradoxical because, as Guillaume de Lorris noted in the *Roman de la Rose,* it is precisely the fact of being idle that allows the aristocratic lover entrance into the Garden of Love.[4] Yet because of the overall design of the *Confessio,* Gower is forced to work

---

the book's discussion of "labor" as a counterexample to the slothful behavior of lovers (34, 161). He asserts that Gower's treatment of work is structured not according to the Three Estates model, but according to the division of believers into those in the active life or contemplative life. In this way, the discussion serves as a foreshadowing and justification of Venus's eventual order in Book VIII for Amans to turn to the intellectual life (169). Kurt Olsson's treatments of Book IV are found in "Aspects of *Gentilesse* in John Gower's *Confessio Amantis,* Books III–V" (*John Gower: Recent Readings,* ed. R. F. Yeager [Kalamazoo, MI, 1989], 225–76) and chap. 10 of his book *John Gower and the Structures of Conversion: A Reading of the "Confessio Amantis"* ([Cambridge, 1992], 119–30). Within his treatment of the *Confessio* as an authored but multi-voiced *compilatio,* Olsson argues that the discussion of love's labor and idleness is a form of "recreation," a genteel pasttime akin to the *demande d'amour,* designed to lead Amans to his eventual recognition of good and "honeste" love in Book VIII (*Structures of Conversion,* 124–25, 226). The discussion is played out against the ambiguity of the sense of *otium,* with meanings ranging from "idleness" and "laziness" through "leisure" and "the fruits of leisure" (ibid., 120). These studies all richly contribute to our understanding of Gower's use of his literary past, but none investigates the influence of changing fourteenth-century labor ideologies on Gower's work.

[3] See Peter Nicholson's "Introduction: The Study of the *Confessio Amantis* in the Twentieth Century," *An Annotated Index to the Commentary on Gower's "Confessio Amantis"* (Binghamton, NY, 1989), 1–20. Most critics, however, see an unambiguously moral lesson emerging at the end of the *Confessio.* See, for example, the comments of Yeager, 265–78. Olsson has written that the discordant "wisdom" of the poem is meant to jar readers into an active, critical search for truth (12–15). For a contrasting view see Hugh White, "Division and Failure in Gower's *Confessio Amantis,*" *Neophilologus* 72 (1988): 600–16.

[4] Here I refer to the character Oiseuse, whom Guillaume makes the gatekeeper of the Garden of Love. See Guillaume de Lorris and Jean de Meun, *Le Roman de la Rose,* ed. Félix Lecoy, 3 vols. (Paris, 1983), ll. 523–616 (I.17–20). For an English translation, see Charles Dahlberg, trans., *The Romance of the Rose* (Hanover, NH, 1983), 37–39. Quotations from the *Roman de la Rose* will be taken from Lecoy's edition and cited in the text by line number.

For a recent discussion of the controversy over the meaning of Oiseuse (leisure or slothful idleness?), see Gregory M. Sadlek, "Interpreting Guillaume de Lorris's Oiseuse: Geoffrey Chaucer as Witness," *South Central Review* 10 (1993): 22–37.

through this very problem in Books IV and VIII. In refocusing our attention on these two books, I hope to enlarge our understanding of the dynamics of Gower's literary creation by presenting it as a site of action at which both literary and social forces (the literary tradition of love's labor as well as traditional and evolving ideologies of labor) are brought into a sustained literary engagement, producing a complex work of literature.

I

Both "romantic love" and "labor" are social constructions refashioned anew to a large extent in the literature of each age.[5] While some classical and medieval literature constructed love, for example, as an affliction, disease, or madness, other works present it as a form of game or religious duty.[6] Beginning at least with Ovid, romantic love was also presented (often comically or ironically) as a form of labor—one that could be taught by means of a "manual."[7] In the *Amores,* Ovid writes: "Qui nolet fieri desidiosus, amet!" [whoso would not be slothful, let him love!]. In the *Ars Amato-*

[5] Peter Berger and Thomas Luckmann, *The Social Construction of Reality* (New York, 1966). See esp. their remarks on language (34–46), the origins of institutionalization (53–67), and roles (72–79). On the interplay of love literature and cultural practice in general but particularly during the Victorian Age, see Robert M. Polhemus, *Erotic Faith* (Chicago, 1990). One of his goals is "to interpret and illuminate the interplay between the novels and the perceived reality of actual people" (3).

There has been a sharp debate on the relationship between literary representation of aristocratic forms of romantic love and medieval social reality. A good review of the debate is found in Robert R. Edwards and Stephen Spector, Introduction, *The Olde Daunce: Love, Friendship, Sex, and Marriage in the Medieval World* (Albany, NY, 1991), 1–8. See also Roger Boase, *The Origin and Meaning of Courtly Love* (Totowa, NJ, 1977), 89–93, 103–9.

[6] Chaucer's depiction of the effects of Palamon and Arcite's love for Emily is a good example of love presented as a form of sickness. See Chaucer's "Knight's Tale" in *The Riverside Chaucer,* ed. Larry D. Benson, 3rd ed. (Boston, 1987), esp. ll. 1356–79. All subsequent quotations from Chaucer will be taken from this edition and cited in the text. Mary Wack fully discusses medieval lovesickness in *Lovesickness in the Middle Ages: The Viaticum and Its Commentaries* (Philadelphia, 1990).

For an example of love presented as a game, see the unedited fourteenth-century *Echecs d'amour,* summarized by Pierre-Yves Badel (*Le Roman de la Rose au XIVᵉ siècle* [Geneva, 1980], 264–76) and trans., at least partly, by John Lydgate (*Reson and Sensuallyte,* ed. Ernst Sieper, 2 vols., EETS, e.s., 84 and 89 [London, 1901]). In particular, ll. 5799–7042.

The Religion of Love was described by C. S. Lewis as being part of Courtly Love (*The Allegory of Love* [Oxford, 1936], 2, 8, 14, passim). A good example of love's being constructed in religious language is seen in Chrétien de Troyes's *Lancelot.* Lancelot reveres Gwenevere's hair as he would religious relics; he enters and leaves her bed with reverence, as if it were an altar; he suffers something akin to martyrdom when he is forced to leave her (*Le Chevalier de la Charrette,* ed. Mario Roques [Paris, 1983], ll. 1460–78, 4648–53, 4689–91, 4716–18).

[7] For an analysis of the self-consciously fictive nature of these manuals, see Peter L. Allen, *The Art of Love: Amatory Fiction from Ovid to the "Romance of the Rose"* (Philadelphia, 1992).

ria, he treats love as a series of three labors (*labores*): finding a lover, winning the lover, making love endure.[8] In the twelfth century, Andreas Capellanus followed Ovid by writing a new, medieval art of love. Although he defines love primarily as *passio* [affliction], the voices in his book often insist that obsessive thought about love must lead the successful lover to work. One of them remarks: "Absque labore gravi non possunt magna parari" [prizes great cannot be won unless some heavy labor's done].[9] In the thirteenth century, the French authors of *Le Roman de la Rose* produced an encyclopedic love allegory, depicting in detail the work of aristocratic lovers and setting this labor specifically in the context of the leisure (*oiseuse*) granted lovers by their privileged social status as members of the aristocracy. In a key passage, Jean de Meun's character Reason defines love as "repos travaillant an touz termes" [the repose always occupied by labor].[10]

If romantic love is to a large degree socially constructed, so is labor.[11] Traditional ways of thinking about work in the Christian Middle Ages were heavily influenced by literature (the Bible and various Patristic writings), by the difficult nature of the work that most medieval laborers performed, and by the traditional social model of the Three Estates.[12] The medieval appreciation of the positive value of creative work, arising ultimately from the depiction of a "worker God" in Genesis, was generally overshadowed by an even more powerful contrasting belief in work as the punishment for original sin.[13] On the one hand, the connotations of the Latin word *labor* were uniformly negative. Starting from well before the advent of the Three Estates social model, *labor* was associated with pain and drudgery, especially the manual agricultural labor of the rural peasant classes. On the other hand,

---

[8] Ovid, "Militat omnis amans" (*Amores*, I.ix, in *Heroides and Amores*, 2nd ed., ed. and trans. Grant Showerman and G. P. Gould [Cambridge, MA, 1986], l. 46). This Ovidian line seems to have been less well known than the contradictory line on idleness from the *Remedia Amoris:* "Otia si tollas,/ periere Cupidinis arcus" [take away leisure and Cupid's bow is broken] (l. 139). Both the *Remedia* and the *Artis Amatoriae* are ed. and trans. in *The Art of Love and Other Poems,* 2nd ed., ed. and trans. J. H. Mozley and G. P. Gould (Cambridge, MA, 1985). For a summary of the "labors" of love in the *Artis Amatoriae,* see ll. 35–40.

[9] Andreas Capellanus, *De amore,* in *Andreas Capellanus on Love,* ed. and trans. P. G. Walsh (London, 1982), 32, 58.

[10] De Lorris, *Roman de la Rose,* l. 4296 (I.133); Dahlberg, *Romance of the Rose,* 95.

[11] See Patrick Joyce, "The Historical Meanings of Work: An Introduction," *The Historical Meanings of Work,* ed. Patrick Joyce (Cambridge, 1987), 1–30.

[12] On typical medieval attitudes toward work, see the essays in *Le Travail au moyen âge: Une Approche interdisciplinaire,* ed. Jacqueline Hamesse and Collette Muraille-Samaran (Louvain-la-Neuve, 1990) and in Allen Frantzen and Douglas Moffat's *The Work of Work: Servitude, Slavery, and Labor in Medieval England* (Glasgow, 1994). A particularly helpful article is Jacques LeGoff's "Le Travail dans les systèmes de valeur de l'Occident médiéval," in *Le Travail au moyen âge,* 7–21. See also George Ovitt's *The Restoration of Perfection: Labor and Technology in Medieval Culture* (New Brunswick, 1987). On the continuities of work attitudes between Antiquity and the Middle Ages, see Birgit van den Hoven, *Work in Ancient and Medieval Thought* (Amsterdam, 1996).

[13] LeGoff, "Travail dans les systèmes," 11–12.

the Latin word *otium*, the opposite of *labor*, meant either "leisure" or "idleness," and, thus, had both positive and negative connotations. As a positive quality, it was associated solely with the aristocracy and with contemplative monks.[14]

Perhaps the most highly developed medieval ideology of work sprang from the moral system of the Seven Deadly Sins and their characteristic antidotes. The roots of *acedia* lay in the tedium and even psychic exhaustion experienced by the early Egyptian desert hermits, who saw *acedia* as the "noonday demon." Over the centuries, however, the meanings of the term expanded to include simple laziness and lack of activity. The subcategories of *acedia* were first established in the writings of John Cassian (b. AD 355), who wrote that the progeny of *acedia* were idleness, somnolence, rudeness, restlessness, wandering about, instability of mind and body, chattering, and inquisitiveness. In this ideology, the primary value of work arose not from what work produced but from its value as an antidote to *acedia*.[15]

What one historian has called "The Age of Anxiety," the late fourteenth century, was a critical time in the history of labor.[16] The depopulation resulting from the Black Plague had an unsettling effect on the value and, thus, the stability of peasant labor. In England this led to the enactment of the Statute of Laborers, which attempted to stifle market forces with respect to workers' wages. Unhappiness with working conditions finally led to the Peasants' Revolt of 1381. In addition, the Lollards rejected the idea of religious mendicancy precisely because the mendicants were not productive citizens. William Langland, appalled at the lack of a strong work ethic among much of the working classes, in the rampaging of his personified Hunger, pointed out the terrible effects of low worker productivity.[17] In his study of medieval preaching, G. R. Owst argues that the sermons of late-fourteenth-century preachers were larded with references to the dignity of work and the necessity of "work for all."[18] Finally, Jacques LeGoff argues

---

[14] On Latin *labor*, see LeGoff, "Travail dans les systèmes," 13–14, and J. Hamesse, "Le Travail chez les auteurs philosophiques du 12ᵉ et du 13ᵉ siècle," *Le Travail au moyen âge*, 115–27. The ambiguous nature of *otium* was perceived at least as far back as Classical Rome. See Jean-Marie André, *L'Otium dans la vie morale et intellectuelle romaine* (Paris, 1966), 9.

Genius refers to Ydelnesse as "the Norrice / In mannes kinde of every vice." See *Confessio Amantis* in *The English Works of John Gower*, ed. G. C. Macaulay, 2 vols., EETS, e.s., 81–82 (1900–01; repr. Oxford, 1979), IV.1086–88. All citations and quotations refer to this edition and will be cited in the text by book and line numbers.

[15] On the origins and development of *acedia*, see Wenzel, *Sin of Sloth*, 3ff. See also John Cassien, *Conférences*, ed. and trans. E. Pichery, Sources Chrétiens (Paris, 1959), V.16.

[16] William Bouwsma, "Anxiety and the Formation of Early Modern Culture," *After the Reformation: Essays in Honor of J. H. Hexter*, ed. Barbara C. Malament (Philadelphia, 1980), 215–46. See also Steven A. Epstein, "Labor and Guilds in Crisis—The Fourteenth Century," in *Wage Labor and Guilds in Medieval Europe* (Chapel Hill, 1991), 207–56.

[17] William Langland, *Piers Plowman: The B Version*, ed. George Kane and E. Talbot Donaldson (London, 1975), VI.115–331.

[18] G. R. Owst, "A Literary Echo of the Social Gospel," in *Literature and Pulpit in*

that the advent of the mechanical clock, which rapidly became installed in city squares during the late fourteenth century, changed old work rhythms and inaugurated new conceptions of urban "work time."[19]

While evidence on typical fourteenth-century attitudes toward work is not consistent, historians such as Margo Todd, Paul Münch, and LeGoff have argued that aspects of what Max Weber identified as the Protestant work ethic (a general belief in the dignity of work, intense concerns about labor productivity, and the belief that time is a commodity to be spent wisely) are to be found in the writings of the early humanists, like Francis Petrarch.[20] It seems reasonable to take the presence of these work concerns, however tentative and unsystematic, to be a sign of early ideological movement toward the full-blown Humanist and, later still, Protestant work ethics.[21]

If "romantic love" and "labor" are to a large extent cultural constructs, they are fashioned in literature out of language—some taken from established literary traditions and some from a writer's contemporary culture. Mikhail Bakhtin argues that ordinary utterances are never ideologically pure but always reflect an ideology, the beliefs of a particular profession, social group, age, political party. "Each word," he writes, "tastes of context and contexts in which it has lived its socially charged life."[22] Gower's social position (among the professional classes that had significant contact with the social worlds of franklins and merchants as well as the more refined world of the aristocracy) would have given him access to the ideologically charged "languages" of several key groups.[23] If one accepts Bakhtin's opinion, then, changes in key ways of thinking about, speaking about, and valuing labor

---

Medieval England, 2nd ed. (New York, 1961), 548–71.

[19] Jacques LeGoff, "Merchant's Time and Church's Time in the Middle Ages," and "Labor Time in the 'Crisis' of the Fourteenth Century: From Medieval Time to Modern Time," in *Time, Work, and Culture in the Middle Ages*, trans. Arthur Goldhammer (Chicago, 1980), 29–52.

[20] Max Weber, *The Protestant Ethic and the Spirit of Capitalism*, trans. Talcott Parsons (New York, 1930); Margo Todd, "Work, Wealth and Welfare," in *Christian Humanism and the Puritan Social Order* (Cambridge, 1987), 118–75; Paul Münch, "The Thesis Before Weber: An Archaeology," in *Weber's "Protestant Ethic": Origins, Evidence, Contexts*, ed. Hartmut Lehmann and Guenther Roth, Publications of The German Historical Institute (Cambridge, 1993), 51–71; and LeGoff, "Labor Time," 48–52.

[21] Owst finds foreshadowings of the Protestant work ethic in fourteenth-century sermons ("Literary Echo," 557). Yeager calls Gower a fourteenth-century Humanist (*John Gower's Poetic*, 13–14).

[22] M. M. Bakhtin, "Discourse in the Novel," in *The Dialogic Imagination*, ed. Michael Holquist, trans. Caryl Emerson and Michael Holquist (Austin, 1981), 293.

[23] On Gower's social position, see John Fisher, "Life Records," in *John Gower: Moral Philosopher and Friend of Chaucer* (London, 1965), 37–70. In particular, Fisher writes: "The different bodies of material show Gower moving in the same two worlds as Chaucer, the upper middle class society of the franklin, merchant, and lawyer, and the aristocratic society of a trusted retainer in a noble household" (41). For further information on Chaucer and Gower's social position, see Paul Strohm, *Social Chaucer* (Cambridge, 1989), esp. 1–46.

among Gower's contemporaries should to some degree be reflected in his literary utterances about work in the *Confessio Amantis*.

II

What language does Gower use to construct "love's labor"? On the level of lexicon, he employs at least six different words to describe love's labor: "travail," "servise," "labour," "werk," "besinesse," and "occupacioun."[24] The word "besinesse," however, was by far Gower's favorite word for love's labor. While he uses the others inconsistently, he employs "besiness" ten times. A review of the denotations and, to the extent the dictionaries allow, the connotations of these words helps us see the range of meanings Gower had to choose from as he constructed his review of love's labor.

Middle English "werk," the word with the longest history in English, descended from Anglo-Saxon "weorc" and had a range of meanings, with apparently neutral to negative connotations, including those covered by the Latin *labor*, i.e., hard, strenuous labor, trouble, and affliction.[25] Several new synonyms for "werk" were borrowed in the thirteenth century but gained wide currency only over the course of the fourteenth century. While the *Middle English Dictionary* has only one or two thirteenth-century citations of "travail," it gives a significantly large number of citations from the fourteenth and fifteenth centuries. Even more strongly than "werk," "travail" seems to have carried the negative denotations and connotations of Latin *labor*.[26] "Servise" entered the English language from French at the beginning of the thirteenth century but, like "travail," is not widely attested until the fourteenth century. Although from the very beginning it carried the sense of generalized effort or assistance to another, it most often carried the suggestion of some kind of legal obligation to a master, such as that owed by a servant, feudal tenant, or knight.[27] It is noteworthy that Gower was almost certainly among the first English poets to use Middle English "servise" to refer to love's labor.[28] Borrowed from Latin or French, Middle

---

[24] For examples of Gower's use of "travail" referring to love's labor, see IV.1105 and 1604. For "servise," see IV.341 and 1130. For "labour," see IV.2023. For "werk," see IV.301 and 317. For "besinesse," see IV.298, 513, 725, 1155, 1261, 1747, 1751, 1757, 2289, and 3492. For "occupacioun," see IV.1257 and 1452.

[25] *Oxford English Dictionary* (OED), ed. J. A. Simpson and E. S. C. Weiner, 2nd ed. (Oxford, 1989), "work," sb., esp. definitions 4, 4b, 6a.

[26] *Middle English Dictionary* (MED), ed. Hans Kurath and Sherman M. Kuhn (Ann Arbor, MI, 1956–), "travail," n., esp. definitions 1(a), 2(b), and 3(a-d).

[27] MED, "servise," n., definition 7: "assistance, help; a helpful act, requested favor" is cited as early as AD 1230. However, definitions 1, 2, 3, and 4, all quite current in the fourteenth century, suggest some kind of legal obligation of the server to the one served. Definition 6, appearing only at the end of the fourteenth century, is: "slavery, servitude, bondage."

[28] MED, "servise," n., definition 5. *Confessio*, VIII.2012, is first on the list of citations here.

English "labour" first appeared at the beginning of the fourteenth century but, again, is not often found in Middle English texts until the end of the century. Like "travail," "labour" carried with it some of the same denotations and negative connotations as its Latin cognate. By the end of the fourteenth century, however, it could also refer specifically to *mental* labor.[29]

While Anglo-Saxon "bisig," from which "businesse" is derived, had a long history in English by Gower's day, its range of meanings expanded in the thirteenth and fourteenth centuries.[30] One instance of Anglo-Saxon "bisignisse" meaning "anxiety" or "solicitude" can also be found.[31] Nevertheless, it seems not to have been in wide circulation until the end of the fourteenth century, when it developed a range of meanings from "industry" and "diligence" to the familiar "task appointed or undertaken; a person's official duty [or] function."[32] "Businesse" could still refer to troubles and anxieties, but unlike the Latin *labor,* it seems to have carried less of the negative connection to *physical* labor. Something similar can be said of "occupacioun." The *MED*'s first citation for this word is dated 1325, but the first citation in which it meant an "activity," an "exercise," a "craft," a "trade," a "profession," or a "business"—denotations that are relevant to this discussion—is dated 1387, precisely when Gower is working on the *Confessio.* What is striking is that, like those of "besinesse," the connotations of "occupacion" were overwhelmingly either neutral or positive.[33] This suggests that "occupacioun" was almost certainly not associated with traditional medieval ideologies that identified work with backbreaking physical toil or with punishment for sin.

Two points stand out from this brief philological survey. First, the thirteenth and fourteenth centuries were times of growth in the part of the English lexicon relating to work. Even more significant, however, than the growth in the *number* of relevant labor words is what seems to have been a significant *semantic* growth in this area. Even long-established words like "work" developed new meanings toward the end of the fourteenth century.[34] As a rule, the newly developed meanings did not bear such negative

---

[29] *MED,* "labour," n., definitions 1(a-c) all refer to hard manual work, in particular, agricultural work. Definition 1(d), however, refers to "mental work," and, here again, a quotation from the *Confessio* (IV.2396) is the first citation. Meanings given under definition 4 (a-c) all refer to generalized troubles and difficulties, mental anguish, and even disease. These latter meanings all developed around the end of the fourteenth century.

[30] *OED,* "busy," a., definition 1.a., "occupied with constant attention," is not found until 1225. Definition 4.a., "constantly or habitually occupied," is not found until about the same time.

[31] *OED,* "business," n., definition 5.

[32] *OED,* "business," sb., definitions 1, 2, 8, and 1.a. See also *MED,* "bisinesse," n., definitions 1 and 2. The entries in the *MED,* even more than those in the *OED,* suggest that "bisinesse" carried far fewer negative connotations than did "werk," "labour," "servise," or "travail."

[33] *MED,* "occupacioun," n., definitions 2, 3(a, b, c).

[34] The plural form, "works," for example, first came to refer to "moral actions

connotations as "strenuous toil," "trouble," and "affliction." Evidence from the history of the English lexicon, then, supports historians' claims that the fourteenth century was a critical time in the history of English labor ideology. The expansion of lexicon and meanings in the labor vocabulary is at least circumstantial evidence suggesting both an interest in work issues and an ideological movement toward the Humanist work ethic.

Second, John Gower seems to have been a participant in the cultural discussion of work. Genius's discussion of labor, and, in particular "mental labor," for example, indicates that Gower was wrestling with work ideologies in general.[35] Gower stretched the traditional English lexicon for "love's labor." He was not only the first to employ more established words like "servise" to denote love's labor, but he also used newly coined words like "occupacioun." Moreover, two of his favorite words for love's labor, "besinesse" and "occupacioun," to a great degree carried positive connotations, suggesting the dignity of work.

Moving from lexicon to the level of argument, one first notes that Book IV's major structuring principle is taken from the traditional schema of the branches of the vice of *acedia*. Genius begins his treatment of sloth in love with the subcategory of "lachesce," procrastination. He continues with treatments of pusillanimity, forgetfulness, negligence, idleness, somnolence, and despair. Particularly revealing of the schema's traditional foundation is the inclusion of pusillanimity and despair, medieval branches of the vice no longer associated with Modern English "sloth."

Under the section on idleness, however, concerns about productivity and the proper use of time arise. When Genius introduces the subject of idleness, he employs a traditional image—the cat who would eat fish without wetting his paws—to suggest that idle men cannot be successful in their endeavors.[36] Since the reason for this confession was Amans's despair over his lack of success in love, Genius asks whether he is guilty of idleness. But Amans vehemently denies that he is idle. On the contrary, he claims to be continually busy with love's labor. When pressed to define his labor, Amans describes how he passes his days trying to meet every desire of his lady:

---

considered in relation to justification" at the end of the fourteenth century (*OED*, "work," sb., definition I.1.b.).

[35] IV.2363–700. The Latin gloss says that the poet "ponit exemplum de diligencia predecessorum, qui ad tocius humani generis doctrinam et auxilium suis continuis laboribus et studiis, gracia mediante diuina, artes et sciencias primitus inuenerunt" [gives examples of the diligence of (his) predecessors, who, by means of continual work and study, originally discovered the arts and sciences for the teaching and aid of the entire human race]. The Latin verse introducing this section explicitly defends the value of mental labor over that of physical labor: "Set qui doctrine causa fert mente labores, / Preualet et merita perpetuata parat" [But he who toils in mind for wisdom's sake / Prevails, for he lays up perpetual meed]. The translation of the latter is taken from Siân Echard and Claire Fanger, *The Latin Verses in the "Confessio Amantis": An Annotated Translation* (East Lansing, 1991), 53.

[36] IV.1105–11. On common medieval images of sloth, see Wenzel, *Sin of Sloth*, 105ff.

> What thing sche bit me don, I do,
> And wher sche bidt me gon, I go,
> And whanne hir list to clepe, I come.
> Thus hath sche fullich overcome
> Min ydelnesse til I sterve. (IV.1160–64)

Among his particular works of love, Amans cites playing with the lady's dog or birds and chatting with her maids. He recites Ovidian songs of love and helps lift his lady onto her horse if she wants to go out riding. If all else fails, he simply waits in attendance and invents what he calls "tariinges," another relatively new term in Gower's English, which carried the negative connotations of the Modern English "loitering."[37] As I remarked earlier, the oft-noted irony here is that much of what Amans defines as "love's labor" is from a Christian moral perspective the essence of idleness.

While Genius at first agreed with Amans that his "tariinges" were legitimate examples of "love's labor," he later attempts to define "love's labor" more closely and introduces a distinction based on gender: the proper labor of women, unlike the "idle" Rosiphelee, is simply to allow themselves to love and be loved, while the proper labor for men is knightly combat.[38] At this point the usually docile Amans begins vigorously to disagree with his confessor. He denies that engaging in battle is truly "love's labor" on grounds that are both moral and pragmatic. Christ, he argues, forbids us to kill other men, even if they are heathens (IV.1659–63). Amans's real objection, however, is grounded in concerns about productivity, for he continues, "What scholde I winne over the Se, / If I mi ladi loste at hom?" (IV.1664–65): what good is work if it does not produce the intended results? To be sure, Amans's position here is inconsistent. Although earlier he argued that he was not guilty of idleness because he kept himself busy, he now admits that just keeping busy, just countering the vice of sloth, is not enough. One's work must produce results. In a key passage, he reasons:

> Bot thogh my besinesse laste,
> Al is bot ydel ate laste,
> For whan theffect is ydelnesse,
> I not what thing is besinesse. (IV.1757–60)

In the traditional schema of the Seven Deadly Sins, the antidote to idleness was simply to be busy, but Amans's position, approaching the Humanist work ethic, is that "besinesse" without productivity is just another example of "ydelnesse." In short, Amans here tests the traditional medieval work ideology and finds it wanting. Indeed, when one considers how Amans here highlights the unproductive nature of his own courtship, one cannot help but believe that he might well have found Chaucer's witty remark about the

---

[37] *OED*, "tarrying," sb., definition 1, first attested in the period 1340–70.
[38] IV.1620–44. See also Genius's insistent comments at IV.1804–10 and IV.2029–39, where he cites the example of Lancelot.

Man of Law appropriate: "Nowher so bisy a man as he ther nas, / And yet he semed bisier than he was" (I.321–22). It is significant that, following this exchange, Genius leads a discussion on the "great workers" of history, emphasizing in each case the productive contributions made by their work (IV.2363–2700).

Book IV of the *Confessio,* then, contains a dialogue among various ideologically colored voices. There is the voice of the traditional medieval ideology of work based on the schema of the Seven Deadly Sins. There are aristocratic voices which speak, on the one hand, of "tariinges" (the fruit of aristocratic *otium*) being the true work of love and, on the other, of knightly combat as love's proper work. There is also, I would argue, the voice of a new work ethic, which insists that legitimate work must also produce concrete results. It is impossible, however, to align these voices neatly with the two major characters, Amans and Genius. Although Amans's position on love's labor through a large part of Book IV seems to be influenced by this new work ethic, he not only endorses his "tariinges" as legitimate work, but he also uses "travail," a word bearing pejorative connotations, as well as the more positive "besinesse" to refer to love's labor. At the same time, although in many ways Genius's presentation of love's labor clearly reflects the traditional ethic of work's value arising from its opposition to *acedia,* it is Genius, not Amans, who not only calls love by the newly borrowed "occupacion" but also warns Amans against the wasting of time (IV.1485–87). In short, Gower's ideology of labor in Book IV is neither simply traditional nor fixed and neatly packaged. It is an ideology in process, mirroring to some extent ideological shifts in his language and his society. Book IV is, then, a "site of action" in which various late-medieval labor ideologies undergo a "sustained literary engagement."

The conclusion of the *Confessio Amantis* adds another layer of complexity. At this point, Amans has finished his confession to Genius, but his spiritual condition, his passion in love, seems no closer to being healed. After relating the story of Apollonius of Tyre, Genius changes his position on love's labor. He now uses the word "servise" to refer to love's labor, and by using that word brings to the foreground the social context of love's work, in particular, the obligations owed by love's servant to the one served. But it is Venus who is served by love labor, and what does she expect? While Genius notes that the rewards of love ("mede") come from "servise" (VIII.2009–12), he says that "servise" must be carried out according to reason, and reason says that love's labor should be directed to procreation. As a result, Genius argues that *for Amans* romantic love is unreasonable "servise," and he counsels Amans to turn his love to a different master, Christ.

For Amans, then, the love of Christ alone is productive. The ultimate reason why Amans's erotic love can never be productive is withheld from the reader until the point when Venus returns to heal Amans of his malady. It is at this point that the link between Amans and the author John Gower is forcefully established (VIII.2321), and the reader finds out that Amans/

Gower is simply too old to enter into a productive relationship with the woman he loves. Venus rejects Amans from her court because his labor can never be productive, but the definition of productivity has changed. Whereas in Book IV Amans conceived productive labor as successful courtship, in Book VIII Venus presents productive labor as successful copulation. Copulation is, after all, another form of love's labor, and the Middle English verbs "swinken" and "labouren" were regularly used to refer to the sexual act.[39] In dismissing Amans, Venus employs metaphors from the worlds of rural labor and business: Amans cannot "plow his field," and he cannot pay the marriage debt (VIII.2421-27, VIII.2431-32). Amans's labor is "an ydel peine" (VIII.2418) because he is impotent. Venus's solution is that he make "a beau retret" (VIII.2416) from the labor of courtship, and to that end she gives him a "Peire of Bedes" with the words "por reposer" engraved on it (VIII.2904-7). Venus removes Cupid's arrow and, in essence, allows Amans/ Gower the privilege of monastic *otium*. He can spend his time praying and writing literature dealing with morality.

At this point, it would be satisfying to conclude that in Venus's remarks, one finds unambiguous evidence of the influence of a new, production-oriented work ideology. However, evidence from the literary tradition of "love's labor" complicates the issue. Once Venus changes the definition of productivity in love, her treatment of love's labor comes very close to that of the character Reason in Jean de Meun's portion of the *Roman de la Rose*.[40] As I mentioned above, Reason defines love as "repos travaillant an touz termes" (4296), but for Reason loving "par amour" is idleness, a "fole emprise" (5761). The real work of love is always procreative copulation. For Reason sexual pleasure is simply the reward given to a good laborer (*cist ovrier*) for reproducing the species (5733-64). It is likely, then, that in Book VIII Gower's presentation of love's labor is rooted just as firmly in the text of the *Roman de la Rose* as it is in changes in contemporary labor ideologies. What we see here, then, is further evidence that both social and literary forces are in play in the final book of the *Confessio*.

To conclude, Gower's treatment of love's labor in the *Confessio* condemns the wasteful idleness of loving "par amour" every bit as strongly as Reason's discourse in *Le Roman de la Rose* did, but the *Confessio* is far from traditional in its treatment of love's labor. Gower's masterpiece does not speak with a single ideological voice, and the ideological "taste" of its condemnation of *acedia* is rooted not only in the traditional rhetoric of "love's labor" but also in the changing labor ideologies of his own culture.

---

[39] *MED*, "swinken," vb., definition 2(c) and "labouren," v., definition 1(a).

[40] On Gower's debt to the *Roman de la Rose*, see Yeager, *John Gower's Poetic*, 34, and Olsson, *Structures of Conversion*, 3.

Remembering Origins: Gower's Monstrous Body Poetic

Eve Salisbury

> *Pacem orate manu, pacem laudate sedentes*
> *magnanimi; pacis solum inviolabile pignus*
>
> [Pray for peace with an open hand.
> Praise peace, high-minded,
> When you sit in judgment's seat, and keep
> Your vow of peace alone inviolate][1]
> —Faltonia Betitia Proba

John Gower's *Vox Clamantis* has often been disparaged by scholars as heavy-handed social criticism neither aesthetically pleasing nor historically accurate. Eric W. Stockton, the poem's translator, for instance, decries the work as "wearisome" and repetitively "lachrymose"; the modern historian, R. B. Dobson, calls it "monotonous" and "pessimistic."[2] G. C. Macaulay's now (in)famous description of the poet's technique as outright "schoolboy plagiarism" has vitiated perceptions of the poem by playing upon our disdain for such practices.[3]

Defining what the poem is by genre has proven to be equally troubled. Called *compilatio*, "satire," "complaint," "lament," "historical narrative," even "encyclopedic political complaint," the poem resists stable, coherent, identifiable, and "pure" taxonomies.[4] Its gargantuan length (10,265 lines

---

I am indebted to Ronald B. Herzman, who noted the monstrous characteristics of an early draft, and Russell A. Peck, whose comments rendered the final product less so.

[1] Faltonia Betitia Proba, *The Golden Bough and the Oaken Cross: The Vergilian Cento of Faltonia Betitia Proba*, ed. and trans. Elizabeth Clark and Diane Hatch (*American Academy of Religion Texts and Translations* 5, 1981), 92.

[2] *Major Works of John Gower: The Voice of One Crying and the Tripartite Chronicle*, trans. Eric W. Stockton (Seattle, 1962), 32. Hereafter cited in the text as "Stockton" followed by page number. R. B. Dobson, *The Peasants' Revolt* (London, 1970), 387. In this work the poem's value as a reliable historical document is questioned simply because it represents a literary and often subjective analysis of contemporary events.

[3] *The Complete Works of John Gower: The Latin Works*, ed. G. C. Macaulay (Oxford, 1902), xxxii.

[4] These classifications derive from Macaulay, ed., *The Latin Works*; Stockton, *Major Works of John Gower*; Paul Miller, "John Gower, Satiric Poet," in *Gower's "Confessio*

of elegiac verse), disturbing subject matter (social and political disorder), internal hybridization of generic forms—dream vision, homily, epistle, beast fable, fictional autobiography, allegory, history—rapid shifts of tense, sudden interruptions of chronology, even the poet's contentious tone, fuel the fires of postmodern critics. Furthermore, revisions, omissions, and the late addition of Book I to the body of the poem in ten of eleven manuscripts, contribute to the difficulty of defining exactly what this work is, where it belongs—literature? history? neither? both?—and what contribution it makes to a postmodern understanding of a medieval past so profoundly removed from us by time.

The fact is, medieval literature generally dispenses with strict adherence to singular generic models, and many medieval authors seem to take delight in mixing genres in various ways. All, for example, that can be said about the *Roman de la Rose* for certain is that it is a dream vision and it is lengthy. Recognizable genres such as *compilatio*, debate, lament, satire, parody, and romance flow together with virtually no acknowledgment of the boundaries between them. Nonetheless, the *Roman de la Rose* sustains a kind of coherence that arises not from its "form" but from its "subject matter." The same may be said for the *Vox Clamantis* whose form is determined by its subject matter rather than by the conventions of unadulterated generic models. Yet the *Vox Clamantis* is a unique literary experiment, one might say Gower's poetic Frankenstein. Of the poetry of the time, it alone cries from the wilderness in an attempt to unveil the corrupt political structures from which the monstrous events of the Rising of 1381 emerge.

Jeffrey Jerome Cohen's attempts to construct a culture theory out of a topos such as monstrosity prove useful at the outset of this essay in grasping Gower's composition strategies. According to Cohen, monsters are "disturbing hybrids whose externally incoherent bodies resist attempts to include them in any systematic structuration ... a form suspended between forms that threatens to smash distinctions."[5] The poem, as monster, assumes an imposing position in both social and literary history. At the juncture between genres and disciplinary fields, it moves in two directions at once; written in a "dead" language, it arises from another language world and threatens to exclude living speakers of English. Moreover, its disruptive prosody, fragments of which are ripped from the texts of other authors from other times and fused together with the poet's own verse, renders the *Vox* disturbingly hybrid. As Cohen further observes: "Monsters are never created *ex nihilo*, but through a process of fragmentation and recombination in which elements are extracted 'from various forms'

Amantis": Responses & Reassessments, Alastair Minnis, ed. (Woodbridge, 1983), 79–105. Janet Coleman, *Medieval Readers and Writers, 1350–1400* (New York, 1981), 128; and Steven Justice, *Writing and Rebellion: England in 1381* (Berkeley, 1994), 208.

   [5] Jeffrey Jerome Cohen, ed. *Monster Theory: Reading Culture* (Minnesota, 1996), 11.

and then assembled as the monster."[6] Gower might well agree since his poem captures the aberrations of society in the very method of his recombinant technique. But it is not schoolboy plagiarism that Gower commits, as Macaulay would have it; rather, it is a technique of Latin *cento* poetry that requires fragments to be taken from the works of venerated ancient *auctores* and rearranged into a "patchwork cloak," differing completely in subject matter from the original texts. An enormous exercise in memory and poetic skill with a tradition extending from the Byzantine past to the late Middle Ages, *cento* is a practice that merits admiration.

It is probable, R. F. Yeager argues, that Gower's *cento* methods derive from a fourth-century Roman poet—Faltonia Betitia Proba—whose *Cento Vergilianus de laudibus Christi* transformed the works of Vergil—the *Aeneid, Eclogues,* and *Georgics*—into a biblical history from Genesis to the Resurrection.[7] Infused with the enthusiasm of a newly inspired Christian convert, Proba's poem marks a significant contribution to the adoption of Vergil's texts into Christian ideology and the promotion of Vergil as a Christian prophet. But by decree of the Bishop of Rome in the late fifth century, influenced perhaps by Jerome's view of *cento* as "puerile" and "silly," or, as some scholars suggest, because this particular *cento* was written by a woman, Proba's poem was relegated to the canonical margins where it was to be used for private reading only. There it remained until it found its way into the manuscripts of monastic libraries where it was considered suitable for the instruction of boys.[8] By the fourteenth century not only were manuscripts containing Proba's work available in England, but positive endorsements from Isidore of Seville in both *De Viris Illustribus* and the *Etymologiae* and Boccaccio in *De Claris Mulieribus* rendered her work a desirable model for experiments in composition.[9]

Gower takes Proba's techniques a step beyond the single-author approach, however, by choosing verbatim fragments from an authorial retinue which not only includes Ovid's *Metamorphoses, Tristia, Fasti, Amores,* et al., but also Peter Riga's *Aurora,* Godfrey of Viterbo's *Pantheon,* Nigel de Longchamps's *Speculum Stultorum,* Alexander Neckam's *De Vita Monochorum,* and others. By splicing fragments from these texts of the past into his own verse, the poet creates a discourse we might call carnivalesque since it relativizes and contradicts itself in a disguised double-voiced manner; it allows the poet a free rein with his critique while at the same time

---

[6] Ibid.

[7] R. F. Yeager, "Did Gower Write *Cento?*," in *John Gower: Recent Readings* (Kalamazoo, 1989), 113–32.

[8] Patricia Wilson-Kastner, et al., *A Lost Tradition: Women Writers of the Early Church* (Washington, 1981), 37. "*Cento* remained a popular work as a school text well into the Middle Ages. Its presence is attested to in the catalogues of many monastic libraries through the twelfth century, often being bound with Aldhelm's *Symposia* and *Enigmas,* poems of Cyprian, Gregory, and Fortunatus, or with works of Adelard and Seneca: all of which were used in the instruction of boys."

[9] Yeager, "Did Gower Write *Cento?*," 122–23.

affords him a measure of personal safety. This most politically charged of
Gower's long poems attacks the failings of all three estates with a fervor
that few other poems of the time can claim. Consisting of seven books, it
begins, in all but one of its eleven manuscripts, with a dream vision of the
Rising of 1381 that inspires in Gower a scathing critique of the rebels. But
because Gower not only indicts the rebels, but members of a powerful
ecclesiastical audience *and* the king, he places himself in political jeopardy,
a position for which the poet, in Eric Stockton's opinion, should be ad-
mired for "speaking out fearlessly to his sovereign, a man who later ruth-
lessly exiled or executed several of the most important nobles of the
realm."[10] Yet it is not without fear that Gower speaks, and his strategies
for constructing a monstrous poetic reflect that concern.

In brief, the term "monstrous" that I am employing in my approach to
the poem, especially the dream vision of Book I, operates in several ways:
(1) It signifies the monstrous human behavior Gower saw enacted in the
Rising of 1381 and the monstrous political structures from which those
events emerged. (2) It reflects his methods of demonstration in the recom-
bination of fragments excerpted from some of the most provocative liter-
ature of the day. (3) It points to a species of maternal imagination inspired
by Proba and her *cento* techniques. By recombining fragments from Ovid
and others Gower's monster startles and instructs simultaneously.

Gower had a strong theological precedent for his constructions of the
monstrous. Both early references in Augustine's *City of God* and a more
complete definition in Isidore of Seville's *Etymologiae* indicate that mon-
sters were thought to be integral "signs" of the divine will with specific
functions of their own.[11] Etymologically related to the Latin *monstrare*,
"to show," and *monere*, "to warn," a monster is a "portent," "prodigy,"
or "omen," a sign of future events that indicates the fulfillment of eschato-
logical history. In *Etymologiae*, under the section entitled "Man and
Monsters," Isidore explains:

> portents are things which seem to have been born contrary to na-
> ture, but in truth, they are not contrary to nature because they exist

[10] Stockton, trans. *Major Works of John Gower*, 13.

[11] *Augustine: Political Writings*, trans. Michael W. Tkacz and Douglas Kries (Indian-
apolis, 1994), 178. Augustine says: "The word 'sign' comes from the verb for portending,
that is, for revealing beforehand; and 'prophecy' from the words for warning beforehand,
that is for announcing the future." (From *City of God*, Book XXI, chap. 8). Isidore of
Seville, *Etymologiarum Sive Originum, Libri xx*, W. M. Lindsay, ed. (Oxford, 1911; repr.
1991), 26–27. The Latin passage reads:
> Portentum ergo fit non contra naturam, sed contra quam est nota natura.
> Portenta autem et ostenta, monstra atque prodigia ideo nuncupantur, quod
> portendere atque ostendere, monstrare ac praedicare aliqua futura videntur.
> Prodigia, quod porro dicant, id est future praedicant. Monstra vero a monitu
> dicta, quod aliquid significando demonstrent, sive quod statim monstrent quid
> appareat; et hoc proprietatis est, abusione tamen scriptorum plerumque corrum-
> pitur. Quaedam autem portentorum creationes in significationibus futuris cons-
> tituta videntur.

by the divine will, since the Creator's will is the nature of every-
thing created.... A portent, therefore, does not arise contrary to
nature but by what nature is understood to be. Portents are also
called "signs," "monstrosities," and "prodigies" because they seem
to "portend" and to "point out," to "demonstrate," and to predict
future happenings.

Isidore's monsters which "seem to be have been born contrary to nature"
refer to abnormal births, both animal and human, thought to be sent by
God to signal cataclysmic change. Their existence was justified by inclu-
sion into the universal order; hence, monsters could not arise "contrary to
nature but contrary to what nature is *understood* to be" (emphasis mine)
because they were born for the purpose of signaling the divine will. Their
function to "demonstrate" or "point out" and "predict future happen-
ings" testified to imminent change in the natural order of things, a signal,
in many cases, of God's negative response to unethical human behavior.
Gower's poetic endeavor embodies the admonitory and premonitory as-
pects of the monstrous; by adopting a prophetic voice that cries from the
wilderness he signals the very changes monsters were thought to portend.

But the etymological tradition from which Isidore writes is not the
only source for understanding how monsters fit into the scheme of things
or even what they were imagined to signify, for among the laity there ex-
isted a [p]opular belief that monsters, at least those recognizably human,
could be formed by the workings of a wayward maternal imagination.
According to Marie Hélène Huet, this persistent belief held that the birth
mother had a formative effect on the fetus if she were engaged in wild
imaginings during copulation, either in the contemplation of external
images or in the wandering of her mind away from the activities taking
place. When the resultant progeny of such unfocused occasion did not
resemble its parents, as anomalous births presumably did not, its resem-
blance was thought to have derived from the images on which the mother
focused at the time of conception. Then, because "monsters" captured the
attention of those who witnessed their emergence into the world, they
were brought immediately to the public arena where they were read as
"prodigies," "omens," and "signs" of impending collective doom.[12] With-
out implicating paternal agency as the cause for the monster's presence in
the world, the hybrid creature pointed back to the unfulfilled desires of the
birth mother. Gower's appropriation of the techniques of Proba—his
desire to transform the texts of authors of the past into an appropriate
vehicle for his subject matter—operates much in the ways of the monstrous
maternal imagination just described. From his unfulfilled desires for an
ideal, peaceful society and the monstrous images that capture Gower's

---

[12] Marie-Hélène Huet, *Monstrous Imagination* (Cambridge, 1993), 6. "Monstrous
births were understood as warnings and public testimony; they were thought to be
'demonstrations' of the mother's unfulfilled desires."

attention as he engages in the act of artistic creation, emerge a deliberate monstrous poetic.

Evidence of the crossover between biological reproduction and literary reproduction is important to delineate here because it provides an explanation of how Gower's monstrous poem is determined not simply by formal concerns, in the "natural" order of art, but by subject matter. Moreover, this process is bound up with medieval notions of matter *per se*. Medieval scholastic literary theory, based upon Aristotle's *Physics* and *Metaphysics*, follows the notions of the Philosopher's four causes governing all activity and change in the universe. Alastair Minnis explains:

> Hence, the author would be discussed as the "efficient cause," or motivating agent of the text; his materials as its "material cause": his literary style and structure, as twin aspects of the "formal cause," the *forma tractandi* and the *forma tractatus* respectively; while his ultimate end or objective in writing would be considered as the "final cause."[13]

But as feminist scholars point out, Aristotle's concepts of human reproduction, as outlined in the *Generation of Animals*, permeates all of his philosophy including that of the *Physics* and the *Metaphysics*. Thus scholastic literary theory, which follows from these texts more closely than it does the *Poetics*, is also implicitly gendered—"matter," the passive principle, or the "material cause," is female, while "form," the active principle, or "efficient cause" is male.[14] The author, acting as mover and purveyor of form or as motivating agent, shapes his text in the manner appropriate to his subject matter. The product of the artist/father's endeavor or the objective in writing is the "final cause," or, in this case, the progeny.

Reproductive mimesis is also present in a tradition of *artes poeticae* that itself fuses poetry and rhetoric together in a hybrid manner. Geoffrey of Vinsauf's *Poetria Nova*, a text Gower knew well, espouses a philosophy of poetry that uses reproductive metaphors to explain the process of molding subject matter. Poetry is "born" out of *materia;* "matter" is then clothed with words and served by poetry which would "make due preparation for attendance upon its mistress."[15] Male authorship mimics the role of the father in this construct; as purveyor of "form," the author shapes his text in the manner deemed appropriate to the subject matter, which passively accepts the form imposed upon it by the author. Matter, because it is the maternal principle in this equation, has the potentiality to become whatever the author desires. Gower's appropriation of *cento* techniques from

---

[13] Alastair Minnis, A. B. Scott, with David Wallace, eds., *Medieval Literary Theory and Criticism c. 1100–c. 1375: The Commentary Tradition* (Oxford, 1988), 3.

[14] See Lynda Lange, for example. "Woman is Not a Rational Animal," in *Discovering Reality: Feminist Perspectives on Epistemology, Metaphysics, Methodology, and Philosophy of Science,* eds. Sandra Harding and Merill B. Hintikka (Boston, 1983), 1–15.

[15] Geoffrey of Vinsauf, *Poetria Nova,* trans. Margaret F. Nims (Toronto, 1967), 17.

Proba complicates the configuration of desire by reversing the "natural" order of art. Rather than imposing his paternity upon the poem, Gower re-members source material in a manner commensurate with Isidore's notion of monsters as "prodigies," "signs," and "omens." Gower has appropriated the power of the maternal imagination to engender a monstrous body poetic suitable to subject matter that functions to point out and to warn his audience of impending collective doom.

To Point Out and To Warn

Because Gower's monstrous progeny both "points out" and warns, it is heavily infused with deictic signs, which, according to Émile Benveniste, exist only in relation to the present moment, the "here" and "now" of the author. Certain demonstrative adjectives, adverbs, or directives—"this," "that," "here," "there," "now," "then," "inside," "outside"—point to the temporal and spatial location of objects as perceived from a particular point of view at a particular moment.[16] In the fourteenth century "pointing" was signaled by some kind of verbal detail, something on the order of *nota bene* devices which call attention to specific passages. Pointing could be accomplished by emphasizing detail in some way, by creating an end rhyme, by repeating a pattern, or deviating from one, by *brevitas, amplificatio,* or by omission.[17] Gower uses these methods of pointing in his Latin poem to "demonstrate" the proof needed to support his assertions. His careful selection of texts combined with his own verse in *cento* style allows his monster to point in two directions simultaneously.

Gower begins the *Vox* with a pastoral prelude to his vision of the Rising of 1381 after situating his narrative within its historical context, "it happened in the fourth year of King Richard." He then creates a setting of Golden Age harmony by fusing fragments of four of Ovid's works: *Metamorphoses, Fasti, Tristia,* and the *Amores* [bold type is mine]:

27 **Purpurea residens velatus veste refulsit**
   Cuius in aspectu secula cuncta patent   *Met.* II. 23–44
   Ante suum solium gradiuntur quotuor anni
   Tempora, que variis compta diebus erant:
   Tunc tamen a dextris stetit alba propinquior estas
32 Serta gerens, et eam cuncta creata colunt.
   Omnia **tunc** florent, **tunc** est nova temporis etas.
   Ludit et in pratis luxuriando pecus.   *Fasti,* I. 156
   Tunc fecundus ager, pecorum *tunc* hora creandi
   Tunc renovatque suos reptile quodque iocos

---

[16] Émile Benveniste, *Problemes de Linguistique Generale* 1, (Paris, 1966), 252–54.

[17] See J. A. Burrow, *Ricardian Poetics: Chaucer, Gower, Langland and the 'Gawain' Poet* (London, 1971).

37 *Prataque pubescunt variorum flore colorum*
    Indocilique loquax gutture cantat avis   *Tristia,* III. xii. 7–8
    *Queque diu latuit **tunc** se qua tolat in auras*
    Invenit occultam fertilis herba viam
    Tuncque pruinosos mollitur Lucifer agros.   *Amores,* I. vi, 65
    Inque suos pullos concitat ales opus.   (*VC* I. i, 27–47)

[Clad in his purple robe (Phoebus) sat gleaming, and all ages lay re-
vealed to his sight. Before his throne passed the four seasons of the
year, which were formed of their respective kinds of days. But at
that time fair Summer stood near his right hand, bearing her gar-
lands, and all created things loved her. Then everything flourished,
then there was a new epoch of time, and the cattle sported wanton-
ly in the new fields. Then the land was fertile, then was the hour
for the herds to mate, and it was then that the reptile might renew
its sports. The meadows were covered with the bloom of different
flowers, and the chattering bird sang with its untutored throat.
Then too the teeming grass which had long lain concealed found a
hidden path through which it lifted itself into the gentle breezes.
Lucifer thawed out the frosty fields, and the mother bird sped to its
work for its young.][18]

The initial line—*purpurea residens velatus veste refulsit* (clad in his purple
robe, [he] sat gleaming)—is excerpted from Book II of *Metamorphoses* where
Ovid describes Phoebus just prior to Phaëton's vision of him. In Ovid's
story, Phaëton, the illegitimate son of Phoebus, insists on driving the char-
iot of the sun despite his father's objections. He fails; the horses career out
of control; the earth is singed with the fiery blast; and Jupiter finally
catapults the rebellious youth out of the sky with a thunderbolt; the boy
then falls into the sea where he drowns. Gower's use of the line to describe
Phoebus establishes a natural order of things, the sun's omnipotence and
temporal power: *cuius in aspectu secula cuncta patent* (all ages lay revealed
in his sight) as he sits in dazzling enthronement. While the king looks calm-
ly over Gower's realm, there is no hint of the disruption soon to occur.
That this *cento* passage comes so soon after Gower's introduction to the
"fourth year of King Richard," suggests a correlation between contem-
porary events and Ovid's text.

From the *Fasti,* Ovid's exposition on the myths and legends associated
with the feast days of the Roman calendar, Gower incorporates fragments
used by Ovid in a dialogue between his narrator and Janus about impend-
ing change. In Ovid's poem, the two discuss whether the year should begin
with spring when—*Ludit et in pratis luxuriando pecus* (cattle cavort wanton-
ly in the fields)—or in the middle of hoary winter. For Ovid, the mythic

---

[18] Ovidian quotations derive from Loeb Library editions of Arthur Leslie Wheeler,
trans., *Tristia* (1953); Grant Showerman, trans., *Amores* (1914); Sir James George Frazer,
trans., *Fasti* (1951); Frank Justus Miller, trans., *Metamorphoses* (1944).

origins of the Roman calendar and the regulation of procreative activities in accordance with them are paramount. The two-faced Janus looks both forward to the spring and backward to the winter, marking a pivotal moment in Nature's cycle. Gower's use of Ovid's quotations suggest that there is a design for universal order—the regulation of the world in which everything behaves according to Nature—in which seasons occur in regular, predictable cycles, in which even rude-minded men find an eager mate. Other lines from the *Fasti* similar in tone and themes of seasonal change—winter to spring—are taken from a discourse on how war is aborted by the intercession of weeping mothers with babes in arms spoken by Mars who promotes the pursuits of peace for the first time. Mars speaks of the Latin mothers who now rightfully observe the rites on his day: "for in their travail they both fight and pray."[19] But the presence of Mars, the Roman god of war, and Janus, a figure of chaos, indicates an underlying potential for disorder despite the gods' assertions to the contrary.

Ovid's *Tristia* supplies the next fragments: *Prataque pubescunt variorum flore colorum / Indocilique loquax gutture cantat avis* (The meadows were abloom with many-colored flowers, the chattering bird sang with its untutored throat). Ovid speaks of springtime in Tomis, the place of exile from which he laments his alienation from Roman society and culture. He specifically laments his separation from Roman festivals where "the stage is full of life ... ablaze with warring passions."[20] From Ovid's fragments, Gower constructs a prelapsarian past, where chattering birds sing according to Nature, before being hideously blasted away by the present moment. Gower changes Ovid's description of Saturnalian Rome in the present tense "*nunc*" to the past tense "*tunc*," to establish a past voice used to comment on the present moment, the "now" of the fourteenth century.

From Ovid's *Amores* Gower adapts a line—*Iamque pruinosus molitur Lucifer axes* (morning star already at its frosty zenith)—which refers to the time at which a lover dreams of amorous conquest while standing outside his lover's locked door. Unable to gain entrance, his hopes of spending the night in secret embrace are shattered by the rising sun. Gower uses the line to reinforce the fragility of his paradisiacal ethos. He refers to the "morning star" as "Lucifer" who, in his classical context, performs a benevolent function of thawing out frosty fields—*pruinosos molitur Lucifer agros*—to facilitate the activities of Nature. Lucifer is Gower's portent for coming events, a sign of thwarted love and impending rebellion. All of these fragments taken verbatim or only slightly adapted have been transferred from their original contexts and recontextualized to establish a setting of tentative harmony, concord, and order, which in the *Vox* is almost instantaneously blasted away by the raging discord of social insurgency. Gower's choice of Ovid's texts creates a temporal duality, that, for Andrew Gallo-

---

[19] Frazer, trans., *Fasti*, 12.

[20] Wheeler, trans., *Tristia*, 149.

way, evokes a "sense of entering a world that is both 'present' and perspectivally 'removed' from the moment of mid-June 1381."[21] The poet is both "here" and "there," "inside" and "outside" the events of *that* time in June.

The heavy concentration of Ovidian texts early in the dream vision of Book I establishes a temporal link to the festivities of the Roman Saturnalia, which, for Gower, empowers his carnivalesque discourse. For Mikhail Bakhtin the festivities of Roman Saturnalia extend to medieval feast-day activities when a "two-faced Janus"—one face of official Church culture, the other, of popular culture—looked to the past for stability and to the future with expectations for change and renewal:

> Roman saturnalia announced the return of the Golden Age. Thus the medieval feast had, as it were, two faces of Janus. Its official ecclesiastical face was turned to the past and sanctioned the existing order, but the face of the people of the marketplace looked into the future and laughed, attending the funeral of the past and the present. The marketplace feast opposed the protective, timeless stability, the unchanging established order and ideology, and stressed the element of change and renewal.[22]

Feast days, including the feast of the ass and the feast of fools, allowed the free expression of mockery and criticism of official Church culture. Nearly every Church feast had its comic folk aspect, which was also traditionally recognized. Such for instance, were the parish feasts, usually marked by fairs and varied open-air amusements, with the participation of giants, dwarfs, monsters, and trained animals. Often these occasions were festive, filled with laughter and uninhibited game playing; just as often such occasions had the potential to turn to violence and disorder. Gower establishes his dual temporal perspective by attaching Ovid's fragments to his own verse, virtually textualizing the tensions between official ecclesiastical order and popular desire for change and renewal. The Golden Age harmony underlying the introductory passages is soon displaced by a description of the disruption of London on the Feast of Corpus Christi. Gower's *cento* techniques establish a carnivalesque discourse invested not only with the rejuvenating effects of parodic laughter, but with the anger of social protest.

The day of the invasion of London by the rebels also marked the city's celebration of the Feast of Corpus Christi, an event which itself had a long history of disorder.[23] In the events of the rebellion that day, what began

---

[21] Andrew Galloway, "Gower in His Most Learned Role and the Peasants' Revolt of 1381," *Mediaevalia* 16, (1993 [for 1990]): 329–47. Galloway argues against the notion that history repeats itself. Rather, Gower is acutely aware of historical and cultural differences.

[22] Mikhail Bakhtin, *Rabelais and His World*, trans. Hélène Iswolsky (Bloomington, 1984), 81.

[23] Miri Rubin, *Corpus Christi: The Eucharist in Late Medieval Culture* (Cambridge,

as a sacred celebration of the body of Christ, became instead an unholy parody attended by mock priests serving real pieces of human flesh upon a mock altar. The vicious decapitation of Archbishop Simon Sudbury, performed on Tower Hill before a "delighted mob of thousands" (Stockton, 359), was depicted by chroniclers as a grotesque inversion of the sacred and the profane, cast within a carnivalesque drama. As told by the *Anonimalle* chronicler, the decapitated head of the archbishop with his mitre conspicuously nailed through his skull was born in a mock Corpus Christi procession through the streets of London to the shrine of Westminster Abbey and finally hung at the city gate as a marker of rebel triumph. The arrangement of Sudbury's mitred head with two other official heads that rolled that day—Robert Hales and William Appleton—recalled the "iconography of the Crucifixion," which, according to Steven Justice, was deliberately constructed to register popular dissatisfaction with the corrupt archbishop's inadequate pastoral care.[24] The aftermath of the archbishop's execution, described by Thomas Walsingham as a "*solemnis ludus*" (a solemn game), then escalated into the random execution of Flemish immigrants as well as those who refused fealty to the rebel cause.[25] What began with shouts of "a revelle! a revelle!," initiated a cycle of violence that ended in screams of terror.

For his description of the horrifying events in London that day Gower chooses a couplet from Peter Riga's *Aurora* (Jud. 225–26), the twelfth-century versified Bible, from the Book of Maccabees:

> *Ecce Iovis festiva dies de Corpore Cristi,*
> *Cum furor accinxit urbis utrumque latus:*
> *Precedens alios Capitaneus excitat unus*
> *Rusticus, ut cuncti consequerentur eum.*
> *Ipse viris multis prefultus conterit urbem,*
> *Ense necat cives, concremat igne domos:*
>
> (*VC*, I. xiii, 919–24)

[Behold, it was Thursday, the Festival of Corpus Christi, when madness hemmed in every side of the city. Going ahead of the others,

---

1991). See also Sarah Beckwith, *Christ's Body: Identity, Culture and Society in Late Medieval Writings* (London, 1994).

[24] Justice, *Writing and Rebellion*, 99. "The rebel parody mocked the archbishop's pretensions to speak in Christ's name, projecting the image of the crucified Christ (which the rhetoric of later Lollardy would seek in the persons of the poor, the 'quick images of God,' rather than in the ornate and bejeweled crucifixes visible in church) behind Sudbury's exposed head, as the standard against which he was measured and found wanting."

[25] Paul Strohm, *Hochon's Arrow: The Social Imagination of Fourteenth-Century Texts* (Princeton, 1992). Strohm argues that the chroniclers used carnivalesque discourse to stigmatize the rebels, make them appear as bumbling, illiterate rustics with neither a cohesive philosophy of dissent nor any organized strategy for accomplishing their goals. Steven Justice also argues for the cohesiveness of the rebel cause and the justice of the actions taken against authority figures like Sudbury. (See *Writing and Rebellion*.)

one peasant captain urged them all to follow him. Supportedby his many men, he crushed the city, put the citizens to the sword and burned down the houses (Stockton, 70).]

The lines from the Book of Maccabees refer to Antiochus' invasion of Jerusalem and the abomination of the Temple by idolatrous sacrifice. Gower uses the quotations to link the notorious tyrant with Wat Tyler, the "peasant captain," on whom he lays considerable blame for instigating mob violence that day. Gower characterizes him as a common English jay who, "well-instructed in the art of speaking" incites the crowd to riot: "so the Jackdaw stirred up all the others with his outrageous shouting, and he drew the people's minds toward war" (Stockton, 65). Gower perceives Tyler to be a tyrant of language, violating his followers with his inflammatory speech acts by demolishing the ethical codes of a rhetorical tradition reaching back to Cicero's *De Oratore*. Not surprisingly, the rebel's murder during a meeting with the king the next day quells the raging seas of Gower's dream vision in Book I where Tyler's death is described as propitiation to the gods.

Gower's choice of the *Speculum Stultorum* to signify the asinine behavior of men furthers the carnivalesque discourse the poet has established from the beginning of Book I. Nigel de Longchamps's twelfth-century beast fable has as its hero an ass named Burnellus, who, discontented with the length of his tail, desires to acquire a longer one. After a series of misadventures, he establishes a new religious order to burlesque those already in existence. Highly satirical and Rabelaisian in character, at the heart of the narrative is Nigel's critique of the corrupt practices of existing monastic orders, lines which Gower appropriates to comment upon the misrule he sees in the monastic orders of his own day. "Burnell's order stands highly esteemed," he says, "since it requires what men wish" (Stockton, 194). His repeated criticism focuses on the inefficacy of those in positions of authority, who should provide examples for their charges, but who fail miserably in the attempt.

Gower's *cento* techniques of recombining texts for monstrous effect are not restricted to Book I, however. In Book II he epitomizes his notion with an anatomization of the Latin word *regula* to demonstrate monstrosities of disfigurement: "The original rule for monks has now become curtailed, for *re* has been subtracted from *regula* so that only *gula* is left" (Stockton, 168). Geoffrey of Vinsauf's *Poetria Nova* states that individual words are governed by rules just as words in a sentence are governed by syntax. Each prefix or "head" directs subsequent syllables which then follow sequentially in order to signify the thing desired. If we take *regula* to mean "order" or "regulation" and "*gula*" to mean "gullet," "throat," "neck," as well as "gluttony," then in a brief verbal *solumnis ludus*, the poet enacts the effects of rampant disregard for regulations. His wordplay points expressly to the monstrosities that ensue when rules governing the daily lives of monks become lax; here the stomach supersedes the head as parts of the body designed for other functions overpower reason. That the prefix of the word has been severed from what follows suggests that linguistic and corporate orders are inextricably linked. Like fragmented words or disrupted syntax, social disorder leads to confusion and violence.

These choices of texts provide another layer of meaning for Gower's remonstrations. Fragments from Neckam's *De Vita Monachorum,* though present in Book II where he criticizes monastic practices, are most heavily concentrated in Books IV through VII, the sections that deal not only with monks, as one might expect, but knights, lawyers, judges, the king, and the state of contemporary society. Gower's primary concern is on a rigid adherence to ethical principles which apply not only to the daily lives of all individuals, but especially to those who define and interpret the law. The poet has little tolerance for corruption among those who dictate the laws by which others are subject. His scathing attack on lawyers, which has caused some to believe that he could not have been a lawyer himself, indicates rather that Gower was so familiar with the profession that he could critique it with the intimate knowledge of an insider. For Gower, an unethical lawyer was like a devouring monster, "swallow[ing] up his native land more than the ravenous Scylla swallows up the waves of the sea... enriching himself with property and the goods of others" (Stockton, 222). Gower's critique focuses on the exploitation of the rights of landowners; he uses the *De Vita Monachorum* to speak against the land-grabbing proclivities of property-hungry barristers.

Neckam's *Vita* spills over into an open letter to Richard II whose own rule, marred by scandal and corruption, might be more accurately called "misrule." Subject to the influence of youthful counselors, the king succumbs to the desires of a fourteen-year-old boy; according to at least one chronicler, extravagant at court and niggardly toward his subjects, sexually exploitative, he mistakes "wrongdoing for joking."[26] As if literalizing the warning capability of the monster, a pointing finger calls attention to the passage in which the poet admonishes the king (see fig. 1):

> O pie rex, audi que sit tua regula regni,
> Concordans legi mixtaque iure dei. (*VC*, VI. viii, 582–83)

[Oh, pious king, listen to what should be your rule for kingship in harmony with the law and joined with God's justice (Stockton, 312).]

Gower pleads with Richard to heed God's directives and subject himself to a higher authority. The pointing finger admonishes, even as the *"tuncs"* and *"nuncs"* of the Prologue, the boy-king who seems to be more like an

---

[26] See Ronald Webber, *The Peasants' Revolt: The Uprising in Kent, Essex, East Anglia and London in 1381 During the Reign of King Richard II* (Lavenham, 1980), 39. The Monk of Evesham writes a contemporary description: "of the common stature ... abrupt and stammering in his speech ... prodigal ... extravagantly splendid ... timid and unsuccessful in Foreign war ... arrogant, rapacious ... remaining sometimes till morning in drinking and other excesses that are not to be named."

actor playing a role, like a boy-bishop at Childermass, rather than a responsible monarch enacting his duties. Described later in the *Cronica Tripartita* as the "ranting Prince of Hell" strutting about the medieval stage, Richard is finally equated with the devouring Charybdis: "Just as the furious Charybdis continually drinks from the raging whirlpool of the salt sea and vomits forth, so did the King spew out, upon a people existing—alas!—without law, the pent-up villainy hidden within his breast" (Stockton, 312). Richard, whether in the *Vox* or the *Cronica*, is presented as a gluttonous monster.

Monstrous Political Bodies

Richard's revolt against his subjects constitutes a violation of the prescribed duty of a monarch to uphold the standards of responsible rule. As "head" of the body politic it is the king's duty to govern the lower members of the corporate organism. The ideal arrangement demands that the head govern justly and that the lower members voluntarily submit to its authority. The body politic becomes monstrous only when its health is impaired by transgressions of proper functions by its members. In a bizarre *effictio* Marsilius of Padua describes the construction of such a monstrous body:

> But no, with respect to the form of this body, which ought to consist in the proper order and position of its parts, it will be seen on close examination, to be like a deformed monster. For if an animal's body had its individual members directly joined to its head, who would not regard it as monstrous and useless for the performance of its proper functions? For if the finger or the hand were joined directly to the head, it would not have its proper position, and hence it would not have its proper power, movement and action. But this does not happen when the finger is joined to the hand, the hand to the arms, the arm to the shoulder, the shoulder to the neck, and the neck to the head, all by proper joints. For then the body is given its appropriate form, and the head can give to the other members, one through the other, their proper individual powers in accordance with their nature and order, and thus they can perform their proper functions. And this form and procedure must be heeded in the ecclesiastic as well as in every civil regime.[27]

The formation of a body politic as well as "every civil regime," for Marsilius, requires the proper order and position of its parts; the normative and official order is established as the standard by which deviation is measured.

---

[27] See *Marsilius of Padua: The Defender of Peace*, trans. Alan Gewirth (New York, 1951–56), 326.

Against that norm is the body politic whose arrangement of parts is re-garded as a monstrous configuration to be "heeded" for ecclesiastic as well as other orders of society.

In 1378 the ecclesiastical body did indeed become monstrous by sprout-ing a second head when the Church, divided by the Great Schism, formed two papacies, one in Avignon, the other in Rome. Like many Englishmen, Gower considers the Avignon papacy to be illegitimate and criticizes Pope Clement's approach to rule: "So the one now called Clement is far from being clement, and he is wrong in keeping this name, for his name lacks a prefix," that is, *in* should precede his name because inclemency is his prac-tice (Stockton, 137). In a brief comment that echoes Geoffrey of Vinsauf's dedication of the *Poetria Nova* to Pope Innocent, Gower says that the Avignon Pope is "wrong to keep his name," since his "inclement" behav-ior denies it. For Gower names should capture the essence of that which is signified if they are to signify truthfully. Gower's brief explication of the Avignon Pope's name, reminiscent of his treatment of *re-gula* in the section critiquing monastic orders, suggests that the pope is a two- faced hypocrite. In a passage about "how churchmen write and talk about things pertaining to peace, but engage in and take charge of things pertaining to war," the hypocrisy of the pope is characterized as a form of threatening militancy. "Thus we have come to send the world not peace but a sword, and we do everything unheard of, no matter what the harm. Thus the head now rages against the body's members, and oppresses those whom accord-ing to its duty it should least offend" (Stockton, 137). Just as the king of England has turned against those he should be leading, so too has this schismatic pope threatened the welfare of the ecclesiastical body.

In view of these metaphorical constructions of monstrous bodies, it is easy to see how Gower's most famous monstrous image, that of Nebuch-adnezzar's statue, might be politically charged. At the beginning of the final section of the poem Gower borrows the well-known image from the *Book of Daniel* to demonstrate the degeneration of human society through history. The monstrous image, as Russell A. Peck observes, "defines an apocalyptical view of history which biblical commentators and medieval writers seized upon to analyze what they saw to be the wretched decline of human enterprise."[28] In Book VII, Gower points explicitly to the alloyed feet, through which he figures contemporary society as the subject of his discussion, but defers his explication until after first pointing to the condition of the statue's head:

> *Nunc caput a status Nabugod prescinditur auri,*
> *Fictilis et ferri stand duo iamque pedes:* (*VC*, VII. i, 5–6)

---

[28] See Russell A. Peck, "John Gower and the Book of Daniel," in *John Gower: Recent Readings,* ed. R. F. Yeager (Kalamazoo, 1989), 159–87.

[The golden head of Nebuchadnezzar's statue has now been cut off,
yet the two feet of iron and clay still stand (Stockton, 254).]

The alloy is weak, a corruptive blending of what cannot adhere. That
Gower chooses the feet of Nebuchadnezzar's monstrous statue as the con-
trolling image for the last book of the poem is significant because it points
back to his analysis of contemporary events. The evocation of the Babylo-
nian tyrant and the period in biblical history when the prophet Daniel
lived in captivity resonates in the events of contemporary England and
Richard's oppression of his own subjects. The king as the "ranting Prince
of hell" cuts himself off from the concerns of his people as the decapitated
head of the statue seems to proclaim. Wat Tyler as the "peasant captain,"
representative of the feet of the body politic, seeks the power of rulership
medieval society is not prepared to relinquish. As figures of the "head"
and the "foot," each transgresses the boundaries of established hierarchical
order. Thus it is noteworthy that Gower draws attention to two primary
body parts—the feet and the head—before continuing his explication.
Unlike Daniel who explicates the statue from head to foot, including the
torso and limbs, Gower not only focuses on the extreme polarities, but
omits the middle parts, the "breast and arms of silver," the "belly and
thighs of bronze," and the "legs of iron." This head, like so many others
in England at this time, has been decapitated so that what remains of the
statue's body is essentially two feet—monstrous indeed! If the statue repre-
sents history, then this is the "here" and "now" of Gower's historical
moment severed so violently from its Golden Age past.

Visualizing the Point

As if transposing his verbal pointing to the visual field, four of the eleven
manuscripts of the *Vox* include an illustration of the poet as an archer with
a drawn bow about to shoot an arrow into the world. In the beautifully
rendered drawing in the Cotton Tiberius MS, Gower is depicted as a
young man wearing a brown hat and a long blue coat with a brown lining
with three arrows attached to his belt. He is aiming a long bow with a
fourth arrow at a target representing the world which is located to his left.
The world, divided into three parts to represent the three estates, marks
the site of the poet's critique. Beyond the world, to its right on the oppo-
site page, the arrow directs the eye to the beginning of the prologue to
Book I of the poem. Located directly above the figure are four lines which
read:

> *Ad mundum mitto mea iacula, dumque saggito;*
> *At ubi iustus erite, nulla sagitta ferit.*
> *Set male viventes hos vulnero trangredientes;*
> *Conscius ergo sibi se speculatur ibi.* (VC, I. Prol.)

[At the world I shoot my darts and arrow, but what is just will receive no arrow. However, I shall harm the transgressors who live evilly; conscious of myself, I shall keep my eye on them (see fig. 2).]

According to Michael Camille "arrows in texts are traditionally guides for the eye, pointing out, like N.B. marks, significant sections."[29] They function as deictic devices to call attention to important passages and features of the text that the author would wish to be remembered.[30] The archer here points to the *nota bene* device located at the beginning of Book II, leading the eye directly to a verbal construction of the poet's identity. The marginal device is located beside the riddling passage and, as effectively as the pointing arrow, directs the reader's attention to it:

> *Scribentis nomen si queras, ecce loquela*
> *Sub tribus implicita versibus inde latet.*
> *Primos sume pedes Godefridi desque Iohanni,*   *Nota nomen*
> *Principiumque sui Wallia iungat eis:*
> *Ter caput ammittens det cetera membra, que tale*
> *Carmine compositi hominis ordo patet.* (*VC*, I. Prol. 19–24)

[If you should ask the name of the writer, look, the word lies hidden and entangled within three verses about it. Take the first feet from "Godfrey" and add them to "John," and let "Wales" join its initial to them. Leaving off its head, let "Ter" furnish the other parts; and after such a line is arranged, the right sequence of the name is clear (see fig. 3).]

The first two letters of the poet's surname derive from Godfrey, probably of Viterbo, the author of the *Pantheon,* one of the texts from which Gower draws verbatim fragments. The name "John" signifies the name of the poet, but resonates with John the Evangelist and John the Baptist both of whom Gower identifies himself with early in the poem. For the final two syllables of his name Gower points to "Wales," which may mean a place of impending rebellion at that time, or John of Wales, whose *Communiloquium* urges preaching to all members of society.[31] The final two letters derive from a metaphoric decapitation of "Ter." The "head" of this word

---

[29] See Michael Camille, *Image on the Edge: The Margins of Medieval Art* (Cambridge, 1992), 107.

[30] Maria Wickert, *Studies in John Gower,* trans. Robert J. Meindl (Washington, DC, 1981). Wickert notes that both the archer and his arrows were frequently used metaphors for the preacher and his sermon. She delineates a tradition from Scripture and Gregory the Great to John Bromyard's use of the arrow as a metaphor for divine message. The sermon in this analogy functions as the arrow which acts as a marker of sin; the preacher enunciates words that point out and threaten the sinner. If Gower is the archer and all other estates belong to the world, even his powerful ecclesiastical audience would be threatened by the pangs of his arrows.

[31] See Jenny Swanson, *John of Wales: A Study of the Works and Ideas of a Thirteenth-Century Friar* (Cambridge, 1989).

is severed just as those in positions of authority have lost their heads. In another example of verbal *solemnis ludus*, Gower has created a poetic identity that itself is a monstrous "sign" pointing in its recombinant (con)-fusion in several directions at once.

In sharp contrast with the formalized portrait of the poet in the Cotton Tiberius MS, is the Laud MS in which the archer appears as a rustic carica-ture; dressed in a haphazard manner, his eyes gaze intently at the audience while his arrow aims precariously at a world containing a tilted castle. This archer and his arrows seem to represent something very different from the formal depiction in Cotton Tiberius—something ludic yet implicitly threat-ening (see fig. 4). Unlike the portrait in the Cotton Tiberius MS, the Laud portrait is located at the beginning of Book III and points not at the begin-ning of Book I, but rather to the critique of the three estates. Unique among the eleven manuscripts, the Laud is the only one that omits the vision of the Rising of 1381; it could be, John H. Fisher suggests, that either it had the first book which was suppressed or else it did not have the first book at all.[32] If it is the case that this is a late copy, then the illustration is not under the control of the author, but rather the copyist whose interpretation of Gower may be a deliberate burlesque of the author. If Gower controls the image perhaps this is self-parody or a self-conscious construction of poetic identity that calls attention to the poet and his message.

When we place the illustrations together and view them side by side, the "this" beside the "that," we see certain similarities and differences that each alone would not reveal. In both Gower assumes a marginal stance in relation to the three estates; he stands outside the world in a proximate position. It is as if he is gaining perspective on his target, distancing himself for a more accurate view. In both illustrations, the archer, a giant in rela-tion to the world, wields a long bow and carries arrows associated with the three arrows of the Apocalypse. The pose in both is similar. But there are several differences: in the Laud MS the archer is dressed in the garb of a common man (a hunter, artisan, or apprentice); he gazes intently at the audience rather than his target, and the world contains a tilted castle. This ludic Gower does not direct his gaze toward the world as the archer in the other picture does. Instead his cockeyed stare focuses rather intently at his ecclesiastical audience. If we understand the operations of carnivalesque dis-course within the poem, the *solemnis ludus* of Gower's *cento* techniques, then these illustrations together may be read as a visual enactment of both sides of the poet's politics: while one figure is formal, the other is ludic; while one represents official order, the other suggests protest and chal-lenge; while one gazes at the world, the other gazes at the ecclesiastical audience. Placed side by side the visual texts contradict and relativize each

---

[32] John H. Fisher, *John Gower: Moral Philosopher and Friend of Chaucer* (New York, 1964), 101–2.

other in a way that underscores the importance of the message being conveyed.

Gower's Monstrous Imagination

R. F. Yeager's suggestion that Proba "possessed a spirit kindred to Gower's own in her concern to treat Christian subjects in her verse" has particular relevance to the monstrous imagination I pointed to earlier.[33] Proba's claim to prophecy and her veneration of Vergil is surely something Gower shares (Book I is filled with allusions to the *Aeneid*), as is the treatment of Christian subjects. But the affinity of the two authors is augmented, it seems to me, by a shared pacifist ethic.[34] The 694-line *cento* begins with Proba's pronouncement that she is no longer going to speak of war, but rather of peace. To carry out that agenda she consciously appropriates Vergilian fragments that are particularly suitable for the ethical transformation she has in mind. In the epigraph at the beginning of this essay for instance—*pacem orate manu, pacem laudate sendentes magnanimi; pacis solum inviolabile pignus*—excerpted fragments are taken from the gods' debate on the war between Turnus and Aeneas in Books X and XI of the *Aeneid*. These carefully chosen excerpts are then recast into a plea for peace spoken by Christ to his disciples. What was in Vergil's text a heated debate on the advantages of war is effectively transformed by Proba into an inspirational homily on the merits of peace.

Proba's pacifist ethic is further promoted by her use of several of Vergil's women—Dido, Creusa, Andromache, Camilla—as she reshapes episodes from their lives in the *Aeneid* into New Testament events. The awakening of Dido's dormant heart to love is used to incite the hearts of "slothful men" to the "good news." Aeneas's poignant farewell to Andromache, Hector's devoted widow, becomes part of the Sermon on the Mount spoken by a transfigured Aeneas. Creusa's ghostly spirit sending Aeneas off on his mission is remodeled into a description of Jesus' miraculous walk on the water. The flight of Camilla's father with his infant daughter carried before him on his breast becomes Mary's flight with her infant son from Herod's massacre. Likewise, Vergil's depiction of Camilla's father feeding her on the "milk of a wild mare" becomes Proba's Mary who nurses her son in the Egyptian wilderness.[35] By changing masculine pronouns Proba emphasizes the pacifying power of the maternal body. Her approach to violence is not to glorify or participate in it, but rather to point to its causes and transform its effects.

There is evidence of this kind of transformation in a bizarre passage in Book V of the *Vox* where Gower borrows from the *Aurora*. In the conven-

---

[33] Yeager, "Did Gower Write *Cento?*," 125.

[34] R. F. Yeager, "*Pax Poetica:* On the Pacifism of Chaucer and Gower," *Studies in the Ages of Chaucer* 9 (1987), 97–121.

[35] Proba, *Golden Bough and the Oaken Cross,* 162.

tion of *effictio* the narrator describes a beautiful woman, the kind of woman for whom knights lust at the expense of their public duties. Gower's lady is comely from head to "perfect foot"; she "possesses a kind of divinity which surpasses the race of man" (Stockton, 199). Conventional, indeed, yet part of this sixteen-line passage is borrowed from the description of Absalom, the rebellious son of King David, while another derives from a Gospel description of the Virgin. As Paul Beichner notes, Gower simply substitutes "several masculine pronouns in the lines about Absalom."[36] In effect Gower has placed the rebellious son within the maternal body as if it could contain the violent impulses of dissent. Found within a chapter on the knight's devotion to courtly love, this curious fusion suggests that rebellion of a personal or social nature can be quelled by "embodiment" in the Virgin Mother. In this subtle detail Gower points to the transformative power of the divine maternal body; as *stella maris*, she calms the raging sea monster that threatens to swallow the narrator in Book I. In Book II where he discusses the three-in-one relation of the Godhead as well as the human and the divine components of Christ Gower pointedly mentions the Virgin Mother's contribution to her son's mortality and her maternal nurturing: "the fact that He suckled at the breast suggests that He is a true mortal; the fact that a new star bore Him suggests that he is God" (Stockton, 107).

Eric Stockton's offhand comment that it "is surprising how little [the Virgin] is mentioned in this poem in view of Gower's reverence for her in the *Mirour de l'omme*" perceives what does indeed seem to be a puzzling absence. Furthermore, the poet's rather negative comments about gender role reversal and lecherous women seem to support a misogynist rejection of *all* women. But if we return to the explanation of pointing as being enacted within the smallest of details, perhaps it is significant that the Virgin Mother's presence has been marked only by small details, signified by *cento* fragments and subtle allusions such as that from the *Aurora* or simply by a well-chosen metaphor. As a "new star" she represents the celestial queen of *Revelation* often depicted in iconography with a crown bearing the twelve stars of the apocalyptic vision; her presence tempers the abjection and fear elicited by the Apocalypse. So too does her understated presence complement Gower's pacifist ethic by recalling Vergil's *Fourth Eclogue* which alludes to the birth of Augustus Caesar as a sign of return to a Golden Age of peace. Christian commentators reinterpreted the lines to prophesy the Virgin Mother's restoration of the reign of peace through the miraculous birth of Christ. Surely Gower would see how the Virgin Mary's sanctified maternal body could transform the effects of sin, or what he calls the "moder of confusion" in *Confessio Amantis*, into order and peace.

---

[36] See Paul Beichner, "Gower's Use of the *Aurora* in the *Vox Clamantis*," *Speculum* 30 (1955): 589.

Despite the praise bestowed upon Proba's *cento* by medieval authors such as Isidore, Boccaccio, and Christine de Pizan in *The Book of the City of Ladies,* modern scholars have tended to regard the genre as a "chimerical undertaking," "repellent," "artificial," and inherently freakish.[37] Yet, as Elizabeth Clark and Diane Hatch suggest, were critics to recognize the resemblance between *cento* and typological methods of adapting the Old to the New Testament there would not only be a reassessment but an overturning of critical biases. Christian writers looked to the Old Testament as the source for Christian prophecy and incorporated fragments from those events into their own texts, so that even the most obscure Hebrew details functioned as "pointers" to Christianity.[38] The *centoist* operation links the Judeo-Christian tradition together to form continuity and unity where there is at the same time ideological and historical difference. It takes but a small intellectual leap to see that the same logic may be applied to the writing of history. Just as a *cento* is constructed by the recombination of fragments from pre-Christian poets or the New Testament made to resemble the Old Testament, so too does the writing of history require the gathering of fragments of information from preexistent sources and recombination into a comprehensible pattern. Often those fragments derive from oral as well as literary and historical sources, from a multitude of voices speaking from a variety of perspectives, shifting and changing over time as more evidence becomes available. The *Vox* is a poetic monster precisely because it embodies all of these sources to comment on fractious times.

As postmodern readers of medieval texts we stand in the "here" and "now" as we look to the past for meaning. Often that process seems alien and foreboding, more often it seems irrelevant to a postmodern world so separated from the Middle Ages by time. Yet the impulses of both modern and postmodern writers to draw from a multitude of sources, to splice them together in innovative ways, and to create pastiches that defy generic classification, constitutes a process similar to that practiced by medieval authors such as Gower. Centonic texts teach us to listen to the voices of

---

[37] Christine de Pizan, *The Book of the City of Ladies,* trans. Earl Jeffrey Richards (New York, 1982), 65–66. "The Roman woman, Proba wife of Adelphus, was equally outstanding and was a Christian. She had such a noble mind and so loved and devoted herself to study that she mastered all seven liberal arts and was an excellent poet and delved so deeply into the books of the poet, particularly Vergil's poems, that she knew them all by heart.... She would put small pieces together, coupling and joining them, all the while respecting the metrical rules, art and measure in the individual feet, as well as in the conjoining of verses, and without making any mistakes she arranged her verses so masterfully that no man could do better." See also David F. Bright, "Theory and Practice in the Vergilian Cento," *Illinois Classical Studies* IX.I (1984): 79–90. "The cento remains for modern readers what it was for Jerome a puzzling and often silly ambition. Proba's evangelical cento brings to mind Dr. Johnson's cheerfully chauvinistic remark: 'A woman's preaching is like a dog's walking on his hinder legs. It is not done well; but you are surprised to find it done at all'" (81). This may be an example of how critical biases are perpetuated.

[38] Proba, *Golden Bough and the Oaken Cross,* 162.

another place and time, to comprehend the monsters of our own time, to conquer our own fear of the Other, whatever form it takes, by exposing its presence, by understanding its operations, and by transforming it into relevant meanings. The *Vox Clamantis* is thus not to be appreciated for its beauty, but for its power to warn us of the potential for monstrousness in ourselves.

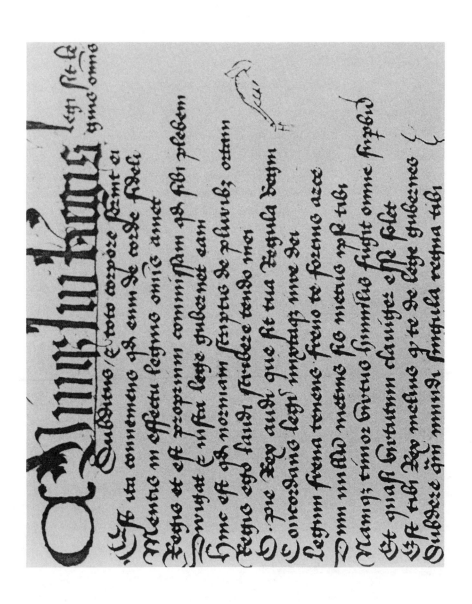

Figure 1. MS All Souls Col., Oxf. 98. *Vox Clamantis*, f. 126ᵛ.

Figure 2. MS Cotton Tiberius A.iv, British Library. *Vox Clamantis*, f. 8ᵛ.

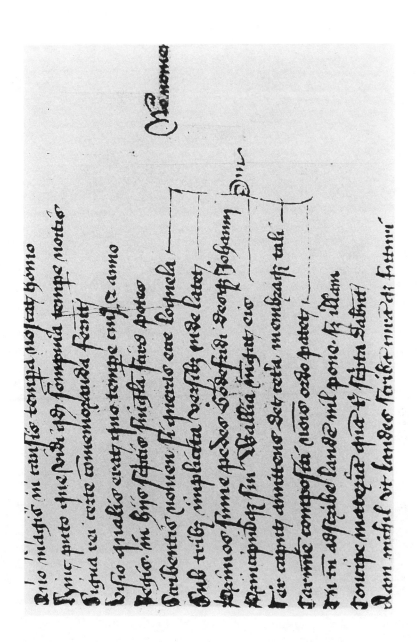

Figure 3. MS All Souls Col., Oxf. 98. *Vox Clamantis*, f. 116.

Figure 4. MS Laud 719, Bodleian Library, Oxford.

Reflections on Gower as "*Sapiens* in Ethics and Politics"

David Aers

Recent scholarship on Gower has been marked not only by its erudition but also by the extremely strong claims made for the subtlety and coherence of Gower's moral and political thought, especially in the *Confessio Amantis*.[1] Because this essay explores aspects of Gower's ethics it seems appropriate to begin with a few examples of the kinds of claims I have in mind. These examples are from recent works which have done a great deal to encourage serious engagement with Gower's writing.

Characteristic of such work is Alistair Minnis's influential essay "'Moral Gower' and Medieval Literary Theory," which sought to demonstrate how coherently Gower's *Confessio Amantis* fulfilled the criteria for "ethi-

---

I would like to thank Winthrop Wetherbee and Nicky Zeeman for discussions related to this essay and Katie Little for turning script to print.

[1] Examples of the work I have in mind are well represented by the following: Jane Chance, *The Genius Figure in Antiquity and the Middle Ages* (New York, 1975), 125–30; A. J. Minnis, "John Gower, *Sapiens* in Ethics and Politics," *Medium Aevum* 49 (1980): 207–29, repr. in Peter Nicholson, ed., *Gower's "Confessio Amantis"* (Cambridge, 1991), 158–80; A. J. Minnis, "'Moral Gower' and Medieval Literary Theory," in A. J. Minnis, ed., *Gower's "Confessio Amantis": Responses and Reassessments* (Cambridge, 1983), 50–78; E. Porter, "Gower's Ethical Microcosm and Political Macrocosm," in A. J. Minnis, ed., *Gower's "Confessio Amantis"* (cited above), 135–62; K. Olsson, *John Gower and the Structures of Conversion* (Cambridge, 1992); R. F. Yeager, *John Gower's Poetic* (Cambridge, 1990); James Simpson, *Science and the Self in Medieval Poetry* (Cambridge, 1995), chaps. 1, 5–9; Larry Scanlon, *Narrative, Authority, and Power* (Cambridge, 1994), chap. 9; Kathryn Lynch, *The High Medieval Dream Vision* (Stanford, 1988), chap. 6. For an attempt to show the coherence and specificity of Gower's political fictions and comments, together with claims that in both *Vox Clamantis* and *Confessio Amantis* "Gower *was* [author's italics] speaking for—on behalf of and in defence of—the people," see Judith Ferster, *Fictions of Advice: The Literature and Politics of Counsel in Late Medieval England* (Philadelphia, 1996), chap. 7: here, 132. Relevant to the concerns of the present essay, and in some ways in dialogue with them, is Frank Grady's "The Lancastrian Gower and the Limits of Exemplarity," *Speculum* 70 (1995): 552–75.; and N. Zeeman, "The Verse of Courtly Love in the Framing Narrative of the *Confessio Amantis*," *Medium Aevum* 60 (1991): 222–40. The Gower texts that I refer to in this essay are the following: *The English Works of John Gower*, ed. G. C. Macaulay, 2 vols. (EETS, e.s., 81 and 82, 1900 and 1901); *The Latin Works*, vol. 4 of *The Complete Works*, ed. G. C. Macaulay (Oxford 1902); *The English Translation of "Vox Clamantis"* in *Major Latin Works of John Gower*, trans. E. W. Stockton (Seattle, 1962).

cal poetry" inherited from Christian-Aristotelian traditions. Minnis noted
that "Gower's *principalis materia* falls within the subject area of ethics"
and that "Gower has taken upon himself the function of *ethicus,* the role
of *sapiens* with a special expertise in ethics and politics."[2] This is the Gow-
er Minnis had described in an earlier article, "John Gower, *Sapiens* in
Ethics and Politics," where it was argued that Gower's *Confessio Amantis*
was an ethical treatise that included substantial political argument.[3] Simi-
larly, R. F. Yeager's book on Gower's poetics presented a poet who com-
pletely meets the "medieval moralist's imperative" to apply traditional
teaching to "edifying use" in present circumstances. Yeager showed how
"public ethics and poetry were never unrelated in Gower's estimation."
The *Confessio Amantis* was the product of a "poet of moral and political
reform," one with a cogent "political program," a profound "program for
societal unity and growth" incorporating a strong tendency to a "pacifist"
ethic.[4] Kurt Olsson's book, *John Gower and the Structures of Confession,*
also saw Gower as successfully "reshaping the values of Ricardian Eng-
land" as he freed his readers from "facile morality."[5]

The dominant version of Gower in current Gower studies, a brilliant
dialogic and utterly coherent moral and political poet, is tenaciously main-
tained in James Simpson's explication of Gower's *Confessio Amantis* in
Sciences and the Self in Medieval Poetry. Simpson rejects the common view
that Christianity provides the unifying force in Gower's moral thought.
He asserts that "Gower's ethics in the *Confessio* are not specifically Chris-
tian."[6] Rather, "Gower, in short, is what might be described as a liberal
humanist" propounding "liberal humanism." The *Confessio Amantis* is a
"humanist psychological allegory" which "might be described as liberal
humanist."[7] What does such a devotedly historicizing scholar mean by
attaching Gower to a term more intelligibly associated with John Stuart
Mill and his heirs? By "humanism" he means to convey that Gower has "a
profound confidence in the powers of human reason, and in the capacity
of human reason to promote human perfection," a respectful engagement
with "classical literature and philosophy" (especially Ovid and Aristotle)
and a view of "politics as a pivotal, if not the supreme science." By
"liberal" he means what he calls "constitutionalist," claiming that "Gower
represents a constitutionalism, whose agreements are arrived at through

---

[2] Minnis, "Moral Gower," 71 and 69.

[3] Minnis, "John Gower, *Sapiens,*" see n. 1.

[4] Yeager, *John Gower's Poetic,* quotations from 115, 201, 265, 241, but see passim; on
the "pacifist" ethic see R. F. Yeager, "*Pax Poetica* and the Pacifism of Chaucer and
Gower," *SAC* 9 (1987): 97–121.

[5] Olsson, *John Gower,* here 1, 14; see also 24, 70–71, and chaps. 13 and 20; similarly,
see Lynch, *High Medieval Dream Vision,* 168, 171, 186–88, 190–98, and Porter, "Gower's
Ethical Microcosm."

[6] Simpson, *Sciences,* 196 n. 40, reiterated on 202 and argued for in chap. 7; contrast
works by Olsson, Lynch, Minnis, and Yeager in n. 1.

[7] Simpson, *Sciences,* 19, 135, 229.

dialogue and through the wisdom of an aged man in an aged world;" "at every point Gower's politics should be described as consensual and constitutionalist."[8] The relations between the allegedly total coherence of Gower's ethics and politics in the *Confessio* and the actual political struggles around the great popular uprising of 1381 or the actual political struggles which involved usurpation, regicide, and the violent maintenance of a usurping dynasty, are not investigated by Simpson, although Gower himself showed no reticence on these matters.[9] The final work I wish to recollect here is Larry Scanlon's study of Gower in *Narrative, Authority, and Power*. In this often brilliantly innovative reading of the *Confessio Amantis*, Scanlon seeks to show that Gower investigated ethics "as a rhetorical project." In doing so, "Gower is every bit as searching and self-conscious about poetic language as Chaucer," bringing this to fruit in a work which combines "anti-clerical critique with a more explicit celebration of lay political authority."[10] Gower is a coherent and "sophisticated political thinker" who understands all authority as the product of human fabrications but values kingship as the most effective form of order.[11] Justice itself is seen "as the king's gift," the product of his "voluntary restraint of his awesome, potentially absolute power."[12] So the *Confessio Amantis* discloses the foundationless nature of all authority while constructing a coherent and unified politics and ethics which belongs to the laicization of power, literacy, and legitimations of power in late medieval England. Here we encounter a very different version of Gower's ethics and politics to ones we find in Simpson or Yeager or Minnis, and yet one thing remains constant: Gower's poetry is a coherent, unified moral and political project.

Even the figure of Genius no longer presents difficulties in such versions of Gower. For example, Simpson sees him as "the increasingly rational imagination" moving the will (Amans) "towards its perfection."[13] Anything that might seem contradictory in Genius's advice is to be read as a deliberately partial moment superseded in the final unities of Gower's theory and art. The sympathetic but nuanced account of Genius

---

[8] Ibid., see *seriatim* 18, 19, 273, 284; see also 294 and chaps. 7 and 9. On the allegedly unproblematic fusion of Aristotle's ethics and politics with Ovid, see 16, 275, and chaps. 5 and 7.

[9] I could find no consideration of the claims that Gower was a "constitutionalist" and a "liberal" in relation to the actual political struggles and options of the period, whether to the popular struggles embodied in the great rising of 1381 or to those around the Lancastrian usurpation. This is a rather peculiar, if revealing, absence in an argument that makes the claims it does about the nature of Gower's politics. In a Marxist vocabulary it might be described as an extraordinarily "idealist" version of politics.

[10] Scanlon, *Narrative*, chap. 9: here quotations from 246 and 247; see similarly 250–52, 255–56, 258.

[11] Scanlon, *Narrative*, 263.

[12] Scanlon, *Narrative*, 286; see too 292.

[13] Simpson, *Sciences*, 194; see similarly 166, 172, 183, 185, 188, 196–97, 254, 258, 260–61; note the anticipations in Lynch, *High Medieval Dream Vision*, 19, 171, 182–85; the anticipation is noted by Simpson himself, *Sciences*, 186 n. 26.

offered by Winthrop Wetherbee seems to have been assimilated to far more securely unifying and homogenizing readings.[14] However, in the view argued for below, it is time to return to a consideration of the kinds of "contradictory positions" that even as sympathetic a reader as Wetherbee found in the *Confessio*.[15] Here it will be argued that "contradictory positions" in the politics and ethics of Gower's writing cannot always or necessarily be read as carefully designed steps on a securely constructed pedagogic ladder belonging to a unified ethical and political system leading us to "perfection." Readers need not set out with assumptions that a work is coherent any more than they need set out with assumptions that it is incoherent.

I begin my own reflections on aspects of Gower's ethical thinking with *Vox Clamantis.* I have recently discussed the poem's responses to the English rising of 1381, and while I am not returning to that analysis here, it seems worth mentioning the relevance of Book I to any consideration of Gower's politics.[16] This is so because the current tendency is to set it aside as scholars derive accounts of Gower's ethics and politics exclusively from the *Confessio.* Yet the "vox" of the *Vox Clamantis,* its language, its prophetic role, and many of its political assumptions, certainly survived the writing of *Confessio Amantis.*[17] Without determining the outcome of any ensuing enquiry, the acknowledgment of this fact might at least encourage us to ask some questions about continuities between works that certainly seem generically incommensurable. And if there are continuities, observing them might even be relevant to our understanding of the complex vernacular work.

Here I confine my comments on *Vox Clamantis* to aspects of Gower's treatment of violence, of war and peace, following in the steps of R. F. Yeager's "Pax Poetica and the Pacifism of Chaucer and Gower."[18] There Yeager maintains that in the "*Vox Clamantis* and the *Confessio* there is an increasing certitude that all wars, including (or perhaps especially) England's with France, are more about money than justice." He argues that Gower sustained a coherent "pacifism" which is "both broad ranging and thoroughly developed," "a strengthening position" based on "legal and

---

[14] W. Wetherbee, "Genius and Interpretation in the *Confessio Amantis,*" in *Magister Regis,* ed. A. Groos (New York, 1986), 241–60; see also, Wetherbee, "Latin Structure and Vernacular Space: Gower, Chaucer and the Boethian Tradition," in *Chaucer and Gower: Difference, Mutuality, Exchange,* ed. R. F. Yeager (Victoria, BC, 1991), 7–35, esp. 29–31.

[15] Wetherbee, "Latin Structure," 29.

[16] Aers, "'Vox Populi' and the Literature of 1381," in the *Cambridge History of Medieval English Literatures,* ed. D. Wallace (Cambridge, 1998), chap. 16; see also Janet Coleman's comments on *Vox Clamantis* in her book, *English Literature in History, 1350–1400* (London, 1981), 126–56, esp. 138–41.

[17] See, for example, the *Chronica Tripertita* and the *Carmen super multiplici viciorum pestilencia:* the former is trans. by Stockton in *Major Latin Works;* the latter in Macaulay, *Latin Works,* 346–54.

[18] See n. 4.

doctrinal authorities that war itself is contrary to most Christian positions."[19] But even if we set aside Gower's constant legitimization of killing on crusades, a legitimization Yeager of course noted, problems emerge which are, we will see, not uncharacteristic of Gower's ethics, in whatever genres he chooses.

In Book III of *Vox Clamantis* Gower turns to the models of the good life offered by the founder of his religion. He tells readers that "Christ used to make peace," that "Christ was gentle [*mitis*]," that Christ suffered "humbly [*humilis*]," was "compassionate [*miserans*]" and did not seek "vengeance," unlike the modern ecclesiastics Gower is criticizing.[20] He reminds readers that "Christ taught us to follow his example of forgiveness" and traced the path of salvation through patience rather than through retaliation. Christian faith, he recalls, is disclosed in love that establishes peace and friendship, not even demanding, let alone defending, things that are one's own; it certainly does not "thirst for the possessions of others."[21] Here the *vox* of John Gower follows very closely the unequivocal and utterly demanding pacifism at the heart of Jesus's teaching in Luke 6:27–38.[22] The poet emphasizes that for a Christian a virtuous life entails following Christ's own "merciful" teaching.[23] Gower sets his outline of the ethics of the Kingdom of God proclaimed by Jesus against the current values and practices of Christians leading the church, those especially obliged to follow "Christ's rule of peace" but now committed to violence and the killing of other Christians.[24]

Three books later the poet addresses the young King Richard directly. As one would expect in a poem that had propounded Christ's teaching on detachment and nonviolence as essential to the Kingdom of God, Christ is invoked as the decisive model for living well. Gower counsels the king in evangelical terms: "conduct yourself like a Christ," be like the "loving Christ" in self-discipline, generosity, and care of the poor.[25] Such are the demands of the founding texts invoked in Book III, and here Gower seems to be developing a consistent ethical counsel. Perhaps, the charitable interpreter may reflect, the first book's indulgence in revengeful violence against the men and women involved in the rising of 1381 was an aberration produced by fear and the deeply internalized norms of class contempt

---

[19] "*Pax Poetica*," 103–4, 108.

[20] III. I.116–17 (reference to book, chap., and page in Stockton's translation; cited in n. 1; I have also occasionally supplied the Latin Text cited in n. 1 where I considered that helpful).

[21] *Seriatim*, III.3.122; III.7.126–7.

[22] An excellent introduction to the issues here is John H. Yoder, *The Politics of Jesus*, 2nd rev. ed. (Grand Rapids, 1994), esp. chap. 2.

[23] III.8.128; the meditation continues in III.9.130–32.

[24] III.9.131; Gower displays a militaristic and worldly understanding of Christians' relationship to Christ's kingship, allegedly derived through his mother and to be gained by the carnal sword: III.9.131–32, III.5.124.

[25] VI.8.234 and VI.11.238–39.

and dehumanization.[26] However, such a genial reading is not sustainable. For from advocacy of evangelical ethics the poet moves to an altogether different paradigm of the virtues. Having just exhorted Richard to conduct himself like the "loving Christ" he commends an altogether different kind of model, "that most illustrious prince, his father," the Black Prince.[27] Gower leaves us in no doubt about the entailments of such a model for the young man whom he has just exhorted to follow the way of Christ, the Christ whose practice and teaching of nonviolence his poem had made clear. The poet reminds Richard, in an unironic celebration of aristocratic violence that could have come from the Chandos Herald's adoration of the Black Prince, how the father:

> plundered [*depredat*] foreign lands ... France felt the effects of him; and Spain, in contemplating the powers with which he stoutly subjected her, was fearful of him. ... he hurled his troops into the midst of his enemies. ... He pursued and destroyed them, he cut them down and killed them just as a wolf driven by hunger. ... his sword was often drunk with the blood of the enemy. Harshly assaulting his foes, he fought and overcame them. His sword point refused to go back into the sheath dry. His hostile blade was sated with enemy gore; a torrent of blood slaked the thirst of his weapons. ... He attacked strongholds, annihilating the people [*Depopulans populos forcia castra ruit*]. In order to seize booty [*Ut predes raperet*], he boldly penetrated deep among his antagonists.[28]

Along with this transformation of the evangelical paradigm we should recall that while Gower had criticized the pursuit of war for material profits, here the self-aggrandizing economic motives of English invasions of France ("to seize booty") are made explicit and extolled as part of the Black Prince's glory.[29] And this is now proposed as a model for Richard,

---

[26] On Book I see works cited in n. 16 together with Andrew Galloway, "Gower in His Most Learned Role and the Peasants' Revolt of 1381," *Medievalia* 16 (1993): 329–47 and S. Justice, *Writing and Rebellion* (Berkeley, 1994), 208–11. (I remain completely unpersuaded by Justice's account of Chaucer's "criticism" of Gower in the *Nun's Priest's Tale* and of his assumed response to the English rising, 208–27: for a far more careful account of Chaucer's political perspectives in this context, see Derek Pearsall, *The Life of Geoffrey Chaucer* [Oxford 1992], 143–51.) On conventional contempt for the peasantry (the majority of European Christians) by the governing and writing classes, see the evidence and references in Lee Patterson, *Chaucer and the Subject of History* (Madison, 1991), 262–74.

[27] Heading to VI.13.241.

[28] See VI.13.241–42. For the Chandos Herald, see "Life of the Black Prince" by the *Herald of Sir John Chandos*, ed. M. K. Pope and E. C. Lodge (Oxford, 1910), text and translation. For the relevant paradigms here see the following: M. Vale, *War and Chivalry* (Athens, Georgia, 1981); M. James, *English Politics and the Concept of Honour* (Cambridge, 1978); S. Knight, *Arthurian Literature and Society* (London, 1983); M. Keen, *Chivalry* (New Haven, 1984); P. Coss, *The Knight in Medieval England* (Stroud, 1993).

[29] On the criticism of economic motivations for war, see Yeager, "*Pax Poetica*," 103–4. Such motivations were pervasive, certainly not confined to those classified as "merce-

"*in exemplum.*"[30] In fact the poet calls on Richard to *surpass* the militaristic deeds of his father.[31] True enough, peace "excels," observes the poet; however, "when our tried and tested rights call for war it should be waged" and the king should seek honor and glory, the familiar goals of the ruling class and its chivalry.[32]

How does all this relate to the evangelical proclamations of Book III and the advice to Richard to follow the loving Christ in Book VI? How does it relate to Gower's understanding of the church, the body of Christ into which all Christians are incorporated, including the French Christians whose slaughter Gower is celebrating? How does Gower's exaltation of violence in defence of "our rights" (that is, the dubious claims of the ruling dynasty to the French crown) relate to his earlier insistence that Christian faith and love "does not thirst for possessions of others, nor does it ever demand things that are its own"?[33] Has the moralist forgotten what he had written about Christ and discipleship in Book III and within Book VI itself? Apparently not, for a little later in Book VI he again instructs Richard to recall "Christ's sacred writings."[34] But to what purpose would one who is exhorted to "surpass" the violence of the Black Prince disturb the dust upon a manuscript of the Gospels? Gower's answer displays no sense of any difficulty here: Christ's words simply warn the king to become a worthy pilgrim "resplendent with the light of virtues," one who remembers that he is made in the image of God and so should "follow Him, conforming to His law"—that is, to the evangelical doctrine the poet articulated clearly enough. So, he writes, "it is to your advantage that you love with all your might Him who fashioned and redeemed you."[35] The poet's moral counsel instructs the addressee to "withdraw" from the world while simultaneously surpassing the military and chivalric triumphs of the Black Prince. Be like the gospels' Christ; follow his unequivocal condemnation of violence and worldly attachment (Luke 6:27–38). Also be like and surpass the Black Prince; that is, plunder, destroy, cut down, kill; make sure your sword is drunk with blood; depopulate lands (i.e., perpetuate massacres and ethnic segregations); make war to seize booty; and through this win honor, glory, and peace.

What are we to make of this? How could the poet, celebrated by scholars as *sapiens* in ethics and politics, produce such contradictory admonitions on such a major moral issue without any signs of discomfort,

---

naries": see H. J. Hewitt, "The Organization of War," in *The Hundred Years War*, ed. K. Fowler (New York, 1971) and *The Organization of War under Edward III* (Manchester, 1966). See also Coss, *The Knight*.

[30] VI.13.241.

[31] VI.13.242.

[32] Ibid. It should be noted that such commitments entailed the unprecedentedly heavy levels of taxation which were the catalyst to the rising of 1381. See n. 16.

[33] III.1.127.

[34] VI.17.246.

[35] VI.17. 246–47.

let alone ironization? My answer involves two strands. They could very loosely be called "cultural" and "literary." The first term directs us to consider the constitution of Christian traditions (plural) in relation to forms of social power and class practices in late medieval Europe. The second strand directs us to consider the genres Gower develops together with the particularities of his own formal choices. In the present case these strands combine to produce the ethical contradictions identified above. This is not the place to provide even an historical sketch of the first strand; all that we need to remember here is that the unequivocal demands Jesus made in passages such as Luke 6:27–38 were mediated by a church committed to the existing organizations of power, including military power. It is no chance matter that the targets of the insurgents of 1381 included the head of the English church, Archbishop and Chancellor Simon Sudbury, or that one of their leaders was a radical priest anathematized and jailed by the ecclesiastical authorities, or that the rebellious peasants at North Walsham were slaughtered by forces under the personal command of the militaristic Bishop Despenser.[36] The shorthand term to designate the church's immersion in the powers of ruling elites is the Constantinianization of Christianity. This has taken numerous forms since the emperor made Christianity the official religion of the Roman empire and its armies, but in all its modalities it entailed a systematic marginalization, or inversion, of Jesus' teachings of nonviolence—teachings at the heart of the proclamation of the Kingdom of God.[37] The contradictions within the first strand enabled the cross to become the symbol around which military power was organized, enabled the eucharist to become a bond among those making war or burning heretics, and enabled pulpits of churches to be instruments of royal propaganda in the years of war against French Christians.[38] Yet it seems that the church's management of the contradictions became normalized and internalized. So it is hardly surprising if they are simply and unironically reproduced by an orthodox Catholic whose estates satire was written from a social position and political assumptions definitively bound up with the governing classes.[39] Not surprising, indeed, but a necessary topic of reflection for those studying Gower's ethics

---

[36] For a good introduction to the late medieval church, especially in the contexts under discussion see P. Heath, *Church and Realm: 1272–1461* (London, 1988), chaps. 3, 7, and 8. On 1381 the best introduction remains R. Hilton, *Bond Men Made Free* (London, 1973) read with R. B. Dobson, *The Peasants' Revolt of 1381* (London, 1970); see also S. Justice, *Writing and Rebellion*, chap. 4.

[37] On the issues here see: Yoder, *Politics of Jesus;* R. H. Bainton, *Christian Attitudes toward War and Peace* (New York, 1960); W. Klassen, *Love of Enemies* (Philadelphia, 1984); on the theology of the just war see: F. H. Russell, *The Just War in the Middle Ages* (Cambridge, 1975).

[38] On the eucharist and the cultural and political roles it played see Miri Rubin, *Corpus Christi* (Cambridge, 1991) and the essays by Rubin and Sarah Beckwith in *Culture and History, 1350–1600,* ed. D. Aers (London, 1992).

[39] Coleman, *English Literature,* 140–41.

and politics.

This brings me to the second strand, the "literary" or more formal. Gower developed a form which facilitated the simple reproduction of the contradictions I have outlined, a mode of literary organization which is markedly paratactic. By this I mean that the poem tends to be compiled in units that are paratactically sealed off from each other *rather than* brought into dialogue. I am certainly not suggesting that a poem whose chief mode of organization is episodic must necessarily generate unexaminedly contradictory positions. An episodic mode of composition can be, in the terms I use here, dialogic rather than paratactic. Episodes can be juxtaposed to produce a carefully organized, complex range of mirrorings, echoes, qualifications, elaborations, perhaps with little connecting narrative. Far from sealing units off from each other and from critical scrutiny, such an organization could encourage a dialogue between conflicting episodes through which the writer explores ethical problems. This is one of the ways in which *Piers Plowman* unfolds.[40] *Vox Clamantis*, however, works very differently. The examples I have considered show how its paratactic mode becomes a powerful impediment to moral inquiry, to sustained critical reflection on the difficulties that are raised. The mode protects the poet from having to confront sharp contradictions in his ethics, let alone from having to explore their sources in the traditions he inherits and the culture he inhabits. Yet the particular contradictions observed above should be extremely serious ones for any Christian moralist, and any study of Gower's ethics needs to identify the poet's failure to *articulate* them as contradictions together with the consequent failure to explore the sources of such contradictions. R. F. Yeager may be right in thinking that there was "a profound division in Gower's own heart" over the practice of war.[41] If so, the poet's paratactic mode enabled him to repress this important "division" from critical exploration. Such occlusion would not be without advantages. It would allow the poet to assert with equal vehemence morally and theologically incompatible positions in areas of real difficulty, asserting whichever position most accorded with contingent demands, including contingent literary demands, as the poet saw them. This might also facilitate the poet's self-presentation as a prophetic and impersonal *vox*, the contemporary figure of the apostle St. John, "the one whom the Isle of Patmos received in the Apocalypse, and whose name I bear," as well as that voice of the people in which God is often disclosed.[42] These are no small claims and the self-representation they in-

---

[40] On the "episodic" form of *Piers Plowman*, see Anne Middleton, "Narrative and the Invention of Experience: Episodic Form in *Piers Plowman*," in *The Wisdom of Poetry*, ed. L. D. Benson and S. Wenzel (Kalamazoo, 1982), 91–92.

[41] Yeager, "*Pax Poetica*," 105.

[42] Prologue to Book I, 50 and VII.25.288: Gower's actual words here are these: "Quod scripsi plebis vox est, set et ista videbis, / Quo clamat populus, est ibi sepe deus" (VII.1469–70).

volve may be more self-gratifying than the figure of the poet in *Piers Plowman*, that irascible, divided, wandering, falling, criticized but tenaciously searching Will, one figure of what it might be to think critically as a Christian moralist in a time of trouble and major dislocations.

Is the analysis offered above of any relevance to *Confessio Amantis*, the vernacular work begun soon after Gower wrote the first book of *Vox Clamantis*?[43] The current scholarship from which this essay set out would lead us to expect that the answer here will be an obvious negative. This may turn out be correct, but I wish to begin a discussion of *Confessio Amantis* which might indicate how its ethical and political dimensions could at least be explored along lines similar to those followed in the preceding discussion of *Vox Clamantis*. Here there is only space to initiate such an exploration, but if this encourages a rather more critically alert engagement with Gower's account of the virtues and "the common good" in the *Confessio* it will have served its purpose even if it is finally shown to be wide of the mark.

On the face of it, the *Confessio* seems to be a thoroughly dialogic poem quite alien to the *Vox Clamantis*. After all, its literary models include the dialogic works of Boethius, Jean de Meun, and Ovid. Its procedures include the invention of different voices and perspectives through which the errant Amans and, according to some accounts, the priest of Venus are educated in substantial ethical and political matters, and, finally, reformed. Despite these facts, the ethical reflections of the *Confessio* manifest examples of the traits I have identified in *Vox Clamantis*. I shall illustrate these by considering the poem's treatment of the contemporary church and Lollardy. Gower's previous works had included sustained criticism of the church which drew heavily on conventional estates satire, antimonastic and antimendicant satire.[44] The *Confessio* returns to these traditions in its consideration of the contemporary church but it does so in ways which may go beyond received conventions for lamenting disparity between current practices and shared ideals. These have been recently analyzed by Larry Scanlon. He shows how Gower's conventional criticism of the clerical estate is combined with a "celebration of lay political authority" which belongs to the new configuration of forces in late medieval England examined in *Narrative, Authority, and Power*.[45] Gower presents "the

---

[43] On the date at which Gower began the *Confessio*, see discussion and references in Simpson, *Sciences*, 293–94, esp. nn. 21 and 22.

[44] For surveys of these traditions: Jill Mann, *Chaucer and Medieval Estates Satire* (Cambridge, 1973); Penn Szittya, *The Antifraternal Tradition in Medieval Literature* (Princeton, 1986); J. A. Yunck, *The Lineage of Lady Meed: the Development of Medieval Venality Satire* (Notre Dame, 1963).

[45] Scanlon, *Narrative*, chap. 9; quotation from 247.

collapse of clerical authority" in his England and calls for an expansion of lay power, particularly monarchic power, with the lay poet devoted to legitimizing the prince's authority which "is always discursively constructed."[46] Here Gower's treatment of the struggle between Pope Boniface VIII and King Philip the Fair is especially illuminating (*Confessio*, II.2798–3071). Scanlon's commentary on this *exemplum*, "no fable" (II.2800) addresses the poet's fascination with "the Church's power to fabricate divine authority."[47] Papal claims to power and the authority of apostolic succession, together with its claims of supernatural authentication, are represented as inventive fictions produced to serve thoroughly material interests. The decisive voice of God turns out to be no more than the projection of an ambitious cardinal who employs a "clergyman of yong age" with a concealed trumpet.[48] In contrast King Philip (the poem's "Lowyz") represents legitimate power, including military power. In the face of a Catholic hierarchy led and represented by Pope Boniface, the lay power, according to the narrator, is entitled to use the violence it commands to displace the duly elected pope (II.2980–3029). This is a very striking image of the lay sovereign's licit role in challenging abuse in the Catholic church, even at its most elevated level. As Scanlon observes, the king and the poet disenfranchise clerical power "by making it entirely spiritual":[49]

> And seiden that the Papacie
> Thei wolde honoure and magnefie
> In al that evere is spiritual;
> Bot thilke Pride temporal
> Of Boneface in his persone,
> Ayein that ilke wrong al one
> Thei wolde stonden in debat. (II.2985–91)

The poem expands lay power while restricting clerical power "to a realm entirely separate from the structures of lay power," a move that involved "an anti-papalism and an anti-clericalism that would be difficult to overstate." However, Scanlon concludes that all this "is not finally anti-ecclesiastic."[50]

For Scanlon this conclusion apparently presents no problems. For him there seems to be no tension, let alone contradiction, in a poem that "disenfranchises clerical power," that undermines the foundational legiti-

---

[46] Ibid., 248–56; quotations from 251 and 250. Genius, Scanlon argues, is a decidedly lay moralist, like his maker: 255–56, 283–84, 292–94. (Perhaps V.1799 may suggest a slightly less consistent identification of Genius than Scanlon, persuasively enough, argues).

[47] Scanlon, *Narrative*, 260.

[48] *Confessio*, II. 2847–2931; Scanlon, *Narrative*, 258–60.

[49] Scanlon, *Narrative*, 262; see also 259–62.

[50] Scanlon, *Narrative*, 260, 262; see also the discussion of the Donation of Constantine at 263–67.

mations of ecclesiastical authority, that presents an "extreme" form of "anti-clericalism" and yet is "not finally anti-ecclesiastical."[51] But to maintain all the terms in this project without incoherence would demand an understanding of church, of "ecclesiastical" power and authority, quite incompatible with orthodoxy *as it was instituted, understood, and enforced* in late-fourteenth-century England. A position can only be antiecclesiastic or not antiecclesiastic in relation to an historically determinate church, an historically specific structure of power, authority, and self-understanding. And here we need to recall certain facts. First, by the time Gower wrote *Confessio Amantis* Wyclif and his followers had developed a major attack on the current authority of the pope and clergy together with a radical program of disendowment enforced by the lay power, especially the king. For them papal and clerical claims to divine authority were as counterfeit as Gower made them appear in Book II of the *Confessio*.[52] Second, by the time Gower was writing this poem the church's authorities had made perfectly clear that such attacks on the church's temporal possessions were unequivocally antiecclesiastic and to be resisted as such. This resistance had been plain enough since the later 1370s. The task was to persuade the lay power, particularly the sovereign, that what was antiecclesiastic would also prove subversive of the foundations of lay power, and that the sovereign needed the wholehearted support of the church.[53] This, in brief, is the specific context in which "I thenke make / A bok for Engelondes sake, / The yer sextenthe of Kyng Richard" (Prol.23–25). The *auctor* of the Prologue and Genius in Book II develop a radical critique of the actually existing church combined with a defence of the secular sovereign's role in challenging the ecclesiastical hierarchy when it is judged to be in serious error—judged, that is, by lay poet and secular lord. In Gower's historical context such critique of the sources and scope of ecclesiastical power and authority, not one confined to itemizing practical failures to meet demanding ideals, was distinctly antiecclesiastical. In Wendy Scase's terms, such writing belonged to a radical and "new" anticlericalism.[54]

Against this, however, one should set some of the confessor's instructions in Book V. Here he undertakes a comparative history of world religions in the course of which he comes to Christianity (V.726–1970; on the Christian faith, V.1737–90). Having given an account of orthodox Chris-

---

[51] Scanlon, *Narrative*, 262.

    [52] By far the best introduction to Wycliffism is Anne Hudson's *The Premature Reformation* (Oxford, 1988); for exemplification of vernacular Wycliffism at the end of the fourteenth century, see the *English Wycliffite Sermons*, ed. Anne Hudson and Pamela Gradon, 5 vols. (Oxford 1983–1996); and William Swinderby's statements summarized in *Registrum Johannis Trefnant*, ed. W. W. Capes (London, 1916), 235–51.

    [53] Pope Gregory XI first condemned Wyclif's teachings on dominion and temporalities in 1377; on the relevant history here see M. Aston, "Lollardy and Sedition, 1381–1431," *Past & Present* 17 (1960): 1–44, reprinted in her *Lollards and Reformers* (London, 1984) and Heath, *Church and Realm*, chap. 6.

    [54] Wendy Scase, *Piers Plowman and the New Anti-Clericalism* (Cambridge, 1989).

tian teaching on the Fall, the Incarnation and Redemption, Genius identi-
fies himself with Christ's power bestowed through apostolic succession in
the Catholic church, a power that "now is falle / On ous that ben of holi
cherche" (V.1797-99[55]). From this identification he (and his *auctor*[56])
warns Amans, an orthodox but morally confused Catholic, about a con-
temporary threat to his church, that guardian of orthodoxy and sole ark of
salvation:

> Now were it good that thou forthi,
> Which through baptesme properely
> Art unto Cristes feith professed
> Be war that thou be noght oppressed
> With Anticristes lollardie (V.1803-7).

This "newe" teaching, he then insists, is one that "goth aboute / To sette
Crites feith in doute" (V.1810-12). How exactly could "lollardie" bring
"Cristes feith in doute"? After all, Lollardy was a form of Christianity
which involved a strong commitment to traditional Christology, to tradi-
tional Trinitarian Doctrine, to the Gospel's account of Christ and its de-
mands of Christian discipleship? The claim is, of course, only intelligible
within a model of "Christes feith" where this is identified with the canon
law, doctrinal determinations, organization and ceremonies of the Roman
church. The narrator continues:

> The seintz that weren ous tofore,
> Be whom the feith was ferst upbore,
> That holi cherche stod relieved,
> Thei oghten betre be believed
> Than these, whiche that men knowe
> Noght holy, thogh thei feigne and blowe
> Here lollardie in mennes ere.
> Bot if thou wolt live out of fere,
> Such newe lore, I rede eschuie
> And hold forth riht the weie and suie,
> As thine Ancestres dede er this:
> So schalt thou noght believe amis. (V.1813-24)

---

[55] This seems one of the many places in the *Confessio* where the text goes against
Simpson's unifying reading of Genius as the soul's rational imagination: here Venus's
priest, still classified as such to the poem's end, is propounding a conventional version
of orthodox Christian doctrine that would fit into any contemporary "lay folk's
catechism."

[56] For an example of Gower's attacks on Wyclif and Wycliffism outside the *Confessio*
see especially the first part of *Carmen super multiplici viciorum pestilencia* (*Latin Works*,
346 ff.); a passage such as *Vox*, III.9.130 represents the commitment of the poet to the
pope's massive authority: "Whatever the Pope does is permissible, as his office indicates.
He can open the heavens and shut the foul pit of hell."

Lollardy is identified with the "new" and counterfeit (ll. 1810–11, 1818–20) while the contemporary church is identified with apostolic foundations, ancient tradition, and an unambiguous "weie" to follow. Yet the poet's defense of the church against Lollardy may be less straightforward than the confidence of the passage might suggest. Any moderately well-informed contemporary reader would note that the appeal to the primitive church was a basic Wycliffite move. From it there followed a wide range of substantial *contrasts* with the contemporary church. How then should one distinguish between different versions of the early church, different claims about continuity and discontinuity? Wyclif and his early followers took patristic sources as seriously as any orthodox exegete or theologian, while they attacked the contemporary church for fabricating novelties in doctrine, discipline, and ecclesiastical institutions. These novelties were presented as a disqualifying rupture with apostolic and patristic traditions, the authentic sources of Christian life to which Wycliffites sought to return.[57] Furthermore, Wycliffites agreed wholeheartedly with the poet's treatment of the Donation of Constantine and its venomous significance for the church (II.3473–96).[58] How precisely does the allegiance of "Anticristes lollardies" to the early church and its hostility to all that the Donation of Constantine symbolized differ from the poet's appeal to those "Be whom the feith was ferst upbore"? In the Prologue to *Confessio Amantis* the poet had *contrasted* the contemporary church and its "clerkes" with those "of daies olde." In those days the church was uncontaminated by the market, committed to non-violence, free from temporal goods, free from worldly honor, devoted to "the bok," preaching, and prayer (Prol. 193–239). "Bot now," the poet laments, the church is dedicated to the carnal sword and rejects Christ's demands that his disciples should pursue nonviolent peacemaking, poverty, patience, and unity. Now "the flock" is "withoute guide" and made the prey of rapacious pseudoshepherds; now the gap between inherited "word" and current norms has become massive (Prol. 240–480). Given this, a reader should wonder how Book V can so *simply* defend the authority of the contemporary church by an appeal to earlier traditions; and wonder too just how to distinguish this appeal and critique from the alleged novelty of Wycliffite arguments. One might almost suspect that the poet is developing some kind of ironic reflection about the utterly contingent and self-interested grounds of all appeals to tradition and authority, an irony directed against both orthodox and Wycliffite arguments, an irony to share with his friend Chaucer, perhaps. But such a response would ignore Gower's virulent attacks on Lollardy in the *Confessio* and elsewhere, ones which accompany defences of the actually

---

[57] These are basic commonplaces in Wycliffite ecclesiology and understanding of tradition and authority: see Hudson, *Premature Reformation,* chap. 7 and 377–78. For the full predestinarian contexts of Wyclif's own address to contemporary conflicts, see his *De Ecclesia,* ed. I. Loserth (London, 1886), esp. chaps. 1, 5, 17, and 18.

[58] On this see Scanlon, *Narrative,* 257–58, 263–67.

existing church; and it would ignore his unequivocal admiration for Archbishop Arundel who led the church toward the triumphant alliance with the lay power which enacted the statute enabling the burning of Lollards.[59] Having set aside this ironic, proto-Nietzschean reading, does one have any explanation of the conflicts in the poet's representations of the church, her authority, and her relation to earlier traditions? Conflicts, it is clear, which the poet does not acknowledge as such, let alone explore. As in *Vox Clamantis,* the explanation is parataxis, a paratactic mode which seals off units from each other and facilitates the propagation of conflicting positions whose conflicts are left unattended, unnoticed.

Even *within* Book V itself this mode can be observed. Here it eases the poet's move from a vehement defense of the church, against critics he classifies as Antichrist's followers, to a description of the same church's catastrophic degeneration from its earlier forms of life (V.1848–1959). Today, Genius declares, "the feith discresceth" and the ark of salvation, Peter's ship, the Roman church has almost sunk (V.1849–1873). Whereas Wycliffites had just been attacked for allegedly undermining "Cristes feith" (V.1810–12), now it seems that the church herself has done the undermining. Indeed this is made explicit as when we learn that the church's own abandonment of earlier tradition has generated both "cokel" sowing heretics and an audience ready "to taken hiede" of these Lollards and their teaching (V.1874–87;[60] see also V.1904–49). The church is vehemently defended and its radical critics demonized; yet soon the church is vehemently attacked as the cause both of these demons and a dissolution of Christian faith, an attack with radical implications. After all, if the contemporary church has become an agent through whom "the feith discresceth," that is, an impediment to saving faith, if it has changed from being the invulnerable ark to a sinking ship, "welnyh dreynt" by worldly attachments, what authority does it have and why should radical reformers be called Antichrist's followers? Undoubtedly the description of the church I have just summarized converges with theirs and raises just the issues they raise. Namely, if the ark has become a sinking ship, actually undermining Christian faith, should disciples of Christ stay on board? Is that God's will? Perhaps. But perhaps not. (Think of that voice from heaven: "Come out, my people, away from her, so that you do not share in her crimes and have the same plagues to bear. Her sins have reached up to the sky, and God has her crimes in mind" [Apoc. 18:4–5].) Yet by what authority does one leave, and to where does one go? At the end of *Piers Plowman,* Con-

---

[59] See the epistle to Arundel translated by Stockton in *Major Latin Works,* 47–48 and note Macaulay's commentary on 340.

[60] Here the Lollards are called "Pseudo": Macaulay's note refers to Rev. 19.20 and Matt. 7.15 as well as relevant passages in *Mirrour de l'Omme* and *Vox Clamantis;* in a context where the poet had already referred to "Anticristes Lollardie" (V.1807) the allusion to the apocalyptic "pseudo" refers again to Wycliffites; in *Carmen* Wyclif is thoroughly diabolized.

science makes the decision to search outside the actually existing church for Piers, *Petrus id est Christus*.[61] But in that long poem, conflicting positions, arguments and emotions have been brought into a critical, often thoroughly vexed, dialogue. Where contraries meet it is not because the poet has not noticed that he may be drawn to conflicting positions but because he seeks to explore them through the juxtaposition. Some contradictions are certainly found to be irresolvable, including ones in Langland's ecclesiology. So at the poem's end we are shown how a contemporary orthodox Christian might have to make the terrifying move Conscience makes.[62] Gower's *Confessio Amantis* includes responses to the church that are as conflicting as many in *Piers Plowman*. But the paratactic mode I have described enables the occlusion of fundamental problems that are ethical, political, and ecclesiological.

This paratactic mode is also displayed in another feature of the passage of Book V under discussion. Genius accuses Lollards of using a kind of ear-trumpet to propagate doctrine whose source is not authentic Christian tradition but their own fabrications: "thei feigne and blowe / Here lollardie in mennes ere" (V.1818–19).[63] We met this act and image in the story of Pope Boniface in Book II. There it disclosed the fabrication of ecclesiastical authority and the effectiveness of such counterfeiting (the cardinals, Pope Celestine, and the whole church accepts Boniface as St. Peter's due successor). What are readers to make of this reiteration? It certainly reveals a striking convergence between the Roman church and "Anticristes lollardie." Are we being invited to cultivate ironic reflection on the grounds of *all* doctrine, on the grounds of *all* claims to unfeigned, uninvented authority in matters concerning the divine? Is the reiteration designed to show that Lollards merely reflect the practices of the church they attack, while the church merely reflects the desires of the Lollards it anathematizes? Are we being led into an antifoundationalism where modern Christians must accept that all they can have access to is self-interested human organizations locked in conflicts over carnal power and material resources? Once more we have to reject such proto-Nietzschean reading as incompatible with too many of Gower's commitments, including his favored self-representations.[64] Whatever contradictions emerge in his treatment of Lollardy, the church, and the grounds of authority, they remain that, unresolved and unacknowledged. There is no intention to initiate a dialogue

---

[61] See *Piers Plowman: The B Version*, ed. G. Kane and E. T. Donaldson (London 1988), XX.368–86 and XV.212.

[62] On the ending of Piers Plowman, see D. Aers, *Chaucer, Langland and the Creative Imagination* (London, 1980), 56–61 and *Community, Gender and Individual Identity* (London, 1988), 63–66; see also James Simpson, *Piers Plowman: An Introduction to the B-text* (London 1990), 243–45.

[63] See also the first part of *Carmen*, esp. lines 30 ff.

[64] On the kinds of intention and self-representation I have in mind see especially the following: Simpson, *Sciences*, chaps. 8–9; Wetherbee (cited in n. 4); Lynch, Yeager, and Minnis (all cited in n. 1).

between contrary positions. It is just here that the paratactic mode helps the poet to escape the consequences of the contradictions he has composed, contradictions with far-reaching and profoundly disturbing consequences for his ethics, politics, and ecclesiological assumptions. The paratactic mode helps to occlude these difficulties, enabling the poet to maintain the stance that although the prophetic pose of the latin *Vox* has been set aside in the *Confessio,* the vernacular Gower remains an auctor in control of his matter, one to whom prince, courtiers, clergy, and people should pay attention, one from whom they have much to learn": "John Gower, *sapiens* in ethics and politics," for sure. The paratactic mode facilitates a paratactic moralism occluding substantial problems. It staves off dialogic relations between units which might force poet, and readers, to address and explore the congruences between aspects of his work and aspects of "Antecristes lollardie." It might force him, and his readers, to suspect that if Lollards are Antichrists in their reformist challenge to the Roman church, then the poet may be one of the smaller horns of the beast. And to escape such acknowledgment who would not use any available rhetorical forms?

Magic and the Metaphysics of Gender in Gower's "Tale of Circe and Ulysses"

Claire Fanger

Recent readings of the *Confessio Amantis* have recognized Gower's central concern with politics and pointed out the ways in which this concern is essentially congruous with the matter of erotic love. James Simpson, referring to an earlier article by Elizabeth Porter, describes this congruity as a function of the fact that, in the *Confessio,* "ethical control of the individual is both productive of, and modelled on, the ideal political order of the state."[1] Porter's own argument opens with the notion that the unity of the *Confessio* derives from

> Gower's assimilation of ideas about the relationship between the ethical health of the individual and the well-being of the body politic derived from the Pseudo Aristotelian *Secretum Secretorum* ... and the influential *De Regimine Principum* of Giles of Rome.... In both, Gower found expressed a view of politics as the extension of ethics into the sphere of public life (Porter, 135).

Porter notes that Gower's reliance on the notion of the human microcosm as a reflection of the greater macrocosm is part of the same allegorical net (ibid, 136–39): the individual and the state, properly governed, will reproduce the order of the cosmos by which they were generated.

Gower's primary concern in the *Confessio,* however, is less with the ideal order reflected in the macrocosm than with its human violation. For pedagogic purposes, the disorder caused by lack of proper self-government may be modeled equally well on a larger scale, in the state, or on a smaller scale, in the domain of erotic love and marriage. Gower's dalliance with erotic love in the *Confessio* serves to generate many exemplary narratives of the ways ethical self-ordering may be disrupted, dwelling upon the violent consequences of that disruption in the social sphere, and insisting,

---

[1] James Simpson, *Sciences and the Self in Medieval Poetry: Alan of Lille's "Anticlaudianus" and John Gower's "Confessio Amantis"* (Cambridge, 1995), 217; referring to Elizabeth Porter, "Gower's Ethical Microcosm and Political Macrocosm," in *Gower's "Confessio Amantis": Responses and Reassessments,* ed. A. J. Minnis (Cambridge, 1983), 135–62.

over the long haul, on the necessity and possibility of their correction, both at the individual and political levels.

To skew this lens only slightly, one can describe Gower's central concern as being a concern with power, both over the self in the ethical domain, and over others in the erotic and political domain. If this concern with power allows the *Confessio Amantis* to be a book about love and about politics at the same time, it almost necessitates that it will be a book about magic as well, for it is in the domain of human power, the sphere of influence with which Gower was most directly concerned, that magical operations are most likely to be used and to cause harm. While natural magic operates among the powers which bind the macrocosm to the individual through heavenly and earthly properties, the darker magics against which Gower expressly warns the reader in Book VI operate most frequently and dangerously among the powers which bind individuals to one another, through words and actions, through politics and love.

A major part of my argument in this essay will hinge on the understanding that Gower's treatment of magic is intrinsic to his concern with power, both erotic and political, and reflects another important facet of his preoccupation with ethical self-ordering and disruptive desire. In the *Confessio*, magic is represented simultaneously as a form of knowledge and a form of coercion. I have argued elsewhere that Gower's treatment of magical power has much in common with his treatment of other domains of knowledge, most especially with his treatment of rhetoric: magic, like language, may be used well or badly, to reveal truth and to help others, or to deceive and coerce others.[2] If magic is frequently depicted as dangerous knowledge, this is as much because knowledge itself is understood to be dangerous as because magic is the epitome of its dangerous form: knowledge is power, and power is dangerous. But this does not make knowledge, in and of itself, a bad thing.[3] Much of the psychological complexity of the *Confessio* is generated by the ambiguities surrounding the status of knowledge. While self-knowledge is synonymous with correct ethical self-

[2] I discuss this point in "A Fourteenth-century Synthesis: Curiosity, Magic and Rhetoric in Gower's *Confessio Amantis*," Part III.3 of my doctoral dissertation "Signs of Power and the Power of Signs: Medieval Modes of Address to the Problem of Magical and Miraculous Signifiers" (University of Toronto, 1993), 278–318. A revised version of this chapter is forthcoming as an article.

[3] Gower's disposition of the relations between power, politics, and self finds echoes in Foucault. In "The Ethic of Care for the Self as a Practice of Freedom: An Interview with Michel Foucault on January 20, 1984," Foucault states: "relations of power are not something bad in themselves, from which one must free one's self. I don't believe there can be a society without relations of power, if you understand them as means by which individuals try to conduct, to determine the behavior of others. The problem is not of trying to dissolve them in the utopia of a perfectly transparent communication, but to give one's self the rules of law, the techniques of management, and also the ethics, the *ethos,* the practice of self, which would allow these games of power to be played with a minimum of domination." In *The Final Foucault,* ed. James Bernauer and David Rasmussen (Cambridge, MA, 1987), 18.

empowerment, which allows more worldly forms of knowledge or power to be rightly used, worldly knowledge may be mistaken for, or otherwise obviate, the operation of self-knowledge. The problematics of magic, as a form of knowledge, are somewhat specialized, but this general pattern may be seen to hold: within the exempla, on the level of narrative, the notion that magic is evil in itself is mostly held in suspension. The evil associated with magic in the exempla is depicted not as an intrinsic consequence of the use of magic, but as a consequence of the reasonable or unreasonable uses to which it is put.

The present essay is conceived as a companion piece to "Curiosity, Magic and Rhetoric in the *Confessio amantis*" (cited above in n. 2). There, I examined the implications of magic understood as a form of knowledge. What I would like to do here is to examine more particularly how issues of knowledge and power are implicated with issues of gender in the poem. My focus will be the "Tale of Circe and Ulysses," the first of the exempla designed to warn against the dangers of magic at the end of Book VI. In brief, I will be arguing that Gower's overriding concern with individual responsibility and ethical self-ordering to some extent overturns the normal narrative expectations deriving from the medieval metaphysics of gender and gives rise to a novel structuring of the relations between magic, power, and gender in this tale. While Gower's underlying assumptions about the metaphysics of gender are no different from those of his contemporaries, the narrative dynamics of his "Tale of Circe and Ulysses" are different in important ways from the tale as it is told in his sources.

I want to begin, not with Gower's own account of the meeting of Ulysses and Circe, but rather with the account as given in Guido delle Colonne's *History of Troy*. Here, Ulysses tells the story of what happened to him:

> And on this island there were two girls, very beautiful sisters, ladies of the island, who were held to be very learned in the art of necromancy and exorcism. And these sisters so firmly captured any sailors Fortune drew to the island (not so much by their beauty as by their magical incantations) that there was no hope of any intruder ever being able to leave. All other business would be forgotten; and then, too, if the girls discovered anyone rebelling against their commands, they immediately turned them into animals.
>
> One of these girls (the one who was more expert in this science) was named Circe, and the other was named Calipsa. Into the power of these two Fortune led me. One of them, Circe, raving with what seemed to be love of me, mixed her potions and bound me so ridiculously with the snares of her incantations that for an entire year I had no means or power of getting away from her. And in this year Circe was made pregnant and conceived a son by me, who afterwards was born and grew and became a very warlike man. Meanwhile I bestowed some thought on the project of my escape. But wrathful Circe found out, and thought to detain me by her

magic art. I, however, who had been similarly well instructed in the art, destroyed and completely annulled every one of her figments by contrary operations. And because art makes sport of art, my arts prevailed so efficaciously against the contrary wiles of Circe that I escaped from the vexed enchantress with all my companions who were then with me.[4]

This passage is of interest to us for two reasons. First, as Macaulay notes, Guido's *History* was one of Gower's sources for the "Tale of Ulysses and Circe," the other being the verse *Roman de Troie* of Benoît de St. Maure, written in the mid-twelfth century. Guido's story was written a little over a hundred years after Benoît's, and while the two stories do differ in detail, their emphases are very similar. Although Gower takes the basic outlines of his narrative from these sources, he makes certain changes which considerably alter the emphases.

But there is another reason to present Guido's version before Gower's: Guido's version represents a view of Circe and her entrapping feminine magics which might be supposed commonplace through and beyond the century and a half intervening between his telling of the tale and Gower's. In her book *Transformations of Circe*, Judith Yarnall describes the view of Circe found in Ovid and the allegorical writers that followed him, which, as she argues, was current from the late classical period until the Renaissance. To Ovid, Circe "personifies a female passion so extreme that it destroys all who impede its satisfaction."[5] Allegorically Circe is no more than a distraction for Ulysses, a feminine temptation in the tradition of Dido, who threatens to turn the pious hero aside from his duty. In Guido's tale, as in Benoît's, there is little question but that we are seeing an aspect of this allegorized Circe; she is clearly to blame for Ulysses' delay,

---

[4] "In hac igitur insula erant due puelle sorores nimium speciose, ipsius insule domine, que in arte nigromancie et exorzizacionibus docte nimium habebantur. Quoscumque igitur nauigantes in hanc insulam fortuna trahebat predicte sorores non tam earum pulchritudine quam earum magicis incantationibus sic tenaciter capiebant quod nulla spes erat intrantibus ab insula posse recedere, omnium aliarum curarum oblitus, adeo quod si quos inueniebant ad earum mandata rebelles, statim eos in bestias transformabant. Harum igitur vna, illa uidelicet que magis docta in hac sciencia erat, Circes suo nomine uocabatur, et alia suo nomine Calipsa. In potestatem igitur harum duarum me fortuna deduxit, quarum vna, videlicet Circes, meo quasi amore bachata, suas inmiscuit pociones, et suarum incantacionum insidiis sic fatue me allexit quod per annum integrum non fuit michi ab ea recedendi facultas. Infra quem annum Circes grauida est facta et concepit ex me filium, qui postea natus ex ea creuit et factus est uir nimium bellicosus. Ego autem circa propositum mei recessus curam adhibui. Sed Circes irata persensit, et suis magicis artibus me credidit detinere. Sed ego, qui de arte eram similiter ualde instructus, contrariis operacionibus omnia sua figmenta destruxi et penitus annullaui. Et quia sic ars deluditur arte, contrariis commentis Circes in tantum preualuerunt efficacius artes mee quod cum omnibus sociis meis qui tunc erant mecum a Circe nimium anxiosa recessi." Guido de Columnis, *Historia Destructionis Troiae*, ed. Nathaniel Edward Griffin (Cambridge, MA, 1936), 258–59. (Translations mine unless otherwise noted.)

[5] Yarnall, *Transformations of Circe* (Urbana and Chicago, 1994), 87.

and in effect she is to blame as well for own impregnation.[6] It is worth looking a bit more closely at the way gender and magic are linked in Guido's tale. The contrast between what is represented in Guido's version and in Gower's is stronger than it might appear.

Although the girls in Guido's tale are said to be very beautiful, it is chiefly their magic (not their beauty) which holds the men on the island. Circe's power of turning men into animals is expressly a punishment for male disobedience, and we must assume that under such conditions the men would not be to blame for succumbing to the force of these women whether they found them desirable or not. Yet there is no indication that any desire is felt by the men; rather the force of erotic longing seems to be experienced only by the women. Circe's desire for Ulysses is the direct motivating factor in her enchantments. If Ulysses experiences any lust on his own behalf it is never mentioned, and is certainly not the motivating force in his own use of magic.

Circe's enchantment is so effective that for one year Ulysses claims to have had "no means of escape." The impregnation of Circe takes place during this time, while Ulysses is in principle bound and held fast by Circe's spells. Nevertheless, escape for Ulysses proves to be a simple matter once he "sets his mind to it"; we find out that he is "similarly well instructed in the art," and in the end he has no difficulty destroying and annulling all of her magical operations. When Ulysses' power is pitted against Circe's power it simply proves to be massively stronger; the question of why he could not have resorted to his own knowledge of the magic arts earlier is left undiscussed.

For Guido there appears to be no simple identification between the power of erotic love and the power of the magic arts. The two are linked primarily as cause to effect: Circe lusts and therefore uses magic to obtain her desires; her magic binds Ulysses, so that he satisfies her lust, and then he uses his magic to counter hers and escape. But his magic is not identified with his own lustful desires in any sense. Circe's magic is debased not only by its weakness in comparison to Ulysses' but also by the triviality of the end for which it is used. Ulysses uses his own magic only to counter her enchantments and to escape from her lust; this is a higher form of magic, both because it is stronger and because its ends are not trivial.

All of these features preserve certain commonplaces of the medieval relations between lust and the feminine as well as the typical role of Circe in her allegorized mode. In all of these points, Guido is more or less repeating what is found at greater length in Benoît, though Benoît's version is more subtle (indeed there are ways in which Guido reads almost

---

[6] Though it is clear that the allegorized Circe is more or less what is being represented by Guido and Benoît, in fact Yarnall does not discuss medieval Circe narratives. Other medieval writers, while recognizing the allegorical Circe, move more strongly against its implications, as for example Christine de Pisan and, as it seems to me, Gower.

like a parody of Benoît). In the polyvalences of Benoît's story we see something of the thematic richness upon which Gower drew, as a brief recapitulation of Benoît's version will show.

Benoît's tale begins with a more elaborate description of the various evils in which the two sorceresses are involved. Circe and Calipsa are said at the beginning to be women with no masters;[7] they lead wandering kings and princes to their hostelry and there enchant them; they have no mercy on any living thing, they make rich men poor and hungry, they take them to bed but this, we are told is no "fine amor" but treason and deception.[8] Ulysses fell into Circe's hands and had no power to escape;[9] and Circe casts strong enchantments to retain him. Benoît's description, however, slyly suggests a mutuality to their erotic pleasure which Guido does not hint at:

> O sei le couche: mout li plaist
> Qu'il la joisse e qu'il la baist;
> E si fait il, c'est la verté. (28759–761)

> [They went to bed: and much it pleased her
> When he made love to her and kissed her;
> He really did this, it's the truth.]

Nevertheless Circe conceives a child while Ulysses is under enchantment, and only after this does Ulysses try to escape.

What makes Benoît's version more subtle than Guido's is that the superiority of Ulysses' magical powers, once revealed to Circe, appear to become something by which her own erotic attachment to him is deepened. As Ulysses prepares to leave, we learn that his knowledge of magic is actually the greater;[10] in fact his own powers are so strong that all Circe's magic (it is not hard to read this as Circe herself) is not worth two coppers to him.[11] Yet his value to Circe appears to increase in the measure that her magic is shown to be of no worth. Circe understands how little she really knew:

> Donc conut bien e vit Circès
> Que poi sot envers Ulixès

---

[7] "Ço dit e conte li Autors / Qu'eles n'aveient pas seignors" (28713–714). Quotations from Benoît de Sainte-Maure, *Le Roman de Troie,* ed. Léopold Constans, vol. 4 (Paris, 1908).

[8] "Tot devoroënt, tot preneient; / De rien vivant merci n'aveient, / Que maint riche home e maint manant / Faiseient povre e pain querant, / O eles cochoënt plusor, / Mais n'i esteit pas fine amor, / Que traïson e decevance" (28739–745).

[9] "Iço retrait danz Ulixès, / Que il chai es mains Circès, / Mais ne li pot pas eschaper" (28747–749).

[10] "S'el sot des arz, il en sot plus" (28775)—as Macaulay notes, a line echoed by Gower.

[11] "Ses uevres, ses conjureisons, / Ses charaies e ses poisons / Ne li valurent pas dous auz" (28779–781).

Maistre a trové a sa mesure
Tel qui ne crient sort ne conjure. (28789–792)

[Then Circe saw and understood:
Beside Ulysses she knew so little
She'd found a master to her measure
In one who feared no spell or potion.]

Circe finds a master to her measure when she finds a man she cannot con-
jure. The word "maistre," implicated at once with its connotations of
pedagogy, mastery, and erotic love, suggests the many ways in which a
woman, at first described as under no male dominion, might have been
mastered by Ulysses' knowledge. Throughout the tale, the ideas of eroti-
cism, power, and magic are much more identified than they ever become
in Guido's version. However two points may be noted: first, that Ulysses
is at least putatively under Circe's enchantment when he impregnates her;
and second, that any sense in which Ulysses might be held blameworthy
for his actions to Circe is suppressed. The fact that Circe has no master to
begin with is entwined with all the other things that make her dangerous
to men; thus the fact that she finds mastery in Ulysses must be seen as, in
a sense, beneficial. At the very least it is no more than she deserved.

Though Gower has lifted most of his narrative from Benoît, and even
(as Macaulay notes) echoes Benoît in a number of lines and phrases, the
dynamic of the situation as Gower represents it is different from that of
either of the sources. The first difference is that Gower's Ulysses, through-
out the tale, remains unbeguiled by Circe. He is never enchanted. That is,
in both sources, we have a period of time when Ulysses is at least putative-
ly "under enchantment" and impregnates Circe, and a subsequent period
of time when Ulysses decides to pit his own magic against Circe's in an
attempt to escape. In Gower's tale, the impregnation episode and the
contest of enchantments are compressed into one. Gower tells how the
queens of the island, Calipsa and Circe, hear of Ulysses arrival and send
for him. "Thes queenes" Gower says, "were as tuo goddesses,"

Of Art magique Sorceresses
That what lord comth to that rivage,
Thei make him love in such a rage
And upon him assote so,
That thei wol have, er that he go,
Al that he hath of worldes good.
Uluxes wel this understod,
Thei couthe moche, he couthe more;
Thei shape and caste ayein him sore
And wroghte many a soutil wyle,
Bot yit thei mihte him noght beguile.[12] (VI.1431–44)

---

[12] All quotations from the *Confessio Amantis* are from G. C. Macaulay, ed., *The*

In Gower's version, the magical contest begins the moment Ulysses steps off the boat; he comes prepared to be magically assaulted, and begins his counterattack immediately. More than this, the love which Circe begins to feel for him, as well as the pregnancy which it occasions, is, in Gower's version, a result of Ulysses' enchantment of Circe (rather than vice versa). After noting that Circe had successfully enchanted Ulysses' shipmates, Gower goes on to write:

> Ther myhte hem nothing desobeie,
> Such craft thei hadde above kinde.
> Bot that Art couthe thei noght finde,
> Of which Uluxes was deceived,
> That he ne hath hem alle weyved,
> And broght him into such a rote
> That upon him thei bothe assote;
> And thurgh the science of his art
> He tok of hem so wel his part,
> That he begat Circes with childe. (VI.1432–61)

Circe's impregnation, indeed her erotic attachment to Ulysses, occurs "through the science of *his* art"; it is not, as in the other stories, a thing Circe brings on herself by her foolish and wanton desires. In Gower's tale, much more than Guido's, the practice of magic is identified with the erotic deception; and erotic deception, which is to say magic arts, are being practiced by both parties at all times.

It is certainly possible here that Gower is taking a trick from Ovid, in whose story Ulysses also has the upper hand from the beginning; but the course of events is clearly dictated as much by the moral Gower was working to convey as by any debt to Ovid. As the frame narrative makes plain, both of the exempla concerning magic at the end of Book VI are designed to show the dangers of magic as a form of intellectual abuse. Integral to the structure of the hinge between Books VI and VII is the notion that no knowledge is properly applicable without selfknowledge;[13] since the perfected self mirrors God, failure to attend to the presence or absence of charity in one's own actions is equivalent to ignorance of God. The two exempla, the stories of Ulysses and of the sorcerer Nectanabus, illustrate the lethal nature of knowledge when it is indulged in purely for its own sake. The two tales have similar structures in this regard: in both, the sorcerer-protagonists (Ulysses and Nectanabus) are learned men shown to

---

English Works of John Gower, 2 vols., EETS, e.s. 81–82 (London, 1900–1901).

[13] A marginal gloss at line 1567 refers this notion to a maxim attributed to (pseudo-) Bernard of Clairvaux: "Plures plura sciunt et seipsos nesciunt" [Many people know much and are ignorant of themselves]. Cf. Latin verse 1.4, "Omnia scire putat, set se Presumpcio nescit, / Nec sibi consimilem quem putat esse parem." [Presumption does not know himself, but thinks / himself all-knowing; equal has he none.] In Siân Echard and Claire Fanger, *The Latin Verses in the "Confessio Amantis": An Annotated Translation* (East Lansing, 1991), 25.

be guilty of misusing the powers granted by their knowledge; and in both, the men are killed by sons conceived through this abuse of power. The crucial gap in the knowledge of each is the understanding of what his own abuse of power may have meant or entailed, the failure to recognize that conforming the self to God's image requires more than earthly science.

With these concerns guiding the narrative of Ulysses and Circe, Gower cannot allow the woman to be the trick in the simple way she appears to be in Guido's or Benoît's version. Instead, Gower pits the male and female protagonists against each other in a contest of knowledge which is also a mutual seduction—almost, indeed, a mutual assault. Since Ulysses binds Circe through magically induced desire and through pregnancy, the child must be read as Ulysses' own doing, his own responsibility; and the end result of the act by which he conceived the child becomes less a cruel accident than an appropriate form of justice. In contrast to the moral structure of the source tales, Gower's Ulysses is not the moral victor by virtue of his superior power. It may be noted that the context provided for ethical judgment of Ulysses' action is not the more courtly one that might be thought applicable from the frame tale (Genius never points out, for example, that adultery is wrong, or that it is unfair to abandon a pregnant mistress). The reader is encouraged rather to think in scrupulously political terms, so that the moral conduct of the parties must be read independently of gender. Both Circe and Ulysses misuse their magical knowledge; Ulysses' superiority of power is merely an increased thoroughness of deception, no standard of virtue. It is not even, in Gower's tale, self defence, properly speaking.

In the end Ulysses is killed by his son, Thelogonus, whom he conceived when he was with Circe on the island. Ulysses' death is brought about by his failure to recognize the son (or even, it appears, to remember the incident with Circe in which a son might have been engendered[14]). The gap in Ulysses' knowledge of himself is emphasized, at this point in the tale, by his inability to read a divinatory dream—a dream which foretells, though Ulysses does not know it, the coming of his son and his own death:

> Him thoghte he syh a stature evene,
> Which brihtere than the sonne schon;
> A man it semeth was it non,
> Bot yit it was as in figure
> Most lich to mannyssh creature,
> Bot as of beaute hevenelich
> It was most to an Angel lich (VI.1525–29)

---

[14] Gower is explicit about the forgetting; at one point he mentions "This Circes, which I spak of late, / On whom Uluxes hath begete / A child, thogh he it have foryete" (1614–16).

Ulysses wishes to embrace the figure, and does so; but the image warns him thereupon that "The love that is ous betuene, / Of that we nou such joie make, / That on of ous the deth schal take" (VI.1544–46). Ulysses asks "What wyht he is that seith him so"; the figure shows him a spear bearing a pennant with three fishes on it, and just before vanishing tells him that it is the sign of an empire.

Who is the dream figure supposed to represent? In all versions of the story, the device on the pennant links the dream figure at least potentially to Thelogonus, who, as we later read, carries such a banner on his spear when he travels to find his father. However it is little wonder that Ulysses does not identify the figure with Thelogonus immediately, not only because he has forgotten the incident with Circe, but also because there are many distracting ambiguities which enter into the dream through the figure's heavenly appearance and oracular speech. When Ulysses seeks to know who the angelic personage is, in no case does the figure name itself, but rather, substituting for a name or explanation a sign which is a mark rather of national than personal identity, thrusts forward the pennant and directs Ulysses to fathom the origin of its device. As noted above, events described later in the narrative identify the banner as bearing the device of Circe's island; this sign Circe gives to her son at the outset of his journey. When Gower describes this event he explains the banner's purpose in a way that expands on the source narratives:

> It was that time such usance,
> That every man the conoiscance
> Of his contre bar in his hond,
> Whan he wente into strange lond;
> And thus was every man therfore
> Wel knowe, wher that he was bore:
> For espiaile and mistrowinges
> They dede thanne suche thinges,
> That every man mai other knowe. (VI.1638–45)

It is an irony characteristic of Gower that the custom evolved to prevent suspicion and mistrust, the bearing of a mark of origin "that every man mai other knowe," is precisely the mark that Ulysses fails to grasp in its ordinary sense.

If we look more closely at the episode of the dream itself, we can see that here too Gower has made alterations to his source narratives which deepen the ambiguity and link the dream figure potentially to Circe in a way that the source tales do not do. Of the features which the three versions share, it may be remarked that the gender of the dream figure is not specified, either in Gower's version or in Guido's. In all the tales, its form is human, its beauty is heavenly, but it appears to have no sex—or if it does have a sex it leans toward the masculine. Benoît's dream figure appears sexless in the description, though Ulysses seems to perceive it as male: "Mout doucement li depreioë / Qu'il m'embraçast: ço desiroë"

(29857–858). [Very sweetly I entreated him to embrace me; I desired this.] And yet despite the neuter or masculine quality of the dream figure, in all versions it is only during the account of the dream that we see Ulysses helplessly in the sway of what appears to be a powerful affective state; Ulysses shows clear signs of loving (or of being in love with) the dream figure in a way that he has not been shown to be with anyone else in the story. The emotion visible in Ulysses in this episode suggests that it would at least be possible to link the figure with a living prototype that is feminine rather than masculine (Circe rather than Thelogonus); yet neither of the source narratives do this at all. Rather they insist on the masculine or neuter qualities of the figure, and indicate by other clues that the link with Thelogonus is to be held primary.

The chief difference between Gower's dream and the dream as it is told in the source narratives is that only in Gower's version is Ulysses allowed to touch the figure. In both sources the figure actively evades Ulysses' grasp; Ulysses is not allowed to embrace it, though he very much desires to do so. And in both sources also, the dream figure's warning hinges on the embrace which Ulysses does not (in the dream) achieve. Guido writes (following Benoît):

> It seemed to [Ulysses] that he wanted more than anything to be able to touch the image, and to gather it firmly in his arms, but it kept on avoiding his embraces and seemed to gaze at him from afar. But then it seemed to him to draw closer and to ask what he desired. And he said: "I'd like us to get together so I can get to know you better." But it said to Ulysses "O how grievous and bitter is your request in this regard: you want to get together with me, but how unhappy this conjunction will be! Indeed from our meeting it must befall that one of us will die."[15]

The conjunction referred to by the dream figure can fairly clearly be read as the meeting of Ulysses and Thelegonus, which, at the time of the vision, is still in the future; it has not yet occurred, though when it does occur, the death of one of them will be the result. The pushing of the conjunction (meeting, embrace) into the future and the statement that "from our meeting it must befall that one of us shall die" anchors the dream figure to an aspect of Thelogonus. Here we find Gower's version different. The figure does not, as in the sources, evade Ulysses' embrace. Ulysses goes forward to it

---

[15] "Videbatur eciam sibi ultra modum appeter ymaginem illam posse tangere et eam suo cogi tenaciter in amplexu, sed illa suos uitabat amplexus et eum uidebatur a longe intueri. Deinde uero ad eum sibi propinquius uidebatur accedere et interrogabat ab eo quidnam uellet. Sed ille dicebat: 'Uolo ut insimul coniungamus ut te forte cognoscam.' At illa dicebat Ulixi: 'O quantum in hoc est tua grauis et amara peticio! Tu enim petis a me ut tibi coniungar. Sed O quantum illa coniunccio erit infelix! Nam ex tali coniunccione necesse est quot unus nostrum exinde moriatur.' " *Historia,* 269–70.

And takth it in his Armes tuo,
And it embraceth him ayein
And to the king thus gan it sein:
"Uluxes, understond wel this,
The tokne of oure aqueintance is
Hierafterward to mochel tene:
The love that is ous betuene,
Of that we nou such joie make,
That on of ous the deth schal take,
Whan time comth of destine;
It may non other wise be." (VI.1538–48)

In Gower's version, the dream figure does not warn of an event which has not yet occurred, but rather prophesies the outcome of a situation already existing: "the love that is ous betuene." This already existing love is marked by the embrace ("the tokne of oure aqueintance") which Ulysses shares with it. The visionary event thus glides back to the incident with Circe, to the only embrace Ulysses has already known (since he has neither met nor embraced the son, though it is the son he will love and not the mother). The dream figure does not offer Ulysses any apparent choice, for the doom which is the outcome of the past event is already foreordained, "Whan time comth of destine." Thus Circe, whom he used by magic, becomes, through a love experienced only in the prophetic vision, an herald of divine retribution for the power play in which Thelogonus was begotten.

It is worth noting here that in Lydgate's version of this story in his *Troy Book,* the dream figure is rendered as clearly feminine, rather than neuter or masculine. Lydgate makes explicit the connection between the dream figure and Circe which Gower merely suggests; and in so doing he also renders completely hetero-normative the suggestion of eroticism which is also present in Guido and Benoît. It seems likely that Lydgate was influenced by Gower in his telling of this tale, for there is no other source in which it is suggested that this figure could be linked to any other living prototype than Thelogonus, and there are other correspondences to Gower's narrative in his ordering of events. Lydgate describes the dream figure in a way that echoes, in spots, the language of Guido and Benoît, but he has clearly shifted the tale into a different genre. The dream figure is

Noon erthely þing, but verraily devyne,
Of port, of chere wonder femynyne,
And, as hym sempte in his fantasye,
Like a þing sent oute of fairie. (2961–64)[16]

---

[16] Quotations drawn from *Lydgate's Troy Book,* ed. Henry Bergen, EETS, e.s. 97 (London, 1908).

Lydgate's fairy-tale rhetoric is consistent throughout the story, which is far more romantic than any of the other versions. He makes of Circe a fatal woman whose beauty is an important part of her attraction (as we have seen, other versions of the tale emphasize the compulsory quality of her magic, deemphasizing the beauty which might have been understood to stir desire in its own right). Lydgate more than any other author turns the episode into something resembling a love story, though one with tragic consequences. When Ulysses speaks to the dream figure he requests to have his will of her immediately. But the language he uses for this demand remains courtly; he calls her "my lyues emperesse"and says,

> My lyf, my deth stant hooly in ʒour grace,
> More of merci requiryng þanne of riʒt
> To rewe on me, whiche am ʒour owne knyʒt ...
> For my desire but I may fulfille,
> þis silfe nyʒt to haue of ʒow my wille,
> To my recure I can no remedie,
> For lak of rouþe but I moste dye. (2990–98)

As in Gower's version, the dream figure allows Ulysses his request, and after they have made love she tells him

> "þin affeccioun
> Wolde fully turne to confusioun
> Of vs boþe, it is so perillous,
> So inly mortal and contagious,
> þat outterly, þer geyne may no red,
> But oon of vs moste anoon be ded—
> þis is þe fyn of þe hatful chaunce
> þat shulde folwe after oure plesaunce."

Thus Lydgate also follows Gower in having the fate prophesied by the dream figure contingent upon a love which already exists—a love which is explicitly referred to Circe, rather than the meeting between father and son which is still to come. As she leaves Ulysses, the visionary Circe tells him that their parting is

> "For euere-more, nowþer for sour nor swete,
> After þis day neuer agayn to mete!"

It is clear, too, from subsequent events, that Circe has in a sense shared the dream experience with Ulysses. Alone among the tellers of this tale, Lydgate has Circe try to prevent her son from going to find his father; it is clear that she foresees Ulysses' doom, and would forestall it if she could. Unlike Gower's version, there is no sense of Ulysses' fate being other than bad luck; in his dream narrative we see no enactment of divine justice, but only natured love and "hateful chance." Circe plays a feminine part which is dictated by fate; she is the direct instrument of Ulysses' doom, but any blame she might bear for being so is softened by the rhetoric of courtly love. Ulysses is equally not held to blame for experiencing emotions and desires which are out of his control.

Gower is much less ready to bow to the emotional dilemmas of the characters in the story and insists upon the personal responsibility of all the participants for their actions. Not only is Ulysses held responsible for his initial erotic mastery of Circe, he is also held responsible for the knowledge which ought to have allowed him to interpret his dream, but did not. Ulysses' failure to understand the dream shows the precariously incomplete nature of his learning, which is extensive only in the worldly sense; the narrator's moral on this point is explicit:

> Men sain, a man hath knowleching
> Save of himself, of alle thing;
> Was nevere yit so wys a clerk,
> Which mihte knowe al goddes werk,
> Ne the secret which god hath set
> Ayein a man mai noght be let.
> Uluxes, thogh that he be wys,
> With al his wit in his avis,
> The mor that he his swevene accompteth,
> The lasse he wot what it amonteth. (VI.1571–78)

It may be noted that Gower has left out the clerks and wise men who, in both source narratives, help Ulysses to interpret his dream. Gower's Ulysses is left alone to ponder its riddle; and in Gower's version, in fact, dream interpretation is listed as one of Ulysses' particular specialties early in the tale, so that Ulysses is made to bear responsibility for knowledge of the dream as he does for his knowledge of Circe. Both kinds of knowledge are traced to the knowledge and power of magic:

> Thurgh Sorcerie his lust he wan,
> Thurgh Sorcerie his wo began,
> Thurgh Sorcerie his love he ches,
> Thurgh Sorcerie his lif he les;
> The child was gete in Sorcerie,
> The which dede al this felonie:
> Thing which was ayein kynde wroght
> Unkindeliche it was aboght;
> The child his oghne fader slowh,
> That was unkindeschipe ynowh. (VI.1769–78)

There is a deceptive simplicity to this bit of doggerel, and an apparent lack of "art" in Gower's telling of the tale generally, which belies the character and importance of the alterations Gower has made to his source narratives. We may note that no previous Ulysses could be said to win his own pleasure or choose his own love "thurgh Sorcerie" in the episode with Circe; it is only in Gower's tale that Ulysses' fate is brought about by the seductive properties of his *own* magic and the power he wields from it.

All of this is thoroughly consistent with the attitude to politics, power, and love Gower espouses in the Prologue to the *Confessio;* the emphasis on individual responsibility for action and the knowledge that informs it is a motif which stretches through the frame tale as well as the individual stories. My enterprise here has been to examine on a more detailed level the way these concerns have influenced Gower's interpretation of one particular tale.

I remarked early on that the narratives by Guido and Benoît conform roughly to our expectations of what the medieval Circe might be like, based on the Ovidian and post-Ovidian allegorical sources examined by Judith Yarnall. Gower's version, I think, does not conform to these expectations in the way that the others do. While Gower certainly does not restore Circe to the semidivine status of Homer's narrative (a divinity which is in fact approached more nearly and more dangerously by Lydgate), Gower also does not render her as the famous harlot or the witch whose evil is seen as the more culpable when set against Ulysses' masculine virtue. In Gower's version, Circe is only human, and bears a human responsibility for her use of knowledge, power, and magic, just as Ulysses does in his turn.

Let me make it clear that I am not arguing that anything in Gower's *Confessio* should be taken as a defense of women, or even as a re-interpretation of the normal medieval metaphysics of gender. It is easy to find traces in his writing of all the expected misogynistic allegories. As in other medieval sources, lust (lechery/*voluptas*) is referred to as a feminine and effeminizing quality which is essentially subversive of (masculine) magnanimity, reason, and proper ethical self-government. In Latin verse VII.5 (on Chastity) Gower refers to such commonplaces when he writes

> Corporis et mentis regem decet omnis honestas
> Nominis vt famam nulla libido ruat.
> Omne quod est hominis effeminat illa voluptas,
> Sit nisi magnanimi cordis, ut obstet ei.
> (Virtue of mind and flesh befits a king
> Lest lustful pleasure ruin his good name.
> That kind of pleasure sissifies a man,
> Who isn't man enough at heart to check it.)[17]

But if it is understood that the rational faculty is weakened and the charitable heart effeminized by lust, it is not precisely the case that in the *Confessio Amantis* reason is set in opposition to the desires of the body, nor that masculine control is set in opposition to feminine subversion. The essential conflicts of the *Confessio,* in the framing tale and many of the exempla, are, I would prefer to say, microcosmic: internal to individual choice and pertaining strictly to the faculty of reason. These conflicts hinge

---

[17] Echard and Fanger, *Latin Verses,* 85.

on the choices made to implement knowledge in ethical or unethical ways. Reason must choose to play Cupid's game (or not); it is no more at the mercy of Cupid's dart than it is at the mercy of the stars.[18] Provided that the processes of reason emerge from self-knowledge and are not perverted to self-indulgence, the desires of the body, and hence the motions of the will, are set in their right order, within the state, within marriage, within the self. This is not an effect of the forceful control or domination of bodily desire by reason, inasmuch as reason is as natural to human consciousness as desire: the right ordering of the human microcosm guarantees fulfillment in both realms. This consequence of the ideal ordering is gestured at many times in the poem, as for example in Book VII, at the end of the "Tale of Sarah and Tobias":

> For god the lawes hath assissed
> Als wel to reson as to kinde,
> Bot he the bestes wolde binde
> Only to lawes of nature,
> Bot to the mannes creature
> God yaf him reson forth withal,
> Wherof that he nature schal
> Upon the causes modefie,
> That he schal do no lecherie,
> And yit he schal hises lustes have.
> So ben the lawes bothe save
> And every thing put out of sclandre. (VII. 5372–83)

It is when the processes of reason are given over, however subtly, to the desires of the body, that conflict and disorder ensue. But what is chiefly taken to task for this disorder is not the desires of the body themselves, but the individual's voluntary concession to them of the power of governance.

What I am getting at is not that Gower allegorized gender differently from his contemporaries, but rather that his stress on the responsibility of the individual for self-knowledge and self-government makes him tend to avoid laying blame for wrong action on the body or its temptations. And though this does not affect his metaphysics of gender (much), it does affect the narrative dynamics of gender. Put simply in terms of what happens in Gower's narratives, it means that rape is never the woman's fault. Lust may be paradoxically effeminizing (where effeminization implies the subversion of reason's power) and tyrannous (inasmuch as Gower's term for the inversion of the right order of power is always tyranny); but the responsibility for the perversion or right use of reason (and power) is always ultimately the responsibility of the human individual. And this

---

[18] The proverbial notion, cited by Gower, that the wise man will rule the stars ("Vir mediante deo sapiens dominabitur astris," Latin verse VII.iv) encapsulates very much the same kind of issues.

does set Gower apart from many of the sources on which he drew. Nowhere is this clearer than in his depiction of what happened between Ulysses and Circe.

It seems important to point to the variety of uses to which the basic medieval metaphysics of gender could be put, not only because I would like to defend the subtle novelties to be found in Gower's artless art, but also as a caution to readers of medieval narratives generally. It is possible for writers to say quite different things within a context that appears superficially similar; it is possible, for example, to take a single tale of the evil of magic, to describe a wizard and a sorceress and a seduction and a dream and a homicide, and have it come out quite differently each time, with the balance of fault and error and the link of both to the feminine all changing in the telling. It is easy to discard the corpus of medieval writing in which the metaphysics of gender are brought into play as in some simple way misogynistic, as Yarnall and others have done. From a more careful reading of the tales medieval writers have told, we can see that there is nothing essentially simple about the way these metaphysics are implemented. It is best not to jump to conclusions about what this all means.

If the power represented by Ulysses and his magical seduction is a dangerous kind of power, for whose abuse he is punished, it may be remarked in a kind of final tangential authorial aside that it is not a very different kind of power from that implemented by Gower himself when he dresses up in lover's garb to tell his story, to seduce his reader with his magical tales in which love and politics are mixed, in which the reader also may choose, like Amans, to be seduced, or choose instead, again like Amans in the end, to become wise. If Gower has used his magic upon us, even as Ulysses did upon Circe, what shall we do about it? It is too late to kill him. Deeply implicated in Gower's metaphysical links between magic and gender is a concept of the ethically oriented cosmos which carries us beyond the Middle Ages to the Renaissance, to its embrace of neo-Platonic ideals, and its tales of Circes whose goddess-like powers are restored, whose femininity partakes, as we all must, in new discourses of power from which we can never be released, but which nonetheless allow us, in a necessarily limited way, our own sphere of action. If we cannot defend John Gower as a feminist, perhaps we may take solace in the diversity of the history of antifeminist metaphysics and ponder the possibilities it offers for the working out of our own stories.

The Sympathetic Villain in *Confessio Amantis*

Hugh White

In her essay, "Moral Chaucer and Kindly Gower," Rosemary Woolf exchanged epithets between the two poets because of what she saw as a characteristic tendency on Gower's part to be too lenient toward vice, Chaucer having a much more strenuous moral vision.[1] In this piece I want to consider whether Gower can indeed be held to demonstrate such a morally dubious sympathy, and if so, what elicits it and why.

One thing which draws sympathetic treatment in *Confessio Amantis* is being a victim of the power of love. But sympathy for such a victim can be sympathy for one who does wrong. The frame narrative offers a case in point. Amans can be seen as a sympathetic victim-villain, one who under the influence of erotic feeling behaves immorally: Genius eventually calls Amans's love "a Sinne" (VIII.2088), but for much of the poem he has dealt with Amans in a friendly, tolerant manner. The view that love is an irresistible and natural force, a view expressed in the poem both by the narrator and by Genius,[2] would seem to underpin such tolerance. The "Tale of Canace and Machaire" offers us incestuous, yet sympathetic, lovers and provides perhaps the most explicit justification in *Confessio Amantis* of an attitude of tolerance toward wrong behavior induced by love:

> For it sit every man to have
> Reward to love and to his miht,
> Ayein whos strengthe mai no wiht:

My thanks to Dr. C. B. White for help on this piece.

[1] Rosemary Woolf, "Moral Chaucer and Kindly Gower" in *J. R. R. Tolkien Scholar and Storyteller: Essays 'In Memoriam,'* ed. Mary Salu and Robert T. Farrell (New York, 1979), 197–218, repr. in *Art and Doctrine: Essays on Medieval Literature*, ed. Heather O'Donoghue (London and Ronceverte, 1986). References are to this reprint. Gower is "moral" at *Troilus and Criseyde* V.1856; for Chaucer as "kindly" according to Coleridge and Matthew Arnold, see Woolf, "Moral Chaucer," 197.

[2] See, for example, besides quotations given in the text, I.29–38, III.166–78, VIII 3138–56; see also John Burrow, "The Portrayal of Amans in *Confessio Amantis*" in *Gower's Confessio Amantis: Responses and Reassessments*, ed. A. J. Minnis (Cambridge, 1983), 5–24 (15f.). Quotations from and references to *Confessio Amantis* are cited from *The Complete Works of John Gower*, ed. G. C. Macaulay, 4 vols. (Oxford, 1899–1902), vols. 2 and 3.

> And siththe an herte is so constreigned,
> The reddour oghte be restreigned
> To him that mai no bet aweie,
> Whan he mot to nature obeie.
> For it is seid thus overal,
> That nedes mot that nede schal
> Of that a lif doth after kinde,
> Wherof he mai no bote finde.
> What nature hath set in hir lawe
> Ther mai no mannes miht withdrawe, (III.344–56)

and Genius goes on to enforce this point by telling the "Tale of Tiresias and the Snakes," in which Tiresias is punished for disturbing the natural sexual order. Genius concludes:

> So mihte it nevere ben honeste
> A man to wraththen him to sore
> Of that an other doth the lore
> Of kinde, in which is no malice,
> Bot only that it is a vice:
> And thogh a man be resonable,
> Yit after kinde he is menable
> To love, wher he wole or non.
> Thenk thou, my Sone, therupon
> And do Malencolie aweie;
> For love hath evere his lust to pleie,
> As he which wolde no lif grieve. (III.384–95)

Now, it would be possible to see the Canace and Machaire story as morally subversive in its attitude to incest, and critics have indeed taken Gower, or Genius, to task over it.[3] We might similarly feel that Genius's early sympathy toward Amans is judged adversely by the unequivocally condemnatory line he takes on Amans's love at the end of the poem (VIII.2060–148). I shall return to the question of Genius's moral perspective later, but, however that stands, I am not sure that either the incestuous brother and sister or Amans in the frame narrative set us back at all sharply on our moral heels. This is partly a matter of their passivity; Amans *does* pathetically little in the course of his amour, whilst Canace and Machaire drift into incest as a natural consequence of being brought up together—it just happens (III.148–78). In both cases there is an absence of positively willed evil action, so that our sympathy does not entail the endorsement of a deliberate choice of evil, or incite us toward applauding the achievement

---

[3] See J. S. P. Tatlock, *The Development and Chronology of Chaucer's Works,* Chaucer Society Publications, 2nd. Series (London, 1907), 173; Henry Ansgar Kelly, *Love and Marriage in the Age of Chaucer* (Ithaca, NY, 1975), 144–45; Thomas J. Hatton, "John Gower's Use of Ovid in Book III of the *Confessio Amantis,*" *Mediaevalia* 13 (1987): 257–74; James Simpson, *Sciences and the Self in Medieval Poetry* (Cambridge, 1995), 172–79.

of what has been thus dubiously chosen. A further absence is that of a victim of the erring lovers' actions. Neither Amans nor Canace and Machaire can reasonably be said to cause harm to others by their questionable behavior.[4] In fact, the lack of deliberate choosing and the failure to inflict harm make it difficult to feel that the designation "villain" is entirely appropriate in these cases.

There are, however, cases where it is appropriate—where there is a deliberate choice of evil, where there is a victim of the evil action—and yet where sympathy still seems to exist for the villain. Take, for instance, the "Tale of Mundus and Paulina." This is how the story is summarized in the Latin commentary:

> sub regno Tiberii Imperatoris quidam miles nomine Mundus, qui Romanorum dux milicie tunc prefuit, dominam Paulinam pulcherrimam castitatisque famosissimam mediantibus duobus falsis presbiteris in templo Ysis deum se esse fingens sub ficte sanctitatis ypocrisi nocturno tempore viciauit. Vnde idem dux in exilium, presbiteri in mortem ob sui criminis enormitatem dampnati extiterant, ymagoque dee Ysis a templo euulsa vniuerso conclamante populo in flumen Tiberiadis proiecta mergebatur.[5]

> [During the reign of the Emperor Tiberius a certain soldier by the name of Mundus, who was at that time a general in command of the Roman troops, pretended in the Temple of Isis, helped by two false priests, to be a god, and under cover of the hypocrisy of a feigned holiness violated in the night the lady Paulina, a most beautiful woman, highly reputed for her chastity. For which they were condemned, this general to exile and the priests to death because of the enormity of their crime. And the image of the goddess Isis was torn out of the temple with the universal consent of the people, thrown into the river Tiber and sunk.]

Clearly Mundus is a villain here, and not a sympathetic one. I think, however, that he is transformed into such by the way Genius tells the story. It is partly a matter of Mundus being a victim of love. There is no mention of this in the Latin commentary, but it is writ large in the English text:

> Ther was a worthi Romein hadde
> A wif, and sche Pauline hihte,
> Which was to every mannes sihte
> Of al the Cite the faireste,
> And as men seiden, ek the beste.
> It is and hath ben evere yit,

---

[4] I take it that it is not reasonable to ascribe the (presumed) death of their baby to Canace and Machaire.

[5] *CA* ed. Macaulay, vol. 2, 56–57.

> That so strong is no mannes wit,
> Which thurgh beaute ne mai be drawe
> To love, and stonde under the lawe
> Of thilke bore frele kinde,
> Which makth the hertes yhen blinde,
> Wher no reson mai be comuned:
> And in this wise stod fortuned
> This tale, of which I wolde mene;
> This wif, which in hire lustes grene
> Was fair and freissh and tendre of age,
> Sche may noght lette the corage
> Of him that wole on hire assote. (I.764–81)

Here we see that Paulina cannot help Mundus's behavior, but also that Mundus cannot help himself; and whilst the commentary offers us the bare *pulcherrima*, the English text revels in Paulina's beauty, thus inciting us to feel that Mundus's action is indeed very understandable.

The point about the power of love made in lines 769ff. is reiterated with specific reference to Mundus:

> There was a Duck, and he was hote
> Mundus, which had in his baillie
> To lede the chivalerie
> Of Rome, and was a worthi knyht;
> Bot yet he was noght of such myht
> The strengthe of love to withstonde,
> That he ne was so broght to honde,
> That malgre wher he wole or no,
> This yonge wif he loveth so,
> That he hath put al his assay
> To wynne thing which he ne may
> Gete of hire graunt in no manere,
> Be yifte of gold ne be preiere. (I.782–94)

Mundus is not explicitly said to have tried to resist the power of love, but that attempt is suggested in lines 786–90, and it would be an honorable one. It seems possible, indeed, that "worthi" in line 785, besides connoting that strength which, according to the topos, is unable to withstand the strength of love (see I.25), also suggests an honor which may have prompted resistance, albeit futile, to illicit love. But even if we are not inclined to see precisely this implication in the "worthi," it does carry favorable implications for Mundus's character, whereas there is no such term of approbation in the Latin commentary.

We should note also how the commentary's second sentence, "Vnde idem dux....," links priests and Mundus in the same grammatical structure in such a way as to suggest that they are to be seen in basically the same moral perspective.[6] In the English, on the other hand, a clear distinction is made between Mundus and the priests, and the reason for it, Mundus's diminished responsibility, is given at some length:

> Bot of the Duck was other wise:
> For he with love was bestad,
> His dom was noght so harde lad;
> For Love put reson aweie
> And can noght se the righte weie.
> And be this cause he was respited,
> So that the deth was him acquited, (I.1048–54)

So much for the disparity of perspective between commentary and text (a disparity in line of course with the perception of certain critics that the Latin commentary mediates a sterner moral vision than the English text[7]). If we now compare Gower's treatment of the story with that in Hegesippus, which Macaulay thought the source, direct or indirect, of Gower's version,[8] we can see how Gower's treatment accords greater sympathy to Mundus. The crucial difference is in the way in which Mundus lets Paulina know that she has unwittingly slept with him. Gower's Mundus says this:

> The myhti godd which Anubus
> Is hote, he save the, Pauline,
> For thou art of his discipline
> So holy, that no mannes myht
> Mai do that he hath do to nyht
> Of thing which thou hast evere eschuied.
> Bot I his grace have so poursuied,
> That I was mad his lieutenant:
> Forthi be weie of covenant

---

[6] It is not entirely clear whether *enormitatem* in the commentary refers only to the priests, or to the priests and Mundus; I suspect the former, but, even supposing this to be probably so, the possibility of doubt shows how little emphasized, in comparison with the English version, is the difference in degree of guiltiness between priests and Mundus.

[7] See Derek Pearsall, "Gower's Latin in the *Confessio Amantis*," in *Latin and Vernacular: Studies in Late Medieval Texts and Manuscripts*, ed. A. J. Minnis (Cambridge, 1989), 13–25; A. J. Minnis, "*De vulgari auctoritate*: Chaucer, Gower and the Men of Great Authority" in *Chaucer and Gower: Difference, Mutuality, Exchange* English Literary Studies Monograph Series, no. 51, ed. R. F. Yeager (Victoria, BC, 1992), 36–74.

[8] *CA* ed. Macaulay, vol. 2, 470 on lines 761ff. In his Oxford D.Phil. thesis, *A Study of the Sources of the Confessio Amantis of John Gower* (1967), H. C. Mainzer suggests that Gower might have had access to the so-called Hegessipus's *De Bello Judaico*, (a Latin version of a work of Josephus), and also to another work of Josephus, latinized as *De Antiquitatibus*. Woolf, "Moral Chaucer," 203 and n. 16, suggests, I think misleadingly, that she has Mainzer's support for regarding Vincent of Beauvais as "in all probability Gower's source," but in any case Vincent is clearly relying on Hegessipus. It seems to me more likely that Gower modeled his story on a Hegessipan version than that he formed it in accordance with the version in *De Antiquitatibus*.

Fro this day forth I am al thin,
And if thee like to be myn,
That stant upon thin oghne wille. (I.940–51)

Winthrop Wetherbee, in his "Genius and Interpretation in the *Confessio Amantis*" sees this as "a coarse joke,"[9] but it is the acme of delicate gentlemanliness when compared with what we find in Hegesippus:

> beata Paulina concubitu dei, magnus deus Anubis, cuius tu accepisti mysteria. sed disce te sicut diis ita et hominibus non negare, quibus dii tribuunt quod tu negaveris, quia nec formas suas dare nobis nec nomina dedignantur. ecce ad sacra sua deus Anubis vocavit et Mundum ut tibi iungeret. quid tibi profuit duritia tua, nisi ut te XX. milium quae optuleram conpendio defraudaret? imitare deos indulgentiores, qui nobis sine pretio tribuunt quod abs te magno pretio inpetrari nequitum est. quodsi te humana offendunt vocabula, Anubem me vocari placuit et nominis huius gratia effectum iuvit.[10]

> [Paulina, blessed in having slept with a god, great is the god Anubis, whose mysteries you have come to know. But learn not to deny yourself, as you do not to gods, to men, to whom the gods give what you have denied, for they do not disdain to give to us their forms and names. Look, the god Anubis summoned Mundus as well to his rites, so that he might unite him with you. What good did your unyieldingness do you except to cheat you of the gain of the twenty thousand which I had offered you? Imitate the more indulgent gods who give us at no cost what it is impossible to get from you at a vast price. But if human names offend you, it was determined that I should be called Anubis and the grace of this name aided the doing of the deed.]

---

[9] Winthrop Wetherbee, "Genius and Interpretation in the *Confessio Amantis*" in *Magister Regis: Studies for Robert Earl Kaske*, ed. A. Groos, et al. (New York, 1986), 241–60, at 252.

[10] Hegesippus, *De Bello Judaico*, ed. C. F. Weber and J. Caesar (Marburg, 1864), II.4, p. 128. The text (and my translation) is questionable at points, but not so as to affect my argument. The version of Mundus's speech in Vincent of Beauvais is almost identical (and other witnesses to Hegesippus's text than the manuscript which Weber uses would bring Vincent even closer to Hegesippus), save that the last two sentences are omitted. See *Speculum Maius* vol.IV (*Speculum Historiale*) (Venice, 1591), VII. 4, p. 75. In the *De Antiquitatibus*, Mundus begins the corresponding speech with a remark about how Paulina has saved him money she might have had and the rest of the speech confronts Paulina openly with what has happened in a way which seems unpleasantly gloating (in contrast, I think, with what Mundus says in *CA*):

> O Paulina,' inquit, 'saluasti mihi viginti miriadas, quas posses familiaribus tuis rebus adjicere. Nunc autem nec meis postulationibus defuisti et damnificationi liberasti. Nam in templo tota nox a te cum Mundo peracta est, nec mei nominis interest voluptas precepta. Nihil enim ad perficiendum negocium offuit, quod Anubus [*sic*] vocitatus sum.'

See *Josephi Iudei Historici Praeclara Opera* (Paris, 1519), f. clxx (my punctuation).

The tones of jeering triumph here, the taunting insinuations that Paulina might as well have behaved, and may as well in future behave, like the prostitute she refused to be, are deeply unpleasant, an unpleasantness exacerbated by the snide cleverness of what is said. Though at the end of Hegesippus's version[11] we are told that Mundus is allowed to go into exile because of the extenuating circumstances (his being overcome by love and beauty), the way in which he speaks to Paulina is deeply unsympathetic—villainous indeed.

Furthermore, in Hegessipus there is some doubt as to whether Mundus is concerned, having had his way with her, to continue his relationship with Paulina. Perhaps, though he casts his remarks as mocking recommendations to a life of general unchastity, Mundus has himself in mind as recipient of her favors when he tells Paulina to learn not to deny herself to men and to imitate the indulgence of the gods; but even if this is so, his domineering imperatives and open references to sexual behavior contrast markedly with the way Gower's Mundus speaks. In Gower, Mundus, considerately avoiding open sexual reference, professes himself the servant in perpetuity of Paulina and allows Paulina to decide whether she will now respond to him. There is no question of mere conquest being sufficient for him. In fact, if we take the "forthi" of line 948 at face value, it would seem that what he has done binds him forever to Paulina and makes him subject to her will; the sexual violation turns out to have been Mundus's act of self-committal, a testimony of his lifelong devotion. So, having consulted Hegesippus to see how Gower might have presented Mundus, we may well be struck by the much greater degree of sympatheticness in the character in Gower—and yet what Mundus has done, of course, is rape Paulina.[12]

Wetherbee thinks that Genius's telling of the "Tale of Mundus and Paulina" fails "to do justice to the positive qualities embodied in Paulina" (Wetherbee, 254). He sees Gower's presentation of this failure as contributing to Book I's examination of "male misperceptions of the feminine"

---

[11] And Vincent of Beauvais's. See reference in n. 10.

[12] Woolf, "Moral Gower," finds a lack of consonance between the end of Gower's tale and what has gone before. She refers to the sparing of Mundus's life quoting I.1051–52, "For Love put reson aweie / And can noght se the rihte weie," and continues "Until that moment, however, Mundus's coldblooded stratagem and his subsequent taunting of Paulina had seemed morally repugnant" (203–4). In fact, as we have seen, the beginning of the tale as well as the end stresses the ineluctable power of love. This, I think, disposes us sympathetically toward Mundus from the outset and should make us less inclined to reach for terms such as "coldblooded" and "taunting." Comparison with other versions suggests that Gower could have made a much better job of it had he been primarily interested in having Mundus appear to offer taunts. Woolf (204) goes on to wonder why "the passions that overcame Mundus should be so much more simply and gently described than those than moved Tarquin (cf. V 3998–4900)" [*sic*.? Arrons? VII 4847–4900]. One might reply that Gower wants the "Tale of Mundus and Paulina" to be the vehicle of certain particular kinds of storial pleasure (which he does not wish to provide in the Lucrece story) and that these pleasures require a basically sympathetic protagonist if we are to accept them; the moral attitude may be affected, that is, by the imperatives of story.

(Wetherbee, 255). However this may be, it is certainly possible to find fault with Genius's perspective.[13] One might argue that though Genius sees an essentially "worthi" personality helplessly smitten, we should be able to penetrate this perspective and see that Genius's vision is blurred, that he is too much on the side of the body and the erotic. This leads him to an unacceptable preparedness to mitigate the horror of Mundus's behavior. Gower, then, would not be doing anything with a tendency to subvert orthodox moral perspectives, but would rather be reinforcing these by causing us to understand that the sympathy for the villain Genius evinces, and which we too might find tempting, is ill-founded and inappropriate.

Now, this kind of ironic perspective on Genius's stories may or may not be a proper one, but I am not sure that it can be used to explain away all the difficulties we find over sympathetic or attractive villains in *Confessio Amantis*. Sometimes Genius attempts, as far as explicit comment goes anyway, no kind of exculpation, and yet the text seems to present us with a sympathetic villain. In the "Tale of Ulysses and Telegonus," for example, we find Genius offering thoroughgoing condemnations of the use of magic which Ulysses exemplifies,[14] but also that in the course of the story Ulysses is rendered rather attractive.

On his return to Ithaca, where he is evidently very welcome to his people (something which inclines us in his favor), Ulysses dreams a mysterious dream, which in fact predicts in a riddling way the manner of his death. This dream, we are told, Ulysses is unable to interpret; in fact, he does rather well: "He dradde him of his oghne Sone" (*CA* VI.1583)—correctly, though he dreads the wrong son. A more ruthless father might have killed his son, but Ulysses merely takes sensible precautions by keeping Telemachus and himself under strong guard. All to no avail, unfortunately. Telegonus, the son conceived on Circe with the help of magic arts and forgotten by Ulysses, goes in search of his father and on reaching him gets involved in the fight in which he gives Ulysses his mortal wound (VI.1657 ff.). What follows engenders profound sympathy for Ulysses, I think. In the first place, Ulysses comes to understand his riddling dream fully, and this not by passive reception, but by an intelligent assessment of clues and seeking of proof (VI.1711 ff.). This tends to redeem Ulysses's earlier inability to interpret the dream with complete accuracy. Then there is the generosity and pathos of these lines:

> Tho wiste Uluxes what it mente,
> And tok him in hise Armes softe,

---

[13] Simpson, *Sciences and the Self,* offers a cogent version of this fault-finding. For Simpson, it is Genius's moral vision early in the text that is in error; both Amans and Genius grow in moral understanding as the poem goes on.

[14] See VI.1375–87 and 1768–81. See also the concluding comments on the "Tale of Nectanabus" (VI.2337–66).

> And al bledende he kest him ofte,
> And seide, 'Sone, whil I live,
> This infortune I thee foryive.' (VI.1744–48)

This is followed by the statesmanly bringing to accord of Telegonus and Telemachus:

> After his other Sone in haste
> He sende, and he began him haste
> And cam unto his fader tyt.
> Bot whan he sih him in such plit,
> He wolde have ronne upon that other
> Anon, and slain his oghne brother,
> Ne hadde be that Uluxes
> Betwen hem made acord and pes,
> And to his heir Thelemachus
> He bad that he Thelogonus
> With al his pouer scholde kepe,
> Til he were of his woundes depe
> Al hol, and thanne he scholde him yive
> Lond wher upon he mihte live. (VI.1749–62)

After which wise, noble, and masterful tying up of ends, Ulysses dies. So when Genius, in summing up, offers this stern condemnation, his words seem, I think, less than entirely appropriate to the Ulysses we have come to admire:

> Lo, wherof Sorcerie serveth.
> Thurgh Sorcerie his lust he wan,
> Thurgh Sorcerie his wo began,
> Thurgh Sorcerie his love he ches,
> Thurgh Sorcerie his lif he les;
> The child was gete in Sorcerie,
> The which dede al this felonie:
> Thing which was ayein kynde wroght
> Unkindeliche it was aboght;
> The child his oghne fader slowh,
> That was unkindeshipe ynowh.
> Forthi tak hiede hou that it is,
> So forto winne love amis,
> Which endeth al his joie in wo: (VI.1768–81)

Nevertheless, though there is an awkwardness in the fit between our feelings about him and the implication of Genius's concluding summary that Ulysses is an evil sorcerer appropriately hoist in his own petard, an awkwardness which means that Ulysses does not take his designated place as villain in an anti-sorcery exemplum piece very comfortably, one might still seek to argue that the admiration we have for Ulysses at the end of the story is in fact supportive of good morality. When we applaud his forgiv-

ing Telegonus and his peacemaking between his two sons, we are taking
pleasure in things that are good. But this is less easy to claim in relation to
our responses to the earlier part of the story. Here Ulysses arrives on the
island of Calypso and Circe. These women are predatory sorceresses of
great power:

> Thes queenes were as tuo goddesses
> Of Art magique Sorceresses,
> That what lord comth to that rivage,
> Thei make him love in such a rage
> And upon hem assote so,
> That thei wol have, er that he go,
> Al that he hath of worldes good
> of the men of his navie
> Thei tuo forschope a gret partie,
> Mai non of hem withstonde here hestes;
> Som part thei schopen into bestes,
> Som part thei schopen into foules,
> To beres, tigres, Apes, oules,
> Or elles be som other weie;
> Ther myhte hem nothing desobeie,
> Such craft thei hadde above kinde.
>   (VI.1433–39; 1445–53)

The women are the initial sinners as far as sorcery goes, and they are the
initial aggressors. Poor Ulysses has to defend himself against their aggres-
sive intentions and magical arts. This he does with great proficiency:

> Bot that Art couthe thei noght finde,
> Of which Uluxes was deceived,
> That he ne hath hem alle weyved,
> And broght hem into such a rote,
> That upon him thei bothe assote;
> And thurgh the science of his art
> He tok of hem so wel his part,
> That he begat Circes with childe.
> He kepte him sobre and made hem wilde,
> He sette himselve so above,
> That with here good and with here love,
> Who that therof be lief or loth,
> Al quit into his Schip he goth. (VI.1454–66)

Ulysses completely turns the tables on the women, escaping "al quit" with
their goods and love. The point I want to make about this is that the
pleasure we take from this part of the story leaves behind moral consider-
ations. We enjoy the sense of the beguiler being beguiled. This requital
does have a moral dimension, as, rather curiously, Ulysses becomes the
enforcer on Calypso and Circe of exactly the process Genius wishes to see

in what happens to Ulysses himself (VI.1379–81). But the basis of our positive response to Ulysses is not, I think, his performance as moral policeman; his being the beguiler of those trying to beguile him *does* give him the moral high ground, but this essentially serves to give permission to our approval not of his innocence or his morality, but of his potent cleverness and his neat reversal of what the women intend: *they* want *his* goods, and *he* gets *theirs*. The crucial thing is not that Circe and Calypso are punished for sin, but that they are outwitted. The satisfactions of the beguiler/beguiled pattern are ultimately aesthetic rather than moral. We are not, I think inclined to tut-tut at Ulysses sleeping with Circe (and Calypso?), because this is an expression of his resourceful cleverness and part of the working out of the pleasing pattern of reversal. Further, if we are men, we may be getting a rather unrespectable pleasure out of this defeat of feminine wiles which involves male sexual enjoyment with no strings of responsibility attached. And, to relate the end of the story to the beginning, these amoral and unrespectable pleasures are, one might argue, validated by the more morally attunable sympathy we feel for Ulysses at the end of the story—though here too, I think, the satisfactions are fundamentally aesthetic and emotional, rather than moral.[15]

Attributing what is problematic for morality in this tale to Genius's faulty perspective is more difficult than in the case of the "Tale of Canace and Machaire," where Genius offers explicit mitigations of what he still calls vice, and where it is possible to see his theory of the power of the natural, which supports his mitigating remarks, as incorrect.[16] In the "Tale of Mundus and Paulina" too, there are explicit remarks on the power of love, as we have seen, which might also be the product of flawed moral vision. Here in the "Tale of Ulysses and Telegonus," however, what Genius says by way of explicit commentary on the story cannot be used to convict him of a dubious moral perspective. If we want to pin the sympathy for Ulysses—a sympathy which runs counter to the explicit moral of the tale and in some respects to any moral perspective—onto Genius, it would seem that we need to hypothesize something along the lines of an

---

[15] In her "Ulysses in Gower's *Confessio Amantis:* The Christian Soul as Silent Rhetorician," *English Language Notes* 24:2 (1986): 7–14, Katharine S. Gittes sees a different relationship between the end of the story and the beginning. She thinks the story shows us the transformation of Ulysses from a lower spiritual state to a higher one, a transformation marked by his words of forgiveness to Telegonus. Gittes writes "When Ulysses speaks words of forgiveness, he is performing a humble and especially Christian act, as Christ forgave those who crucified him. In a sense, Ulysses is repudiating his previous disobedience of God's law in performing sorcery, and in doing so, he becomes more virtuous" (14). As well as making this criticism of Ulysses for sorcery, Gittes (12) stresses Ulysses's failure as lover and political leader (he is unfaithful to Penelope and he loses many of his men to the magic power of Circe and Calypso). Gower does not, however, advertise these failures, and I think Ulysses's sorcery is presented within the tale in a more positive light than Gittes allows. For me, Gittes's piece shows how a determination to read morally can lead to a certain insensitivity to Gower's narrative procedures.

[16] See Simpson, *Sciences and the Self,* 179.

unwitting tendency in Genius to approve behavior in love which he consciously repudiates, a tendency arising, no doubt, from an overcommitment to sexual love and sometimes manifesting itself in the way he tells his stories. To me this seems rather implausible, a somewhat desperate attempt to recuperate for morality aspects of the story which do not arise as a product of the author's moral concern. I think it more likely that here we come face to face with the unreconciled distinctness of two principles operating in the creation of *Confessio Amantis*, the desire to write moral *lore* and the drive to offer storial pleasure, *lust*.[17] I think that this unreconciled distinctness can be seen also in the "Tale of Mundus and Paulina."

Now, what I have noted about the sympatheticness of Mundus thus far could, I acknowledge, fairly easily be put down to a faulty perspective on Genius's part. There is, however, a further element in our finding Mundus congenial, something which is distinguishable from Genius' presentation of him as an essentially "worthi" victim of love and which aligns him with Ulysses in the "Tale of Ulysses and Telegonus," and that is a resourceful cunning. Mundus finds a way of getting what he wants and it is a very imaginative way. This is not, be it noted, something of which Genius approves. Yet only a supinely insensitive acquiescence in Genius's moral disapproval (or a self-inflicted politically correct unresponsiveness) will stop us delighting in the inventiveness which allows Mundus to sleep with Paulina.[18] We might see in it a parallel with the *Miller's Tale*, where Nicholas uses religion to further his sexual aims, and this parallel will encourage us to relish in Gower's story the high arrogance of Mundus's impersonation of a deity, the insouciant daring blasphemy of it. And though he cannot know this, Mundus's pagan blasphemy, enjoyable as it is in its own rite, as it were, also allows his Christian readers (rather as with Nicholas's Flood parody) to take a guilty pleasure in the blasphemy of a parody of the Annunciation.[19] Further, the wittiness of Mundus's reply to Paulina is offered for our enjoyment, as is what Wetherbee designated its coarseness.[20] For we are here, I would suggest, in a world approximating that of

---

[17] See Prologus 12–21 (and also VIII.3106–14).

[18] Credit for inventiveness redounds upon Mundus even though the plan may not be entirely his (see I.815–35; in fact, however, I suspect we do read the whole procedure as Mundus's plan because he initiates the meeting with the priests and seems to have something in mind: "He drowh hem unto his covine" (I.819)). Note in these lines the dry joke aligning Mundus's private meeting with the priests with "schrifte" (I.818), a confession ending not in absolution of sin, but in a plan for committing it.

[19] On the use of the Annunciation in Gower (taken as working to rather more serious ends than I propose here) see Patrick J. Gallacher, *Love, the Word, and Mercury* (Albuquerque, NM, 1975).

[20] Wetherbee, "Genius and Interpretation," 252. Mundus displays arrogance, blasphemous daring, wit, and coarseness in Hegesippus and Vincent of Beauvais, but the unsympatheticness of Mundus in these versions makes it difficult for us to take pleasure in them. See nn. 10 and 12. There is less wit, I would judge, in the speech of the *De Antiquitatibus*'s Mundus, and readerly admiration for him in this version is mitigated by the fact that it is his servant woman Ida who invents the plot to win Paulina.

fabliau, where we admire cleverness and wit, bawdy humor and sexual success. Wetherbee's genteel, considerate, feminist perspective may be a possible one on this tale (though how much do we really care about this pathetic, deluded Isis-worshipper?), but it is not, I think, the only one from which it should be read. I mentioned earlier that the stories of Amans and Canace and Machaire do not incite us to applaud the achievement of dubiously chosen ends. I think that we are permitted to adopt a perspective on the story of Mundus and Paulina from which we find ourselves doing exactly that.

As with the "Tale of Ulysses and Telegonus," Gower allows the "Tale of Mundus and Paulina" to flourish along lines not determined solely by moral concerns. As far as sympathy for the victims of love goes, one might argue that this is created by an attitude to love on Gower's part which exists in the ethical realm: love is irresistible, so you cannot blame those who are overcome by it.[21] Here the pleasure of our sympathy would be attunable to and support a particular moral vision. But the celebration of resourceful cunning in the sexual sphere allows us to see that not all of Gower's effects are in the service of ethical instruction, whether orthodox or not. He is interested, like Chaucer, in writing good stories, and knows, like Chaucer, that though a good story can be a moral one, it can alternatively, or in addition, offer pleasures that have little to do with morality and which indeed are morally dubious. Good stories can be good because they evoke the snigger and the leer and offer the pleasures of surrogate sex. Consider Geta and Amphitrion:

> Of Geta and Amphitrion,
> That whilom weren bothe as on
> Of frendschipe and of compaignie,
> I rede how that Supplantarie
> In love, as it betidde tho,
> Beguiled hath on of hem tuo.
> For this Geta that I of meene,
> To whom the lusti faire Almeene
> Assured was be weie of love,
> Whan he best wende have ben above
> And sikerest of that he hadde,
> Cupido so the cause ladde,
> That whil he was out of the weie,
> Amphitrion hire love aweie
> Hath take, and in this forme he wroghte.
> Be nyhte unto the chambre he soghte,

---

[21] My view would be that this is indeed Gower's deepest attitude to love, for all the registering in *Confessio Amantis* of the idea that it is possible to restrain love in accordance with the demands of reason. See Hugh White, "Division and Failure in *Confessio Amantis*," *Neophilologus* 72 (1988): 600–16.

Wher that sche lay, and with a wyle
He contrefeteth for the whyle
The vois of Gete in such a wise,
That made hire of hire bedd arise,
Wenende that it were he,
And let him in, and whan thei be
Togedre abedde in armes faste,
This Geta cam thanne ate laste
Unto the Dore and seide, 'Undo.'
And sche ansuerde and bad him go,
And seide how that abedde al warm
Hir lief lay naked in hir arm;
Sche wende that it were soth.
Lo, what Supplant of love doth:
This Geta forth bejaped wente,
And yit ne wiste he what it mente;
Amphitrion him hath supplanted
With sleyhte of love and hire enchaunted: (II.2459–92)

Genius offers the story as part of a po-faced condemnation of the vice of supplantation, but we surely register the wit and bravado with which this particular supplantation is contrived. Geta is not made sympathetically pathetic,[22] as one might claim for Paulina; we merely laugh at his bewilderment.[23] It is good fun, though certainly not clean; there is the lurking suggestion that women do not much mind who is in bed with them provided he can perform (what, exactly, we may ask, is implied in "With sleyhte of love and hire enchaunted"?). And what happens afterwards, when Almeene finds out? We do not know,[24] but nowhere is there a suggestion that she minds what has happened to her. She does not offer herself up to a Wetherbean seriousness of vision. There seems little, in fact, to prevent Amphitrion commanding a leering, laddish respect, as he offers a fantasy of sexual conquest, of both woman and rival, and sexual enjoyment.

The imperatives of story are not inevitably moral; rather, as these examinations of some of Gower's sympathetic villains suggests, they have the potential to take narrative in morally dubious directions. And Gower

---

[22] Geta is "bejaped." Though MED offers the meanings "disappointed, disillusioned" (1b), which imply no kind of stricture on the person so designated, I suspect "bejaped" at least usually invites a degree of contempt for one who has fallen for a trick, or been made to look a fool. I think "deceived" would not be an adequate substitute for "bejaped" here. OED perhaps rightly offers only "to play a trick on, to befool" as meanings for "bejape."

[23] In his "Gower's Geta and the Sin of Supplantation," *Neuphilologische Mitteilungen* 87 (1986): 211–17, Stephen K. Wright remarks on the "unusual comic vitality" (213) of the conclusion of Genius's story.

[24] Or has she already found out? Might line 2488 tell us that Almeene, having experienced his performance, is happy to acknowledge that Amphtrion rather than Geta is now her "lief"?

is not necessarily prepared to haul his stories back into a realm where morality has the dominion, not even by ironizing the voice which tells us the dubious stories. He is not prepared to coordinate *lust* with *lore* absolutely. Rather he invites, or perhaps merely enables, our surrender to the pleasures of the text. These pleasures may be more or less attunable to moral perspectives, but they are sometimes, surely, guiltily immoral. One might see this, perhaps, as a correlate in the texture of Gower's text of the admission at the level of its discourse of the abiding power of the pursuit of the pleasures of love to shatter moral order.[25] Delivering storial pleasure can involve a sanctioning of what the moral vision disregards or repudiates. The desire to offer the pleasures of story incites an investment on Gower's part in the *fully* human, both in what story represents and in what it appeals to. But to engage with these vitalities may be to find oneself seduced from the path of seriousness and virtue. That, I suspect, is why at the end of the poem Gower's moralist self has to leave behind the compelling instabilities of both love and storytelling and content himself with praying for peace.

---

[25] On the irreconcilability of love and morality in *Confessio Amantis* see White, "Division and Failure."

PART III. TEXTS AND MANUSCRIPTS

Glossing Gower: In Latin, in English, and *in absentia:* The Case of Bodleian Ashmole 35

Siân Echard

This essay began its life as a footnote to a larger project on the manuscripts of Gower's *Confessio Amantis.* As part of that project I explore Gower's assertion, in the opening Latin verses of the *Confessio,* that he intends to write in Hengist's tongue "Carmente metra iuuante"[1]—with Carmen, goddess of Latin letters, aiding his verse.[2] Carmen's role in Gower's English poem is manifested by the presence, in almost all the manuscripts, of a complete Latin apparatus, one which includes the quirky and difficult verses, the apparently simpler Latin prose commentary or glosses, and the usual Latin trappings of many medieval books, vernacular and Latin alike, such as incipits and explicits, running titles, and speaker markers. The verses and glosses are Gower's own[3] and are usually seen as the means by which Gower creates and affirms his *auctoritas,* his link to the Latin literary tradition.[4] Such a link need not, however, imply a simple, master-apprentice relationship, and I perceive the role of the Latin in the poem to

---

[1] Quotations from the *Confessio Amantis* are based on *The English Works of John Gower,* ed. G. C. Macaulay, 2 vols., EETS, e.s. 81–82 (Oxford, 1900–1901).

[2] See my "With Carmen's Help: Latin Authorities in the *Confessio Amantis,*" *Studies in Philology* 95 (1998): 1–40.

[3] The Gower manuscripts display a surprising degree of consistency, and many are of quite high quality. It was once argued that these factors suggested Gower must have overseen production of many *Confessio* manuscripts, perhaps even in his own scriptorium. While the work of Malcolm Parkes and others has now established that latter idea to be unlikely, it is still generally agreed that Gower had a great deal to do with the earliest manuscripts of his poem, and most, although not all, readers are content that the marginalia are his own and not the work of a (later) glossator. Derek Pearsall, "Gower's Latin in the *Confessio Amantis,*" in *Latin and Vernacular: Studies in Late-Medieval Texts and Manuscripts,* ed. A. J. Minnis (Cambridge, 1989), 13–25, argues that the "consistency and care" with which the Latin is treated in the manuscripts is a good indication that Gower was himself the originator of the apparatus (14). Summarizing the position of various writers on Gower manuscripts, R. F. Yeager notes that most critics "appear content that Gower composed marginal glosses for his own poems"; see "English, Latin, and the Text as 'Other': The Page as Sign in the Work of John Gower," *Text* 3 (1987): 255.

[4] Pearsall, "Gower's Latin in the *Confessio Amantis,*" is a notable example. He argues that the Latin serves to "stabilize" (14) the English, and later characterizes it as acting as a "fixative" (18) for the "slippery" vernacular.

be in fact quite complex. I agree here with those writers who remark on the multiplication of voices in the text which the presence of the Latin—or rather, Latins—creates. These multiple voices offer different levels of interpretation, and they do not always agree with one another. Winthrop Wetherbee, for example, resists the notion that the Latin is "an end in itself," and characterizes the interplay between the different voices as a Boethian dialogue which includes the "dogged, schoolmasterly moralism" of the glosses and the gnomic voice of the verses.[5] R. F. Yeager argues that Gower saw the manuscript page as a physical environment for (multiple) voices, and it is not, of course, inevitable that these voices will always be harmonious.[6] But because even the most sympathetic readers tend to find the Latin and English verses much more interesting than the Latin glosses, it is often the case that criticism of the poem overlooks one or more of these voices.

It may be that terminology encourages the underestimation of the importance of the Latin prose. "Glosses" are often seen as little more than academic footnotes. Worse, glossing may be perceived as a kind of pedantry which points so insistently at *moralitas* that it shuts down any possibility of multivocality, or even of ambiguity. "Gloze" had certainly acquired a negative field of meaning in Gower's own day, one which is echoed in our own tendency to see glosses as colonizing the text and displacing its meaning. Yet if "gloss" is a negative term, the more neutral label "prose summary" is scarcely more helpful, because it implies that the role of the Latin prose in Gower's text is simply to provide a précis of a very long poem. If it does not actually harm Gower's poem in this reading, the Latin prose nevertheless makes no real contribution to the work of the English poetry.

But this apparatus, I am convinced, *is* Gower's, and it is enormous; this is a great deal of labor if its goal is to permit a reader to avoid reading. Certainly there is a self-conscious connection to the academic Latin tradition here. The physical framing of the poem by Latin in the manuscripts does give the poem the appearance of other "authoritative," glossed manuscripts, including the Ovid manuscripts which we assume Gower must have used.[7] But this connection cannot offer a complete reckoning of the Latin, largely because Latin's linguistic richness cannot be reduced to so fundamentally simple a role. The Latin language in Gower's day is not, as we often tend to assume, a monolith, an unambiguous source of, or

---

[5] Winthrop Wetherbee, "Latin Structure and Vernacular Space: Gower, Chaucer and the Boethian Tradition," in *Chaucer and Gower: Difference, Mutuality, Exchange,* ed. R. F. Yeager (Victoria, B.C., 1991), 9–10.

[6] Yeager, "English, Latin, and the Text as 'Other,'" argues Gower invested a great deal in the actual look of the page, conceiving of it as "a totality, an *environment*—that is, as a space to be inhabited poetically and spoken from," 263.

[7] Wetherbee, "Latin Structure and Vernacular Space," 27, suggests Ovid manuscripts as the model.

pointer to, authority. Gower's wordplay in the verses is a first piece of evidence that this is not so; the juxtaposition of the voices of verse, gloss, and English text is another. I have argued elsewhere that Gower's Latin problematizes the question of authority in the *Confessio* by presenting to the reader a cacophony of potentially authoritative voices.[8] The "look" of the page, then, is part of this larger project, through its invocation, in the visual appeal to the glossed manuscript tradition, of the paradigm of authority. But paradigms can be questioned, and appearances can be deceiving.

If Gower's Latin apparatus was intended to complicate the reception of his poem, can we recover any evidence that the audience found the work problematic? The treatment of the Latin apparatus in the manuscripts offers some clues as to the attitude of some of Gower's audience toward that apparatus. The "best" manuscripts of the tradition, such as Oxford, Bodleian Library, MS Fairfax 3 and San Marino, Huntington Library MS El.26.A.17, the Ellesmere-Stafford MS, come complete with the full program of Latin verses and Latin prose apparatus;[9] the Latin is integral here, although we cannot tell for certain *how* its role was understood.[10] But there are variations in the amount of the Latin in the manuscripts: some omit or reduce the glosses but not the verses, some omit the speaker markers while others multiply them, and a few manuscripts have almost no Latin at all.[11] Even when one allows for variations in manuscript

---

[8] Echard, "With Carmen's Help."

[9] "Full" must, of course, be understood in the context of the manuscript recensions. There are groups of glosses, most notably in the section on the gods in Book V and in the scientific section of Book VII, which are absent in some copies. The situation is further complicated by the fact that some manuscripts may have had more than one exemplar, as is suggested by the common tendency for manuscripts with text-column placing of the glosses to insert in the margins those glosses sometimes omitted in different recensions. (I continue the common practice of citing Macaulay's recensions here, although I am aware of Peter Nicholson's reservations about the system; see "Gower's Revisions in the *Confessio Amantis*," *Chaucer Review* 19 [1984]: 123–43, and "Poet and Scribe in the Manuscripts of Gower's *Confessio Amantis*," in *Manuscripts and Texts: Editorial Problems in Later Middle English Literature,* ed. Derek Pearsall [Cambridge, 1987], 130–42.)

[10] The layout and treatment of this apparatus does however offer some tantalizing hints as to how fifteenth-century readers would have been guided through the poem. I discuss the effects of elements such as red or black ink and marginal or text-column placement in my "Latin Authorities in the *Confessio Amantis*." There are several articles on the miniatures in the manuscripts which also offer a sense of how readers might have perceived the text; see, for example, Jeremy Griffiths, "*Confessio Amantis:* The Poem and Its Pictures," in *Gower's Confessio Amantis: Responses and Reassessments,* ed. Alastair J. Minnis (Woodbridge, Suffolk, 1983), 163–78; Peter C. Braeger, "The Illustrations in New College MS 266 for Gower's Conversion Tales," and Patricia Eberle, "Miniatures as Evidence of Reading in a Manuscript of the *Confessio Amantis* (Pierpont Morgan MS M.126)," both in *John Gower: Recent Readings,* ed. R. F. Yeager (Kalamazoo, 1989), 275–310, 311–64; and, most recently, Joel Fredell, "Reading the Dream Miniature in the *Confessio Amantis*," *Medievalia et Humanistica* 22 (1995): 61–94.

[11] The copies with no Latin prose are all first recension: they are the Chetham and Ashmole manuscripts which form the basis of this article; Oxford, New College MS 326; and Princeton, NJ, Princeton University Library, Garrett MS 136. Of these, Ashmole

production and finishing, sufficient evidence remains to show that not all Latin is created equal, for the manuscripts suggest a tendency to regard the glosses as more dispensable than the verses, and some of the marginalia as more dispensable than the rest of it. The Latinity of Gower's poem is nevertheless central in all but a very few manuscripts, suggesting that we should pay more heed than we do to the whole of the apparatus, verse and prose. It may be a paradox that, in order to illustrate this point, I turn now to two of the minority of manuscripts which seem to reject the Latin, in whole or in part. Yet I will argue that the resistance of one of these manuscripts to the Latin prose in fact underlines the complex role played by that prose. The inability or refusal of both of these manuscript produc- ers to render the Latin program calls our attention most insistently to Car- men's voice even as, for readers of the poem in these versions, that voice falls silent.

Oxford, Bodleian MS Ashmole 35, omits the Latin verses but provides an English equivalent for the Latin prose.[12] The manuscript is of little interest to Macaulay, who classifies it as first recension unrevised, makes a few brief comments about its physical appearance, and then moves on. It is not one of the manuscripts that he regularly consults in his collation. He does not date it or suggest provenance. Kate Harris has dated it to the second half of the fifteenth century;[13] I would add that the manuscript has features of some second- and third-recension texts—in the pattern of glosses in Book V, for example—and that it has linguistic features which suggest the Midlands, most notably the "fadur" spelling which spreads from the West Midlands to the other Midlands, except the East, in the fifteenth century.[14] Several leaves of the manuscript have been lost. It is not a deluxe production, but it is quite neat, showing evidence of fairly frequent correction. Once into Book VII, there seem to be many more errors, and the apparatus, hitherto deployed with care, starts to be omitted or to be placed in such a way that the glosses disrupt the sense of the narrative. After fol. 152ʳ, around VII.2493, the blanks for the glosses have been left empty. The blanks, and the occasional cramping of the glosses, suggest that the apparatus, as was common practice, was copied after the

---

and New College 326 also omit the Latin verses. The copies with a partial Latin prose program include manuscripts from all recensions: Cambridge, St. John's College, MS B.12 (1a); Cambridge, Trinity College MS R 3 2 and London, British Library MS Addi- tional 12043 (2); and Geneva, Bibliotheca Bodmeriana MS 178 and Oxford, Wadham College MS 13 (3).

[12] A single couplet from the Latin verse which opens Book VI, and four lines from the verse which opens Book VII, are the exceptions here. It is possible that they have been accorded special treatment because they began these books, but the absence of comparable cases earlier in the manuscript, and the fact that neither of these poems is complete, suggests to me that their survival is accidental rather than deliberate.

[13] Kate Harris, "Ownership and Readership: Studies in the Provenance of the Manuscripts of Gower's *Confessio Amantis*," D. Phil., University of York, 1993, 102.

[14] See Karl Brunner, *An Outline of Middle English Grammar*, trans. Grahame K. W. Johnstone, 1963, 31, n. 3; fadir becomes fadur.

English text. The hand is the same throughout.

Manchester, Chetham's Library MS A.7.38 is unlike Ashmole in that it retains the Latin verses, but it too jettisons the Latin marginalia, here in favor of a much-reduced macaronic mix of English and Latin. It is a larger volume than Ashmole, parchment rather than paper, and assigned by Macaulay to the first recension unrevised. Kate Harris disputes his date of the late fifteenth century, arguing instead for some time between 1533 and 1537.[15] While it may have more pretensions to beauty than does Ash-mole—the scribe uses a display script for glosses and the first words of the Latin verses—this is nevertheless still a rather modest and even messy manuscript. Ashmole's earlier date and fuller program make it the focus of this essay, but Chetham is also of considerable interest: although it con-tains an abridged version of the poem, suggesting that space or time were concerns for its producer and/or intended audience, it does preserve a framework, albeit a sketchy one, of marginal glosses. Both of these manu-scripts, then, go to some lengths to preserve an interpretative framework for the poem, although this framework is no longer Gower's Latin one.

The Ashmole apparatus is entirely, even insistently, English. Chetham makes use of both English and Latin, and tends to use Latin when the glosses are longer than a word or two. While the vices and virtues in Chetham are often cataloged in English, the more learned material in Books V and VII in particular tends to receive Latin glossing. Chetham also preserves the Latin verses. In Ashmole, by contrast, there is no Latin at all.[16] The glosses are here replaced by extensive English substitutes—not the simple names so characteristic of Chetham, but summaries, often quite long. Chetham's practice of listing sins, vices, and major character names in the margins invites comparison with those few manuscripts that provide tables of contents to the *Confessio*. While there is no such table in Chet-ham, the marginal glosses could be seen as a preliminary step toward the creation of one, and in any case serve a similar, cataloging function.[17]

---

[15] Harris, "Ownership and Readership," 163–64. In "John Gower's *Confessio Amantis:* The Virtues of Bad Texts," in *Manuscripts and Readers in Fifteenth Century England: The Literary Implications of Manuscript Study,* ed. Derek Pearsall (Cambridge, 1983), Harris argues that this manuscript and Princeton University Library, Garrett 136 were both copied from the same version, a copy which must have preserved considerable portions of the apparatus (28–29). Garrett differs from Chetham, however, in the com-plete absence of any program of notes, whether English or Latin; the Latin verses are retained.

[16] That is, with the exception of the few lines of verse noted above. There are markers for the speeches of Genius and Amans, but even here, in keeping with the obvious linguistic preferences of the glossator, Amans has become Louer.

[17] Kate Harris has argued that the addition of running titles (in hands of the fifteenth through the seventeenth centuries) in manuscripts such as New York, Columbia Univer-sity, Plimpton MS 265; London, British Library MS Harley 3869; and Cambridge, Cam-bridge University Library MS Mm.II.21, suggest the processes necessary for producing an index or table of contents; see "Ownership and Readership," 232–34. I discuss complete tables of contents in manuscript and print versions of the *Confessio* in my "Pretexts: Tables of Contents and the Reading of the *Confessio Amantis,*" *Medium*

Ashmole's program is far more extensive. These English glosses are treated as are the Latin glosses in many other manuscripts; that is, they are placed in the text columns in red.[18] It seems, then, that the Ashmole scribe or his source wishes to preserve the content and even the appearance of authority, the framework of interpretation, while abandoning the language which we are accustomed to see as the assurance of that authority. The omission of the verses is particularly interesting. They are the part of the Latin program most likely to survive in those copies with an incomplete frame, as they have done in the Chetham manuscript and in its near relative, Princeton, NJ, Princeton University Library, MS Garrett 136. In the case of Ashmole, it would seem that the Latin verses have been understood to belong neither to the framework of authoritative commentary nor to the poetic body of the text. Are we to take their omission as a sign that this glossator is resisting the difficulties which they raise? Or is he simply not up to the task of translation?

Even without the verses, the reduction and translation of the Latin prose is no minor task for the Ashmole scribe or his source. The Latin glosses and speaker markers, as represented in the Fairfax MS, total about 21,000 words, and the Ashmole glosses about 14,000; when we allow for the fact that Latin is naturally more compressed a language than is English, then we can estimate the Ashmole apparatus as just over half the length of the normal program. Chetham's program is far more modest, with most books limited to a handful of one- or two-word markers. What is remarkable about Ashmole's recasting of the Latin apparatus is nevertheless not simply its bulk nor its language, but rather the principles of selection, reduction, and emendation which appear to have been exercised. In other words, this curiosity of the manuscript tradition becomes a valuable source of information about how at least one of Gower's near-contemporary readers reacted to his text, in terms of both content and framing.

First, it is clear that the Ashmole scribe or his source created the notes with a manuscript with the usual Latin apparatus near at hand. There are times when the glossator is clearly translating: "Tho þat be called of God as Aaron" (fol. 2ʳ) for "Qui vocatur a deo tanquam Aaron" (at Prol.434), or "Here he telleþ þat euery kyngdom diuided in it self is desolate," (fol. 4ʳ) for "quod omne regnum in se diuisum desolabitur" (at Prol.967). Sometimes a Latin grammatical form of a name will slip into the gloss; thus Tiresias, rendered as such in the English verse, appears in one gloss (but not the other in which Tiresias is mentioned) as Tiresiam (fol. 46ᵛ); the Latin original (at III.731) was accusative. Sometimes the English version is quite garbled, apparently the result of word-by-word translation from the Latin. One example of this approach and its results is the Cornix gloss.

Aevum 66 (1997): 270–87.

[18] The earliest manuscripts of the tradition tend to use marginal Latin, usually in black. I discuss manuscript treatment of the Latin program at length in "With Carmen's Help."

The Latin reads:

> Quia litigantes ora sua cohibere nequiunt, hic ponit Confessor exemplum contra illos qui in amoris causa alterius consilium reuelare presumunt. Et narrat qualiter quedam auis tunc albissima nomine coruus consilium domine sue Cornide Phebo denudauit; vnde contigit non solum ipsam Cornidem interfeci, set et coruum, qui antea tanquam nix albus fuit, in piceum colorem pro perpetuo transmutari. (at III.783)

> [Since those who are quarreling don't know how to keep their mouths shut, the Confessor offers an exemplum here against those who presume to reveal the counsel of another in love's cause. And he tells how a certain bird, then most white, crow by name, revealed to Phebus the counsel of his lady Cornix. Whence it happened, not only was that Cornix killed, but the crow, which before was white as snow, was changed forever into the color of pitch.][19]

And here is the Ashmole version:

> Here þe confessor declareþ A yen þo þat
> tellen out þe consel of a noþer / and telleþ
> howe þer was a brid white /. told þe consel
> of his ladi vnto phebus so þat fortuned
> her to be sleyne not only she but þe
> brid also whiche first was white and after
> transformed into blak and is called a rauon. (fol. 46ᵛ)

There are several features of interest here—this is one example of a general tendency to assimilate the glosses to a single opening formula (Here the Confessor declareth, telleth etc.) regardless of their treatment in the original—but note in particular how a strict adherence to the Latin syntax (*set et corvum*) produces in English the temporary impression that the bird, too, is killed.

Certainly there are times when the glossator has slipped. Sometimes he appears simply to misunderstand the Latin, as when he characterizes the Acteon story as illustrating "on liefful heryng" (fol. 5ᵛ), or in this case, when he gives Achilles two teachers:

> Here þe confessor spekeþ that it be
> houeþ A knyght in his youþe to vse
> hym to hardynesse / As Achilles was
> first lerned with Chiro and Centaurus to
> hurte and slee euery day A lyon or a

---

[19] All translations of the Latin prose are my own. As always, I am grateful to Claire Fanger for her advice: any infelicities which remain are naturally mine.

tigre so þat þis Achilles was as
bolde ouer a lion as ouer / an asse. (fol. 69ʳ)

The Latin begins "Hic loquitur quod miles in suis primordiis ad audaciam prouocari debet. Et narrat qualiter Chiro Centaurus Achillem, quem secum ab infancia in monte Pileon educauit."[20] Ashmole's "and" could of course be a slip of the pen rather than of the mind, or a similar slip in the source. There are enough errors elsewhere, however, to allow one to suppose a mistake of translation rather than of copying. The glossator often seems, for example, to have been reading the English too quickly, as when he puts speaker markers in the wrong places. He marks a speech of Perseus's (fol. 32ʳ) as the lover's, and Abraham's speech to Dives (fol. 131ʳ) as the Confessor's.[21] The Cornix and perhaps the Achilles glosses suggest a similar hasty practice with respect to the Latin.

The question of the speaker markers brings me back to my sense that this glossator has definite principles for his adaptation and abbreviation of the Latin framework. While the program of glosses is shortened, the Confessor/Amans markers—here Confessor/Louer—represent the only category of gloss where the glossator actually adds to what was probably in the original.[22] About one-third of the surviving manuscripts have very few speaker markers. While it is probable, given the frequency of the markers and their close correspondence to the "standard" program as found in manuscripts such as Fairfax, that the Ashmole glossator's exemplar was one of those manuscripts with a fairly complete set, there are in fact some twelve markers which are now unique to this manuscript (two of these are the errors described above). There is another dozen or so which the Ashmole manuscript shares with only a small number of manuscripts.[23] The Chetham manuscript, by contrast, contains only two mark-

---

[20] At IV.1963: Here he says that a soldier ought to be induced to be audacious from his childhood. And he tells how Chiro the Centaur raised Achilles from his infancy with himself on Mount Pileon.

[21] (Fol. 32ʳ) louer (II.1653); Perseus is speaking, but "louer" appears in the left margin, where the corrections usually are in this manuscript; (fol. 131ʳ) conff (VI.1048); here the speaker is Abraham, addressing Dives.

[22] Like many manuscripts, Ashmole does render the longer *opponit / respondet* and *Confessio Amantis* forms with single names, an assimilation which could have been in the source manuscript(s) or could have been performed by the Ashmole glossator himself.

[23] I discuss the question of the speaker markers at length in my "Dialogues and Monologues: Manuscript Representations of the Conversation of the *Confessio Amantis*," forthcoming in *Middle English Poetry: Texts and Traditions in Honour of Derek Pearsall*, ed. Alastair Minnis (York, England: York Medieval Press). My base text for the count is the Fairfax MS, which has 280 name markers for the speeches of the Confessor and Amans. The 31 markers found in Ashmole which are *not* part of the Fairfax program are at **I.1922**; II.11, 16, 221; III.19, 831, 852, 855, **945**, 1083, 1670, 1722, **2230**; IV.913, 1222, 2190, 2200, 2204; V.353, **399, 4710, 4868**, 6103, 6417, 6485, 7586; VI.100, **687, 948, 1048**, 1227. The unique readings are in bold type. I have not been able to assess the program in Geneva, Bibliotheca Bodmeriana MS 178, but Ashmole's particular character with respect to speaker markers is, I think, clear.

ers.[24] There seems to me to be sufficient evidence to conclude that the speaker markers were of particular interest to the Ashmole glossator, and that he may in fact have originated the unique readings. Many of his additions to the usual program complete pairs, so that the speeches of both Genius and Amans are marked where Fairfax and similar manuscripts might mark only one of the conversants (typically Genius). The fact that the Ashmole glossator abbreviates freely elsewhere would seem to indicate that, even if he had a source with the extra markers, he would have left them out had they not conformed to his overall plan for the apparatus. The speaker-markers punctuate the text, dividing it into digestible chunks. It seems, then, that the glossator retains and improves this part of the Latin program in the interests of increasing the accessibility of his text.

This glossator is certainly not interested in cataloging everything. He rarely reproduces the source glosses which are the most obvious link to the academic Latin tradition. The *Nota* glosses which draw attention to allusions or proverbial wisdom are also often omitted; where they are included, they are generally assimilated to the favored "Here" formula. The Chetham manuscript, on the other hand, has a fairly high incidence of *Nota* glosses, given the far greater brevity of its program, although these are often substitutes for Latin glosses which may not have had this form. Both Chetham and Ashmole have a fairly high incidence of glossing in Books V and VII, in the sections on the Greek gods and on the scientific material, so "learned" material is clearly of interest to them. But while the Chetham manuscript retains Latin forms, albeit reduced ones, for these glosses, Ashmole consistently anglicizes even obvious Latin: Chetham's "De me*rc*urio" (fol. 96ᵛ) would be too Latinate for this glossator, who writes of the "ster*re*" called "me*rc*urie" instead (fol. 142ᵛ). These features of the Ashmole manuscript may suggest that the glossator is addressing a different kind of audience than perhaps originally envisioned for the poem, one to whom the facilitation of general reading in the vernacular, with a seasoning of certain popular lore, is more important than the immersion in the Latin academic and literary tradition suggested and required by Gower's original program.

The glossator's approach to abbreviation in the case of the Latin prose summaries to the *Confessio*'s embedded narratives would seem to support this idea. As I have already suggested, the glossator often assimilates the summaries to a single syntactic pattern, a factor which suggests either an attempt to ease reading, or a certain lack of imagination. In addition, the

---

[24] Or perhaps three; fol. 8ᵛ has "opp. conf." at Prol.708, while fol. 9ʳ has "resp. A" at Prol.712 and "C" at Prol.745. These markers may have survived because they are early in the text and because they could be identified as glosses, given their longer form. It is not unusual to find a handful of markers early on in a manuscript which later abandons them, and even an apparent intent to pursue a full program can later be discarded: compare, for example, London, British Library Additional MS 12043, whose full program in Book I is abandoned at II.278, after which there are no more markers in the text.

glossator routinely omits many details, some of them fairly esoteric, from
the summaries. Here, for example, is his treatment of the Arion gloss:

> Here it telleþ A gode ensample of vnite *and*
> pees amonges men as of AAron[25] *and* oþer. (fol. 4ᵛ)

The original is much longer:

> Hic narrat exemplum de concordia et vnitate inter homines prouo-
> canda; et dicit qualiter quidam Arion nuper Citharista ex sui cantus
> cithareque consona melodia tante virtutis extiterat, vt ipse non
> solum virum cum viro, set eciam leonem cum cerua, lupum cum
> agna, canem cum lepore, ipsum audientes vnanimiter absque vlla
> discordia adinuicem pacificauit. (at Prol.1053)

> [Here he recounts an exemplum about the concord and unity which
> ought to be occasioned among men; and he says how once a certain
> Arion, a harper, was held to be of such great virtue on account of
> the harmonious music of his song and his harp, that he immediately
> and without any discord brought into harmony all those who heard
> him—not only man with man, but indeed the lion with the deer,
> the wolf with the sheep, the dog with the rabbit.][26]

Arion's classical history as a harper has disappeared, along with the poetic
rendition of the effects of his music, but the emphasis on unity, the essence
of the symbolism of Arion, *is* retained. Chetham, on the other hand,
reduces the gloss to "The harpe of Arion" (fol. 5ʳ). That is, Ashmole
preserves Arion's symbolic meaning, while Chetham preserves his harp
but not its sense.

Longer examples of a similar nature in Ashmole are the glosses to the
stories of Florent and of Narcissus; in each case, the details are pared away,
to dramatic effect. Narcissus's story is reduced in this way:

> Here in special þe confessor tretes *with*
> þe louer a yenst þo þat presume he*m*
> self so þat þei þynke þat no woman
> myght be her pere / And telleþ howe
> narcizus was mychieued be þat vice (fol. 16ᵛ)

Narcissus is "mychieued" by vanity, but the details are very unclear. The
Latin reads:

---

[25] Arion is rendered Aaron, with a heavy line above the final -n: because this scribe
often uses such a mark, normally indicative of abbreviation, where no addition of -n or
-m is called for, I have not expanded it here. The English verse reads "aaron" expuncted,
then "arian."

[26] While "nuper" normally means "recently," Gower seems to use it throughout the
Confessio to introduce narratives of the past; the sense is almost "Once upon a time."

Hic in speciali tractat Confessor cum Amante contra illos, qui de propria formositate presumentes amorem mulieris dedignantur. Etnarrat exemplum, qualiter cuiusdam Principis filius nomine Narcizus estiuo tempore, cum ipse venacionis causa quendam ceruum solus cum suis canibus exagitaret, in grauem sitim incurrens necessitate compulsus ad bibendum de quodam fonte pronus se inclinauit; vbi ipse faciem suam pulcherrimam in aqua percipiens, putabat se per hoc illam Nimpham, quam Poete Ekko vocant, in flumine coram suis oculis pocius conspexisse; de cuius amore confestim laqueatus, vt ipsam ad se de fonte extraheret, pluribus blandiciis adulabatur. Set cum illud perficere nullatenus potuit, pre nimio languore deficiens contra lapides ibidem adiacentes caput exuerberans cerebrum effudit. Et sic de propria pulcritudine qui fuerat presumptuosus, de propria pulcritudine fatuatus interiit. (at I.2275)

[Here in particular the Confessor speaks with the Lover against those who, presuming on their own beauty, disdain the love of women. And he tells the exemplum of how a certain prince's son, Narcissus by name, was out and about one springtime, hunting a certain stag, alone with his dogs. Becoming very thirsty, he was compelled to drink from a certain spring, and so lay down; where, seeing his own beautiful face in the water, he thought that he saw that nymph whom the poets call Echo before his eyes in the water. He was immediately captured by love of her, so that he implored her, with many endearments, to take herself out of the spring. But since he could not succeed in this in any way, he became weak with a great langor, and he fell against the nearby stones, striking his head so that his brains flowed out. And thus the one who was presumptuous about his own beauty, died infatuated with his own beauty.]

The Ashmole glossator has pared away all of the details of the classical story, even going so far as to remove the clear reference to Narcissus's death. This radical reduction has the effect of removing a potential conflict between Latin gloss and English text, for the English seems to suggest suicide more clearly than does the Latin. At least Narcissus and his vice remain; in the case of the Florent gloss, it is not even clear whom we are to read about:

> Here þe confessor declareþ An example
> a yenst disobedience vnto þe comendacion
> of obedience whiche is gode to here
> And as hit apereþe folowynge (fol. 11ᵛ)

Compare this to the Latin:

Hic contra amori inobedientes ad commendacionem Obediencie Confessor super eodem exemplum ponit; vbi dicit quod, cum quedam Regis Cizilie filia in sue iuuentutis floribus pulcherrima ex eius Nouerce incantacionibus in vetulam turpissimam transformata extitit, Florencius tunc Imparatoris Claudi Nepos, miles in armis strenuissimus amorosisque legibus intendens, ipsam ex sua obediencia in pulcritudinem pristinam mirabiliter reformauit. (at I.1407)

[Here the Confessor offers an exemplum against those who are disobedient in love, to the commendation of Obedience, in which he says how, when a certain most beautiful daughter of the King of Sicily was transformed, in the flower of her youth, into a hideous crone by the spells of her wicked stepmother, Florent, nephew of the then-emperor Claudius, a knight most skilled in arms and one who followed love's laws, restored her miraculously to her former beauty, through his obedience.]

Ashmole does not name the participants, nor does it even make clear that the obedience in question is obedience *in love*. Both these examples in fact seem to generalize the moral content, concentrating on the point of the exemplum rather than on the narrative itself. A last example is offered by the "Tale of Albinus and Rosemund," abbreviated to the extent that one could be forgiven for missing the connection between Albinus's and Rosemund's actions, as well as their whole connection to the story:

> Here þe confessor scheweþ an example
> A yenste þo þat bostone of hir own
> lewdenesse as wel in loves cause as
> oþer / And telleþ howe Albin*us* first
> kyng of lombardes in batail kilde
> Gurmu*n*de *and* of his hed made a cup *and*
> wed his dought*er* / *and* she myshieued [*sic*] hi*m* //.
>
> (fol. 17ᵛ)

We are not told here exactly why Rosemund would have wished to "myschieue" Albinus, nor what exactly she did to him. The gruesome detail of the skull cup remains and might perhaps be enough to capture a reader's attention, but that reader would have little further sense of what to expect. As for Chetham, it has "Narcius" (fol. 14ᵛ) and "Albin*us and* Gormonde" (fol. 15ʳ), with nothing at all for Florent. The names might be enough for a reader seeking to locate stories already known: several Gower manuscripts have later readers' additions which suggest the use of marginal notations as mnemonic or indexing devices, and many of the notations in Chetham correspond to this pattern. By contrast, the Ashmole glosses, despite their brevity, offer more than this indexing function. Yet the above examples show that abbreviation, often to the extent of loss of sense, is a primary mode for this glossator. What do his glosses accomplish, then?

First, it would be misleading to suggest that abbreviation is the Ashmole glossator's only mode. He also on occasion adds detail, a fact which is all the more remarkable precisely because of the ruthless excision of

many parts of the Latin summaries. While this feature too could appear to
be intended to enhance accessibility—he provides details which are missing
from the original Latin—it should be noted that these additions routinely
do what the Latin glosses might be expected to do, but do *not* do; they
tame the multivocality of the text. It seems that this glossator has noticed
that the pages of the *Confessio* are structured around an occasionally caco-
phonous conversation between Latin verse, Latin gloss, and English text.
It seems further that he has decided to put an end to this conversation.

His treatment of the story of Nauplus is one such case. In the usual
Latin gloss, the stress is on Nauplus's words, and there is no reference to
the trick, to Ulysses's unwillingness, or to any dishonor. The Latin gives
the impression that Nauplus's wise words have turned Ulysses from uxo-
riousness:

> Hic dicit quod amoris delectamento postposito miles arma sua pre-
> ferre debet: Et ponit exemplum de Vlixe, cum ipse a bello Troiano
> propter amorem Penolope remanere domi voluisset, Nauplus pater
> Palamades eum tantis sermonibus allocutus est, quod Vlixes thoro
> sue coniugis relicto labores armorum vna cum aliis Troie magnani-
> mus subiba. (at IV.1815)

> [Here he says that a soldier ought to put aside the delights of love
> and prefer his arms: and he offers the exemplum of Ulysses. When
> he wanted to stay at home, away from the Trojan War, out of his
> love for Penelope, Nauplus, the father of Palamides, counseled him
> with such words that Ulysses left the marital bedchamber and with
> the others, brave, undertook the labor of arms at Troy.]

The English telling of the story is quite a bit more ambivalent about
Ulysses than is the Latin summary. In addition to detailing the tricks each
character played, it adds references to shame, lust, and sloth in Nauplus's
speech, and the effect of that speech is to make Ulysses "halvinge
aschamed" (IV.1885), so that, "be him lief or loth" (IV.1889), he sets forth
to Troy. While we all know that he performed great exploits there, the
English text does not mention that fact at this place. Ulysses's function in
this book is to be an exemplum of the dangers of uxoriousness, and the
stress in the English on the shamefulness of his behavior underlines that
exemplary function, while the Latin's stress on love and its approving
"magnanimus" might temper the negativity of the portrait. In other
words, the English part of the poem seems in this case to fit tale to moral
more closely than does the Latin. This kind of loose fit between the inter-
pretative framework (Carmen's contribution) and the English verse is, for
many readers, one of the most fascinating aspects of the *Confessio*. And yet
the evidence of the Ashmole gloss would seem to suggest that one reader
found it more negatively problematic:

> Here þe confessor sheweþ an example
> howe þe kyng Namplus praied wit

> oþ*er* grekes Vlixes to go wiþ hem
> to þe siege of troye / And þan þis
> Vlixes feyned a sleight to be at
> home wiþ Penolope his loue w (stroked out)
> which sleight was aft*er* knowe to hi*m* a
> a grete dishono*r* as it apereþ after /. (fol. 68ʳ)

In this gloss, we read of the "sleight" practiced by Ulysses, and of the "grete dishonor" which his behavior earned him. We are not even told that he agreed in the end to go to Troy. The Ashmole Ulysses is, then, unquestionably a negative example, and the details which make him so seem to have come from a reading of the English part of the poem. Gloss and text now "fit." And this is not an isolated example.

In the case of the story of Piramus and Thisbe, the Ashmole glossator makes additions which, while they help the gloss to make more sense, might be said to undermine its point. The Latin summary of the story has Piramus kill himself simply because he comes to the appointed meeting-place and does not find Thisbe:

> Hic in amoris causa ponit Confessor exemplum contra illos qui in sua dampna nimis accelerantes ex impetuositate seipsos multociens offendunt. Et narrat qualiter Piramus, cum ipse Tisbee amicam suam in loco inter eosdem deputato tempore aduentus sui promp-tam non inuenit, animo impetuoso seipsum pre dolore extracto gla-dio mortaliter transfodit: que postea infra breue veniens cum ipsum sic mortuum inuenisset, eciam et illa in sui ipsius mortem impe-tuose festinans eiusdem gladii cuspide sui cordis intima per medium penetrauit. (at III.1331)

> [Here the Confessor tells an exemplum against those who, in love's cause, often injure themselves, hastening to their doom out of rash-ness. And he tells how Piramus, when he did not find Thisbe, his beloved, at hand at the place arranged between them for the time of his own arrival, with a rash spirit drew his sword for grief and pierced himself mortally. She, coming shortly afterwards, when she had found him thus dead, in her turn hastened rashly to her own death, and penetrated the intimate depths of her heart with the very same sword.]

There is no mention here of the bloody scarf or of the lion, so that, in the voice of the Latin gloss, Piramus is indeed an example of foolhardiness and self-murder. In the English part of the poem, however, he is in the grips of Cupid's inescapable will: "Cupide hath so the thinges schape, / That thei ne mihte his hand ascape" (III.1351–52). He does come across the bloody scarf, and while he should perhaps have been a little less hasty with the sword, we are told quite clearly that he "demeth sikerly / That sche be ded" (III.1427–28). His actions are understandable, if not wise, and gloss and text seem, if not exactly contradictory, at least differently focussed.

The Ashmole glossator offers this solution:

> Here þe confessor sheweþ an example
> A yenst al þo þat in loues cause þorowe
> wraþ wiþ hem self / slee hem self / As
> Piramus kild hym self be cause he went
> þe wolf had sleyn Tisbee his love / And
> when she came And fonde piramus
> her love ded with a swerd . wiþe same
> sworde she kilde her self and þat was pite (fol. 49ᵛ)

While the supplying of Piramus's motive may seem to go against what we have seen in the case of the Nauplus gloss—it makes him *less* effective an example against the vice with which the section is dealing—it does in another sense accord with the practice in that example, in that it brings the gloss in line with the English text. It also allows the audience to feel from the outset the sympathy (or at least understanding) which the English verse might evoke. Thus in supplying the crucial missing motive, the Ashmole glossator again shuts down the ambiguities which arise from the juxtaposition of the different voices on the page. That is, Gower's original construction allows for different readings, and leads us to question the authority of the Latin framework, by showing us how the Latin withholds crucial information contained in the English. The same might be said of the Narcissus gloss, discussed above. This sort of tension, at least, is gone from Ashmole 35.

The Ashmole glossator proves his preference for the English text in his frequent use of whole phrases and lines of it to supplement and even to radically alter his glosses. Sometimes a simple change is nevertheless tantalizing; in these next examples, the glossator has made use of the English text to generalize the moral comment from men alone, to men and women. These are the glosses on jealousy and chastity. The jealousy gloss is similar in length to its Latin original, but the content differs:

> Here þe confessor declareþ vnto
> þe louer / the cely malady which
> is called Ielosie whiche is in
> a man or woman In maner / of
> A feuer / cotidian (fol. 82ʳ)

The Latin has simply "Nota de Ialousia, cuius fantastica suspicio amorem quamuis fidelissimum multociens sine causa corruptum ymaginatur" (at V.455: A note about Jealousy, whose fantastical suspicion often without cause imagines the most faithful lover to be corrupt). The last line in the Ashmole version comes from the English ("A Fievere it is cotidian," V.464) and the woman, who appears in only a few lines at the end of that passage (V.569 ff.) and disappears entirely in the gender-neutral Latin version, is here made part of the discussion from the beginning.

The story of the value placed by the Romans on chastity is similarly generalized. The Latin reads: "Hic loquitur de virginitatis commendacione, vbi dicit quod nuper Imperatores ob tanti status dignitatem virginibus cedebant in via" (at V.6361: Here he speaks in praise of virginity, where he says that once Emperors ceded the roadway to virgins, because of the great dignity of their state). While the Latin's "virginibus" can certainly mean virgins of either sex, the Ashmole glossator makes it clear that this is so:

> Here he spekeþ howe þat þe emperoure
> of rome muste obeie to virgyne where
> so euer he mete wiþ hir notonly the
> chaste woman but þe man also (fol. 116ʳ)

Again, the Ashmole glossator abandons the potentially ambiguous neutrality of Latin for a clear statement which is also found in the English verse. There virginity is explicitly of great dignity, "Noght onliche of the wommen tho, / Bot of the caste men also" (V.6367–68).

Sometimes the Ashmole glossator discards the Latin almost completely and fills out his notes instead with material from the English, as in the case of the reference to the signs of the zodiac in Book V:

> Here þe confessor sheweþ and declareþ
> Howe þe false goddes were first be
> gonne as of olde tyme / som byleued
> vnto þe forme of þe xii signes And
> some to bestes and some oþer / but þe
> feyþe of Cristis lawe is more clerer /
> þan al oþer / but first he declareþ of
> þe feiþ of þe men of Caldees ./ (fol. 83ᵛ)

There is little contact here with the usual Latin gloss:

> Quia secundum Poetarum fabulas in huius libelli locis quampluribus nomina et gestus deorum falsorum intitulantur, quorum infidelitas vt Cristianis clarius innotescat, intendit de ipsorum origine secundum varias Paganorum Sectas scribere consequenter. Et primo de Secta Chaldeorum tractare proponit. (at V.747)

> [Because the names and deeds of many false gods are inscribed in places in this book, after the fables of the Poets, that their infidelity might be noted more clearly by the Christian, he intends consequently to write about their origins according to various sects of the pagans. And first he proposes to treat the sect of the Chaldeans.]

The signs of the zodiac are probably mentioned in the Ashmole version here because of the reference to "the signes tuelve" at V.752; the reference to beasts from the section that begins at V.791 ("For thei diverse bestes there / Honore"). The reference to the fables of the poets does *not* appear in the English.[27] Again the result of the Ashmole glossator's preference for the English is to mesh the commentary and the English more closely.

It seems that the glossator is reading around in the text, rather than simply transferring material from what is immediately adjacent to the commentary. A particularly striking example occurs in the reference to the four elements in Book VII. The Latin is quite brief:

> Hic interim tractat de creacione quatuor Elementorum, scilicet terre, aque, aeris et ignis, necnon et de eorum naturis, nam et singulis proprietates singule attribuuntur. (at VII.203)

> [Here in the meantime he deals with the creation of the four Elements, namely earth, water, air, and fire, and of their natures, for also singular properties are attributed to each one.]

The English version in Ashmole includes a fifth element:

> Here he telleþ of the first
> creacion of the elementes þat
> is to seye erþe water / aier / *and*
> fire And more ouer / he telleþ
> of a noþer elemente whiche
> is called orbis And of thei*re*
> nature and singuler / prop*ri*etes
> As it telleþ pleynly here after /. (fol. 139ᵛ)

This gloss appears at VII.203; "orbis" appears over four hundred lines later, at VII.613, in both Latin and English. Here, then, the conforming of commentary to the English text has been enhanced by the glossator's reading ahead.

Is any of this real evidence for a recognition of the multivocality of Gower's text, followed by a systematic attempt to tame that multivocality into a single voice, the voice of the English part of the poem? There are enough errors and ineptnesses in the Ashmole glosses to make me cautious, despite the passages to which I have drawn attention. And yet my final impression of this glossator is of someone who has a strong sense of what the text "should" look like *and* what it should say. I close with one final example, the passage that opens Book I:

> This booke is dyuyded into viii p*ar*tes
> Wherof þe First parte specifieþ of Pride
> and of þe braunches of pride And a parte
> of þe v witt*es* þat towchen to loves cause.
> And also Iohn Gower whiche was maker

---

[27] At least, not in so many words. Amans is told to refer to "Ovide the Poete" at V.878, after the description of Jupiter, and the account of Diana refers to the "Cronique of this fable," V.1270.

> of þis boke made *and* deuysed it to be in mane*r*
> of a confession þat þis said Iohn Gower
> was confessid yn vnto a *p*rest whiche
> was called Genius whom Venus þe
> goddesse of loue sent vnto þe said Gower
> to confesse hym þat he had trespast a-
> yenst Venus *and* hir courte / And calleþ hym
> self a louer/ *and* Genius Venus clerk is called confesso*r*.
> (fol. 4ᵛ)

All but one of the books in the Ashmole manuscript begin with a gloss, followed by provision for a large initial, followed by the English text proper, a layout which gives visual emphasis to the importance of these headnotes. The usual Latin opening to Book I stresses the subject and title of the book:

> Postquam in Prologo tractatum hactenus existit, qualiter hodierne condicionis diuisio caritatis dileccionem superauit, intendit auctor ad presens suum libellum, cuius nomen Confessio Amantis nuncu-patur, componere de illo amore, a quo non solum humanum genus, sed eciam cuncta animancia naturaliter subiciuntur. Et quia nonnulli amantes ultra quam expedit desiderii passionibus crebro stimulan-tur, materia libri per totum super hiis specialius diffunditur. (at I.1)

> [Here, after the material treated thus far in the Prologue, how nowadays division of condition triumphs over the delight of char-ity, the author turns to the present book, whose name is the Con-fession of a Lover, to write about that sort of love by which not only the human race, but also all living things, are naturally sub-dued. And since many lovers are stimulated frequently beyond what is appropriate by the passions of desire, the matter of this book throughout gives especial attention to these cases.][28]

Chetham, too, refers to the author and the title: "How the auctor nameth the werke Confessio Amant*is*" (fol. 5ʳ). The alternate opening gloss in Ashmole lays out the divisions of the work far more explicit than either of these, and its emphasis on the author's responsibility for the text is con-siderably more marked in that it names the author and repeats that name three times.

Is the Ashmole glossator moved simply by a desire to leave nothing to the imagination, or at least to later discovery? Gower is named in the Latin prose which accompanies the Prologue, and he announces his name in the English at the end of Book VIII. It appears that the Ashmole glossator is particularly eager not to postpone the English acknowledgment of the

---

[28] I have rendered "nonnulli" as "many" rather than "some," because Gower seems to intend "many" on most occasions when he uses the word.

maker of the book. I think it possible that the Ashmole glossator is here resisting what he might see as a subterfuge in the original poem. The voice of the lover in Book I declares repeatedly his intention to tell forth his own experience truly, as a service to lovers; his speech, from lines 61–87, is full of verbs of telling, showing, and bearing witness. The Latin verse to I.ii echoes the note of self-sacrifice and warning in its own, higher register: "Me quibus ergo Venus, casus, laqueauit amantem, / Orbis in exemplum scribere tendo palam" (So openly I bring myself to write / Of nets I tumbled in, for me outstretched / By Venus; thus a lover warns the world).[29] It would seem, then, that English and Latin poetic voices alike are uniting to assure the reader of the truth and value of the exempla/ensamples to follow, a truth and value grounded in their status as the real experiences of the speaker (and it should be noted that the first-person voice is very unusual in the Latin verses). And yet the Latin prose gloss to line 61 makes the fiction perfectly clear:

> Hic quasi in persona aliorum, quos amor alligat, *fingens* se auctor esse Amantem, varias eorum passiones variis huius libri distinccionibus per singula scribere proponit. (at I.61; my emphasis)

> [Here as if in the person of others whom love binds, the author *feigns* himself to be a lover (or Amans), and proposes to write in the various sections of this book about their various passions.]

The contrast between the repeated expressions of good faith (in English and Latin verse) and the acknowledgment of feigning (in Latin prose) is pointed. The Ashmole version's references to devising and making are not perhaps so potentially pejorative as "fingens," but the insistence on authorship, on poetic creation, is if anything heightened by the repetition of the poet's name and by the placement of this gloss at the head of Book I. There seems to be a desire here to underline—perhaps to make accessible—the fiction revealed in the Latin prose (an impulse which may be shared by those manuscripts in which the Confession portrait clearly suggests Gower). And while the source of the "truth" here may indeed have been that Latin prose, it is most often the case that the Ashmole glossator "corrects" the gaps between English and Latin through recourse to the English part of the poem. Perhaps here, too, the primary impulse for the Ashmole glossator's displacement of the Latin original is not another Latin gloss, but rather the naming which occurs in the English of Book VIII. The result, in any case, is to install the English author at the head of his English text, the unambiguous source of all that it contains.

For Winthrop Wetherbee, the uneasy fit between Latin and English in the *Confessio Amantis* is part of Gower's desire "to make explicit and central the confrontation between traditional Latin *auctoritas* and a vernacular

---

[29] The translation is from Siân Echard and Claire Fanger, *The Latin Verses in the Confessio Amantis: An Annotated Translation* (East Lansing, MI, 1991), 17.

with its own claims to meaning."[30] The failures of the Latin program raise the profile of the English part of the poem. Perhaps the anglicizing Ashmole glossator is, wittingly or unwittingly, an accomplice in this act. The examples above suggest he may have recognized the confrontation between English and Latin, if not necessarily its meaning. He is, in practical terms if not theoretical ones, indisputably a champion of the vernacular. Despite the invocation of Carmen in the Prologue, Gower declares at the end that his intention was "in englesch forto make a book" (VIII. 3108). The Ashmole glossator appears to have taken him at his word. His presentation of Gower's text is, to borrow from the title of this volume, an English "re-visioning" of the poem in its linguistic parts and its complex whole.

---

[30] Wetherbee, "Latin Structure and Vernacular Space," 10.

Selection and Subversion in Gower's *Confessio Amantis*

A. S. G. Edwards

The very act of selection is self-evidently a subversive one, isolating a portion of a work from its larger design, placing it in contexts where it can, at least potentially, assume new possibilities of meaning. Such processes of selection were common in Middle English manuscripts, particularly in the treatment of those of the great medieval English vernacular triumvirate, Chaucer, Gower, and Lydgate, albeit in rather different ways.

In the case of Chaucer the chief emphasis seems to have fallen on narrative selections. Thus, about a quarter of the surviving manuscripts of the *Canterbury Tales* are selected individual narratives or groups of narratives. Sometimes, such groupings are made apparently on a generic principle, as in a collection like British Library MS Harley 1239 that brings together Chaucer's romances from the *Canterbury Tales* ("Knight's," "Man of Law's," "Wife of Bath's," and "Franklin's" tales) together with *Troilus*. Others combine Chaucer's religious tales with similar material from other sources, such as Lydgate's saints' lives. Only one manuscript of the *Canterbury Tales* includes any non-narrative selection, an extract from the description of the Parson in the General Prologue.[1] Similarly, the only surviving selections from the *Legend of Good Women* involve the excerption of individual legends, those of Dido and Thisbe.[2] It is only in some of the

---

The fullest account in print of selections from Gower occurs in A. E. Hartung, ed., *Manual of the Writings in Middle English* (New Haven, CT, 1986), 7, 2408–9. I am grateful to Priscilla Bawcutt, who identified the extract in the Boston Public Library manuscript and to Dr. Kate Harris who made me aware of the Longleat extract, neither of which is noted there. Dr. Harris's University of York D. Phil. thesis "Ownership and Readership: Studies in the Provenance of the Manuscripts of Gower's *Confessio Amantis*" (1993) contains an opening chapter (27–75) "A Survey of the Ownership of the Manuscripts Containing Extracts from the *Confessio Amantis*" which has proved helpful to my own concerns. It is hoped that this useful work will be published in the near future.

[1] British Library (henceforward BL) MS Add. 10340, f. 41; for description see J. M. Manly and Edith Rickert, *The Text of the "Canterbury Tales,"* 8 vols. (Chicago, 1940), I, 48–51 (henceforward Manly/Rickert).

[2] In Bodleian Library MS Rawlinson C. 86, fols. 113–119^v and Cambridge University Library MS Ff. 1. 6, fols. 64–67^v respectively; for descriptions see Janet Cowen and George Kane, eds., *The Legend of Good Women*, Medieval Texts and Studies, no. 16 (East Lansing, 1995), 7–8, 13–14.

extracts from *Troilus* that there is any preoccupation with lyric passages in Chaucer among the surviving selections.[3]

With Lydgate the situation is rather different. The only one of his major works to be extensively excerpted was his *Fall of Princes*,[4] although there were a few extracts from his *Life of Our Lady*.[5] In its complete form the *Fall* survives in about forty manuscripts. But there are at least as many manuscripts, if not more, that contain selections from the *Fall*. These selections consist chiefly of passages chosen from the various hortatory envoys Lydgate added to his work rather than from his actual accounts of the falls of great men. It was clearly the tone of sonorous exhortation rather than the narratives of history that commended his work to a number of early readers. These tendencies to briefer, more exclamatory passages offer a parallel to the non-narrative briefer selections from Chaucer's *Troilus*. (There is one instance where a passage from Lydgate's *Fall of Princes* is combined with one from *Troilus* to form a lyric.)[6]

Both the number and nature of the selections from Gower differ from those for Chaucer and Lydgate. In the first place, there are considerably fewer selections from the *Confessio* than from the works of Chaucer and Lydgate mentioned above. Out of the sixty-one surviving manuscripts or seemingly independent fragments I know of, only nine are demonstrably the result of conscious selection,[7] and three of these are very brief.[8] One may speculate why this should be so. Perhaps the answer lies in part, at least, in the early and rapid consolidation of the form of the *Confessio* in the commercial London book trade. One can point to the now well-known activities of Scribe D, who, in whole or in part can be associated

---

[3] For a full list of these passages see B. A. Windeatt, ed., *Troilus & Criseyde* (London, 1984), 75–76.

[4] For a list of these see A. S. G. Edwards, "Selections from Lydgate's *Fall of Princes:* A Checklist," *The Library*, 5th series, 26 (1971): 337–42 and Nigel Mortimer, "Selections from Lydgate's *Fall of Princes:* A Corrected Checklist," *The Library*, 6th series, 17 (1995): 342–44.

[5] These occur in three manuscripts; see Rossell Hope Robbins, "A New Lydgate Fragment," *English Language Notes*, 5 (1967–68): 243–47, which contains some helpful general comments on other selections from longer poems.

[6] This occurs in Cambridge University Library MS Ff. 1. 6, fols. 150–151.

[7] I leave out of this count Trinity College, Oxford MS D. 29, a particularly complex merging of passages from the *Confessio* with material from other vernacular sources; for some preliminary comments see Kate Harris, "John Gower's *Confessio Amantis:* The Virtues of Bad Texts," in *Manuscripts and Readers in Fifteenth-Century England*, ed. D. Pearsall (Cambridge, 1983), 31–33; Dr. Harris has in preparation a more extensive study of this manuscript which I have been fortunate to read in draft. It may be noted that this manuscript has Augustinian associations, a fact of some interest in view of the appearance of other Gower selections in BL Harley 7333, on which see below.

[8] The fullest published list of Gower manuscripts is in Hartung, ed., *The Manual* (see headnote above), which lists 64; but Rawl. C. 82 receives two entries there (50 and 51), BL Add 38181 is a post-medieval transcript of Takamiya 32, 64 is a part of 49. Neither the Boston or Longleat fragments are noted. The status of some of the fragments (62 and 63) is unclear; possibly they could be leaves from manuscripts surviving elsewhere.

with eight copies of the *Confessio* copied between the 1390s and the first two decades of the fifteenth century.[9] Even though this scribe copied different states or stages of Gower's poem, he was copying a finished poem in a remarkably uniform way. Indeed one can point to several factors—the *ordinatio* of the Latin apparatus, the presentation of verse form and layout —that were established early in the textual tradition of the poem and which made excerption more difficult.

Derek Pearsall has spoken, for example, of the particular effect of the Latin apparatus to "package" or "case" the poem in ways which may also have helped to inhibit selection.[10] In addition, while the rhyme royal stanza used by Chaucer and Lydgate naturally breaks the work down into chewy chunks of a comfortable size, the couplet verse of the *Confessio*, especially in the regular 42-line, double column format of many of the manuscripts, crenellated with its Latin apparatus, does not lend itself as naturally or as obviously to the processes of excerption. Hence the majority of the selections are of longer self-contained narratives or collections of such narratives, most obviously isolable as separate units.

There may also have been an element of pre-selection related to the commercial factors I have mentioned. The frequency with which the same extracts occur is striking:[11] "The Three Questions" appears in five of the selections (Balliol, CUL Ee, CUL Ff, Harley 7333, Takamiya); the "Tale of Tereus" in three (Harley, Takamiya, CUL Ff), and the tales of "Apollonius" (Balliol, CUL Ff), "Constance" (Balliol, Harley) "Adrian and Bardus" and "Demetrius and Perseus" (Takamiya, Balliol) in two each. This degree of recurrence in selection would seem to raise the question of whether the coincidence of such selections derives from antecedent exemplars, rather than individual taste. Kate Harris suggested some years ago that at least some of the surviving selections, notably Cambridge Ee and the Takamiya manuscript, do seem to reflect a common ancestor.[12] It is less easy to determine whether such exemplars were the product of the book trade, though the most likely explanation for the circulation of such extracts is as commercial "booklets."

Certainly the kinds of manuscripts with which these narrative selections are associated are generally composite or accretive ones, some forms of which can be clearly linked to aspects of commercial book production at varying levels of accomplishment. Both Takamiya and Ee were evidently professionally produced, as was Rawlinson, which has been shown to

---

[9] On Scribe D see A. I. Doyle and M. B. Parkes, "The production of copies of the *Canterbury Tales* and the *Confessio Amantis* in the early fifteenth century," in *Medieval Scribes, Manuscript & Libraries,* ed. M. B. Parkes and Andrew G. Watson (London, 1978), esp. 192–96.

[10] Derek Pearsall, "Gower's Latin in the *Confessio Amantis,*" in *Latin and Vernacular,* ed. A. J. Minnis (Cambridge, 1989), 13–25 (esp. 14, 20).

[11] I use short forms for referring to the manuscripts; for full details see Appendix.

[12] Harris, "John Gower's *Confessio Amantis,*" 34.

have been originally a fascicular manuscript, the distinct booklets of which now exist separately.[13] Harley 7333 was compiled to a high professional standard for the Augustinian Abbey of St. Mary le Pratis in Leicester which seems to have links to the metropolitan book trade (it seems partly derived from an exemplar or exemplars linked to the London scribe John Shirley).

These commercial factors may also be connected to larger aspects of collocation, in which selections from Gower recurrently occur with Chaucer or in Chaucerian contexts, particularly with his narrative works: Takamiya 32 includes the *Canterbury Tales,* Harley 7333 the *Canterbury Tales* and some of Chaucer's lyrics, CUL Ee. 2. 15 the "Man of Law's Tale," while CUL Ff. 1. 6 contains selections from the *Legend* and some lyrics. Even briefer selections, like that in the Boston manuscript, occur in Lydgate's *Siege of Thebes,* itself a continuation of the *Canterbury Tales,* while the only other verse apart from the Gower extract in the Gonville & Caius manuscript is Chaucer's "Purse." Balliol 354 and Rawl. D. 82 are the only one of the larger selections that do not contain any of Chaucer's works. The extent of the Chaucerian presence even in amateur compilations like Ff. 1. 6, may suggest the residual pressures of commercial exemplars.[14] These persistent collocations underscore the fact that Gower's identity was closely linked to Chaucer's in ways that—perhaps subversively—compromised the distinct identity of the former for posterity.

These possibly commercial factors are one reason why the briefer extracts are especially interesting. Where such extracts occur they offer evidence of an unusually deliberate attempt at subversion of Gower's original design as they reconstitute his massive narrative collection as attenuated lyric or isolable precept, resisting the pressures of layout and verse form in particularly decisive ways.

Perhaps unsurprisingly, few readers attempted such an audacious reconstitution. Selections of this kind occur in only three manuscripts. Two are very brief. One is a passage of twelve lines in Gonville & Caius, Cambridge MS 176/97, p. 23, selected from Book IV (IV. ll. 1623–34), one of a series of brief passages (including an extract from Chaucer's "Purse") added to the main texts of what is primarily a scientific and medical collection. The lines are titled "A pure balade of love" and have indeed been printed as an amatory lyric.[15] It is easy to understand why they should be readily accepted as a free standing short poem. They are taken

---

[13] See Kathleen L. Smith (Scott), "A Fifteenth-Century Vernacular Manuscript Reconstructed," *Bodleian Library Record* 7 (1966): 234–41.

[14] See Kate Harris, "The Origins and Make-Up of Cambridge University Library MS Ff. 1. 6," *Transactions of the Cambridge Bibliographical Society* 8 (1983): 299–333, esp. 309–12 on links to London exemplars.

[15] H. A. Person, ed., *Cambridge Middle English Lyrics* (Seattle, 1962), 38 (his text is reprinted here). The identification of this extract as Gower's was made by Ethel Seaton, *Sir Richard Roos* (London, 1961), 458.

from a passage delivered by Confessor to Amans on the ways in which love expresses itself in knightly service in foreign lands, with no hint of the wider frame of reference from which they come:

> Kny3tes in travayle for to serve
> Wherof the may thanke deserve
> Where as thes men of Armes be
> Some most ouer the gret see
> So that by lande and by ship
> The most travayle for wurship
> And make many hasty rodes
> Somtyme vnto ynde sumtyme to Oþe Rodes
> And somtyme in to tartary
> So that the heriaultes on theym crye
> Viallant viallant Lo wher he goith
> And then he gyvith hym gold & cloth

One of the other two short extracts occurs on a flyleaf of Boston Public Library f. med 94 where it forms one of several additions made in the late fifteenth or early sixteenth centuries to a manuscript of Lydgate's *Siege of Thebes*. It comprises thirteen lines, this time from Book VII (ll. 1811–23). They are a passage from "King, Wine, Women and Truth," summarizing the narrative question: ("of thinges thre which strengest is, / The wyn, the womman or the king," VII. 1812–13). The passage is copied in a sixteenth-century hand, presumably that of one of the Campbells of Glenorquhay, who were the earliest recorded owners of the manuscript. Why it should have commended itself as an attractive subject to Scottish lairds is unclear, unless it was a reflection of recurrent personal preoccupations.

The third brief passage, in Longleat 174, fols. 159–160, also contains a slightly longer extract from the same book, running to about seventy lines (VII. 1281–1348) added in a hand that does not appear anywhere else in the manuscript and seems to have been done later than the main transcription.[16] It differs from the Boston extract from Book VII in containing expository rather than narrative material, chosen from Gower's account of astrological and herbal significance of the fifteen stars. The significance of the extract must lie here in the larger context of the manuscript itself, which is a compilation chiefly of medical materials, in a number of hands. It affords us one of the most unlikely incarnations of Gower as a medical *vade mecum*, the doctor's friend.

All of these extracts evidence forms of idiosyncratic excerption and adaptation to isolate brief passages from any narrative context. Such activities seem wholly removed from the activities of professional scribes or

---

[16] This extract was discovered by Kate Harris and is to be discussed by her at length in a forthcoming paper in a Festschrift for Derek Pearsall; for a preliminary discussion see her thesis, "Ownership and Readership," 49–56, to which I am indebted.

compilers. The extracts reveal ways of personalizing the text to reflect highly individual responses that shift the work into new modes, abandoning narrative to wholly re-contextualize the poem in these fragmentary forms.

The other selections from Gower retain the element of narrative while isolating individual tales. Most of the manuscripts contain several tales and usually they are non-sequential. Indeed only one manuscript, Rawlinson, contains a single extended consecutive portion of Gower's poem (VII. 2377–2970).[17]

But while the commercial factors I have noted may have a role in the choice of these narrative selections, it is possible to suggest that in certain instances there may have been other pressures of a discernibly purposive kind operating in the process of excerption. Some of these pressures can be illustrated by Cambridge University Library, Ee.2.15. This manuscript seems to be a professional, if relatively low-grade, manuscript production[18] that seeks to accommodate its Gower selections into a larger compilational design. This design is clearly generic, reflecting the influence of devotional, particularly hagiographic models: the other principal contents of the manuscript are the "Man of Law's Tale" from the *Canterbury Tales,* and selections from the *South English Legendary,* together with Lydgate's *Life of St. Edmund.* It also contains two extracts from Gower, the "Three Questions" (I. 3124–3315) and the "Trump of Death" (I. 2083–2253). Both find a place without overmuch difficulty into this devotional framework. The "Three Questions" offers an explicitly Christian representation of the virtue of Humility:

> Thurgh which the hihe trinite
> As for decerte of pure love
> Unto Marie from above ...
> His oghne Sone adoun he sente,

---

[17] Whether this manuscript can be properly designated a selection is open to question. The manuscript as it is presently constituted comprises 34 leaves. The first 24 leaves (in three gatherings of 8 leaves each, signed a-c), form a codicologically distinct unit containing the prose *Siege of Thebes* and *Siege of Troy.* The final ten leaves form a single (unsigned) gathering containing the passage from Gower comprising VIII. 2377–2970, Amans's final encounter with Venus. The text begins at the top of the recto of fol. 25 with a two-line red initial and stops at the bottom of fol. 33[v] without any indication of closure. The difference in quiring and signatures suggests that the collocation of Gower with these prose texts is fortuitous. It also raises the question of whether there was once likely more of the Gower than has survived. This seems probable given the lack of formal incipits or explicits, but how far the text might have extended before the surviving passage cannot be determined.

[18] For description see Manly/Rickert, I.126–129. The manuscript itself begins at fol. 18 being preceded by a codicologically unrelated fragment of Mirk's *Festial.* It is written on parchment in a single trained, if rather loose, hand and decorated throughout the verse portions in a systematic way with rubricated marginal headings on the recto of each leaf, red flourishing at the end of each line and occasional, fairly elaborate, painted initials (e.g., fols.. 18, 31[v], 48, 59[v], 79[v], 107).

Above alle othre and hire he ches
For that vertue which bodeth pes: (I. 3276–81)

The "Trump of Death" episode is also concerned with humility, of course, concluding with the exhortation "... sithen that so is / That thou canst drede a man so sore / Drede god with al thin herte more" (I. 2244–46). Affirmation of trust in God's power links not just the two Gower episodes but all of the narrative extracts that the volume contains in ways that re-shape Gower into a larger pious, quasi-hagiographical context.

These selections and the pious environment in which they are placed can be contrasted with those Gower selections in Takamiya 32. Here extracts from the *Confessio* occur with the *Canterbury Tales, Gamelyn, Parthonope of Blois* as well as the *Adulterous Falmouth Squire,* the *Visio Tundale,* and the *Speculum Misericordie.* The overall impression is of a very different kind of collection from the Cambridge one, one in which secular, particularly romance, modes predominate. This is true not simply of the obvious romance texts like *Parthonope* and *Gamelyn* but also of the *Adulterous Falmouth Squire* which occurs elsewhere in such well-known romance collections as Cambridge University Library Ff. 2. 38[19] and even the *Visio Tundale,* which appears in another romance collection, BL Cotton Caligula A. ii[20] and in BL Royal 17. B. xliii, the principal content of which is *Sir Gowther,*[21] as well as in National Library of Scotland MS 19. 3.1, a primarily religious collection that also includes both *Sir Gowther* and *Sir Isumbras.*[22] The Gower selections fall into two groups: the bulk appear near the beginning of the manuscript, comprising five extracts from Books I ("Three Questions"), V ("Tereus"), VI ("Nectanabus"), II ("Demetrius and Perseus") and V ("Adrian and Bardus"); after the *Canterbury Tales*—the major work in the manuscript—comes part of "Nebuchadnezzar's Dream," from the Prologue and Book I of the *Confessio.* There seems no thematic or topical purpose to these collocations. Here the pressures on the assembling of the collection seem not to have been generic, as with Ee.2.15; they are much more loosely formal, in the emphasis on the narrative mode. Indeed, the Gower selections have clearly been editorially adjusted, in part at least, to facilitate their presentation as a series of discrete narratives, cut off from any indication of any larger design or interrelationship.[23] The re-creation of parts of Gower's poem in this

[19] For a full description see the Introduction by Frances McSparran and Pamela Robinson to *Cambridge University Library MS Ff. 2. 38* (London, 1979), xxi–xxv.

[20] For description see Gisela Guddat-Figge, *Catalogue of Romances containing Middle English Romances* (Munich, 1976), 168–72.

[21] For description see George Warner and J. P. Gilson, *Catalogue of Western Manuscripts in the Old Royal and King's Collections,* 4 vols. (London, 1921), II.223–4.

[22] For description see Philippa Hardman, "A Medieval 'Library in Parvo,'" *Medium Aevum* 47 (1978): 262–73.

[23] Cf. Manly/Rickert: "The stories from Gower ... are complete but have been edited slightly at beginning and ends, and the text has been treated very freely" (I.109).

assemblage of separate narrative poems seems designed to make them congruent with the distinctive romance emphases of the collection as a whole.

The final large, commercially derived collection, BL Harley 7333, also has as its chief poetic contents the *Canterbury Tales* and other shorter poems by Chaucer. It also includes Gower narratives some of which appear elsewhere ("Constance," "Tereus," and the "Three Questions"), selections which suggest that they all quite probably derive from some pre-selected commercial Gower 'anthology.' This possibility together with the manuscript's production over a period of time, possibly decades, limits the usefulness of any attempt to seek any very clear controlling purpose or purposes to the manuscript's design, into which the Gower selections could be accommodated. All that can be said is that the selections seem generally didactic in nature and hence were perhaps felt congenial to the sensibilities of the house of Augustinian canons that owned it. Certainly other texts in the manuscript, notably the *Canterbury Tales,* have been edited in ways which seem designed to consider such sensibilities.[24]

It may appear that such commercially derived selections are similar in their narrative and generic emphases to those I have noted from the *Canterbury Tales.* But we find in some of the longer selections produced outside the commercial milieu processes that involve recontextualizations of parts of the *Confessio* that seem, at least intermittently, to respond to pressures that are not simply those of literary form. This seems to be the case in parts of the so-called Findern manuscript (Cambridge University Library Ff. 1.6), put together over a period of some years, by a Derbyshire family in the fifteenth century. The manuscript is particularly noteworthy for its collection of lyric texts, many of them unique to this collection and possibly written by members of the family, who may also have been responsible for much of its transcription. It also contains some narrative texts, including, apart from the *Confessio* passages, an extract from Chaucer's *Legend of Good Women,* the romance *Sir Degrevaunt,* and the *Alexander-Cassamus* fragment.[25]

In Findern, the "Three Questions" also occurs (fols. 45–51), preceded by Gower's "Tale of Tereus" (beginning imperfectly, fols. 3–5) and "Rosiphelee" (fols. 5–10ᵛ), grouped as a sequence, while those of "Ceyx and Alcione" (fols. 81–84) and "Apollonius" (fols. 84ᵛ–95) occur later in the manuscript as a separate sequence. To consider the significance of the first of these groupings it is necessary to entertain the possibility that at least some parts of this family collection may have been compiled in a way that sought to reflect the gendered consciousness of those assembling it. That

---

For some illustrations of the medieval editing of Takamiya see Kate Harris, "John Gower's *Confessio Amantis,*" 38–39.

[24] For a summary account of such editing see Manly/Rickert, I.212.

[25] For a full description see the Introduction by Richard Beadle and A. E. B. Owen to *The Findern Manuscript: Cambridge University MS Ff. I. 6* (London, 1977), xix–xxx.

the manuscript was compiled in large part for a female audience and per-
haps to some extent even composed and copied by women are possibilities
that recent research has raised,[26] and which are strengthened by the
Gower selections. A common element in the narratives of the "Three
Questions," "Tereus," and "Rosiphelee," is their focus on female charac-
ters and the different kinds of power and authority their lives can be
shown to possess in the political, spiritual, and emotional spheres. In the
case of the "Three Questions" the narrative turns on the crucial, exposi-
tory role of the knight's daughter as interpreter of the questions. The tale
of "Tereus" is, in actuality—and even more so in the incomplete version
in Findern—a narrative of Procne and Philomene: it is their voices of
female complaint that the narrative affirms, establishing for women "the
falshod of hire housebonde" (V. 6020). "Rosiphelee" (IV. 1114–1466) con-
cerns itself exclusively with a female subject as an exemplum of idleness in
love.[27]

One cannot push such gendered assumptions very far, at least in terms
of the Gower extracts. The later two narratives, those of "Ceyx and
Alcione" (IV. 2746–2926) and "Apollonius" (VIII. 271–846) stand apart
from this pattern of female sympathy. They occur separately from the
other selections, in a later part of the manuscript, added in different hands
from those that copied the earlier extracts.[28] It is particularly striking that
the portion of the tale of "Apollonius" in this part of the manuscript
comprises a selection that virtually ignores the figure of Antiochus's
daughter, the chief focus of pathos in the narrative. Doubtless as the
manuscript evolved over time, different factors came to shape the various
components of its construction. In such a piecemeal collection it is the
collocation of these narratives at the local level, together with their links
to materials similar in subject matter that serves to establish such a limited
degree of contextual coherence as the selections may possess.

The seemingly intermittent discernible design of the selections in
Findern points to the difficulties of finding purposive patterns to some of
the other selections. This is particularly so in the manuscript containing
the largest number, Balliol 354. This was copied by the London grocer,
Richard Hill, in the early sixteenth century and contains eleven different

---

[26] For this argument see Sarah McNamer, "Female Authors, Provincial Setting: The
Re-Versing of Courtly Love in the Findern Manuscript," *Viator* 22 (1991): 279–310 ; see
also A. S. G. Edwards, "Gender, Order and Reconciliation in *Sir Degrevaunt*," in
Readings in Middle English Romance, ed. Carol Meale (Cambridge, 1994), 53–64 (esp.
63–64).

[27] It may be relevant to note that several of the lyrics argued to have been written by
women occur in the early part of the manuscript, where this group of Gower extracts
occurs; see the two lyrics on fol. 20ᵛ, and those on fols. 28ᵛ, 56, and 69ᵛ, nos. 1–5 in
McNamer, "Female Authors, Provincial Setting," 303–5.

[28] It may be suggested that there seems to have been a break in the sequence of the
manuscript's construction just before the appearance of the Gower selections, following
fol. 76ᵛ; see Beadle and Owen, *Findern Manuscript,* xxiii.

extracts from the *Confessio*. A number of these do occur in other manu-
scripts: "Apollonius," "Constance," "Demetrius and Perseus," "Adrian
and Bardus," and the "Three Questions"; but the majority have no
parallel among surviving witnesses. Is this a series of personal, idiosyncratic
choices from a complete manuscript? Or do the parallels elsewhere point
to Balliol's derivation from some pre-selected exemplar? Certainly the
extent of Hill's very wide reading, both of Gower and other works, as
reflected in this manuscript, gives some support to the former possibili-
ty.[29] He may be a literary Jack Horner, extracting what, for him, were
choice plums. Yet the appearance of the same selections in other manu-
scripts may strike a cautionary note. What is clear, as with the Takamiya
selections, is the extent of the re-shaping of his sources into a series of
"self-contained narrative units."[30] Yet the range of Hill's taste seems
much wider, encompassing both narrative and lyric and didactic verse.
Here, even more than with the other selections, it does not seem possible
to shape the evidence of selection into more satisfyingly compelling forms.

But overall, the evidence of the selections from the *Confessio* does
demonstrate several points of some relevance to those interested in matters
of reception and reader-response.[31] First, clear evidence of individualized
responses is limited and generally reflected in very short extracts like those
in the Gonville & Caius and Longleat manuscripts. More generally, the
process of excerption reveals how far the selections are removed from the
original design of the *Confessio*. Most obviously what is lost is any concern
with the larger penitential framework, with its emphasis on confession and
correct instruction and the attendant preoccupation with sin. Among those
manuscripts containing selections, only Findern leaves any vestiges of the
dialogic mode, the exchanges between Genius and Amans that give the po-
em such direction and structure as it possesses, in its extracts from the pro-
logues to the tales of "Rosiphelee" and "Ceix and Alcyone" (from Book
IV). The isolation of narrative from original moral context, its transforma-
tion into a form that is situationally and formally chameleon-like, adapt-
able to whatever ethical context that the selector reconfigures it for, includ-
ing no context at all, forms the most notable act of narrative subversion in
the selections from the *Confessio Amantis*.

---

[29] For a description of the contents of Balliol see R. A. B. Mynors, *Catalogue of the Manuscripts of Balliol College Oxford* (Oxford, 1963), 352–54.

[30] The term is Kate Harris's; see her dissertation, "Ownership and Readership," 46–47, for some analysis of Hill's methods.

[31] For a general survey of such questions of reception see Neil Gilroy-Scott, "John Gower's Reputation: Literary Allusions from the Early Fifteenth-Century to the Time of *Pericles*," *Yearbook of English Studies* 1 (1971): 30–47, and Derek Pearsall, "The Gower Tradition," in *Gower's Confessio Amantis: Responses and Reassessments*, ed. A. J. Minnis (Cambridge, 1983), 179–97.

Appendix: Selections from the "Confessio Amantis"[32]

1. Bodleian Library, Rawlinson D. 82, fols. 25–33 (VIII.2377–2970).

2. Oxford, Balliol 354, fols. 55–96: VIII.271–2028 ("Apollonius"); II.587–1612 ("Constance"); II.1613–1865 ("Demetrius and Perseus"); V.4937–5162 ("Adrian and Bardus"); V.4937–5162 ("Pirithous, Galba and Vitellius"); VI.975–1238 ("Dives, Delicacy of Nero"); II.3187–3507 ("Constantine and Silvester"); I.2785–3066 ("Nebuchadnezzar's Punishment"); III.1201–1300 ("Diogenes and Alexander"); III.1331–1680 ("Pyramus and Thisbe"); V.141–312 ("Midas"); fols. 171ᵛ–175: I.3067–3402 ("Three Questions").

3. Cambridge University Library Ee. 2. 15, fols. 38–47: I.3124–3315 ("Three Questions"); I.2083–2253 ("Trump of Death").

4. Cambridge University Library Ff. 1. 6, fols. 3–10ᵛ: V.5921–6052 ("Tereus"); IV.1114–1466 ("Rosiphelee"); fols. 45–51: I.3067–3425 ("Three Questions"); fols. 81–84: IV.2746–2926 ("Ceix and Alcyone"); fols. 84ᵛ–95: VIII.271–846 ("Apollonius").

5. Cambridge, Gonville & Caius College 176/97, p. 23: IV.1622–34.

6. British Library Harley 7333, fols. 120–129ᵛ: V.5551–6052 ("Tereus"); IV.587–1608 ("Constance"); I.3067–3425 ("Three Questions"); II.291–372 ("Traveller and the Angel"); V.2031–2272 ("Virgil's Mirror"); V.2273–2390 ("Two Coffins"); V.2391–2498 ("The Beggars and the Pasties").

7. Warminster, Longleat 174, fols. 159ʳᵃ–160ʳᵃ: VII.1281–1348.

8. Tokyo, Takamiya 32, fols. 3–5: I.3067–3402 ("Three Questions"); fols. 5ᵛ–8ᵛ: V, 5551–6048 ("Tereus"); fols. 8ᵛ–11ᵛ: VI, 1789–2358 ("Nectanabus"); fols. 11ᵛ–13: II, 1613–1864 ("Demetrius and Perseus"); fols. 13–14: V, 4937–5162 ("Adrian and Bardus"); fols. 158–162ᵛ: Pr. 585–1088, I.2785–3042 ("Nebuchadnezzar's Dream").

9. Boston Public Library f. med 94, fol. 74ᵛ: VII.1811–23.

---

[32] It should be noted that the line numbers I give are to some degree approximate; quite often the opening and, on occasion, the closing lines have been altered as a result of the removal of the selection from a larger narrative context. Nor do these numbers take account of omissions of individual lines, or groups of lines, within the extract.

Printing the *Confessio Amantis:* Caxton's Edition in Context

Martha W. Driver

Addressing the reader in his 1532 edition of Gower's *Confessio Amantis,* Thomas Berthelette warns that in the edition printed by his predecessor William Caxton, there are copious misreadings "cleane contrarye in sentence and in meanynge" and omissions of "lynes and columns, ye, and sometyme holle padges." According to Berthelette, Caxton's "chaunging of wordes, and misordrynge of sentences" has marred Gower's original to such an extent that even the most learned reader would find the text difficult, and what, asks Berthelette, "can be a greater blemysshe vnto a noble auctour"? For these reasons, Berthelette explains he "toke some peyne to prynte it more correctly than it was before." In compiling his new edition of the *Confessio,* Berthelette tells us he has consulted manuscripts, "the wrytten copies," as well as "the prynt copie"; his edition is one of the earliest forays into Gower scholarship. Berthelette's prefatory material is also unabashedly self-promoting. In the previous edition published by Caxton, "this moost pleasant and easy auctor could not wel be perceyued," says Berthelette, but he, Berthelette, in this new and improved edition, has now made Gower, that "pleasant and easy" author, for the first time visible, "sette forth in his owne shappe and lykenes."[1] Writing about Caxton's edition some 450 years later, Norman Blake comments that "Caxton's edition of the *Confessio* exhibits more signs of carelessness in the printing than usual."[2] If we look again at Caxton's *Confessio,* however, we

---

[1] Despite these criticisms, Caxton's *Confessio Amantis* [RSTC 12142] served as one important source for the two editions published by Berthelette, the first in 1532 [RSTC 12143] and the second in 1554 [RSTC 12144]. For more on Berthelette, see Tim William Machan, "Thomas Berthelette and Gower's *Confessio,*" in *Studies in the Age of Chaucer* 18 (1996): 143–66. See also *The English Works of John Gower,* ed. G. C. Macaulay. 2 vols. *Early English Text Society,* e.s., vols. 81 and 82 (London, 1900). Gower in print is also discussed by Derek Pearsall in "The Gower Tradition," in *Gower's Confessio Amantis: Responses and Reassessments,* ed. A. J. Minnis (Cambridge, 1983), 179–97. Reference numbers for books are taken from the *RSTC: A Short-Title Catalogue of Books Printed in England, Scotland, and Ireland, 1475–1640,* first comp. by A. W. Pollard and G. R. Redgrave, 2nd ed. begun by W. A. Jackson and F. S. Ferguson, completed by Katharine F. Pantzer (London, 1976, 1986). I wish to thank Jonathan Alexander for reading a draft of this paper.

[2] N. F. Blake, "Early Printed Editions of *Confessio Amantis,*" in *Mediaevalia* 16

find that what appears to be carelessness may, in fact, be traced to Caxton's models, his manuscript exemplar or exemplars, to conventions of Continental printing practice, and finally to the volatile political scene of the 1480s.

Caxton printed the *Confessio Amantis* on 2 September 1483, though the colophon tells us the book was "fynysshed the ii day of Septembre the fyrst yere of the regne of Kyng Richard the thyrd / the yere of our lord 1493," a date that is clearly wrong. There are actually two versions of the colophon, which, to the best of my knowledge, have not been otherwise noted. One copy in the British Library includes the following, presumably unfinished, colophon, which I term version one:

> Enprynted at Westmestre by m
> Willyam Caxton and fynysshed the
> day of Septembre the fyrst yere of th
> reyne of kyng Richard the thyrd / the
> yere of our lord a thousand / CCCC
> lxxxxiii

Other Gower editions, those in The Pierpont Morgan Library and another in the British Library, for example, conclude this way:

> Enprynted at Westmestre by me
> Willyam Caxton and fynysshed the ii
> day of Septembre the fyrst yere of
> the regne of kyng Richard the thyrd /
> the yere of our lord a thousand / CCCC /
> lxxxxiii /

No reference to what appears to be a preliminary pull in the first British Library edition is made by de Ricci, Blades, or Duff; nor does the *Revised Short-Title Catalogue* or Norman Blake say anything about it. My guess is that Caxton was correcting as he went along. The version one colophon represents a first, unfinished state of text. We see Caxton experimenting as well in other ways: arabic numerals designate some page numbers in the book while roman numerals appear on others, in apparently random fashion. The types also shift, Caxton using type 4, a type he had used since 1480, for the first four-fifths of *Confessio Amantis,* then finishing the volume, from quire Z, with a new state of type 4 (4*). The type is set in two columns, running forty-six lines to a full page.[3]

(1993): 294. See also Blake's argument that Caxton was probably working from only one Gower manuscript exemplar in "Caxton's Copytext of Gower's *Confessio Amantis,*" repr. in *William Caxton and English Literary Culture,* ed. by N. F. Blake (London, 1991).

[3] One Caxton copy in the British Library (BL G 11627) has the unfinished colophon, though I presume there are other examples extant. The finished colophon predominates as shown in the second example taken from Caxton copies in the Pierpont Morgan Library and the British Library (Morgan ChL f1780, BL IB 55077). The preliminary pull

Gower's *Confessio* is the first "big book" to be set by Caxton in a two-column format, though the brief *Doctrine to Learn French and English* appeared in this way in 1480. Norman Blake has suggested that the two-column printing "makes the finished edition seem more of a clerkly than a poetic book," thus packaging Gower "in a way that seems to set him off from Chaucer and many of the other poems published by our first print-er."[4] I doubt, however, that Caxton was doing anything other than he usually does, that is, following his exemplar. If one compares, for example, the layout of the opening of Caxton's Book I with a page from Morgan M125, a *Confessio* manuscript written and illuminated in England about 1420, the observer will note that both texts employ a two-column format with forty-six lines per page. And, as Malcolm Parkes and Ian Doyle have also observed, there are fifteen early manuscripts of the *Confessio Amantis* "written forty-six lines to a column and two columns to a page." In a footnote contributed, no doubt, by Doyle to their well-known essay "The Production of Copies of the *Canterbury Tales* and the *Confessio Amantis* in the Early Fifteenth Century," we learn that "it is reasonable to suppose that this layout may have derived ultimately from the author's own copies. However, the inclusion of the Latin prose commentary within the col-umns of some of these copies and variations in the size of the spaces occupied by the miniatures disturb page-for-page parallels throughout."[5] In following the page formats of his manuscript exemplar or exemplars, Caxton is tracing, at one or two removes, the original text layout which ultimately derives from Gower's own copies of the *Confessio*.

A perfect copy of Caxton's *Confessio* has 222 leaves, quired in eights, with four blanks. According to Duff, the blanks are leaves 1, 8, 9, and 222, though almost all surviving copies lack the blanks or blanks may occur elsewhere in the volume. For example, the Royal copy in the British Library has four blanks, two in the first quire, and two in the last quire.[6] Blanks also occur at the beginnings and usually at the endings of the eight

---

is not mentioned by Seymour de Ricci in *A Census of Caxtons,* Bibliographical Society Illustrated Monographs 15 (Oxford, 1909), or by William Blades in *The Life and Typo-graphy of William Caxton: England's First Printer,* vol. 2 (London, 1861–1863; repr. New York, n.d.), or in E. Gordon Duff's *Fifteenth-Century English Books, A Bibliography of Books and Documents Printed in England and of Books for the English Market Printed Abroad,* Bibliographical Society Illustrated Monographs 18 (Oxford, 1977). For discussion of types, see *William Caxton: An Exhibition to Commemorate the Quincentenary of the Introduction of Printing into England* (London, 1976), 57.

    [4] Blake, in "Early Printed Editions of *Confessio Amantis,*" 296. Caxton's *Doctrine to Learn French and English* [RSTC 24865] was originally 26 leaves, extant now only in fragments.

    [5] A. I. Doyle and M. B. Parkes, "The production of copies of the *Canterbury Tales* and the *Confessio Amantis* in the early fifteenth century," in *Medieval Scribes, Manuscripts and Libraries: Essays presented to N. R. Ker,* edited by M. B. Parkes and A. G. Watson (London, 1978), 165, n. 6.

    [6] E. Gordon Duff, *William Caxton* (Chicago, 1905; repr. Burt Franklin, 1970), 94. The Royal copy is C.11.C.7, formerly IB55078.

books, presumably spaces left for woodcuts or another sort of illustration, that was never supplied, though enterprising later readers sometimes fill them in with material of their own. In Morgan PML 689 (fig. 1), for example, there is a drawing in brown ink of two women and a man in tunic, armor, and sandals between the rubrics *Explicit Liber Quartus* and *Incipit Liber Quintus*. One woman holds what may be a money bag as the man gestures toward it, a scene perhaps related to the theme of Avarice treated in Book V; though, given the pseudoclassical dress of the three figures and the item in question (which bears a distinct resemblance to male genitalia), the drawing may be a visual comment on other action described in Book V, the castration of Saturn by his son Jupiter who (102ᵛ) "kyt of with his owne honde / His genytalles whiche also fast / In to the depe see he cast /" and the creation of the goddess Venus: "Wherof the grekes afferme & seye / Thus when they were cast awey / Cam Venus forth by wey of kynde."[7]

On folio 2 of the Caxton edition (fig. 2), the Prologus, is a twenty-line gap across both columns and an eight-line gap in the lower left column. At the beginning of Book I (which would follow blank leaves 8 and 9 in a perfect copy) is a fourteen-line gap in the left column. Book II opens with a twenty-one-line gap in the left column, and at the end of Book II, there is a twelve-line space. Thirteen-line gaps occur between the Latin introduction and the Middle English text at the beginnings of Book III and IV. After Book IV ends, there is a twenty-one-line space. These are clearly not random spaces left by the compositor, though Blake blames the two-column format for what he calls the "untidy gaps": "The edition is printed in two columns per page throughout, but this results in untidy gaps in many places. It is natural to think," Blake continues, "that this space was left for an illustration, and that means a woodcut."[8] Given the different space sizes, which range from twenty-one lines to six, one might posit that the planned picture program was to include both narrative and emblematic scenes.

Between the Latin *incipit* and Middle English text of Book V, there is a three-line gap, and in the second column of the opening text a twelve-line gap. Within the text of Book V is a six-line gap between the Latin text and the beginning of the Middle English tale of Calisto. In one copy, a sixteenth-century reader has supplied a note beside the space: "The tale of Calistona / how she was turnyd / to a Bere."[9] Book V closes with a

---

[7] There are also notations in the Morgan copy, for example, on fol. 17ʳ "Perseus and yᵉ Gorgones," and on fol. 40ʳ, "The Bloudy Banquet." Among the reader additions in Caxton editions is an inscription supplied at the start of Liber Primus of British Library G11627 by a John Fremen in 1570: "When fortune doth fayell then frendship is gon / And nature agayne doth want that she lent / But that nothing is gotten by Vertue A lone / Will euer endure, and neuer be Spente / John fremen / Anno dm 1570." Fremen has also supplied some notes in the edition.

[8] Blake, in "Early Printed Editions of *Confessio Amantis*," 294–95.

[9] This is from the BL edition [G11627], seemingly in the hand of John Fremen who

sixteen-line space; Book VI opens with a thirteen-line space before the Latin prologue, ending with a six-line space at the *explicit*. In Book VII, there is a brief space of six lines within the Latin introduction and another six-line space in the text, introducing the line "EMouge these old tales wyse Of phylosophres." At the beginning of Book VIII, we then find a seventeen-line blank. The evident pattern of gaps indicates there was to have been illustration at beginning and ends of books, perhaps with pictures introducing the stories of Calisto and the wise philosophers. Including the blank leaves, space has been left in the text for some eighteen illustrations.

Of the blanks, Blake remarks that "Certainly if the woodcuts had been included, the edition would have looked far better."[10] To our eyes, yes, but the leaving of blanks in early printed books for pictures to be supplied later is quite a common practice, particularly a bit earlier among Caxton's colleagues on the Continent. We frequently find large folio books, some ornamented with decorative pen flourishing and other hand-elements, that have spaces for illustration, a final stage in the finishing process. Printers like Jan Veldener, Arendt de Keiser, and Colard Mansion, Caxton's early colleague in Bruges, to name a few, produced a number of books with spaces left for pictures never completed.[11]

---

also supplied the poem at the start of the volume.

[10] Blake, in "Early Printed Editions of *Confessio Amantis*," 295.

[11] One important example is John Rylands 12619, a copy of Boethius's *De Consolatione Philosophie* printed by Colard Mansion on 28 June 1477. Blanks have been left in the Rylands copy at the start of five books. The only known copy of Mansion's Boethius finished with hand-painted borders and illuminations is Cambridge University Library Inc.I.F.3.1 (3304), illustrations which are closely related to those in a finished Boethius printed in Ghent by Arend de Keyser in 1485 now in the Fitzwilliam Museum (C.E. Sayle, *Catalogue of the Early Printed Books Bequeathed to the [Fitzwilliam] Museum by Frank McClean*, Cambridge, 1916, 338). The edition of Boethius printed by de Keyser has been called "the most spectacular to come on the book market in late fifteenth-century Europe," ranking "among the most impressive incunables produced in the Low Countries" (Alain Arnould and Jean Michel Massing, eds., *Splendours of Flanders: Late Medieval Art in Cambridge Collections, The Fitzwilliam Museum* [Cambridge, 1993], 163). Some copies remain unfinished, with extensive blanks (for example, Cambridge University Library Inc.2.F.7.1). There are, however, 12 copies extant which have been supplied with miniatures and borders, including CUL Inc.1.F.7.1. (3464), British Library IC 50105, and Rosenwald 535, discussed in *Vision of a Collector: The Lessing J. Rosenwald Collection in the Library of Congress* (Washington, DC, 1991), item 30. The *Vision of a Collector* catalogue incorrectly states that most of the Arend de Keyser copies contain blanks and that "only one other illuminated copy (in the Bibliothèque Royale, Brussels) is recorded." For more on Veldener and his relationship with Caxton, see: Paul Needham, "William Caxton and His Cologne Partners: An Enquiry Based on Veldener's Cologne Type," in *Ars Impressoria: Entstehung und Entwicklung des Buchdrucks: Eine internationale Festgabe für Severin Corsten zum 65. Geburtstag*, ed. Hans Limburg, Hartwig Lohse, and Wolfgang Schmitz (München, 1986), 103 ff.; Lotte Hellinga, *Caxton in Focus* (London, 1982), 49–51; Wytze and Lotte Hellinga, *The Fifteenth-Century Printing Types of the Low Countries*, 2 vols. (Amsterdam, 1966), 24, 49, 66, and pls. 61–64; Colin Clair, *A History of European Printing* (London, 1976, 74; and *William Caxton* (cited in n.3), 12–14, 28–29.

Mansion was a scribe, bookseller, translator, and later the printing partner of Caxton. He maintained a shop from 1454 through the early 1480s, supplying books to Duke Philip and Louis de Bruges, Seigneur de la Gruthuyse, the friend of Edward IV, among other patrons. There are six printed editions, seven if we include his re-edition of Ovid's *Metamorphoses*, known with certainty to have been published by Mansion; the Hellingas have further posited that Mansion collaborated with Caxton on the four French texts Caxton printed in Bruges. Several other volumes have also been attributed to Mansion and bear further investigation. We shall also see that both Caxton and Mansion produced deluxe manuscripts at the same time they were beginning their printing careers.[12]

D. G. Scillia's "The Master of The London Passional: Johann Veldener's 'Utrecht Cutter,'" in *The Early Illustrated Book: Essays in Honor of Lessing J. Rosenwald*, ed. Sandra Hindman (Washington, DC, 1982), 23–40, discusses illustration in early Veldener editions. See also Driver, "Illustration in Early English Books: Methods and Problems," *Books at Brown* 33 (1986): 1–57, and "The Illustrated de Worde: An Overview," *Studies in Iconography* 17 (1996): 349–403.

[12] Books known to have been produced by Colard Mansion include: *La Penitance d'Adam*, trans. from Latin to French by Mansion and copied after 13 October 1472. An illuminated MS on vellum, the text was copied in Bruges(?) by Mansion(?) for Louis de Gruthuyse(?), this formerly belonged to Louis XII (now Paris, Bibliothèque nationale de France, MS franc. 1837). The text opens: "Cy commence un petit traitie intitule de la penitance Adam, translate du latin en francois au commandement de hault et puissant seigneur Monseigneur de la gruthuse, conte de wincestre &c par Colard Mansion son compere et humble seruiteur"; Pierre D'Ailly, *Le jardin de devotion*, printed in Bruges in 1476(?) with the colophon: "Primum opus impressum per Colardum mansion. Brugis Laudetur omnipotens." This may be Mansion's first printed work. Wytze and Lotte Hellinga argue that this is the first book Mansion printed as an independent printer, having collaborated with Caxton on the four French texts printed by Caxton in Bruges. See Wytze and Lotte Hellinga, *Colard Mansion: an original leaf from the Ovide Moralisé, Bruges, 1484* (Amsterdam, 1963), 10. In this volume, the Hellingas further comment, "It is a striking fact that neither Colard Mansion nor Caxton published books under his own name until the latter had left the Continent and had settled in Westminster as a printer and publisher" (8); Giovanni Boccaccio, *De la ruine des nobles hommes et femmes*, trans. into French by Laurent de Premierfait and printed in Bruges by Mansion in 1476; Boethius, *Consolation de philosophie* printed in Bruges on 28 June 1477, trans. into French with the commentary of Renier de Saint-Trond. Blanks have been left for illumination at the start of five books (supplied in Cambridge University Library copy); Jean Boutillier, *La somme rural*, printed in Bruges, 1479, with three blanks; Alain Chartier, *Le quadrilogue invectif*, printed in Bruges between 1479–1484(?); and two editions of *Ovide, Metamorphoses*. This prose adaptation in French was compiled by Mansion and printed by him in Bruges in May 1484. Printed on paper in black ink with red rubrication, the text is illustrated by 34 woodcuts, which are hand-colored in some editions. A re-edition printed in black ink only on paper also appeared in 1484. Twenty-eight of the 49 quires are reset. The colophon cites Mansion's name but omits his printer's mark, perhaps indicating the volume was completed by another printer. The index of the *Short-Title Catalogue of Books Printed in the Netherlands and Belgium and of Dutch and Flemish Books Printed in Other Countries from 1470 to 1600 Now in the British Museum* (London, 1965) also mentions a 1478 Psalms collection printed by Mansion, but the only cross-reference is to a copy of the Meditations by Pierre d'Ailly on the Penitential Psalms, in French with Latin and French text of the Psalms, printed in Bruges by Caxton in 1475(?) [IB 49408]; the Works of St. Dionysius, called the Areopagite, printed ca. 1480, "Per Colardum Mansionis"; and a copy of *Labuse en court*, printed

In 1477, Mansion printed a French translation of Boethius, making provision for miniatures to be added at the beginning of each of the five books. The pattern of gaps is similar to that found in Caxton's *Confessio*, with blank leaves or spaces preceding the text of some books and blanks occurring at the end of others, and like the *Confessio*, it is a big book, a folio printed on paper. In the John Rylands Library copy (fig. 3), for example, note the substantial gaps occurring at the end of Book II and at the beginning of Book III. The Cambridge University Library Boethius is the only copy surviving with the miniatures supplied, along with penwork initials and marginal decoration. According to the recent *Splendors of Flanders* catalogue, the Mansion Boethius was sold in 1482 "at the Bruges guild of St. John the Evangelist for ten shilling groot (Weale 1872). The receipt does not mention whether the copy was illuminated or not, but since the sum corresponds approximately to one day's wages for a mason in Bruges at the time, it is more likely to allude to an unillustrated copy."[13] In Caxton's day, even books we would consider unfinished were salable, though these were less expensive than illuminated copies.

In 1476, Mansion published Laurent de Premierfait's translation of Boccaccio's *De casibus illustrium virorum et mulierum*, a luxuriously laid-out book with spaces provided for ten illustrations, one for the introduction and nine others at the start of each of the nine books, probably, it is thought, originally left for miniatures, as in the Boethius. Nine copper engravings with Boccaccio subjects then came into Mansion's hands, and he included them in some editions. Several illustrated copies are extant: one in the Museum of Fine Arts in Boston (formerly in the collection of the Marquess of Lothian at Newbattle Abbey), another in the Bibliothèque d'Amiens, and another copy in private hands in Schweinfurt, Germany. Loose engravings have also survived.[14]

---

in Bruges by Mansion, also ca. 1480. In the *Colard Mansion* volume, the Hellingas remark: "In the eight years that Colard Mansion referred to himself as a printer, 24 editions, it is now assumed, were produced by his press, 13 of them with his name or device" (8). Other books attributed to Mansion and cited by the Hellingas, include: *La doctrine de bien vivre en ce monde* by Jean Gerson; *L'Art de bien mourir;* two works by Surse de Pistoye (*Controversie de noblesse, Debat entre trois chevalereux princes*); *Le Doctrinal au temps present* by Pierre Michault; and *Les advineaux amoureux*. The Hellingas reproduce the frontispiece miniature from Mansion's copy of *Le dialogue des creatures*, which shows the author translating, writing, or copying from the exemplar at his desk (Vienna: Oesterreichische National-Bibliothek. Cod. Vindob. 2572, leaf 1^r). Further work on establishing the Mansion bibliography remains to be done.

[13] Arnould and Massing, eds., *Splendors of Flanders*, 164.

[14] Ibid., 166. The catalogue reproduces one of the engravings: "Boccaccio presents his Book to Mainardo Cavalcanti" (no. 56). The first space in the copy of Mansion's Boccaccio in the Pierpont Morgan Library (ChL 1692M) is filled in with a pen-and-wash drawing of Adam and Eve appearing to the author, with a penwork border, which includes a scene of St. George slaying the dragon. This illustration may have been copied from an engraved example because a similar scene of Boccaccio as author, seated at his writing desk, interviewing Adam and Eve occurs in those editions with engravings. In the Morgan copy, there are blanks otherwise at the start and end of each book. Book IV, for

The style of the copper engravings illustrating some editions of Mansion's Boccaccio is said to be similar to that of the frontispiece engraving of the *Recuyell of the Histories of Troy,* translated and printed by Caxton in Bruges, ca. 1473–74 and dedicated by him to Margaret of York, the wife of Charles the Bold and sister of Edward IV. While Otto Pächt tentatively identified the artist as the Master of Mary of Burgundy, identifying him as the artist of the Boccaccio engravings as well, Lotte Hellinga has more cautiously commented, "There is not much to suggest a link between Caxton and Mansion's engravings, but their technique would not exclude the possibility that they were executed by the same engraver."[15] The styles of the two illustrations, of the introduction of Boccaccio presenting his book to Mainardo Cavalcanti, surrounded by the Pope, the emperor, a king, a ruler, and a prelate (fig. 4) and of the *Recuyell* frontispiece (fig. 5) are similar, but not identical. The medium, engraving, is perhaps deceptive, creating an initial impression of similar style, though it is certainly likely that the engravings were made in the same locale and, as Hellinga suggests, "by the same engraver."

The blanks left in Caxton's *Confessio* are thus found to be similar to

---

example, ends at the bottom of column two, the verso is blank, and Book V begins in the middle of the next folio. This is typically the pattern throughout. Ten spaces have apparently been left for illustrations. In a recent article, "Reading an engraving: William Caxton's dedication to Margaret of York, Duchess of Burgundy" (in *Across the Narrow Seas: Studies in the history and bibliography of Britain and the Low Countries Presented to Anna E. C. Simoni,* ed. Susan Roach [London, 1991], 13, n.7), Lotte Hellinga-Querido cites several other of Mansion's Boccaccio editions with engravings: in the University Library of Göttingen; in the Annmary Brown Memorial of Brown University, Providence, RI; and in the Huntington Library. The Huntington copy is cited as item 5015 (9316) by Herman Ralph Mead in *Incunabula in the Huntington Library* (San Marino, CA, 1937). The engravings are reproduced and the editions described in Henri Michel, *L'Imprimeur Colard Mansion et Le Boccacce de La Bibliothèque D'Amiens* (Paris, 1925), 27ff., though Michel does not mention the Morgan copy and omits mention of several others in his discussion of states of the edition. Henry P. Rossiter, writing on "Colard Mansion's Boccaccio of 1476" (in *Essays in honor of George Swarzenski,* ed. Oswald Goetz [Chicago and Berlin, 1951]), comments, along with Michel, that the source manuscript used by Mansion for his edition "was one he borrowed from Louis de Bruges, Seigneur de la Gruthuise, his friend, godfather to one of his children, and owner of a fine library, who often employed him in his capacity of scribe and illuminator" (104). Rossiter further remarks that the printer Jean du Pré published a Boccaccio edition in 1484 "illustrated with engravings freely adapted from some of the engravings in Mansion's work" (108). Another work with blanks printed by Mansion is *La somme rural* by Jean Boutillier, printed in Bruges in 1479, in which three blanks (on fols. 132^v, 134^v, 136^v), presumably left for trees of affiliation and consanguinity charts, have been left. See n. 12.

[15] Hellinga-Querido, *Across the Narrow Seas,* 2. Rossiter recounts the apocryphal story told by Alfred von Würzbach attributing the Boccaccio engravings to the female artist Ida van der Ameye, whose name is found on the list of the Bruges Guild of Illuminators for 1467, said by Würzbach to be the wife of Israhel van Meckenem (109). For brief further mention of Ida, see Henry Meier, "Some Israhel Van Meckenem Problems," in *The Print Collector's Quarterly* 27, 1 (February, 1940): 27f., which also reproduces a print by van Meckenem, *Dance at the Court of Herod* (Print Room, New York Public Library), showing women in high-belted dresses and hennin similar to those represented in the *Recuyell* frontispiece.

those found in other Continental books, which might be variously filled in with engravings, woodcuts, or drawings, all methods employed by Caxton (as well as Mansion) to illustrate books during his career. And there is some evidence to suggest that an edition of the *Confessio* was planned several years before it appeared in print, perhaps even while Caxton was working in Bruges under the patronage of Margaret of York. J. A. W. Bennett pointed out in 1950 that there are unmistakable verbal similarities between Caxton's *Confessio* and the translation of Ovid made by Caxton in 1480, which exists today in one deluxe manuscript edition. As has been noted by Derek Pearsall, Bennett discovered that "In his translation of Ovid's *Metamorphoses* (1480), Caxton introduced into the story of Ceix and Alcione some striking phrases from Gower's version of the same story in Ovid. Perhaps [Caxton] was already working on the text of the *Confessio*," presumably by the 1470s. Norman Blake further comments that the verbal echoes of Gower in Caxton's Ovid translation reveal definitively "a knowledge of Gower's text since the phrases in question are hardly likely to have been current at the time as vogue expressions."[16]

Like Mansion, who produced one or more deluxe manuscripts, probably for Louis de Gruthuyse, while simultaneously engaged in a printing career, Caxton was also directly responsible for at least one deluxe manuscript, his translation of Ovid, which, to judge from its script and decoration, was made in Bruges. As in the other books we have seen, a cycle of illustrations intended to introduce each of the fifteen books was planned, and in this case, only four of these were ever finished.[17] The other books

---

[16] J. A. W. Bennett, "Caxton and Gower," *Modern Language Review* XLV (1950): 215–16. See also: N. F. Blake, *Caxton and His World* (Elmsford, NY, 1969), 131; Blake, "Caxton's Copytext of Gower's *Confessio Amantis*," in *William Caxton and Literary Culture* (London, 1991), 187; Blake, "Early Printed Editions of *Confessio Amantis*," 291; and Derek A. Pearsall, "The Gower Tradition," in *Gower's "Confessio Amantis": Responses and Reassessments*, ed. A. J. Minnis (Woodbridge, Suffolk, 1983), 188.

[17] Mansion produced *La Penitance d'Adam* after 13 October 1472. This is an illuminated manuscript on vellum thought to have been copied by Mansion himself for Louis de Gruthuyse. Michel further reproduces a contract between Mansion and Seigneur de Gazebeeke for the copying and illumining of a French translation of Valerius Maximus (43). The Ovid manuscript has been reproduced in facsimile as *The Metamorphoses of Ovid, translated by William Caxton 1480* (New York, 1968). Illustrations are discussed by Kathleen L. Scott, *The Caxton Master and His Patrons*, with preface by J. A. W. Bennett (Cambridge, 1976), 3ff. In his colophon, Caxton concludes: "Thus endeth Ouyde hys booke of Methamorphose translated & fynysshed by me William Caxton at Westmestre the xxii. day of Appryll. the yere of oure lord anno.iiii.ᶜiiii ˣˣ. And the xx yere of the Regne of kynge Edward the fourth." Though Caxton says the book was finished in Westminster, the script and decoration argue for Bruges production. In his introduction to *The Caxton Master*, Bennett comments that the Ovid manuscript is written "in a formal book-hand of the type commonly used in publishing houses of fifteenth-century Flanders" and "We must assume that the scribe made a fair copy of a text supplied by Caxton" (xi), that is, that the manuscript was written by a Flemish scribe working presumably in his native Bruges from copy Caxton supplied. There is also some precedent for this among Caxton's printed books. Paul Needham has noted that Caxton's first printed edition of the *Histoire de Jason* [RSTC 15383] by Raoul Le Fevre was "Printed

of Caxton's Ovid open with blanks covering about two-thirds of the text space. For his Middle English translation, it is thought that Caxton consulted the Ovid manuscripts in the library of Louis de Bruges. The same manuscript sources in Louis's library were also used by Mansion for his last book, a French prose translation of the Moralised Ovid, published May 1484, shortly before Mansion disappeared from Bruges records. Mansion has commonly been said to have been unable to pay the debts incurred by the expense of printing this large volume with its thirty-four woodcuts, but actually, there are two issues of the Ovid, both printed in 1484: the second is printed in black ink only and twenty-eight of the forty-nine quires have been reset. This suggests a rather different scenario, the financial success of the first issue inspiring a second printing within months. Mansion himself presumably died shortly thereafter, perhaps before this second issue, which lacks his printer's mark, was off the press. The record here is incomplete, as it is for much of printing history.[18]

The connections between Mansion's edition of Ovid and Caxton's

---

in Bruges with type 1 after Caxton had removed to Westminster with type 2, ca 1475–76" (in *The Printer & the Pardoner*, Washington, Library of Congress, 1986), 84. Blake, in his essay "Manuscript to Print," cites a manuscript copy of *Jason*, now Glasgow University Library, MS Hunterian 410, "written in a Flemish hand" on the "same paper sorts as found in Caxton's prints" (in *William Caxton and English Literary Culture*, London, 1991), 297, another piece of evidence suggesting that Caxton continued to maintain an active working relationship with his Bruges publishing contacts even several years after relocating to England. For another view on the origin of the Ovid, see Martin Lowry, "Sister or Country Cousin? The Huntington *Recuyell* and the Getty *Tondal*," in *Margaret of York, Simon Marmion, and The Visions of Tondal*, ed. Thomas Kren (Malibu, 1992), 108, who points out, "Even if we assume that much of the work on the Ovid manuscript was done in Bruges, bibliographies agree in attributing around twenty books to Caxton between his return to England in the autumn of 1476 and the spring of 1480, when the colophon ... was written." Lowry further mentions the exemplars used by Caxton, which include MSS belonging to Louis de Gruythuse and his brother-in-law, along with British Library, Royal MS 17 E IV, copied for Edward IV.

[18] Mansion's *Ovid Moralisé* is his last big book, trans. by him into French prose, and the first book printed by Mansion to be illustrated with woodcuts. His text is based on the *Ovidius moralizatus* of Bersuire and the early fourteenth-century *Ovide Moralisé*. Printed in red and black, the text has 34 woodcuts illustrating gods, goddesses, and a variety of narrative scenes. The two Mansion editions are briefly discussed by Robert H. Lucas, "Mediaeval French Translations of the Latin Classics to 1500," in *Speculum: A Journal of Mediaeval Studies* XLV, 2 (April 1970): 243. In their discussion of Mansion's two Ovid editions, the Hellingas relate that the second issue was originally discovered by Henry Bradshaw. Bradshaw also noted that Mansion had incurred debts, leaving Bruges in September 1484, and that "in October 1484 the Chapter of the Cathedral re-let his tenement to Jean Gossin *copiste des livres* on the condition that Gossin pay the arrears in rent which Mansion left unpaid." Bradshaw speculated in a private letter, subsequently printed by Campbell, that Gossin completed the second Ovid: "I cannot doubt for a moment, that he was allowed to make what profit he could out of the waste remaining sheets of Mansion's latest production" (10–11). For more on Mansion's influence on French printers and further imaginative speculation (this time, definitely tongue-in-cheek) upon his sudden disappearance from Bruges, see Sheila Edmunds, "From Schoeffer to Vérard," in *Printing the Written Word: The Social History of Books, circa 1450–1520*, ed. Sandra Hindman (Ithaca, 1991), 36–37, 38–39, 40.

manuscript remain unclear. It is commonly said, for example, that Mansion's edition was used by Caxton to prepare his translation. There is, however, a small problem with dates, since the Mansion edition appeared in print four years *after* Caxton says he made his manuscript translation. Close comparison of the two translations shows occasional similarities of expression and of the general ordering of stories, but very different emphases and narrative detail, suggesting that the two have a common source and are not directly influencing each other. But what is important here is to place Caxton, thinking of Gower, as he translates Ovid in the 1470s, from manuscripts in the library of Louis de Gruthuyse, the powerful friend of Edward IV.

How to fill the gaps in Caxton's *Confessio* is a scholar's parlor game, which has been played with varying degrees of dexterity and skill in other instances, for example, the well-known example of the *Troilus* manuscript in Corpus Christi College, Cambridge (CCC 61).[19] Most *Confessio* manuscripts have only two pictures, illustrating Nebuchadnezzar and the Lover with Confessor. We see, for example, a typical representation of Nebuchadnezzar's Dream of Precious Metals from Morgan M 690 (fig. 6), an early-fifteenth-century copy of the *Confessio*. Caxton, however, has left very little space—only four lines—before the story of Nebuchadnezzar's dream, probably an indication that no illustration was planned for this portion of text. There are also two extant manuscripts of the *Confessio Amantis* with more fully developed picture cycles: Oxford, New College, MS 266, which once had thirty-two miniatures, of which nineteen remain, and Morgan M126, with 108 miniatures.

There seems little or no connection between New College MS 266 and Caxton's edition. The miniatures in MS 266 occur primarily within the text, not at the start and end of books as indicated by the blanks in Caxton's edition, and illustrate the longer tales, perhaps as a visual aid to the reader, as Peter Braeger has suggested. Its pictures are English in style, associated with the workshop of William Abell.[20] Morgan M 126, in

---

[19] On the relationship between Caxton's and Mansion's copies, see also Norman Blake, "Manuscript to Print," 415, who mentions a prologue translated "from the French version which Caxton used as his source, which was printed by Colard Mansion in Bruges in 1484." For discussion of blanks, see, for example, Elizabeth Salter, in *Troilus and Criseyde: a facsimile of Corpus Christi College Cambridge 61*, intros. by Salter and M. B. Parkes (Cambridge, 1978), 15–23. Her excellent essay is reprinted as "The Troilus Frontispiece," in *English and International: Studies in the Literature, Art and Patronage of Medieval England*, ed. Derek Pearsall and Nicolette Zeeman (Cambridge, 1988), 267 ff.

[20] Peter C. Braeger, "The Illustrations in New College Ms. 266 for Gower's Conversion Tales," in *John Gower: Recent Readings*, ed. R. F. Yeager (Kalamazoo, 1989), 275–97. J. J. G. Alexander, in "William Abell 'lymnour' and 15th Century English Illumination," *Kunsthistorische Forschungen Otto Pächt zu seinem 70. Geburtstag*, ed. Artur Rosenauer and Gerold Weber (Wien, 1972), 168. Braeger comments that "In style and in subject matter the pictures in New College MS. 266 contrast sharply with those of the other heavily-illustrated *Confessio* manuscript, Morgan M 126," with miniatures executed

contrast, like Caxton's Ovid manuscript, has Anglo-Flemish connections and was produced about the same time and intended for the same aristocratic circles. While there is also not a great deal of evidence linking Morgan M126 directly with Caxton's *Confessio* edition, the pictures in M126 do tend to come, as also indicated in Caxton's edition, between the Latin rubric and the Middle English text. Furthermore, this deluxe manuscript, with its 108 miniatures, and Caxton's edition, with its eighteen blanks, represent stages in the history of the *Confessio*, which may now be set against a larger political backdrop.

Morgan M126 was copied in the 1470s, about the same time Caxton was reading Gower and translating his Ovid. The Morgan catalogue describes the illumination of M126 as Anglo-Flemish, and it is not entirely impossible that the manuscript was made in Bruges. Comparison of the hand of the Caxton Ovid manuscript, which has been described as "a formal book-hand of the type commonly used in publishing houses of fifteenth-century Flanders," with the hand of M126 reveals similarity of stylistic features. The script of the Ovid manuscript is more rounded than that of M126 and lacks many of the display elements, but both hands employ decorative cadels on ascenders and strapwork initials, and both use a thick downstroke on long-**s** and **f**, showing consistent use of an angular horned **g**, double **f**, single-compartment **a**, with looped ascenders on **h**, backward strokes on the ascender of **d** (more pronounced in M126), occasional use of 2-shaped **r**, and the secretary form of **w**. The calligraphic hand of M126 further shows the influence of "lettre bastarde." Decorative cadels and strapwork initials, found in both manuscript hands, are more regularly employed in manuscripts copied in the 1470s or later, these features coming into use in deluxe printed books of about the same period.[21]

"in an Anglo-Flemish style" (n. 3, 297–98). For an introductory essay on illustration in Gower's *Confessio Amantis* manuscripts, see Jeremy Griffiths, "*Confessio Amantis*: The Poem and Its Pictures," in *Gower's Confessio Amantis: Responses and Reassessments*, ed. A. J. Minnis (Cambridge, 1983), 163–78.

[21] The use of decorative cadels was in vogue with the early printers by the 1480s. Antoine Vérard, for example, often includes cadels on his title pages. For examples, see John Macfarlane, *Antoine Vérard* (London, 1900 for 1899), figs. LV–LXIII, LXX, LXXIV. For "lettre bastarde," see M. B. Parkes, *English Cursive Book Hands 1250–1500* (Oxford, 1969), 15, item 15. The letter forms of both manuscripts (excluding the calligraphic elements in M126) most resemble item 12ii in Parkes, a folio from MS Rawlinson Poetry 32, copied ca. 1470. An identity for the M126 scribe has been suggested. In a note in the Morgan catalogue, Kathleen Scott attributes the script of MS M126 to the scribe Ricardus Franciscus, as does Paul Christianson in *A Directory of London Stationers and Book Artisans 1300–1500* (New York, 1990), 107, who cites Jeremy Griffiths and Kathleen Scott as his source. The scribe Franciscus copied a number of MSS, one dated 1447 and signed of the *Statutes of London* (now Huntington Library MS HM 932). Most of the MSS attributed to him, however, date from the 1470s and later. His name is suggestive (Richard the Franciscan?), but very little else is known about him. Kate Harris briefly mentions "the vogue scribe" Franciscus, associating him with Morgan M126, in her essay, "The role of owners in book production and the book trade," in *Book Production and Publishing in Britain, 1375–1475*, ed. Jeremy Griffiths and Derek Pearsall

The artists of Morgan M126, vaguely identified as "Anglo-Flemish" in the catalogue, have produced vivid, if crudely rendered, miniatures. It is a commonplace that "crude" style of illustration in manuscripts is synonymous with English origin. In this case, however, details of decoration and costume suggest at least one Continental illuminator working alongside another artist. In the scene where Tereus is shown cutting out Philomena's tongue, for example (fig. 7), we see three kinds of headgear worn by women, the hennin, the butterfly veil, and the puff-ball hat, also called the *balzo,* defined as "a bulbous headdress, consisting of a wire or possibly a willow understructure which was then covered by a textile ... [and] often covered with gems, usually pearls, and with velvet."[22] While the butterfly veil is quite frequently seen in English manuscripts made from the 1450s onward,[23] the hennin and *balzo,* which is ubiquitous in this manuscript, are more frequently found in Continental manuscripts. The hennin, for example, is the female headgear of choice in the presentation scene to Margaret of York (see fig. 5), and we find it worn in almost all representations of Margaret as well as by other female figures in the *Hours of Engelbert of Nassau* painted by the Master of Mary of Burgundy. We might also

---

(Cambridge, 1989), 178. In a note to her essay, Harris mentions her paper "Pierpont Morgan MS M126: An Occasion for Illustration," read at the New Chaucer Society Conference, York, 6–11 August 1984 (n. 78, 193), hers presumably the earliest Franciscus identification, though unpublished. Patricia Eberle, in a note to "Miniatures as Evidence of Reading in a Manuscript of the *Confessio Amantis* (Pierpont Morgan MS M. 126)" in *John Gower: Recent Readings,* ed. R. F. Yeager, 355 n. 51, mentions that Malcolm Parkes, having examined reproduced pages from M126, "suggests that the scribe may well be Ricardus Franciscus." Close comparison of M126 with sample documents signed by or attributed to Franciscus indicates that if not by Franciscus, M126 has been copied by a scribe similarly trained in the transcription of documents. For more on Franciscus, see Richard Hamer, "Spellings of the Fifteenth-Century Scribe Ricardus Franciscus," in *Five Hundred Years of Words and Sounds: A Festschrift for Eric Dobson,* ed. E. G. Stanley and Douglas Gray (Cambridge, 1983), 63–73, and Kathleen L. Scott, *Later Gothic Manuscripts 1390–1490,* ii, in A Survey of Manuscripts Illuminated in the British Isles, ed. J. J. G. Alexander, 6, (London, 1996), 318–19, 321, 322–24, 331. There are others who would wish to identify the hand of the Ovid manuscript as Caxton's own. See the questions raised by Martin Lowry in "Sister or Country Cousin? The Huntington *Recuyell* and the Getty *Tondal*" in *Margaret of York, Simon Marmion, and The Visions of Tondal,* ed. Thomas Kren (Malibu, 1992), 108.

[22] Jacqueline Herald, *Renaissance Dress in Italy 1400–1500,* in The History of Dress Series, ed. Aileen Ribeiro (Atlantic Highlands, NJ, 1981), 50. For discussion of the illustrative program of Morgan M 126, see Patricia Eberle, "Miniatures as Evidence of Reading," 311–64.

[23] One can find illustrations of butterfly veils throughout the fifteenth century, though in English MSS, these tend to appear after 1450. This style of veil was apparently in fashion in England from the 1450s to 1480s. Examples may be seen in Morgan MS M 876, copied in the mid-fifteenth century, and in Morgan M 775, a mid- to late-fifteenth-century compendium written and illuminated for Sir John Astley. See also Carol Meale, "Book Production and Social Status," in *Book Production and Publishing in England,* 213–14, pl. 21. A reproduction of a miniature showing Margaret of York wearing a butterfly veil in a manuscript of the *Vie de Sainte Colette* occurs in Hellinga-Querido, *Across the Narrow Seas,* fig. 2.

compare the low-cut belted dresses worn by the buxom ladies of the Tereus illumination with the dresses worn by Margaret of York in the *Recueyell* representation and elsewhere.[24]

The *balzo*, on the other hand, originates in Italy and is rarely, if ever, seen in English manuscripts. There are, however, examples to be found in the miniatures of Flemish manuscripts, particularly those associated with the Master of Mary of Burgundy and Simon Bening of Bruges.[25] They also appear in modified form in woodcuts produced in Flanders and the Netherlands in the late fifteenth century. Compare the *balzo* worn in the Tereus scene with the banded puff-ball cap worn by Herodias, the woman at the table (fig. 8), in the illustration of Salome with the head of John the Baptist. This woodcut, which recurs in editions of the *Vita Christi* of Ludolphus of Saxony, printed at Zwolle by Petrus van Os in the 1490s, has been attributed to a woodcutter from Antwerp.[26]

Internal evidence in Morgan M 126 suggests a royal patron, most probably a woman. The arms of England, identified as those of Edward IV, later used as well by Edward V and Richard III, appear on fol. 103 in a miniature (fig. 9) introducing the story of Emperor Frederick and the two beggars. Within banderoles ornamenting decorative initials are several inscriptions which the Morgan descriptive catalogue records as "Belle Lavine," "Une le Roy," and "Roy Lavine." "Roy Lavine" says the Morgan catalogue, may be the scribe's name. These are all misreadings which overlook the playfulness of the scribe, who writes the inscriptions forward, backward, and even upside down.[27] "Vive le roy" (fig. 10) and

---

[24] See also Margaret's costume and hennin in a miniature from a French manuscript, Jean Miélot's *Romuléon*, reproduced in *Margaret of York, Simon Marmion, and The Visions of Tondal*, 32, fig. 1, also figs. 2, 8, 10, 14, 16, 17, 19, 21. For illustrations of the Book of Hours of Engelbert of Nassau, see *The Master of Mary of Burgundy*, intro. by J. J. G. Alexander (New York, 1970). Other illustrations of Margaret may be seen in Christine Weightman, *Margaret of York: Duchess of Burgundy 1446–1503* (New York, 1993).

[25] Dame Philosophy wears a modified *balzo* in the illuminated copy of Arendt de Keyser's *Boethius*, printed in Ghent in 1485 (reproduced in Arnould and Massing, eds., *Splendors of Flanders*, fig. 57). We also see women in the foreground of a miniature of Christ nailed to the Cross in the Hours of Mary of Burgundy, painted by the Master of Mary of Burgundy (reproduced *Renaissance Painting in Manuscripts: Treasures from the British Library*, ed. Thomas Kren [New York, 1983]), fig. 1, and a woman wearing jeweled *balzo* (in this case, with some hair showing) at the center of the *Genealogical Tree of John, Duke of Lancaster*, painted by Simon Bening of Bruges, pl. XII.

[26] M. J. Schretlen, *Dutch and Flemish Woodcuts of the Fifteenth Century* (1925; repr. New York, 1969), 36.

[27] The inscriptions in the banderoles in ascenders and descenders of the text of Morgan M 126 have been supplied by the scribe. A complete list follows: fol. 34ᵛ in red, in banderole around ascender top margin, "I wold fayn please my lady"; fol. 39ᵛ in black ink in banderole around ascender top margin (left column), "fido con no domini"; in red ink in banderole around ascender in top margin (right column), "ma vie endure qd R"; fol. 41ᵛ in red, in banderole around ascender, top margin, "prenes engre mon (coeur) [drawing of a heart]"; fol. 42 in black, in banderole around ascender top margin, "viue Le roy Edward IVe illegible?"; fol. 50ᵛ in banderoles around ascenders in Explicit and Incipit, first column: in red "aue marie gracia," in black "viue la belle"; fol. 67ᵛ in

"Vive la belle" (fig. 11) occur, along with "ave maria" and other Marian prayers throughout the manuscript (figs. 12, 13). Evidence of a female patron or owner may be further deduced from the first notation to appear in the manuscript: "I wold fayn please my lady." Another proclaims, "viue Le roy Edward IVe." There are also several mottoes: "fido con no domini"; "ma vie endure qd R"; "prenes engre mon (coeur)" with a drawing of a heart; "a mon plesir qd R." None of these can be readily traced, though there are at least three other manuscripts in which the "prenes engre" inscription occurs.[28]

---

banderole around ascender in Incipit, first column, in red "viue Le Roy"; fol. 70ᵛ in banderole around descender, in second column, in red "aue maria"; fol. 91 in banderole around ascender in first column, in red "viue La belle"; fol. 95 in banderole around ascender in first column, in black "viue le Roy"; fol. 99 in banderole around descender in second column, in black "Aue maria gra*cia* plena domin*us*"; fol. 101 in banderole around ascender in second column (text reversed), in black "a mon plesir qd R"; fol. 103 royal arms of England, crowned, in miniature; fol. 103ᵛ in banderole around ascender first column, in red, "viue Le Roy"; fol. 104 in banderole around ascender second column, in red "aue maria gra*cia*"; fol. 135ᵛ in banderole around ascender, first column, in red, "aue maria gra*cia*"; fol. 137 in banderole around ascender, second column, in red "aue maria gracia plena"; fol. 139ᵛ in banderole around ascender, first column, in black, "aue gra*cia* plena"; fol. 140 in banderole around descender, first column, in black, "Aue maria gracia plena domin*us*" and in banderole around ascender, second column (reversed), in black, "Ecce ancilla domin*us* fiat." The predominance of Marian prayers and other inscriptions would seem to indicate a royal woman patron.

[28] See Carol M. Meale's essay "'Prenes: engre': an early sixteenth-century presentation copy of *The Erle of Tolous*," in *Romance Reading on the Book: Essays on Medieval Narrative Presented to Maldwyn Mills*, ed. Jennifer Fellows, et al. (Cardiff, 1996), 221–36. Meale has found the inscription "Prenes: Engre" in a banderole in a drawing of a man presenting a woman with a book in Oxford, Bodleian Library, MS Ashmole 45, fol. 2ʳ, a copy of *The Erle of Tolous*, copied 1520–30 and commissioned "by a prosperous member of the middle classes" (233). In a note, Meale mentions that a scroll with a similar inscription occurs in a "copy of Boccaccio's *Genealogiae deorum* dated to the second half of the fifteenth century, now Exeter Cathedral Library, MS 3529" (235, n. 29). Ker describes this manuscript in *Medieval Manuscripts in British Libraries*, II (Oxford, 1977, 836–37, item 3529) as having been probably "copied from the edition printed at Cologne c 1473 . . . A scroll below the last words on f. 166v bears 'Prandez en gre. moun cur,' perhaps a Grey family motto, in the main hand." The manuscript was written in England, a "gift to the Benedictine abbey of St Augustine's Canterbury: 'Bocacius de Geneologia deorum de adquisicione D' patricii Grey. de librario sancti Augustini extra Cant." In a note, Ker remarks that Patrick Grey, whom he elsewhere describes as "dom Patricius Grey" (in Ker, ed., *Medieval Libraries of Great Britain: A List of Surviving Books*, 2nd ed. [London, 1964], 164), had the keeping of this volume in the St. Augustine's catalogue, ca. 1500. I have not been able to ascertain whether this Grey was related to Elizabeth Woodville's first husband. There was also another important early collector, William Grey, whose 98 MSS survive at Balliol College, Oxford. I wish to thank Julia Boffey for her help in locating Carol's published article and also for Julia's observation of a later use of "prenes engre," also in the context of a female patron or reader, which occurs at the end of John Skelton's *The Garland of Laurell*. This segment of Skelton's poem is not preserved in the single extant manuscript (BL Cotton Vitellius E.x), which is fragmentary, but the inscription does occur in variant forms in the editions printed by Richard Faques, or Fawkes, in 1523 (STC 22610) and by Thomas Marshe in 1568 (STC 22608). *The Garland*, a dream allegory, was composed when Skelton was the guest of the Countess of Surrey and is dedicated to her and her ladies, containing the famous compli-

If "Le roy" refers to Edward IV, as one of the inscriptions indicates, the identity of "La belle" is more difficult to ascertain. According to the *Dictionary of National Biography*, the father of Elizabeth Woodville, Edward's queen, "was regarded as the handsomest man in England," while she herself is cited in the wardrobe books of Margaret of Anjou, whom she served in the capacity of lady of the bedchamber, as "Lady Isabella Grey." The name "Isabella," explains the *DNB*, "was in those days a mere variation of Elizabeth." The name "Dame Isabella" or Elizabeth Grey occurs also in earlier documents, appearing, for example, on a list of the ladies who were sent out from the English court to France in 1445. This seems convincing enough evidence to link "La Belle" of the inscriptions with Isabella or Elizabeth Woodville, beautiful daughter of the handsome Sir Richard Woodville and wife of Edward IV.[29]

Elizabeth also had an enviable collection of manuscripts, including Arthurian romances in French (BL Royal MS 14.E.III), the *Life of our Lady* (Yale Univ Lib MS 281) and the Collected Works of Christine de Pisan (Harleian 4431), which had formerly belonged to her mother Jacquetta of Luxembourg, the Duchess of Bedford. This last book also has the signature of Louis de Bruges and was presumably given to him in gratitude after Jacquetta's death for his kindness in befriending Edward IV during his Bruges exile of 1470–1471. The Huntington Library copy of Caxton's *Recuyell of the Histories of Troy*, with its unique presentation frontispiece, was also formerly owned by Elizabeth Woodville, who was, of course, the sister-in-law of Margaret of York.[30]

---

mentary lyrics to the Countess of Surrey, Mistress Margaret Hussey and others. Published by Faques soon after it was completed, *The Garland* is the only poem by Skelton to appear in print in his lifetime. Among modern editions that retain the "prenes engres" reading at the end of the poem are: *John Skelton: The Complete English Poems*, ed. John Scattergood (Harmondsworth, 1983), 357, and *English Verse between Chaucer and Surrey*, ed. Eleanor Prescott Hammond (New York, 1965), 367. Kathleen Scott, in *Later Gothic Manuscripts*, 319, has found examples of the motto 'prenes en gre je vous en prie' (which she attributes to Charles d'Orléans) in Oxford, University College MS 85, a tract of *Le Quadrilogue Invectif* composed by Alain Chartier in 1422 and copied ca. 1470 by Ricardus Franciscus.

[29] Leslie Stephen and Sidney Lee, eds., *The Dictionary of National Biography*, vol. X (London, 1973), 614. See also George Smith, *The Coronation of Elizabeth Wydeville, Queen Consort of Edward VI* (London, 1935), 27, who cites the name Dame Isabella or Elizabeth Grey as found interchangeably "in earlier documents of Queen Margaret's officials."

[30] Margaret of York, sister of Edward IV, was among the immediate party in the coronation ceremonies of Elizabeth Woodville, following the Duchess of Buckingham, who "bare up the Quenys trayne," and walking with the Duchess of Suffolk, another sister of Edward IV, and the Duchess of Bedford, Elizabeth Woodville's mother. She married Charles the Bold, Duke of Burgundy, three years later. A book commissioned by Elizabeth and mentioned in her account rolls, title unknown, was copied for £10 ("per manus Willelmi Wulflete, clerici nuper cancellarii universitatis Cantebrigiensis, £10, ut in precio unius libri eidem domine regine venditi"). The scribe William Wulflete or Wolflete, formerly a master of Clare Hall, was Chancellor of Cambridge University. See A. R. Myers, in "The Household of Queen Elizabeth Woodville, 1466-7," *Bulletin of the*

During his exile, when he spent the winter of 1470–1471 at the home of Louis de Gruthuyse, Edward himself had been influenced by Louis to begin buying books, the first king to establish a royal library. As Doyle remarks, "there is no evidence of a continuous library before Edward IV," and as Margaret Kekewich has pointed out, Edward's "sojourn in Bruges as a guest to the pro-Yorkist Seigneur de Gruthyse, must have provoked a desire to possess some sumptuous Flemish manuscripts."[31] Given the visual evidence provided by Morgan M126, script, iconography, and the pervasive inscriptions, I strongly suspect it was made for a woman in the circles of Edward IV, most probably for the beautiful Elizabeth Woodville, at a time when Caxton too was enjoying Yorkist patronage.

After moving from Bruges and the household of Margaret of York, Caxton set up shop in Westminster, an advantageous location seen by some historians as another mark of Yorkist favor. And, as is well known, Anthony Woodville, Lord Rivers, brother of the queen, was an early sponsor of Caxton, supplying him with copy for four of his first books. Woodville translated the *Dicts and Sayings of the Philosophers,* which Caxton printed in three editions (two before 18 Nov 1477, another in 1480[?]).[32] There is also the famous Lambeth Palace manuscript of this

---

John Rylands Library 50 (1967–68): 481. The Huntington Library copy of the *Recuyell* contains the ownership inscription: "This book is mine Queen Elizabeth late wife unto the most noble King Edward the Fourth of whose both souls I beseech Almighty God take to his infinite mercy above." In a footnote in *William Caxton: A Biography* (New York, 1977, 63 n. 1), George D. Painter points out that "The inscription is not in the Queen's autograph, but written by 'Thomas Shukburghe the Younger,' persumably a secretary who was putting her library in order after her widowhood in 1483; so it is quite possible that she possessed the book long before." Elizabeth Woodville was also a learned benefactress of a college at Cambridge, according to John Speed's *The History of Great Britain Under the Conquests of ye Romans, Saxons, Danes and Normans* (printed in London, 1650). Queen's College, Cambridge, was begun by Margaret, wife of Henry VI, and completed after her death by "Q. Elizabeth, wife to King Edward 4. [who] obtained licence to finish the same, which shee accomplished in the sixt of Edward 4" (801ᵛ). Books owned by Elizabeth Woodville are also cited briefly by Margaret Kekewich, in "Edward IV, William Caxton, and Literary Patronage in Yorkist England," *Modern Language Review* 66, 3 (July 1971): 486.

[31] A. I. Doyle, "English Books In and Out of Court from Edward III to Henry VII," in *English Court Culture in the Later Middle Ages,* ed V. J. Scattergood and J. W. Sherborne (London, 1983), 174. Doyle comments that Edward IV "appears to have been the first king to commission books in quantity, although from abroad." In "Founders of the Royal Library: Edward IV and Henry VII as Collectors of Illuminated Manuscripts," Janet Backhouse reproduces a list of books belonging to Edward IV now in the Royal Collection of the British Library (in *England in the Fifteenth Century: Proceedings of the 1986 Harlaxton Symposium,* ed. Daniel Williams [Woodbridge, Suffolk, 1987], 39–41. Her essay concerns "the elaborate and costly copies of historical and literary works commissioned for formal use within the royal residences." She further comments that "None of Edward's library books was produced in England," all having been "imported from the professional workshops of Flanders" (24). See also Kekewich, "Edward IV, William Caxton, and Literary Patronage in Yorkist England," 482.

[32] According to the *RSTC,* there are three editions of the *Dicts and Sayings,* translated "out of Frenshe by lord Antone [Wydeville] erle of Ryuyers [from the version of G. de

text (Lambeth Palace MS 265), copied from the printed edition onto vellum, "a precise copy of Caxton's printed edition of 1477, even to including all its editorial insertions and comments" with its frontispiece author portrait (fig. 14), executed in the English style:

> The well-known opening miniature is small (85 x 100mm) and neatly executed. It represents on the left Rivers, kneeling on his right knee, wearing armour and a surcoat with his intricate coat of arms; he is handing a book to the King … On the right is the King, crowned and seated, flanked on his left by the Queen and in the foreground, the little Prince. On the King's right, in the background, stand six courtiers, one of them royally dressed like the King and the Prince, but wearing no crown or coronet.[33]

In the miniature, we can readily identify Edward IV, Elizabeth, the young prince, and Rivers, the noble audience for whom Caxton produced some of his earliest works in England. The *Dicts and Sayings* was translated by Rivers for the edification of young Edward, Edward IV's son. Rivers further translated the *Moral Proverbs* of Christine, printed by Caxton on 20 February 1478, for the boy prince, along with the *Cordiale* (24 March 1479) of Gerard of Vliederhoven.[34] In 1477, Caxton dedicated *The History*

Tignonville]" and printed by Caxton. These are STC 6826, printed before 18 November 1477, "fynisshed the xviii day of Nouembre [17 Edw. IV]." STC 6828 has the same colophon, though it may have been published as late as 1480(?). STC 6829 also appeared in 1477. The next edition was not published [STC 6830] until 1528 by Wynkyn de Worde. According to most sources, the Lambeth Palace manuscript was copied (on vellum) from Caxton's imprint, though Doyle remarks, "Earl Rivers' version of the *Dicts and Sayings of the Philosophers* was copied, from a different exemplar than that used for the printed edition, by an accomplished clerical scribe and completed about a month later than it in 1477, probably as a Christmas presentation to Edward IV as shown in the well-known miniature" ("English Books In and Out of Court," 180–81). For more on this manuscript, see Blake, "Manuscript to Print," 421, and Hellinga, *Caxton in Focus,* 77–80, who says, "The manuscript was demonstrably copied from a copy of Caxton's first edition of the *Dicts,* but contains many of the textual features of the second edition which were partly inserted as discreet corrections." Before Rivers's version, the text had been translated by one unidentified author and by Stephen Scrope, Sir John Fastolfe's stepson.

[33] Anne F. Sutton and Livia Visser-Fuchs, "Richard III's Books: Mistaken Attributions," in *The Ricardian: Journal of the Richard III Society* IX, 118 (September 1992): 303, 304. Sutton and Visser-Fuchs identify the tonsured figure kneeling in the foreground as "the original author, Guillaume de Tignonville" (304), but Doyle, in "English Books In and Out of Court," says in a footnote "If the figure in the foreground on his knees with Rivers is the scribe, Haywarde, he was a cleric, from his garb perhaps a member of a college; and St James in the Fields, where he wrote, may be the same hospital of that name at Westminster. … It cannot be Guillaume de Tignonville, the original author, unless the miniaturist misunderstood the status of the Provost of Paris" (181 n. 54).

[34] *The morale prouerbes of Cristyne* [RSTC 7273], trans. in verse by A. Wydeville, "therle Ryueris," is also mentioned briefly in Driver, "Mirrors of a Collective Past: Reconsidering Images of Medieval Women," in *Women and the Book: Assessing the Pictorial Evidence,* ed. Lesley Smith and Jane Taylor (London, 1997), 79. There are three MSS extant of the *Cordiale* of Gerardus de Vliederhoven [RSTC 5758], copied from Caxton's

of Jason to the young Prince of Wales, in his preface linking *Jason* to the
Recuyell, mentioning the early patronage of Margaret and the connections
between the story of Jason and the Order of the Golden Fleece. Caxton
sends the volume to Elizabeth, the prince's mother, so she might then
"presente this sayde boke vnto the most fayre and my moost redoubted
yong lorde." Edward IV was the patron of *Godfrey of Bologne,* printed by
Caxton in 1481, and of Caxton's *Polychronicon,* which appeared in 1482.[35]
Several of these printed books were subsequently copied into manuscript
format, exemplifying the fluidity between manuscript and print in this
period, and perhaps hinting that manuscripts might be preferable to print,
a snobbery which reaches its apex in English court circles of the Renais-
sance. Caxton's edition of the *Confessio Amantis* was itself soon copied
after it was printed, extant as Bodleian Library Hatton MS 51, which has
been transcribed from Caxton's imprint of 1483 with blanks occurring in
the same places in the text. The manuscript is believed to have been copied
about 1500.[36] The aforementioned books, the *Dicts and Sayings,* Chris-
tine's *Moral Proverbs,* the *Cordiale,* the *History of Jason, Godfrey of Bologne,*
and the *Polychronicon,* are among the most popular printed by Caxton
prior to his *Confessio,* which, I would argue, was planned long before it
appeared, when the political climate was somewhat more stable than it was
to become.

Printed just after the *Confessio* is Caxton's *Golden Legend,* and here we
see a decided shift in Caxton's political leanings. The work was commis-
sioned by William, Lord Arundel, an old-line Yorkist, who joined Hast-
ings against the Woodvilles at the approach of Edward's death in the
spring of 1483. Arundel's badge and motto, a horse and an oaktree lettered

print. See Blake, "Manuscripts to Print," 295. According to Needham in *The Printer &
the Pardoner,* the first edition of the *Cordiale,* trans. by Jean Mielot, was printed while
Caxton was still in Bruges.

[35] Kekewich, "Edward IV, William Caxton, and Literary Patronage," 487. The first
edition of *The History of Jason* was "printed in Bruges ... after Caxton had removed to
Westminster" (Needham, *The Printer & the Pardoner,* 84). There are two MSS related to
the second edition of *The History of Jason* [STC 15383], Glasgow University Library MS
Hunterian 410, described by Blake (in "Manuscript to Print," 297) as "written in a
Flemish hand" (297) and CUL MS Dd.3.45, written in a late fifteenth-century hand. The
first of these looks to have been the copy-text for Caxton's print. In his preface, Caxton
says he intends "by the supportacion of our most redoubted liege lady / most excellent
princesse the Quene to presente this sayde boke vnto the most fayre and my moost
redoubted yong lorde. My lord Prynce of Wales." *Godfrey of Bologne* [STC 13175],
translated "out of ffreusshe [sic] by W. Caxton," may be seen in the Pierpont Morgan
Library. Lister M. Matheson has demonstrated links between the *Polychronicon* [STC
13438] of Ranulphus Higden, edited and printed by William Caxton in 1482, and Cam-
bridge, Peterhouse MS 190, Glasgow Hunterian 83 (T.3.21) and BL Harley 3730 (see
Speculum 60 [1985]: 593–614).

[36] Bodleian Library Hatton MS 51 has been copied in brown ink on vellum with
some rubrication. Profile heads appear on ascenders (fols. ii, 1ᵛ, 11ᵛ, 27, 27ᵛ, 56ᵛ) and on
calligraphic initials (fols. 8, 33ᵛ, 48ᵛ, 59/60), but the blanks in the text remain. There is
sporadic and sometimes incorrect foliation. The MS is believed to have been copied ca.
1500.

"My Truste Is" (fig. 15) appear on the second leaf of text.[37] Another big book, printed, like the *Confessio*, in double columns, the *Golden Legend* consists of 449 leaves with copious illustrations, including nineteen narrative scenes and fifty-one woodcuts of saints with their emblems.

In the six months between the death of Edward IV and the printing of the *Confessio Amantis*, Richard seized the throne (June 1483); Anthony Woodville, Earl Rivers, was executed (25 June 1483); and the boys were imprisoned in the Tower. September 1483 marked the beginnings of the Lancastrian uprising in support of that most unlikely pretender Henry Tudor. It seems no coincidence that Caxton replaced the customary dedication of the *Confessio* to Richard II with the later version, the dedication by Gower to Henry of Lancaster, who was to become Henry IV. Caxton's *Confessio* thus represents a shift in Caxton's connections to royal circles of power and patronage; its very unfinishedness shows us a text in transition in an uncertain time.

---

[37] The copy of Caxton's *Golden Legend* [RSTC 24873] in Longleat House also retains the scene of the murder of Thomas à Becket, which has been ripped out of most surviving copies. The first edition was printed after 20 November 1483, with a second edition [RSTC 24874] issued ca. 1487.

Fig. 1. Drawing Added by Later Reader. John Gower, *Confessio Amantis*, f97ᵛ. Westminster, William Caxton, 2 September 1483. PML 689 The Pierpont Morgan Library, New York (courtesy of The Pierpont Morgan Library).

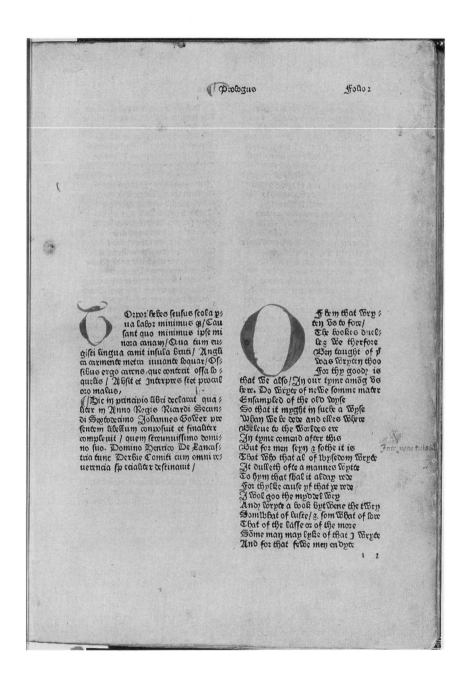

Fig. 2. Prologus. John Gower, *Confessio Amantis*, f2. Westminster, William Caxton, 2 September 1483. PML 689 The Pierpont Morgan Library, New York (courtesy of The Pierpont Morgan Library).

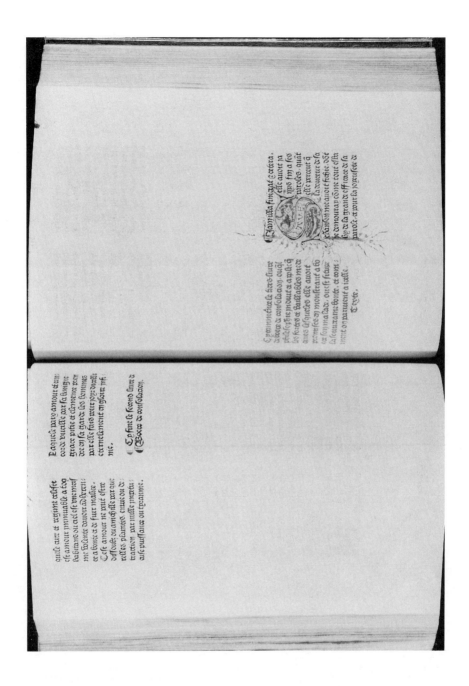

Fig. 3. Opening of Book III. Boethius, *Consolation de Philosophie,* ff 105ᵛ–106. Bruges, Colard Mansion, 1477. Rylands 12619 The John Rylands Library, Manchester (by permission of The John Rylands Library).

Fig. 4. Boccaccio Presents His Book to Mainardo Cavalcanti. Boccaccio, Giovanni, *De casibus illustrium virorum et mulierum*. Trans. Laurent de Premierfait, f3. Bruges, Colard Mansion, 1476. Museum of Fine Arts, Boston (by permission of the Museum of Fine Arts).

Fig. 5. Presentation Scene. Le Fèvre, Raoul, *Recuyell of the Histories of Troy*. Trans. William Caxton, frontispiece. Bruges, William Caxton, 1473–1474. Henry E. Huntington Library, San Marino (courtesy of the Huntington Library and Art Gallery).

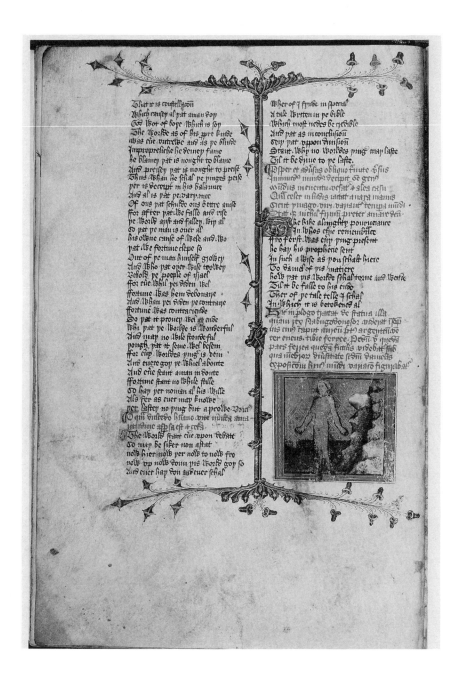

Fig. 6. Nebuchadnezzar's Dream of Precious Metals. John Gower, *Confessio Amantis*. Morgan M 690, ca. 1430, f4ᵛ. The Pierpont Morgan Library, New York (courtesy of The Pierpont Morgan Library).

Fig. 7. Tereus Cutting Out the Tongue of Philomena. John Gower, *Confessio Amantis.*
Morgan M 126, after 1470, f122. The Pierpont Morgan Library, New York (courtesy
of The Pierpont Morgan Library).

CXXIII

eñ salich te maken dan te verderuē. op dat se siende hoer boescheit vnpelt sijnde voert aen aflaten souden vā hē te willen doodē wāt de tijt zijnre doot noch nz comen was noch oec alsulckē doot en hadde hi niet ver coren te steruen. Te weten pst dat crist9 doot in vierderhande manierē is aenghe lept gheweest. wat dpe sommighe woudē hem dooden mitten sweerde als herodes doen ihesus gheborē was. Die sommighe om van boué neder te worpē ghelijc nv de se van nazareth doen wilden Die sommi ghe om te steruen. te weten die iodē inden tempel Die sommighe om hē te crupcen. te weten oec die iodē Alsoe wort oer cristus noch gheestelijc gheecrupst van ōs als wij weder keeren tot voergaēdē sunde. hi wort ghesteent in onser oerhertichet hi wort ter neder ghewoorpen in wanhopen. eñ mptsē

sweerde woort hi ghedoot in blasphemerē

Ghebet.

Here ihesu criste die di also voetmoedicht hebbes tot allen dpesten. dattu niet en heb bes vonweerdicht te hebben die officie des lesens. eñ na die weldaet dpen vā nazareth gedaē. lijflsamelic hebbes otsae quaet voer goet. alstu du dp hebbes sond wederstoot latē lepdē van hē die dp vā boué nedwerpē wildē. Goede ihesu gheeft mp dese gracie dz ic dp nauolgēde begheeren moet mp te crōme tot allē dpestē der oetmoedicheit. eñ mi blijdelijc heuset bewijsen gheeft oec on recht lijbsamelic te vdragē eñ daer af ghes wrake te sueckē Eñ alle mijn vianden van herten te minnē eñ hē weldaet te bewijsen Amen.

Van die onthoefdinghe eñ doot sin te ians baptisten Dat lriij capittel.

Fig. 8. Salome with the Head of John the Baptist. Ludolphus of Saxony, *Vita Christi*, f 123. Zwolle, Petrus van Os, 1495. PML 20613 ChL fl656. The Pierpont Morgan Library, New York (courtesy of The Pierpont Morgan Library).

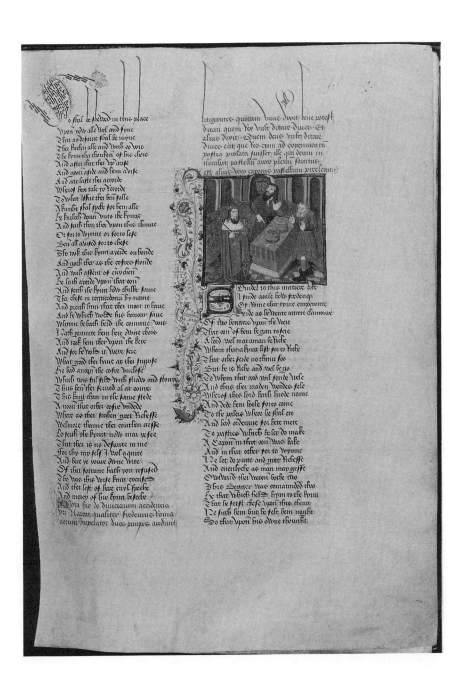

Fig. 9. Emperor Frederick and the Two Beggars. John Gower, *Confessio Amantis*. Morgan M 126, after 1470, f 103. The Pierpont Morgan Library, New York (courtesy of The Pierpont Morgan Library).

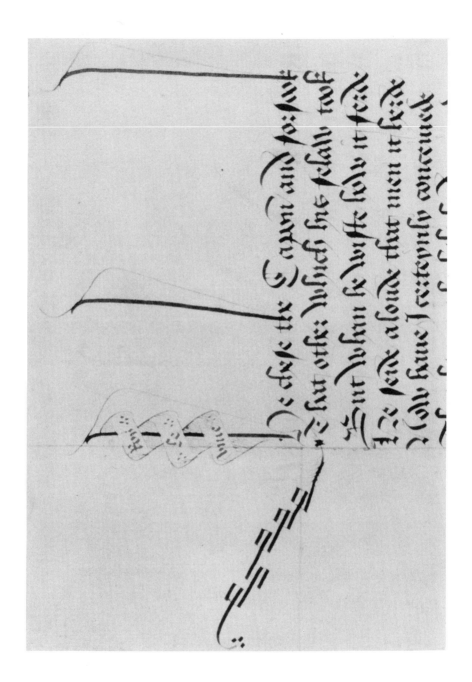

Fig. 10. "viue Le Roy" (detail). John Gower, *Confessio Amantis*. Morgan M 126, after 1470, f 103ᵛ. The Pierpont Morgan Library, New York (courtesy of The Pierpont Morgan Library).

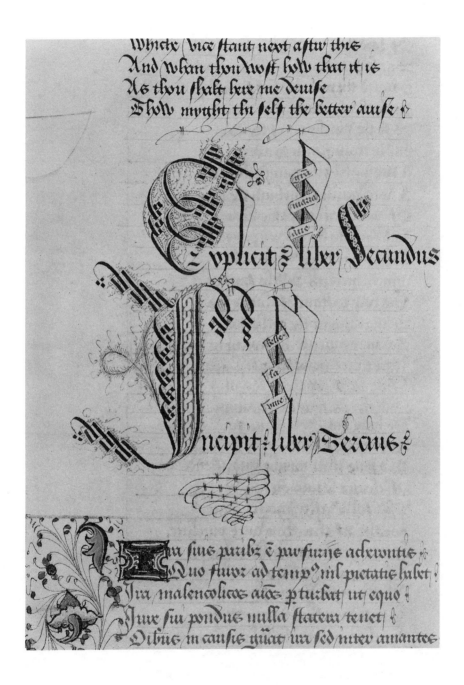

Fig. 11. "viue la belle" "aue marie gra<u>cia</u>" John Gower, *Confessio Amantis*. Morgan M 126, after 1470, f 50ᵛ. The Pierpont Morgan Library, New York (courtesy of The Pierpont Morgan Library).

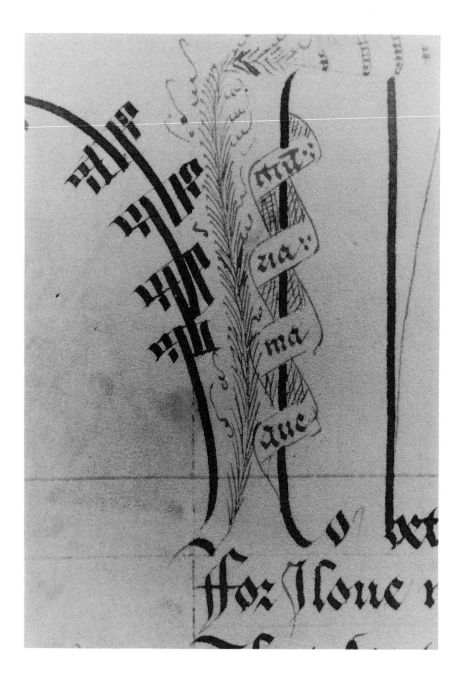

Fig. 12. "aue marie gra<u>cia</u>" (detail). John Gower, *Confessio Amantis*. Morgan M 126, after 1470, f 104. The Pierpont Morgan Library, New York (courtesy of The Pierpont Morgan Library).

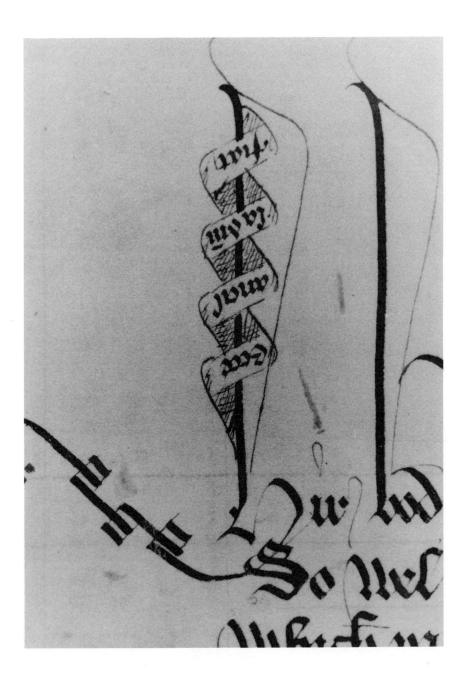

Fig. 13. "Ecce ancilla do̱mi̱nus fiat" (detail, reversed). John Gower, *Confessio Amantis.* Morgan M 126, after 1470, f 140. The Pierpont Morgan Library, New York (courtesy of The Pierpont Morgan Library).

Fig. 14. Presentation of the Book. *Dicts and Sayings of Philosophers*, trans. Anthony Woodville, Earl Rivers. MS 265, finished 29 December 1477, frontispiece. Lambeth Palace Library, London (courtesy of Lambeth Palace Library).

Fig. 15. Badge and Motto of William, Lord Arundel. Jacobus de Voragine, *The Golden Legend*. Trans. William Caxton. Westminster, William Caxton, 20 November 1483. Longleat House, Warminster, Wiltshire (by permission of the Marquess of Bath, Longleat House).

Contributors

David Aers is Professor of English and Religion at Duke University in Durham, North Carolina.

Patricia Batchelor is a Lecturer in the Department of English, at Marquette University, Milwaukee, Wisconsin.

María Bullón-Fernández is Assistant Professor of English at Seattle University in Seattle, Washington.

Thomas Cable is Blumburg Centennial Professor of English at the University of Texas at Austin.

Martha W. Driver is Professor of English at Pace University in New York City.

Siân Echard is Assistant Professor of English at the University of British Columbia in Vancouver, British Columbia.

A. S. G. Edwards is Professor of English at the University of Victoria, in British Columbia, Canada.

Claire Fanger is a Visiting Professor in the Department of English at the University of Western Ontario in London, Ontario.

Kurt Olsson is Professor of English and Dean of the College of Letters and Science at the University of Idaho.

Russell A. Peck is John Hall Deane Professor of Rhetoric and Language at the University of Rochester in Rochester, New York.

Dhira B. Mahoney is Associate Professor of English at Arizona State University, Tempe, Arizona.

Gregory M. Sadlek is an Associate Professor of English at the University of Nebraska at Omaha.

Eve Salisbury is a Visiting Assistant Professor of English at SUNY Geneseo, Geneseo, New York.

Larry Scanlon is Associate Professor of English at Rutgers, the State University of New Jersey, New Brunswick, New Jersey.

Hugh White is a Lecturer in the Department of English, University College, London, England.

R. F. Yeager is Professor of Literature and Language at the University of North Carolina at Asheville, Asheville, North Carolina.